Foundations of American Contract Law

Foundations of American Contract Law

JAMES GORDLEY

OXFORD
UNIVERSITY PRESS

Oxford University Press is a department of the University of Oxford. It furthers the University's objective of excellence in research, scholarship, and education by publishing worldwide. Oxford is a registered trade mark of Oxford University Press in the UK and certain other countries.

Published in the United States of America by Oxford University Press
198 Madison Avenue, New York, NY 10016, United States of America.

CIP data is on file at the Library of Congress

ISBN 978–0–19–768608–9

DOI: 10.1093/oso/9780197686089.001.0001

Printed by Integrated Books International, United States of America

Note to Readers
This publication is designed to provide accurate and authoritative information in regard to the subject matter covered. It is based upon sources believed to be accurate and reliable and is intended to be current as of the time it was written. It is sold with the understanding that the publisher is not engaged in rendering legal, accounting, or other professional services. If legal advice or other expert assistance is required, the services of a competent professional person should be sought. Also, to confirm that the information has not been affected or changed by recent developments, traditional legal research techniques should be used, including checking primary sources where appropriate.

(Based on the Declaration of Principles jointly adopted by a Committee of the American Bar Association and a Committee of Publishers and Associations.)

Contents

Table of Authorities

CASES

166 Mamaroneck Ave. Corp. v. 151 E. Post Rd. Corp., 575 N.E.2d 104 (N.Y. 1991) 90
1464- Eight, Ltd. & Mills Management Corp. v. Joppich, 154 S.W.3d 101 (Tex. 2004) 67

Aerial Advertising Co. v. Batchelor's Peas, [1938] 2 All E.R. 788 (K.B. 1938) 171–72
Academy Chicago Publishers v. Cheever, 578 N.E.2d 981 (Ill. 1991) 94
Air Products & Chemicals, Inc. v. Fairbanks Morse, Inc., 206 N.W.2d 414
(Wis. 1973) 246n.52
Air Safety v. Teachers Realty Corp., 706 N.E.2d 882 (Ill. 1999) 254–55
Alaska Children's Services, Inc. v. Smart, 677 P.2d 899 (Alaska 1984) 288–89
Alderson v Madderson, 5 Ex. D. 293 112
Alfred Marks Realty Co. v. Hotel Hermitage Co. 156 N.Y.S. 179 (A.D. 1915) 107
Allegheny College v. National Chautauqua County Bank, 159 N.E. 173 (N.Y. 1927) 17
American Cotton- Oil v. Kirk, 68 F. 791 (7th Cir. 1895) 89–90
Am. Home Improvement, Inc. v. MacIver, 201 A.2d 886 (N.H. 1964) 57
AM International, Inc. v. Graphic Management Associates, Inc., 44 F.3d 572
(7th Cir. 1995) 254–55
American Fidelity Fire Ins. Co. v. Kennedy Bros. Construction, Inc.
670 S.W.2d 798 (Ark. 1984) 288–89
Amoco Oil Co. v. Burns, 437 A.2d 381 (Pa. 1981) 186
Amoco Oil Co. v. Ervin, 908 P.2d 493 (Colo. 1995) 185
Anaheim Co. v. Holcombe, 426 P.2d 743 (Or. 1967) 217
Anderson v. Aul, 62 N.W.2d 304 (Wisc. 2015) 212
Anderson Bros. v. O'Meara, 306 F.2d 672 (5th Cir. 1962) 109
Angel v. Murray, 322 A.2d 630 (R.I. 1974) 100
Anglia Television Ltd. v. Reed, [1971] 2 All E.R. 690 (C.A.) 309–10
Antonini v. Thrifty- Nifty Homes, 76 So.2d 564 (La.App. 1955) 216
Arc Electric Construction Co. v. George A. Fuller Co. 247 N.E.2d 111 (N.Y. 1969) 228
Arcadian Phosphates, Inc. v. Arcadian Corp, 884 F.2d 69 (2nd Cir. 1989) 141
Armstrong & Latta v. City of Philadelphia, 94 A. 455 (Pa. 1915) 278–79
Armstrong Rubber Co. v. Griffith, 43 F.2d 689 (2d Cir. 1930) 278–79
Arnold v. Arnold (C.A.), 14 Ch. D. 270 114–15
Ashland Management, Inc. v. Janien, 624 N.E.2d 1007 (N.Y. 1993) 283
Atlantic Richfield Co. v. Razumic, 390 A.2d 736 (Pa. 1978) 186
Austin Instrument Co. v. Loral Corp. 272 N.E.2d 533 (N.Y. 1971) 127–28

Bagley v. Smith, 10 N.Y. 489 (1853) 283–84
Baer v. Chase, 392 F.3d 609 (3rd Cir. 2004) 92–93
Bainbridye v. Firmstone, (1838) 8 A. & E. 743 16–17
Beachcomber Coins, Inc. v. Boskett, 400 A.2d 78 (N.J. App. Div. 1979) 107
Bead Chain Mfg. Co. v. Saxton Products, Inc. 439 A.2d 314 (Conn. 1981) 289
Beirne v. Alaska Housing Authority, 454 P.2d 262 (Alaska 1969) 82
Bentley v. Slavik, 663 F. Supp. 736 (S.D. Ill. 1987) 108

Beraha v. Baxter Health Care Corp. 956 F.2d 1436 (7th Cir. 1992)....................188
Best v. United States National Bank of Oregon, 739 P.2d 554 (Or. 1987)..........182, 183
Bilman v. Hensel, 391 N.E.2d 671 (Ind. App. 1979)....................217
Blanchard v. Ely, 21 Wend. 342 (S. Ct. N.Y. 1839)....................285–86
Board of Control of Eastern Michigan University v. Burgess, 206 N.W.2d 256 (Ct. App. Mich, 1973)....................67
Bollinger v. Central Pennsylvania Quarry & Construction Co., 229 A.2d 741 (Pa. 1967)....................255–56
Brant Const. Co., Inc. v. Metropolitan Water Reclamation Dist. of Greater Chicago, 967 F.2d 244 (7th Cir. 1992)....................229
Brawley v. U.S., 96 U.S. 168 (1877)....................88, 90, 181, 182
British Columbia Saw Mill Co. v. Nettleship, [1868] LR 3 CP 499....................276n.66
Brown v. Cara, 420 F.3d 148 (2d Cir. 2005)....................141–42
Brown Machine, Inc. v. Hercules, Inc., 770 S.W.2d 416 (Mo. App. 1989)....................245–46
Brown v. Oliver, 256 P. 1008 (Kan. 1927)....................254
Budget Marketing, Inc. v. Centronics Corp, 927 F.2d 421 (8th Cir. 1991)....................140
Burger King v. Family Dining, Inc. 426 F.Supp. 485 (E.D.Penn. 1977)....................218–19

Cabot Corp. v. AVX Corp. 863 N.E.2d 503 (Mass. 2007)....................124
Capps v. Georgia Pac. Corp., 453 P.2d 935 (Or.1969)....................123
Carr v. Maine Cent. R.R. Co., 102 A. 532 (N.H. 1917)....................27–28
Chang v. First Colonial Savings Bank, 410 S.E.2d 928 (Va. 1991)....................70
Channel Home Centers v. Grossman, 795 F.2d 291 (3d Cir. 1986)....................142
Chase Precast Corp. v. John J. Paonessa Co. 566 N.E.2d 603 (Mass. 1991)....................109–10
Chatlos Systems, Inc. v National Cash Register Corp. 670 F.2d 1304 (3d Cir.1982)....................303, 304
C. Itoh & Co. (America), Inc. v. Jordan International Co., 552 F.2d 1228 (7th Cir. 1977)....................246
City of Everett v. Estate of Sumstad, 631 P.2d 366 (Wash. 1981)....................108
City of New Orleans v. Firemen's Charitable Association, So. 486 (La. App. 1891)....................327
Clementi v. Nationwide Mut. Fire Ins. Co., 16 P.3d 223 (Colo. 2001)....................221
Coggs v. Bernard (1703) 2 L. Raym. 909....................16–17, 19
Cohen v. Ratinoff, 195 Cal. Rptr. 84 (Cal. App. 1983)....................187
Cold Blast Transp. Co. v. Kansas City Bolt & Nut Co., 114 F. 77 (8th Cir. 1902)....................88
Cole- McIntyre- Norfleet v. Holloway, 214 S.W. 817 (Tenn. 1919)....................77–78
Columbia Hyundai, Inc. v. Carll Hyundai, Inc., 484 S.E.2d 468 (S.C. 1997)....................243
Comfort v. McCorkle, 268 N.Y.S. 192 (Sup. Ct. 1933)....................29
Commonwealth v. Fremont Investment and Loan, 897 N.E.2d 548 (Mass. 2008)....................130
Community Design Corp. v. Antonell, 459 So.2d 343 (Fl. App. 1984)....................92
Compare Lee Oldsmobile v. Kaiden, 363 A.2d 270 (Md. App. 1976)....................308–9
Congregation B'nai Sholom v. Martin, 173 N.W.2d 504 (Mich. 1969)....................17
Contemporary Mission v. Famous Music Corp., 557 F.2d 918 (2d Cir. 1977)....................283
Continental Sand and Gravel v. K & K Sand and Gravel, 755 F.2d 87 (7th Cir. 1985)....................302–3
Cook Associates v. Wanick, 664 P.2d 1161 (Utah 1983)....................278–79
Cotnam v. Wisdom, 104 S.W. 164 (Ark. 1907)....................323
Cramer v. Grand Rapids Show Case Co. 119 N.E. 227 (N.Y. 1918)....................290
Crane v. C. Crane & Co. 105 F. 869 (7th Cir. 1901)....................89
Credit Alliance Corp. v. Andersen & Co, 483 N.E. 2d 110 (N.Y. 1985)....................155–56
Cydrus v. Houser, No. 98CA2425, 1999 Ohio App. LEXIS 5746 (Ohio Ct. App. Nov. 29, 1999)....................108

Dalrymple v. Ed Shults Chevrolet, Inc., 380 N.Y.S.2d 189 (A.D. 1976), aff'd, 363 N.E.2d 587 (N.Y. 1977) 27
Davis v. Outboard Marine Corp. 415 N.W.2d 719 (Minn. App. 1987) 169
Deadwood Elks Lodge No. 508 v. Albert, 319 N.W.2d 823 (S.D. 1982) 91
De Cicco v. Schweitzer, 221 N.Y. 431 (1917) 19
De Joseph v. Zambelli, 139 A.2d 644 (Pa. 1958) 119–20
Designer Direct, Inc. v. DeForest Redevelopment Authority, 313 F.3d 1036 (7th Cir. 2002) 28–29, 188
Devecman v. Shaw, 14 A. 464 (Md. 1888) 40, 44
Diamond Fruit Growers, Inc. v. Krack Corp., 794 F.2d 1440 (9th Cir. 1986) 246
Diatom, Inc. v. Pennwalt Corp., 741 F.2d 1569 (10th Cir. 1984) 246
Dixon v. Wells Fargo, N.A. 798 F.Supp. 2d 336 (D.Mass. 2011) 138
Donovan v. RRL Corp., 27 P.3d 702 (Cal. 2001) 239
Dorton v. Collins & Aikman Corp., 453 F.2d 1161 (6th Cir. 1972) 245–46
DPJ Co. Ltd. Partnership v. F.D.I.C., 30 F.3d 247 (1st Cir. 1994) 309
Drennan v. Star Paving Co, 333 P.2d 757 (Cal. 1958) 73–74

Earl of Durham v. Legard, 34 Beav. 611 114–15
EarthInfo, Inc. v. Hydrosphere Resource Consultants, Inc., 900 P.2d 113 (1995) 324
East Providence Credit Union v. Geremia, 239 A.2d 725 (R.I. 1968) 27
Edelman Arts, Inc. v. Art Intern. (UK) Ltd., 841 F.Supp.2d 810 (S.D.N.Y. 2012) 222
Elsinore Union School District v. Kastorff, 353 P.2d 713 (Cal. 1960) 239
Embry v. Hargadine, McKittrick Dry Goods Co, 105 S.W. 777 (Mo. App. 1907) 235–36
enXco Development Corp. v. Northern States Power Co. 758 F.3d 940 (8th Cir. 2014) 208, 209–10
Estate of Nelson v. Rice, 12 P.3d 238 (Ariz. Ct. App. 2000) 108
European American Bank & Trust v. Staubs & Kaye 477 N.Y.S.2d 146 (AD 1984) 155–57
Eustis Mining Co. v. Beer, Sondheimer & Co., 239 F. 976 (S.D.N.Y. 1917) 173

Federal Wall Paper Co. v. Kempner, 244 Fed. 240 (1917) 260, 262
Feld v. Levy & Sons 335 N.E.2d 320 (N.Y. 2009) 180–81
Fera v. Village Plaza, 242 N.W.2d 372 (Mich. 1976) 290
Firestone & Parson, Inc. v. Union League of Phila., 672 F. Supp. 819 (E.D. Pa. 1987) 108
First Presbyterian Church v. Dennis, 161 N.W. 183 (Iowa 1917) 17
Fleming v. Beck, 48 Pa. 309 (1864) 278–79
Fortune v. Nat'l Cash Register Co., 364 N.E.2d 1251 (Mass. 1977) 186
Foster v. United Home Imp. Co., Inc. 428 N.E.2d 1351 (Ind. App. 1981) 288–89
Fox v. Catholic Knights Ins. Soc., 665 N.W.2d 181 (Wisc. 2003) 212
Frampton v. Cent. Ind. Gas Co., 297 N.E.2d 425, 427 (Ind. 1973) 132
Franklin v. Demico, Inc. 347 S.E.2d 718 (Ga. App. 1986) 287
Freeman v. Clute, 3 Barb. 424 (S. Ct. N.Y. 1848) 285–86
Freund v. Washington Square Press, 314 N.E.2d 419 (N.Y. 1975) 282–83
Frostifresh Corp. v. Reynoso, 274 N.Y.S.2d 757 (Sup. Ct. 1966), rev'd on other grounds, 281 N.Y.S.2d 964 (App. Div. 1967) 57

Galati v. Am. W. Airlines, Inc., 69 P.3d 1011 (Ariz. Ct. App. 2003) 133
Gale v. Leckie (1817) 2 Stark. 107 283–84
Gardner Zemke Co. v. Dunham Bush, Inc., 850 P.2d 319 (N.M. 1993) 245–46
Gartner v. Eikill, 319 N.W.2d 397 (Minn. 1982) 107
Gianni v. R. Russell & Co. 281 Pa. 320 (1924) 255–56
Glenn v. Clearman's Golden Cock Inn, 13 Cal. Rptr. 769 (Ct. App. 1961) 132

Goldman v. Weinberger, 475 U.S. 503 (1986) 135
Griffen v. Colver, 16 N.Y. 489 (Ct. App. 1858) 285–86
Griffith v. Brymer (1903) 19 T.L.R. 434 (KB Div.) 107
Grobarchik v. Nasa Mtg. & Inv. Co., 186 A. 433 (N.J. Sup. 1936) 224
G.W. Grun Roofing & Construction Co. v. Cope, 529 S.W. 2d 258
(Tex. Civ. App. 1975) 316

Hadley v. Baxendale, 9 Exch. 341, 156 Eng. Rep. 145 (1854) 117–18, 152, 273, 274–76, 277–79, 290
Hamer v. Sidway 27 N.E. 256 (N.Y. 1891) 39–40
Hand v. Dayton- Hudson, 775 F.2d 757 (6th Cir. 1985) 119
Hardin v. Dimension Lumber Co. 13 P.2d 602 (Or. 1932) 169–70
Harless v. First Nat'l Bank, 246 S.E.2d 270 (W. Va. 1978) 132
Hazlett v. First Fed. Sav. & Loan Ass'n, 127 P.2d 273 (Wash. 1942) 29
Higgins v. California Petroleum & Asphalt Co. 52 P. 1080 (Cal. 1898) 169
Highly v. Phillips 5 A.2d 824 (Md. 1939) 172
Hill v. Waxberg 237 F.2d 936 (9th Cir. 1956) 137
Hobbs v. Massasoit Whip Co 33 N.E. 495 (Mass. 1893) 77
Holiday Inns of America, Inc. v. Knight, 450 P.2d 42 (Cal. 1969) 213, 214
Holman Erection Co. v. Orville E. Madsen & Sons, Inc., 330 N.W.2d 693
(Minn. 1983) 73–74
Holst v. Guynn, 696 P.2d 632 (Wyo. 1985) 216
Hughes v. Abell, 867 F. Supp. 2d 76, 82 (D.C. Cir. 2012) 130
Hunt Const. Group, Inc. v. National Wrecking Corp., 587 F.3d 1119
(D.C. Cir. 2009) 221
Hutchison v. Thompkins, 259 So.2d 129 (Fla. 1972) 308–9

Ingram v. Bigelow, 138 N.Y.S.2d 217 (S. Ct. 1954) 325–26
Inman v. Clyde Hall Drilling Co. 369 P.2d 498 (Ala. 1962) 222–23
International Transportation Ass'n v. Bylenga, 236 N.W. 771 (Mich. 1931) 119
International Underwater Contractors, Inc. v. New England Tel. and
Tel. Co. 393 N.E.2d 968 (Mass. App. 1979) 124
Izadi v. Machado (Gus) Ford, Inc., 550 So.2d 1135 (Fla. App., 1989) 70–71

Jacob & Youngs v. Kent, 129 N.E. 889 (N.Y. 1921) 211, 297–98
James T. Taylor & Son, Inc. v. Arlington Independent School District,
335 S.W.2d 371 (Tex. 1960) 240
Johnson v. Capital City Ford Co., 85 So.2d 75 (La. App. 1955) 70
Jones v. Star Credit Corp., 298 N.Y.S.2d 264 (Sup. Ct. 1969) 57
Johnson v. Otterbein University, 41 Ohio 527 (Ohio 1885) 17
Johnston Realty & Inv. Co. v. Grosvenor, 217 N.W. 20 (Mich. 1928) 57
Joseph Martin, Jr., Delicatessen, Inc. v. Schumacher, 417 N.E.2d 541 (N.Y. 1981) 91
Jungmann & Co. v. Atterbury Bros. 249 N.E. 123 (N.Y. 1928) 204

KGM Harvesting Co. v. Fresh Network, 42 Cal. Rptr. 2d 286 (Cal. App. 1995) 272, 330
Kendall v. Ernest Pestana, Inc., 709 P.2d 837 (Cal. 1985) 187
Kenford Co. v. Erie County, 493 N.E.2d 234 (N.Y. 1986) 282–83
Keyer v. Driscoll, 159 N.W.2d 680 (Wisc. 1968) 298
Kham & Nate's Shoes No. 2, Inc. v. First Bank of Whiting, 908 F.2d 1351
(7th Cir. 1990) 198–99, 200–1
Kirke La Shelle Co. v. Paul Armstrong Co. 188 N.E. 163 (N.Y. 1933) 171
Koch v. Streuter, 83 N.E. 1072 (Ill. 1908) 64–65
Koehring v. Glowacki, 253 N.W.2d 64 (Wis. 1977) 243

Komraus Plumbing & Heating, Inc. v. Cadillac Sands Motel, Inc., 195 N.W.2d 865 (Mich, 1972) . . . 119
Koufos v. C. Czarnikow, Ltd. [the Heron II], [1969] A.C. 350 [H.L. 1967] . . . 279–80
Krell v. Henry, (1903) 2 KB 740 . . . 107
Kukuska v. Home Mutual Hail- Tornado Insurance Co. 235 N.W. 403 (Wis. 1931) . . . 78, 79

Laclede Gas Co. v. Amoco Oil Co. 522 F.2d 33 (8th Cir. 1975) . . . 310–11
La Cumbre Golf & Country Club v. Santa Barbara Hotel, 271 P. 476 (Cal. 1928) . . . 109–10
Laemmar v. J. Walter Thompson Co. 435 F.2d 680 (7th Cir. 1970) . . . 122
Laidlaw v. Organ, 15 U.S. 178 (1817) . . . 55, 110
Laurin v. DeCarolis Construction Co. 363 N.E.2d 675 (Mass. 1977) . . . 323–24
Lawrence v. Cain, 245 N.E.2d 663 (Ind. App. 1969) . . . 172–73
Lawrence v. Fox, 20 N.Y. 268 (1859) . . . 152–53, 154–55
Lee v. Joseph E. Seagram & Sons, Inc. 552 F.2d 447 (2d Cir. 1977) . . . 93
Lefkowitz v. Great Minneapolis Surplus Store, Inc., 86 N.W.2d 698 (Minn. 1957) . . . 70–71
Lemmon v. Cedar Point, Inc., 406 F.2d 94 (6th Cir. 1969) . . . 186
Lewanee Cnty. Bd. of Health v. Messerly, 331 N.W.2d 203 (Mich. 1982) . . . 108
Lexington Products Ltd. V.B.D. Communications, Inc., 677 F.2d 251 (2d Cir. 1982) . . . 283
Lingenfelder v. Wainwright Brewing Co, 15 S.W. 844 (Mo. 1891) . . . 99–100
Linsell v. Halicki, 215 N.W. 315, 316 (Mich. 1927) . . . 64–65
Locke v. Warner Brothers, Inc. 66 Cal. Rptr. 2d 921 (Cal. App. 1997) . . . 184–85
Lonergan v. Skolnick, 276 P.2d 8 (Cal. App. 1954) . . . 70
Lopez v. Reynoso, 118 P.3d 398 (Wash. App. 2005) . . . 253–54
Lucy v. Zehmer, 84 S.E.2d 516 (Va. 1954) . . . 236–37
Lumley v. Gye, 118 Eng. Rep. 749 (Q.B. 1853) . . . 329
Lumley v. Wagner, 42 Eng. Rep. 687 (Ch. 1852) . . . 329
Luttinger v. Rosen, 316 A.2d 757 (Conn. 1972) . . . 215

Machinery Hauling, Inc. v. Steel of West Virginia, 384 S.E.2d 139 (W. Va.1989) . . . 125
Market Street Associates v. Frey, 941 F.2d 588, 594 (7th Cir. 1991) . . . 184, 198–99, 200
Markov v. ABC Transfer & Storage Co. 457 P.2d 535 (Wash. 1969) . . . 138
Marvell Light & Ice Co. v. General Electric Co. 259 S.W. 741 (Ark. 1924) . . . 290
Masterton & Smith v. The Mayor &c of the City of Brooklyn, 9 Hill 61, 68 (S. Ct. N.Y. 1845) . . . 285–86
Martin v. Hamilton State Bank, 723 S.E.2d 726 (Ga. Ct. App. 2012) . . . 199
Martinez v. Socoma Companies, 521 P.2d 841 (Cal. 1974) . . . 151
Masterson v. Sine, 436 P.2d 561 (Cal. 1968) . . . 253
Masterton & Smith v. The Mayor &c of the City of Brooklyn, 9 Hill 61, (S. Ct. N.Y. 1845) . . . 285–86
Mattei v. Hopper, 330 P.2d 625 (Cal.1958) . . . 69, 73, 184, 224, 226
Mayerson v. Washington Mfg. Co. 58 F.R.D. 377 (E.D. Penn. 1972) . . . 122
McEwen v. McKinnon, 11 N.W. 828, 830 (Mich. 1882) . . . 278–79
McNeil v. Reid, 9 Bing. 68 . . . 283–84
Merritt Hill Vineyards Inc. v. Windy Heights Vineyard, Inc., 460 N.E.2d 1077 (N.Y. 1984) . . . 222
M. F. Kemper Const. Co. v. City of Los Angeles, 235 P.2d 7 (Cal. 1951) . . . 238
Mineral Park Land v. Howard, 156 P. 458 (Cal. 1916) . . . 95n.154, 215
Minnesota Lumber Co. v. Whitebreast Coal Co., 43 N.E. 774 (Ill. 1895) . . . 88
Miller v. Othello Packers, Inc. 410 P.2d 33 (Wash. 1966)
Miles Homes Division of Insilco Corp. v. First State Bank, 782 S.W.2d 798 (Mo. Ct. App. 1990) . . . 27, 29
Miller v. Coffeen, 280 S.W.2d 100, 104 (Mo. 1955) . . . 64–65
Mills v. Wyman, 20 Mass. (3 Pick.) 207 (1825) . . . 315

MindGames Inc. v. Western Publ. Co., Inc., 218 F.3d 652 (7th Cir. 2000) 284
Mineral Park Land Co. v. Howard, 156 P. 458 (Cal. 1916) 95–96
Mississippi & Dominion Steamship Co., v. Swift, 86 Me. 248, 258 (1894) 139
Mitchell v. Lath, 160 N.E. 646 (N.Y. 1928) 253, 254
Moch v. Rennselaer Water Co, 159 N.E. 896 (N.Y. 1928) 151–52, 156
Moolemaar v. Co- Build Companies, Inc., 354 F.Supp. 980 (D.Va. 1973) 91
Morgan v. Stagg, 1987 WL 18703 (Tex. Ct. App.) 325–26
Morin Building Products, Co. v. Baystone Construction, Inc, 717 F.2d 413
(7th Cir. 1983) 227
Morse, Inc., 206 N.W.2d 414 (Wis. 1973) 246
Morton Shoe Co., Re 40 B.R. 948 (Bankruptcy Ct., D. Mass., 1984) 38
Moulthrop v. Hyett, 17 So. 32 (Ala. 1895) 278–79
Mutual Life Insurance Co. of New York v. Tailored Woman, Inc,
128 N.E.2d 401 (N.Y. 1955) 189–90

Nash v. Thousand Island Steamboat Co., 108 N.Y. Supp. 336 (A.D. 1908) 283–84
Nebraska Wesleyan University v. Griswold's Estate, 202 N.W. 609 (Neb. 1925) 17
Neri v. Retail Marine Corp. 285 N.E.2d 311 (N.Y. 1972) 269–70
New England Insulation Co. v. General Dynamics Corp., 522 N.E.2d 997
(Mass. App. 1988) 137–38, 181
New York Cent. Ironworks Co. v. United States Radiator Co., 66 N.E. 967
(N.Y. 1903) 88–89, 90, 181–82
Nolan v. Whitney 88 N.Y. 648 (1882) 228
Northern Commercial Co. v. United Airmotive, 101 F. Supp. 169 (D. Alaska 1951) 27
NPS, LLC v. Minihane, 886 N.E.2d 670 (Mass. 2008) 308

Oakwood Village, L.L.C. v. Albertsons, Inc., 104 P.3d 1226 (Utah 2004) 191
Oglebay Norton Co. v. Armco, Inc., 556 N.E.2d 515 (Ohio, 1990) 91
Officer v. Chase Ins. Life & Annuity Co., 541 F.3d 713 (7th Cir. 2008) 212
Oliver v. Henley, 21 S.W.2d 576 (Tex. Civ. App., 1929) 70
Olwell v. Nye & Nissen Co. 173 P.2d 652 (Wash. 1956) 323
Olympus Hills Shopping Center, Ltd. v. Smith's Food & Drug Centers, Inc.
889 P.2d 445 (Utah 1994) 190–91, 324
Oppenheimer & Co. v. Oppenheim, Appel, Dixon & Co 660 N.E.2d 415
(N.Y. 1995) 207, 209–10
Oscar Barnett Foundry Co. v. Crowe, 86 A. 915 (N.J. Err. & App. 1912) 325–26
O'Sullivan v. Mallon, 390 A.2d 149 (N.J. Super. Ct. 1978) 132
O.W. Grun Roofing & Constr. Co. v. Cope, 529 S.W.2d 258 (Tex. Civ. App. 1975) 297–98

Pacific Gas & Electric Co. v. G.W. Thomas Drayage and Rigging Co. 442 P.2d 641
(Cal. 1968) 174–75
Palmateer v. Int'l Harvester Co., 421 N.E.2d 876 (Ill. 1981) 132
Paul W. Abbott, Inc. v. Axel Newman Heating & Plumbing Co 166 N.W.2d 323
(Minn. 1969) 169
Perma Research & Devel. Co. v. Singer Co., 542 F.2d 111 (2d Cir. 1976) 284
Petermann v. Int'l Brotherhood of Teamsters, Chauffeurs, Warehousemen &
Helpers of Am., Local 396, 344 P.2d 25 (Cal. Ct. App. 1959) 132
Philadelphia, W. & B.R. Co. v. Howard, 54 U.S. (13 How.) 307 286
Phillips v. Moor 71 Me. 78 (1880) 80, 81
Pierce v. Ortho Pharmaceutical Corp. 417 A.2d 505 (N.J. 1980) 135
Precision Testing Laboratories, Inc. v. Kenyon Corp. 644 F.Supp. 1327
(S.D.N.Y. 1986) 137

Prescott v. Jones, 41 A. 352 (N.H. 1898) 29
Pyeatte v. Pyeatte 661 P.2d 196 (Ariz. 1983) 93–94

Raffles v. Wichelhaus 2 H. & C. 906; 33 L.J. Ex. 160 102
Rancourt v. Verba, 678 A.2d 886 (Vt. 1996) 107
Red River Commodities, Inc. v. Eidsness 459 N.W.2d 805 (N.D 1990) 210–11
Renner v. Kehl, 722 P.2d 262 (Ariz. 1986) 107
Ricketts v. Scothorn 77 N.W. 365 (Neb. 1898) 18, 20, 40
RLM Assocs. v. Carter Mfg. Corp., 248 N.E.2d 646 (Mass. 1969) 186
Robinson v. Harman, (1848) 1 Ex. Rep. 850 . . . . 260, 262
Rogers v. Galloway Female College, 44 S.W. 454 (Ark. 1898) 17
Rombola v. Consindas, 220 N.E.2d 919 (Mass. 1966) 283
Rotolith, Ltd. v. F.P. Barker & Co. 297 F.2d 497 (1st Cir. 1962) 248
Ryder Truck Rental, Inc. v. Central Packing Co. 341 F.2d 321 (10th Cir. 1965) 189

Sabo v. Fasano 201 Cal. Rptr. 270 (Cal, App. 1984) 81–82
Salisbury v. Northwestern Bell Telephone 221 N.W. 2d 609 (Iowa 1974) 38
Sanders v. FedEx Ground Package Sys., Inc 188 P.3d 1200 (N.M. 2008) 190
Sandoval v. Bucci (In re Estate of Bucci), 488 P.2d 216 (Colo. Ct. App. 1971) 40, 44
Schweiso v. Williams, 198 Cal.Rptr. 238 (Cal. App. 1984) 187
Scott v. Moragues, 80 So. 394 (Ala. 1918) 68
Seaver v. Ransom 120 N.E. 639 (N.Y. 1918) 146, 147–48
Security Stove & Mfg. Co. v. American Ry. Express Co. 51 So.2d 572 (Mo. App. 1932) 309–10
Seidenberg v. Summit Bank 791 A.2d 1068 (N.J. Super., 2002) 189
Sherwood v. Walker 33 N.W. 919 (Mich.1887) 107–8
Siegel v. Spear & Co., 138 N.E. 414 (N.Y. 1923) 27
Silver Air v. Aeronautic Development Corp. Ltd., 656 F.Supp. 170 (S.D.N.Y. 1987) 222
Simon v. Etgen, 107 N.E. 1066 (N.Y. 1915) 28–29, 188
Simmons v. Patchett, [1857] 26 LJQB 195, 197 275–76
Slack v. Munson 61 So.2d 618 (La. App. 1952) 215
Smith v. Hughes L.R. 6 Q.B. 597 103–4
Smith v. Zimbalist, 38 P.2d 170 (Cal. App. 1934) 108
Snell v. Cottingham, 72 Ill. 161 (1874) 278–79
Snepp v. United States 444 U.S. 507 (1980) 322
Soltani v. Western & Southern Life Insurance Co. 258 F.3d 1038 (9th Cir. 2001) 222
Southern Calif. Acoustics Co. v. C.V. Holder, Inc., 456 P.2d 975 (Cal. 1969) 73–74
Stare v. Tate, 98 Cal. Rptr. 264 (Cal. App. 1971) 238, 241
State Sec. & Realty Co. v. Shaffer, 142 N.W. 1058 (Mich. 1913) 64–65
Steiner v. Mobil Oil Corp., 569 P.2d 751 (Cal. 1977) 246
Sturlyn v. Albany, (1587) Cro. Eliz. 67 . . . . 14–15, 16
Sumerel v. Goodyear Tire & Rubber Co., 232 P.3d 128 (Col. App. 2009) 238
Sundance Cruises Corp. v. American Bureau of Shipping, 7 F.3d 1077, 1084 (2d Cir. 1993) 278–79
Super Valu Stores, Inc. v. Peterson, 506 So.2d 317 (Ala. 1987) 290
Swift Canadian Co. v. Banet, 224 F.2d 36 (3d Cir. 1955) 109

Tameny v. Atl. Richfield Co., 610 P.2d 1330 (Cal. 1980) 132
Taylor v Bradley, 39 N.Y. 129 (1868) 283–84
Teachers Ins. & Annuity Ass'n of America v. Tribune Co. 670 F.Supp. 491 (S.D.N.Y. 1987) 138–39
Tractebel Energy Mtg. Inc. v. AEP Power Mktg, Inc., 487 F.3d 89 (2d Cir. 2007) 281

Toker v. Westerman, 274 A.2d 78 (N.J. Dist. Ct. 1970)....57
Toys, Inc. v. F.M. Burlington Co. 582 A.2d 123 (Vt. 1990)....91
Transatlantic Financing Corp. v. United States, 363 F.2d 312 (D.C. Cir. 1966)....96–97
Travelers Ins. Co. v. Bailey, 197 A.2d 813 (Vt. 1964)....240
Trident Center v. Connecticut General Life Ins. Co., 847 F.2d. 564 (9th Cir. 1988)....174–75
Trombetta v. Detroit, Toledo & Ironton R.R., 265 N.W.2d 385 (Mich. Ct. App. 1978)....132
T.W. Oil, Inc. v. Consolidated Edison Co., 443 N.E.2d 932 (N.Y. 1982)....113, 306

Udell v. Cohen, 122 N.Y.S.2d 552 (S.Ct. 1953)....169
Ultra- Mares Corporation v. Touch, 174 N.E 441 (N.Y. 1934)....155–56
Union Carbide Corp. v. Oscar Mayer Food Corp., 947 F.2d 1333 (7th Cir. 1991)....244
United Elec. Corp. v. All Service Elec., Inc., 256 N.W.2d 92 (Minn. 1977)....27, 29
United States v. Algernon Blair, 479 F.2d 638 (4th Cir. 1973)....316, 317
United States Naval Institute Press v. Charter Communications, Inc, 936 F.2d 692 (2nd Cir. 1991)....326
U.S. Shipping Board Merchant Fleet Corporation, to Use of U.S. v. Aetna Casualty & Surety Co., 98 F.2d 238 (D.C. App. 1938)....221

Van Gulik v. Resource Development Council for Alaska, 695 P.2d 1071 (Alaska, 1985)....150–51
Valiulis v. L'Atelier Wholesale Antiques, 519 So. 2d 312 (La. Ct. App. 1988)....109
Varel v. Banc One Capital Partners Inc. 55 F.3d 1016 (5th Cir. 1995)....217–18
Vermillion v. AAA Pro Moving & Storage, 704 P.2d 1360 (Ariz. Ct. App. 1985)....132
Victoria Laundry (Windsor) Ltd. v. Newman Industries, Ltd. [1949] 2 K.B. 528 (Ct. App.)....274–75, 276
Vitex Mfg. Corp. v. Caribtex Corp. 377 F.2d 795 (3d Cir. 1967)....271–72

Wagenseller v. Scottsdale Memorial Hospital, 710 P.2d 1025 (Ariz. 1985)....133–34, 136
Wakeman v. Wheeler & Wilson Manufacturing Co., 4 N.E. 264 (N.Y. 1886)....285–86
Walgreen Co. v. Sara Creek Property Co. 966 F.2d 273 (7th Cir. 1992)....311, 324
Walter v. Keith, 382 S.W.2d 198 (Ken. App. 1964)....91
Wasserman's Inc. v. Middletown, 645 A.2d 100 (N.J. 1994)....308
Weaver v. American Oil Co, 276 N.E.2d 144, (Ind. 1971)....59, 61
Webb v. McGowin 168 So. 196 (Ala. Ct. App. 1935), cert denied, 169 So. 199 (Ala. 1936)....314–15
Wertheim v. Chicoutimi Pulp Co., [1911] A.C. 301....260, 262
West Virginia Transp. Co. v. Sweetzer, 25 W.Va. 434 (1885)....125, 126
Western Hills v. Pfau 508 P.2d 201 (Or. 1973)....184, 224
White v. Guarente, 372 N.E. 2d 315 (N.Y. 1977)....155–57
Wickham & Burton Coal Co. v. Farmer's Lumber Co., 179 N.W. 417 (Iowa 1920)....88
Williams v. First Gov't Mortg. & Invs., 225 F.3d 738 (D.C. Cir. 2000)....130
Williams v. Walker- Thomas Furniture Co, 350 F.2d 445 (D.C. Cir. 1965)....60, 61, 131
Wilson v. Amerada Hess Corp. 773 A.2d 1121 (N.J. 2001)....185
Wisconsin & Mich. R.R. v. Powers, 191 U.S. 379 (1903)....18–19
Wright v. Wilson, 10 Tenn. 294 (Ct. Err. & App. 1829)....64–65
Wollums v. Horsley, 20 S.W. 781 (Ky. 1892)....57, 58
Wood v. Boynton, 25 N.W. 42 (Wis. 1885)....108

Y.J.D. Restaurant Supply Co. v. Dib, 413 N.Y.S.2d 835 (S. Ct. 1979)....325

Zigas v. Superior Court 174 Cal. Rptr. 806 (Ct. App. 1981)....150

RESTATEMENTS

LEGISLATION

Statutes

Foreign legislation

FRANCE

GERMANY

SWITZERLAND

UNITED KINGDOM

TRANSNATIONAL LAW

PART I
PROLOGUE

1

The Search for System

I. The systems come unstuck

Our goal will be to rethink the foundations of contract law in a way that will be helpful in understanding the law of American common law jurisdictions. We will begin by describing why its foundations need to be reconsidered.

One of the great enterprises of the nineteenth century in common law and civil law was to systematize the law of contracts. By the late twentieth century, as Grant Gilmore observed, "The systems have come unstuck and we see, presently, no way of gluing them back together again."[1]

The systems were positivist, conceptualist, and, for the most part, voluntarist. They were positivist in that they purported to provide the best explanation of the texts that had legal authority in a particular jurisdiction. In common law countries, the authoritative texts were the decided cases. In some civil law countries, such as France, they were the provisions of civil codes. In others, such as much of Germany, they were the Roman legal texts collected in the sixth century under the Emperor Justinian in what came to be called the *Corpus iuris civilis*.

These systems were conceptualist. As many rules as possible were to be inferred from a small number of concepts. Conceptualism went hand in hand with positivism. The concepts were thought to be explicit or implicit in the authoritative texts. Consequently, the rules inferred from them had the same authority as the texts themselves. A jurist who reached a conclusion that could not be inferred from the texts was not interpreting the law but making it.

These systems were voluntarist although their emphasis on the will had triggered a reaction even in the nineteenth century. Nineteenth-century jurists defined contract in terms of the expressed will of the parties.[2] The innovation was

[1] GRANT GILMORE, THE DEATH OF CONTRACT 102 (1974).

[2] *See* 1 SAMUEL COMYN, A TREATISE OF THE LAW RELATIVE TO CONTRACTS AND AGREEMENTS NOT UNDER SEAL 1 (1809); JOHN NEWLAND, A TREATISE ON CONTRACTS, WITHIN THE JURISDICTION OF COURTS OF EQUITY 1 (1821); JOSEPH CHITTY, JUN., A PRACTICAL TREATISE ON THE LAW OF CONTRACTS, NOT UNDER SEAL; AND UPON THE USUAL DEFENCES TO ACTIONS THEREON 3 (1826); 2 JAMES KENT, COMMENTARIES ON AMERICAN LAW 450 (Charles M. Barnes ed., 13th ed. 1884); C.E. Dodd, *On the Construction of Contracts—Assent—Construction*, 12 LEGAL OBSERVER J. JURIS. 249, 249 (1836); WILLIAM W. STORY, A TREATISE ON THE LAW OF CONTRACTS NOT UNDER SEAL 1 (1844); Professor Carey, *A Course of Lectures on the Law of Contracts*, 4 L. TIMES & J. PROP. 448, 463 (1845); 1 THEOPHILUS PARSONS, THE LAW OF CONTRACTS 6 (3d ed. 1857); STEPHEN MARTIN LEAKE, THE ELEMENTS OF THE LAW OF CONTRACTS 7–8 (1867).

Foundations of American Contract Law. James Gordley, Oxford University Press. © Oxford University Press 2023.
DOI: 10.1093/oso/9780197686089.003.0001

not the idea that the parties enter into contracts by expressing their will to do so. The Roman jurists had said as much.[3] The innovation was to treat the will of the parties, in the words of A. W. B. Simpson, as "a sort of Grundnorm from which as many rules of contract law as possible were to be inferred."[4] We remember the nineteenth and early twentieth centuries as an age of will theories of contract.

One problem with these theories was that they were blind to the idea of purpose. A notorious example is Christopher Columbus Langdell's claim that, as a matter of logic, a contract cannot be formed until the offeree's acceptance of an offer is received by the offeror. By definition, there can be no contract without mutual assent and no mutual assent without communication. Some scholars had argued that the interests of the parties would be better served by the common law rule, which had been adopted before the rise of the will theories, that an acceptance is effective on dispatch. According to Langdell, "The true answer to this objection is that it is irrelevant."[5] As in mathematics, consequences were derived from definitions without regard to purposes.

Another problem with these theories is the implausibility of maintaining that the will of the parties can be the source of all of their contractual obligations. Oliver Wendell Holmes and Samuel Williston objected that the law reads many terms into a contract to govern matters for which the parties did not provide and, indeed, which they had never envisioned. As Willison said, "[t]o assume first that everybody knows the law, and, second, that everybody thereupon makes his contract with reference to it and adopts its provisions as terms of the agreement, is indeed to pile fiction upon fiction."[6] Holmes and Willison proposed "objective theories" in which a contract is defined as the consequences which the law attached to what the parties had said or done. They did not explain why the law attached one set of consequences rather than another.

Another problem was that the law sometimes does not enforce terms to which the contracting parties did assent. It does not enforce a promise to give away money or property even though one party expressed the will to give and the other the will to accept. The law sometimes does not enforce a harsh bargain. Yet even in the nineteenth and early twentieth centuries, courts gave relief from unfair bargains while claiming that fairness did not matter. In 1952, the *Uniform Commercial Code* recognized that fairness does matter. The *Code* allowed a court to refuse to enforce a term that is "unconscionable."[7] A similar provision was adopted in 1981 by the *Restatement (Second) of Contracts*.[8] The *Second*

[3] DIG. 2.14.1.3.

[4] A.W. B. Simpson, *Innovation in 19th Century Contract Law*, 91 L.Q. REV. 247, 266 (1975).

[5] CHRISTOPHER COLUMBUS LANGDELL, SUMMARY OF THE LAW OF CONTACTS 20–21 (2d ed. 1880).

[6] 2 SAMUEL WILLISTON, THE LAW OF CONTRACT § 615 (1920).

[7] U.C.C. § 2-302 (AM. LAW INST. & UNIF. L. COMM'N 1977).

[8] RESTATEMENT (SECOND) OF CONTRACTS § 208 (AM. LAW INST. 1981).

Restatement explained other traditional doctrines as ways to prevent unfairness, for example, to prevent one party from speculating at the other's expense.

The systematization of American contract law culminated in the *Restatement (First) of Contracts*, for which Samuel Williston served as Reporter. It reflected the positivism and conceptualism of the age. Although it was intended to formulate rules that would best fit the decided cases, it was not as systematic as Willison wished it to be. It shifted back and forth between the objective theory that he endorsed and a concern for the will of the parties. It sometimes sacrificed logic to practical concerns about purpose.

The *Restatement (Second) of Contracts* was published soon after Gilmore declared that the systems had come unstuck. The drafters were in no position to glue them together again. As Gilmore had pointed out, no one knew how to do that. By inertia, much of the *First Restatement* passed into the *Second*. Concerns about fairness and the purposes of the parties were addressed on an ad hoc basis. Sometimes the drafters did so by adding epicycles to already complicated doctrines. Sometimes they retreated into obscurity. Its formulations have now been adopted by many courts, sometimes uncritically, sometimes without attention to their own prior decisions. We will be concerned with these formulations. They illustrate how difficult it is to devise solutions piecemeal without rethinking the foundations of contract law.

II. Contract theory before the nineteenth century

We will be borrowing ideas from an earlier theory of contract law that was built by continental jurists in the sixteenth and seventeenth centuries and was never confidently abandoned until the rise of the will theories.

The architects belonged to a school of philosopher-jurists known to historians as the "late scholastics" because their method, like that of the medieval scholastics, was based on reconciling conflicting authorities. They wished to reconcile Roman law, as interpreted by the medieval jurists, with Aristotelian philosophy, as interpreted by Thomas Aquinas. Among the leaders were Domingo de Soto (1494–1560), Luis de Molina (1535–1600), and Leonard Lessius (1554–1623).

The work of the late scholastics deeply influenced the founder of the northern natural law school, Hugo Grotius (1583–1645). The structure of their theory and many of their conclusions were borrowed by him and his followers, and so spread through northern Europe, paradoxically, during the very centuries in which Aristotelian philosophy lost its once unquestioned authority. Eighteenth-century jurists such as Robert Pothier (1699–1772) explained contract in much the same way. A century later, the ideas on which this earlier theory was built no longer made sense to common law or civil law jurists.

According to the earlier theory, there are two purposes or *causae* for which parties make contracts and the law enforces them. One is to exercise liberality. The other is to receive an equivalent in exchange for what one gives. The late scholastics were drawing on Aristotle. According to Aristotle, liberality meant, not simply conferring a benefit gratuitously, but doing so "to the right people, the right amounts, and at the right time, with all the other qualifications that accompany right giving."[9] According to Aristotle, voluntary transactions such as sale and lease are acts of commutative justice in which the parties exchange resources of equivalent value.[10]

In a contract entered into out of liberality, one party may or may not have intended to confer a benefit on the other at his own expense. He might have intended to do the other party a favor that would cost him nothing. For example, he might loan property or money for which he has no present use. Or he might agree to look after another's property believing that he could do so at no extra cost. Such contracts were binding on consent but the party who had agreed to do the favor could back out if it he found that he could not do so without cost to himself.[11] Alternatively, one party may have wished to benefit the other at his own expense. For example, he promised to give the other money or property. Liberality meant not merely giving it away but doing so sensibly. The concern that a party act sensibly was said to explain the rule, taken from Roman law, that such a promise was not binding without a formality. By the Middle Ages, the formality had become subscription to the document before a notary. It was also said to explain two exceptions to this requirement which had been recognized by civil law: a promise to those about to marry (*proper nuptias*)[12] and a promise to an institution (*ad pias causas*).[13] In these situations, it was thought, a would-be donor was likely to have acted sensibly.

In contracts of exchange, the principle of equality was said to explain why Roman law, as interpreted by the medieval jurists, gave a remedy for *laesio enormis*, a deviation of more than half from the just price. The just price was

[9] Aristotle, Nicomachean Ethics IV.i. 1119b–1120a.

[10] *Id.* V.ii 1130b–1131a; V.i 1131b–1132b. Fourteenth-century jurists familiar to Aristotle had first formulated the doctrine of *causa* by using these Aristotelian ideas. Bartolus de Sassoferrato, Commentaria Corpus Iuris Civilis in Omnia quae extant opera to Dig. 12.4.16 no. 3; to Dig. 44.4.2.3 (1615); Baldus de Ubaldis, Commentaria Corpus Iuris Civilis to C. 3.36.15 no. 3; to C. 4.30.13 no. 14 (1577); Baldus de Ubaldis, In decretalium volumen commentaria to X 1.4.11 no. 30 (1595). But they did not incorporate this doctrine into a larger theory. See James Gordley, Philosophical Origins of Modern Contract Doctrine 49–57 (1991).

[11] 3 Ludovicus Molina, De iustitia et iure tractatus disp. 279, no. 10 (1614).

[12] 4 Antonius de Gamma, Decisionum Supremi Senatus Lusitaniae Centuriae dec.no. 348, no. 5 (1622). It was accepted by Molina, *supra* note 11, at no. 7.

[13] Julius Clarus, Sententiarum receptarum liber quartus lib. 4 § Donatio q. 17. no. 1 (1595); 2 Antonius Gomezius, Variae resolutiones iuris civilis, communis et regii cap. 4, no. 10 (1759). It was accepted by Molina, *supra* note 11, at no. 2; Leonardus Lessius, De iustitia et iure, ceterisque virutibus cardinalis lib. 2, cap. 18, dub. 13, no. 102 (1628).

identified with the market price under competitive conditions.[14] A remedy was given only for gross violations for pragmatic reasons such as the stability of commerce.[15]

The principle of equality was also said to explain the terms that the law read into a contract of exchange in the absence of any express provision. In Roman law, as interpreted by the medieval jurists, a seller warranted his goods against defects absent a provision to the contrary. The reason, it was said, is that otherwise the buyer would have paid more than the goods were worth.[16] Molina said that the seller could expressly disclaim this warranty, but only if he reduced the price so that equality was preserved.[17]

For the will theorists, the ideas on which the earlier theory had been built were unacceptable. They believed that it would be paternalistic for the law to concern itself with whether a party had acted sensibly or whether a contract was fair. They were puzzled that the law required a formality before it would enforce a promise to give away money. In contracts of exchange, Joseph Story said:

> [E]very person who is not from his peculiar condition under a disability is entitled to dispose of his property in such a manner and upon such terms as he chooses; and whether his bargains are wise and discreet or profitable or unprofitable or otherwise, are considerations not for courts of justice but for the party himself to deliberate upon.[18]

Moreover, for the nineteenth-century jurists, the idea of a just price or equality in exchange seemed meaningless. Value, Joseph Story said, "must be in its nature fluctuating and will depend upon ten thousand different circumstances. One man in the disposal of his property may sell it for less than another man would."[19] According to Chitty and Metcalf, there were "no means" for determining whether an adequate price had been paid.[20] William Wentworth Story

14 *See, e.g.*, Glossa Ordinaria to C 4.44.2 to *auctoritate iudicis* (1581).

15 *See* Domenicus Soto, De iustitia et iure libri decem lib. 6, q. 2, a. 3 (1553); Molina, *supra* note 11, at disp. 348; Lessius, *supra* note 13, at cap. 21, dub. 2.

16 Molina, *supra* note 11, at disp. 353; Lessius, *supra* note 13, at cap. 21, dub. 11; Hugo Grotius, De iure bellis ac pacis libri tres II.xii.9.1 (1688).

17 Molina, *supra* note 11, at disp. 353.

18 1 Joseph Story, Equity Jurisprudence as Administered in England and America 337 (1918). Similarly, Chitty, *supra* note 2, at 7; 12 Charles Greenstreet Addison, A Treatise on the Law of Contracts 163 (1911); Story, *supra* note 2, at 435; Leake, *supra* note 2, at 311–12; Joel Bishop, Commentaries on the Law of Contracts 18 (2d ed., 1887); John Smith, The Law of Contracts 96 (1847); John Newland, Contracts within the Jurisdiction of Courts of Equity 357 (1821); Louis Hammon, The General Principles of the Law of Contract 692 (1912).

19 Story, *supra* note 18, at 339.

20 Chitty, *supra* note 2; Theron Metcalf, Principles of the Law of Contracts as Applied by Courts of Law 163 (1878).

thought that the determination would require "a psychological investigation into the motives of the parties,"[21] a view also held by Addison.[22]

When they spoke of equality in exchange, however, the earlier writers did not mean that each party personally placed the same value on the goods he gave as on those he received. If they had, the parties would not exchange. As Aristotle said, the shoemaker does not exchange with the shoemaker but with the house builder.[23] Nor did they believe that the just price of goods was an intrinsic or stable property of them like their color. They identified the just price with the price on a competitive market,[24] which, they knew, fluctuates from day to day and place to place in response to need, scarcity, and cost.[25] Neither party became richer or poorer at the moment of the transaction although either might find himself richer or poorer the next day. The risk that the market price would change after the contract was made was an inherent risk of selling or buying property, just as the risk that property would be destroyed by fire was an inherent risk of ownership. A party who loses if prices fall would have gained if prices had risen. As Soto said, a merchant must bear his losses if "bad fortune buffets him, for example, because an unexpected abundance of goods mounts up," and he may sell for more if "fortune smiles on him and later there is an unexpected scarcity of goods . . . [f]or as the business of buying and selling is subject to fortuitous events of many kinds, merchants ought to bear risks at their own expense, and, on the other hand, they may wait for good fortune."[26] Similarly, Lessius noted, "this is the condition of merchants, that as they may gain if they receive goods at small expense, so they lose if the expense was disproportionate or extraordinary."[27] A party who was unwilling to bear the losses he had sustained because the market price had fallen is like a party who tries to repudiate a contract because the property he purchased has since been destroyed. He assumed a risk and is trying to escape its consequences.

Later we will consider the merits of this position. For now, it is enough to see the contrast with the will theories. The will theories arose in an age of conceptualism in which rules of law were supposed to follow logically from concepts such as the will. The earlier theory was teleological rather than conceptualist. The rules were supposed to serve the purposes for which the parties contracted. For the will theorists, the will of the party was the sole source of their obligations. The earlier theorists recognized that sometimes the parties are bound by terms that they did not will and sometimes they are not bound by terms that they did.

21 STORY, *supra* note 2, at 435.

22 ADDISON, *supra* note 18, at 12.

23 Aristotle, *Nicomachean Ethics* V.v 1133a.

24 As noted by JOHN NOONAN, THE SCHOLASTIC ANALYSIS OF USURY 82–88 (1957); Raymond de Roover, *The Concept of the Just Price and Economic Policy*, 18 J. ECON. HIST. 418 (1958).

25 See SOTO, *supra* note 15, at lib. 6, q. 2, a. 3 (1553); MOLINA, *supra* note 11, at disp. 348; LESSIUS, *supra* note 13, at lib. 2, cap. 21, dub. 4; GROTIUS, *supra* note 16, at II.xii.14.

26 SOTO, *supra* note 15, at lib. 6 q. 2 a. 3.

27 LESSIUS, *supra* note 13, at lib. 2, cap. 21, dub. 4.

PART II
ENFORCEABILITY

2
A Critique of Current Doctrine

I. An outline

Current doctrine is ably summarized by the *Restatement (Second) of Contracts*.

A contract is defined as an enforceable promise. "A contract is a promise or a set of promises for the breach of which the law gives a remedy, or the performance of which the law in some way recognizes as a duty."[1]

A promise is enforceable if it is made under seal, if it is made for consideration, or, under some circumstances, if the promisee acted in reliance on it.

Seal is a formality that was established in the Middle Ages when people of importance owned seals or signet rings which they used to make an impression in wax on a document when they wanted to be legally bound. The *Second Restatement* defines a seal as "a manifestation in tangible and conventional form of an intention that a document be sealed."[2] It "may take the form of a piece of wax, a wafer or other substance affixed to the document or of an impression made on the document."[3] "[I]n most States in which the seal retains significance a seal may take the form of a written or printed seal, word, scrawl or other sign."[4]

Consideration is defined by the presence of a bargain. According to § 71 of the *Second Restatement*:

> (1) To constitute consideration, a performance or a return promise must be bargained for.
> (2) A performance or return promise is bargained for if it is sought by the promisor in exchange for his promise and is given by the promisee in exchange for that promise.
> (3) The performance may consist of
>   (a) an act other than a promise, or
>   (b) a forbearance, or
>   (c) the creation, modification, or destruction of a legal relation.

[1] Restatement (Second) of Contracts § 1 (Am. L. Inst. 1981).
[2] *Id.* at § 96(1).
[3] *Id.* at § 96(2).
[4] *Id.* at § 96(3).

Foundations of American Contract Law. James Gordley, Oxford University Press. © Oxford University Press 2023.
DOI: 10.1093/oso/9780197686089.003.0002

Section 79 provides that "there is no additional requirement of . . . equivalence in the values exchanged." According to § 208, however, a court may refuse to enforce an "unconscionable" bargain. "[G]ross disparity in the values exchanged may be an important factor in a determination that a contract is unconscionable."[5]

The *Restatement (First) of Contracts* recognized, for the first time, another situation in which a promise might be enforceable: it might have been relied upon by the promisee. Section 90 of the *Second Restatement* provides, in language similar to § 90 of the *First*:

> A promise which the promisor should reasonably expect to induce action or forbearance on the part of the promisee or a third person and which does induce such action or forbearance is binding if injustice can be avoided only by enforcement of the promise.[6]

Section 90 was adopted to avoid difficulties which arose from the requirement that a promise not under seal is enforceable only if it was made for consideration. To understand those difficulties, we need to examine the origins of the doctrine of consideration.

II. From a law of writs to a law of contract

i. Consideration as bargained-for detriment

Before the nineteenth century, common lawyers did not think in terms of categories such as contract and tort. The common law was organized by writs. Since the Middle Ages, a plaintiff needed to bring the facts of his case within the scope of a writ to sue in the common law courts. Otherwise, though he might be entitled to a remedy as a matter of justice, he had to seek it elsewhere: for example, in a manorial court, a municipal court, a merchants' court, or an ecclesiastical court. By the eighteenth century, two writs were used to enforce a promise: covenant and assumpsit. Covenant could be used to enforce a promise made under seal, which was a formality in which an impression was made on a document on which the promise was written. Assumpsit could be used to enforce a promise which had "consideration." Whether it did was determined by a body of lore to be found in the decided cases. Only in the nineteenth century was consideration defined, as it is today, as bargain or exchange.

[5] *Id.* at cmt. c.
[6] *Id.* at § 90.

In the nineteenth century, the common lawyers explained that the common law actions of covenant and assumpsit constituted a law of contract. They developed a systematic body of contract law for the first time. They did so, like jurists on the continent, on premises that were positivist, conceptualist, and voluntarist. The continental jurists, however, were replacing one theory of contract law with another. The common lawyers were developing a theory for the first time. They borrowed a great deal from continental writers. They claimed that the ideas they borrowed best explained liability in covenant and assumpsit.

In this transformation, a leading role was played by treatise writers. As A. W. B. Simpson noted, before the nineteenth century, there was little literature on what we call the common law of contract.[7] Aside from the reports of the decided cases, there were only a few pages in William Blackstone's *Commentaries on the Laws of England* (1766). The first treatise on the common law of contract was written by John J. Powell in 179.[8] Thereafter, treatises appeared in ever-growing numbers.

The treatise writers identified consideration with a bargain or an exchange. To do so was an innovation. Previously, as John Dawson noted:

> "Consideration" was only one of the words employed to precipitate the vague sensation that it was necessary to stop somewhere. . . . [T]he term "consideration" on its first appearance merely expressed obscurely the feeling that there should be some sufficient reason, ground or motive that would justify enforcement of a promise.[9]

The common law courts had found consideration for promises to bargain or exchange. But they had found consideration for other promises which they wished to enforce without the formality of a seal. They held that there is consideration for a promise by a parent to give money to a prospective son-in-law after his marriage. One can hardly imagine a prospective son-in-law asking for such a promise to be made under seal. They held there was consideration for the promisor to look after and return property when it was borrowed gratuitously or gratuitously entrusted to his care. It would be unreasonable to expect such promises to be made under seal. One party was doing the other a favor.

Beginning with William Blackstone,[10] common lawyers identified consideration with the civil law concept of *causa*. John J. Powell[11] and William

[7] A.W.B. Simpson, *Innovation in Nineteenth Century Contract Law*, 91 L.Q. REV. 247, 250–51 (1975).

[8] JOHN J. POWELL, ESSAY UPON THE LAW OF CONTRACTS AND AGREEMENTS 1 (1790).

[9] JOHN P. DAWSON & WILLIAM BURNETT HARVEY, CONTRACT AND CONTRACT REMEDIES CASES AND MATERIALS 540 (1959).

[10] 2WILLIAM BLACKSTONE, COMMENTARIES ON THE LAWS OF ENGLAND 444–46 (1766).

[11] POWELL, *supra* note 8, at 331.

Taylor[12] did so in England and likewise Samuel Comyn,[13] William Wentworth Story,[14] and Theophilus Parsons in the United States.[15] As A. W. B. Simpson said, the common lawyers seemed to regard consideration as a local version of the doctrine of *causa.*[16]

As we have seen, according to that doctrine, there are two *causae* or good reasons why the parties would make a contract or the law would enforce one: to exercise liberality and to obtain an equivalent in exchange for what one gives in return. The common lawyers identified consideration with the *causa* of a contract of exchange. According to Blackstone, as "[t]he civilians hold . . . there must be something given in exchange, something that is mutual and reciprocal."[17] In civil law, promises to give away money or property usually required the formality of notarization to be enforceable. Identifying the consideration with the *causa* of a contract of exchange made the common law look like the civil law. Contracts to confer a benefit gratuitously were enforceable in covenant which required the formality of a seal. Contracts to exchange were enforceable in assumpsit.

The fit was far from perfect. As noted, the common law courts had found consideration in transactions that are not bargains in any ordinary sense. One example was a promise by a parent to give money to a prospective son-in-law. Another was a promise to look after and return property that the promisee had loaned gratuitously, or that the promisor had gratuitously agreed to keep safe for him. Continental lawyers had classified them as acts of liberality, and distinguished them from other acts of liberality, such as promises to give away money or property, which were intended to enrich one party at the donor's expense. The latter required a formality to be binding; the former did not. If the promises in these transactions had consideration, and consideration meant bargain, there was a problem. These transactions were not bargains.

Moreover, sometimes common courts found there to be consideration by drawing a remote analogy to exchange. They did so to enforce promises that were not an exchange in the ordinary sense, and in which consideration was not a recompense in any ordinary sense of the word. To demand that the consideration be adequate or equal to the value of what was promised would defeat the very purpose that the judges were trying to achieve, which was to enforce promises in which the consideration was not a recompense. Thus, it came to be said, in the famous words of *Sturlyn v. Albany*,[18] that "when a thing is done, be it never

[12] WILLIAM TAYLOR, A TREATISE ON THE DIFFERENCES BETWEEN THE LAWS OF ENGLAND AND SCOTLAND RELATING TO CONTRACTS 16 (1849).

[13] 1SAMUEL COMYN, CONTRACTS AND AGREEMENTS NOT UNDER SEAL 8 (1809).

[14] WILLIAM W. STORY, A TREATISE ON THE LAW OF CONTRACTS 431, 431 n.1 (1851).

[15] 1 THEOPHILUS PARSONS, THE LAW OF CONTRACTS 355 (1860).

[16] Simpson, *supra* note 7, at 262.

[17] BLACKSTONE, *supra* note 10, at 444.

[18] Sturlyn v. Albany, Cro. Eliz. 67, 78 Eng. Rep. 327 (QB 1587).

so small, this is a sufficient consideration to ground an action." In *Sturlyn*, the plaintiff had leased to a third party who had granted his estate to the defendant. The plaintiff demanded the rent from the defendant who promised to pay if the plaintiff would show him a deed proving that the rent was due. The showing of the deed was said to be consideration.

Another problem was that, according to the doctrine of *causa* each party to an exchange received an equivalent for what he gave. The common law courts did not examine the adequacy of consideration. Had the idea of equality in exchange been accepted in the nineteenth century, the common lawyers might have responded in two ways. They might have said that in principle an exchange required equality but that the law did not do so in practice. Christopher Columbus Langdell claimed that:

> the law has never in theory abandoned the principle that a consideration must be commensurate with the obligation which is given in exchange for it; that, though the smallest consideration would in most cases support the largest promise, this is only because the law shuts its eyes to the inequality between them; and hence any inequality to which the law cannot shut its eyes is fatal to the validity of the promise.[19]

Or the common lawyers might have said that although common law courts did not examine the adequacy of consideration, to do so was the task of courts of equity. Courts of equity gave relief when a contract was so unfair as to be "unconscionable."

The idea of equality in exchange was not accepted in the nineteenth century. Treatise writers such as Sir Frederick Pollock explained that the reason that the common law did not examine the adequacy of consideration is that there is no such thing as a just price.[20] As Simpson noted, although courts of equity gave relief from unconscionable contracts, the rationale for doing so changed. Courts now claimed that the harshness of terms mattered because it is "evidence of fraud, not as an independent substantive ground, and not as constituting hardship."[21] The harshness of the terms did matter, however, although they were unwilling to admit it. They gave relief when the disadvantaged party never alleged that he had been defrauded.[22] Indeed, had they really been giving relief for fraud, they would not have needed a doctrine of unconscionability.

[19] Christopher Columbus Langdell, Summary of the Law of Contracts 70–71 (1880).

[20] Frederick Pollock, Principles of Contract: Being a Treatise on the General Principles Concerning the Validity of Agreements in the Law of England 172 (4th ed. 1885).

[21] A.W.B. Simpson, *The Horwitz Thesis and the History of Contracts*, 46 U. Chi. L. Rev. 533, 569 (1979).

[22] James Gordley, The Philosophical Origins of Modern Contract Doctrine 154–57 (1991).

Pollock found a way around these difficulties. Like previous treatise writers, he identified consideration with a bargain or exchange. He formulated a new definition of bargain to explain the cases in which courts had found consideration when the parties had not made a bargain in any ordinary sense. It became known as the "bargained-for-detriment" formula for consideration. In the United States, it was accepted enthusiastically by his friend Oliver Wendell Holmes.[23] Holmes's admirer Samuel Williston wrote a version of it into the *First Restatement of Contracts*[24] for which he served as Reporter, whence it passed into § 71 of the *Second Restatement*, quoted earlier.

According to Pollock, "Consideration means not so much that one party profited as that the other abandons some legal right in the present, or limits his legal freedom of action in the future, as an inducement for the act or promise of the first."[25] "[I]t is enough that . . . the party giving it does thereby undertake some burden, or lose something which in contemplation of law may have value."[26] He began by quoting Thomas Hobbes: "The value of all things contracted for is measured by the appetite of the contractors, and therefore the just value is that which they be contented to give."[27] This "idea," he said, "is characteristic not only in English positive law but in the English school of jurisprudence and politics."[28] The rule that a court will not "enter into an inquiry as to the adequacy of consideration is reached 'by a deduction' from this principle."[29] "And the legal rule is long-standing and illustrated by many cases." He quoted the passage cited earlier from *Sturlyn v. Albany*.[30] "The principle of all these cases may be summed up in the statement made in so many words by the judges in more than one of them, that the promisor got all that he bargained for."[31]

His definition enabled him to classify a transaction as an exchange because "the promisor got all that he bargained for" even though the transaction was not an exchange in the ordinary sense. "Marrying the promisor's daughter at his request is put as a good consideration" for a promise to pay money to the promisee after the marriage takes place.[32] For Pollock, the marriage was "the price of the

[23] Oliver Wendell Holmes, Jr., The Common Law 193–94 (1881). *See* Letter from Oliver Wendell Holmes, Jr., to Frederick Pollock (June 17, 1880) *in* 1 Holmes–Pollock Letters 14–15 (M. Howe ed., 2d ed. 1961).

[24] Restatement (First) of Contracts § 75 (Am L. Inst. 1932).

[25] Pollock, *supra* note 20, at 172.

[26] *Id.*

[27] *Id.* The quotation is from Thomas Hobbes, Leviathan I.xv, 102 (1935).

[28] Pollock, *supra* note 20, at 172.

[29] *Id.*

[30] (1587) Cro. Eliz. 67.

[31] Pollock, *supra* note 20, at 174.

[32] Frederick Pollock, Principles of Contract at Law and in Equity, Being a Treatise on the General Principles Concerning the Validity of Agreements, with a Special View to the Comparison of Law and Equity, and with References to the Indian Contract Act, and Occasionally to Roman, American, and Continental Law 151–52 (1st ed. 1876).

promise" and "all that [the promisor] bargained for."[33] Promises to care for and return objects borrowed gratuitously were also bargains. Pollock cited *Bainbridye v. Firmstone*,[34] which held that "[i]f a man who owns two boilers allows another to weigh them, this is a good consideration for that other's promise to give them up after such weighing in as good condition as before."[35] So were promises to care for and return objects gratuitously deposited with the promisor. In *Coggs v. Bernard*,[36] a porter was held liable for damaging a cask of rum which he had promised gratuitously to carry to the owner's lodgings. According to Pollock, in such a case "the bailor parts with present legal control of the goods; and this is so far a detriment to him, though it may be no benefit to the bailee, and the bailee's taking possession of the goods if for the bailor's use and convenience."[37]

American courts put this formula to a new use: to enforce promises to give money or property to a charitable institution. Sometimes, but not always,[38] they held that the promise was induced by some commitment made by someone else: for example, the commitments of other subscribers to donate money,[39] or in the commitment of a charity to name a fund after the donor,[40] to locate a college in a particular town,[41] or even to use the money for charitable purposes.[42]

In the United States, as we will see, these results were later explained by the doctrine of promissory reliance. Yet the bargained-for-detriment formula endures. In part, the reason is inertia. In part, it is the belief that this formula accurately describes the traditional English common law. In part, the reason is that courts use the formula for an entirely different purpose: to refuse to enforce promises in business transactions where neither party is playing Santa Claus. They have done so, paradoxically because these promises are often unfair even though, according to the bargained-for-detriment formulation, fairness isn't supposed to matter.

ii. Promissory reliance

According to the doctrine of "promissory reliance" or "promissory estoppel," a promise made without a seal and without consideration is enforceable if the

[33] *Id.* at 152.
[34] (1838) 8 A. & E. 743.
[35] POLLOCK, *supra* note 32, at 154.
[36] (1703) 2 L. Raym. 909.
[37] POLLOCK, *supra* note 20, at 173.
[38] Johnson v. Otterbein University, 41 Ohio 527 (Ohio 1885) (no consideration).
[39] Congregation B'nai Sholom v. Martin, 173 N.W.2d 504, 510 (Mich. 1969); First Presbyterian Church v. Dennis, 161 N.W. 183, 187–88 (Iowa 1917).
[40] Allegheny College v. National Chautauqua County Bank, 159 N.E. 173, 176 (N.Y. 1927).
[41] Rogers v. Galloway Female College, 44 S.W. 454, 455 (Ark. 1898).
[42] Nebraska Wesleyan University v. Griswold's Estate, 202 N.W. 609, 616 (Neb. 1925).

promisor could reasonably expect the promisee to act in reliance on it, and the promisee suffered some harm by doing so. It was formulated to enforce some promises that lacked consideration under the bargained-for-detriment formula and others that supposedly did not.

One type of promise that lacked consideration had been noted by Williston in 1920 in his influential treatise on contracts.[43] He cited the Nebraska case of *Ricketts v. Scothorn*.[44] Kathy Scothorn's grandfather had given her a note for $2,000 so that she could quit her job, which she did. He died before the note was paid. The court required his executors to pay the note on the ground that she quit work in reliance on the promise.[45] The court had said that the executors were required to pay because Scothorn had quit work in reliance on the promise. Williston suggested that the courts might be allowing reliance by the promisee to serve as a substitute for consideration. Nevertheless, he said, although that idea is "by no means without intrinsic merit, if generally applied it would much extend liability on promises and . . . at present it is opposed to the great weight of authority."[46] A few years later, despite what he had called "the great weight of authority," he wrote the doctrine into § 90 of the *First Restatement*.

Williston and Corbin also believed that this doctrine better explained why courts had enforced promises in the situations discussed earlier which are not bargains in any ordinary sense. In support of the new doctrine, Williston cited the cases enforcing promises made in prospect of marriage and to charitable institutions.[47] The married couple supposedly relied on the parent's promise by marrying. The charitable institution supposedly had spent money in reliance on the donor's promise.

Corbin had arrived at the reliance principle at almost the same time but by a different route. In his 1919 edition of Anson's *Principles of the Law of Contract*, he claimed that when courts find consideration they are sometimes holding the promisor liable because of "subsequent facts consisting of acts in reliance on the promise."[48] Although he did not say so expressly, he seems to have been thinking

[43] 1SAMUEL WILLISTON, THE LAW OF CONTRACTS § 139 (1920).

[44] FREDERICK POLLOCK, PRINCIPLES OF CONTRACT AT LAW AND IN EQUITY 650 n.1 (Gustavus Wald & Samuel Williston eds., 7th English ed., 3d American ed. 1906).

[45] 77 N.W. 365 (Neb. 1898).

[46] 1 SAMUEL WILLISTON & GEORGE THOMPSON, A TREATISE ON THE LAW OF CONTRACTS § 139 (1937).

[47] *Id.* He also mentioned to give land when the promisee had moved on and made improvements.

[48] WILLIAM R. ANSON, PRINCIPLES OF THE LAW OF CONTRACT WITH A CHAPTER ON THE LAW OF AGENCY § 118 at 116 n.3 (Arthur L. Corbin ed., 14th English ed., 3d American ed. 1919). He had come close to this position a year earlier when he disapproved of a statement by Holmes that "[i]t is not enough that the promise induces the detriment or that the detriment induces the promise if the other half is wanting." Wisconsin & Mich. R.R. v. Powers, 191 U.S. 379, 386 (1903). Corbin said, "[t] here are all too many decisions enforcing a promise where the only consideration was some expected action in reliance upon it for us to adopt [this statement] without reserve." Arthur L. Corbin, *Does a Pre-existing Duty Defeat Consideration?—Recent Noteworthy Decisions*, 27 YALE L.J. 362, 368 (1918).

of the cases in which courts had found consideration for gratuitous loans and deposits of property.[49] These, again, were the sort of cases that Pollock had devised his formula in order to explain.

One can see why Williston and Corbin thought that the doctrine of consideration could not explain such cases. To speak of a bargain was either artificial or wrong. When a promise is made in prospect of marriage it is artificial to call the marriage "the price of the promise" and "all that [the promisor] bargained for."[50] Also, it may be simply untrue. The parent may have promised money to the prospective son-in-law only after begging his daughter not to marry him. Pollock's line of reasoning was pushed to its logical extreme by Judge Benjamin Cardozo in the celebrated case of *De Cicco v. Schweitzer*.[51] A father had promised money to a prospective son-in-law who was engaged to his daughter at the time the promise was made. Since he was already legally obligated to marry her under the law of the day, it would seem that by marrying he had done nothing that he was not already bound to do. Cardozo found consideration in a right that the suitor had not given up: the right to break off the engagement with the daughter's consent. It would be either artificial or incorrect to think that the father was induced to make the promise by the suitor's commitment to insist on the marriage even if his daughter wanted to break it off.

It is artificial to say that promises to charities have consideration. It is possible, of course, that the promise was made, in part, to induce the promisee to name a fund after the donor or to locate a college in a particular town. But courts enforced such promises without any evidence as to the promisor's motivations.

The same can be said of promises to repay loans or to take care of and return borrowed property. It may be that the borrower promised, in part, to induce the lender to lend. But it is artificial to say that receiving the loan was the "price" of his promise.

In a case such as *Coggs v. Bernard*, moreover, the bargained-for-detriment formula does not work at all. The porter did not promise to take care of the cask of spirits in order to induce the owner to entrust it to him. As Gunter Treitel noted, "parting with possession is hardly a detriment" to the promisee.[52]

Williston and Corbin thought that the doctrine of promissory reliance provided a better explanation of why these promises are enforced. It does not. Those who marry only for love are not relying on a parent's promise of money. They would have married anyway. A court will not ask whether they would have done

[49] In the text Corbin was editing, Anson had listed them as exceptions to the normal requirements of consideration. Anson, *supra* note 48, at § 122 at 119; §§ 133–35 at 132–35. In contrast, Williston, while uncomfortable with these cases, seems to have thought that they could be explained as instances of genuine consideration or else as tort actions. 1 Williston, *supra* note 43, at § 138.

[50] Pollock, *supra* note 32, at 152.

[51] 221 N.Y. 431 (1917).

[52] G.H. Treitel, The Law of Contract 142 (8th ed. 1991).

so or not. To avoid contradicting the case law the *Second Restatement* provides that "a marriage settlement is binding . . . without proof that the promise induced action or forbearance."[53] The reason, according to Melvin Eisenberg, is that "[o]nce a person has been promised that he will be compensated if he takes a given act, it will be impossible for either the person or a court to sort out whether and to what extent the act was motivated by the promise of compensation."[54] But suppose there were no doubt. Can it really be that, in principle, the promisee who swore that money never mattered should lose? Or that, in principle, a promisee who married for money should win?

Courts have enforced promises to charities without any proof that the charitable institution relied on it. Accordingly, the *Second Restatement* also provides that "a charitable subscription is binding without proof that the promise induced action or forbearance."[55]

Moreover, surely a borrower must repay a loan even if the lender did not rely on his promise to do so. In *The Merchant of Venice*, Antonio loaned his friend Bassanio money to woo the fair Portia, a loan which Bassanio would be able to repay if he married her. Suppose that Antonio thought there was no chance at all that Portia would marry Bassanio and made the loan anyway because he would rather lose the money than imperil his friendship. Surely, if Bassanio succeeded, he must repay the loan.

Suppose a porter were entrusted with a cask of spirits by a passenger trying to board a cruise ship who had just been told that no one could not bring liquor onboard. Suppose the porter were the only person to whom the passenger could have entrusted the cask because no one else was in sight. It may be that the porter should not be liable for the least negligence in looking after it, as they would if had been paid to do so.[56] But it would be remarkable if the porter had no duty to do so at all.

With one exception, then, the doctrine of promissory reliance does not explain the cases cited in its support when it was formulated. The exception is a case like *Ricketts v. Scothorn*,[57] in which the promisee relies on a donative promise. Yet the doctrine has not only survived but also flourished. As with the doctrine of consideration, courts have used it in business transactions. As we will see, they have used it to enforce agreements that are perfectly fair but would be unenforceable under the doctrine of consideration.

[53] Restatement (Second) of Contracts § 90(2) (Am. L. Inst. 1981).

[54] Melvin A. Eisenberg, Foundational Principles of Contract Law 129 (2018).

[55] Restatement (Second) of Contracts § 90(2) (Am. L. Inst. 1981).

[56] The traditional rule was that his duty of a gratuitous bailee was less stringent than one of ordinary care. Dobbs, Hayden, and Bublick treat this "supposed rule" as a historical relic, citing Thomas M. Cooley, The Law of Torts 628–33 (1879). Dan B. Dobbs et al., Law of Torts § 121 at 379–80, 380 n.13 (2d ed. 2016). But one can cite any number of modern cases supporting it.

[57] Pollock, *supra* note 44, at 650 n.1.

iii. Reorganizing our doctrines

Doctrines should be formulated to group together cases in which the result should be the same for similar reasons. As they are presently formulated, the common law doctrines fail to do so.

We can learn from the traditional civil law. Like the common law, it enforced promises of gifts of money and property only if a formality is completed. The civil law formality is notarization. The common law formality is the seal. Once a seal called the promisor's attention to the importance of the transaction: an imprint was made on wax dripped on a document. The English still require that an impression be made on paper. But the seal can be used to make any promise binding. American lawyers have used it not only in important transactions such as gifts of money and property but ubiquitously. As the *Restatement* observes, "in most States in which the seal retains significance a seal may take the form of a written or printed seal, word, scrawl or other sign."[58] Lawyers understand the meaning of that word, scrawl, or sign, but laymen often do not. The formality no longer calls attention to the importance of a transaction. Many states have abolished it, leaving no formality by which a would-be donor can bind himself. Later we will examine substitutes which provide the protection of a formality such as notarization. It would be better to be clear about their role in binding commitments to make gifts of money or property.

Before codification, as we have seen, the civil law had recognized two exceptions to the need for a formality. Promises to give money or property to those about to marry (*proper nuptias*) were binding without it, as were promises to give to charities (*ad pias causas*). These promises were held to have consideration by eighteenth-century English courts and nineteenth-century American courts, respectively. To explain why they had consideration, the bargained-for-detriment formula transmuted them into bargains. When that explanation seemed artificial, Americans turned to the doctrine of promissory reliance. It would be better, like the civil law, to recognize that these promises are enforceable for special reasons, reasons that have nothing to do with consideration or reliance.

Roman law had distinguished a contract to loan money or fungibles gratuitously (*mutuum*), a contract to loan an object for the use of the borrower gratuitously (*commodatum*), and a contract to look after another's property gratuitously (*depositum*). In Roman law, these contracts were binding upon delivery of the object loaned or bailed. The late scholastics believed that they should be binding upon consent, and that rule was eventually adopted by civil law. But no civil lawyers ever claimed that they were binding because they were really

[58] Restatement (Second) of Contracts § 96(3) (Am. L. Inst. 1981).

contracts of exchange or because one of the parties relied upon the promise of another. The common lawyers did. According to the bargained-for-detriment formula, these transactions were bargains. According to the doctrine of promissory reliance, the promises made pursuant to these transactions were enforceable because promisees had relied on them. It would be better to recognize, like the civil law, that they are gratuitous contracts, that they are enforceable for reasons that have nothing to do with bargain or reliance, and that they do not require the same scrutiny as promises to give away money or property.

According to the bargained-for-detriment formula, each promise made by the parties to a contract of exchange has consideration. If Sally sells Bill her Mustang for $30,000, her promise has consideration because he promised to give up his right to the money, and his promise has consideration because she promised to give up her right to the car. By this formula, Pollock managed to define contract without using the idea of equivalence in value, in contrast to the civilians who spoke of *causa*. According to Pollock, one could not speak of an equivalent. The *Second Restatement* agreed with Pollock that as long as the relinquishment of a legal right was bargained for "there is no additional requirement of . . . equivalence in the values exchanged."[59] Yet, under § 208, it gives relief from an "unconscionable" bargain. "[G]ross disparity in the values exchanged may be an important factor in a determination that a contract is unconscionable."[60] As we will see, a principal use of the doctrine of consideration is to deny enforcement to promises made in a commercial context that are likely to be unfair. The idea of equivalence has been thrown out one door and allowed to come back in through another. It would be better to consider why and when such a contract should not be enforced because of a disparity in the values exchanged.

[59] *Id.* at § 79.
[60] *Id.* at cmt. c.

3
Promises to do Favors

I. Favors in a non-commercial context

One who promises a gift of money or property wishes to benefit the other party at one's own expense. As we will be using the term, one who promises to do another a favor wishes to confer a benefit on the other without incurring any cost.

A promise to loan money or property gratuitously is not enforceable at common law. It lacks consideration. So does a gratuitous promise to accept another's property for safekeeping. After a loan has been made or property has been entrusted to the other party, however, that party's promise to look after it and return it is enforceable. Before the nineteenth century, common law courts held that such a promise had consideration. As we have seen, they had a pragmatic reason for doing so. If they had denied that there was consideration, the promise could not be enforced by an action in assumpsit. It would have to be enforced in covenant, and that required a seal. When one party is doing another a favor, it would be unrealistic to expect such a promise to be made under seal.

When consideration was identified with bargain in the nineteenth century, the bargained-for-detriment formula was contrived, in part, to characterize these transactions as bargains, and so explain why there was consideration. The doctrine of promissory reliance was devised, in part, to avoid the artificiality of this characterization.

To explain the rules that govern these transactions, some scholars have turned to the law of torts. Corbin, at one point, suggested that the basis of liability might be the tort of negligence.[1] The problem is that, to be liable for negligence, a person must have been under a duty of care. If liability is in tort, this duty does not arise from their promise.

Dan Dobbs, Paul Hayden, and Ellen Burdick suggested that the defendant is liable in tort in cases such as *Coggs*, in which a porter gratuitously agreed to take charge of a cask of spirits, because "the relationship of the parties . . . may require the defendant to take affirmative steps to avoid harm to the plaintiff."[2]

[1] Although his preferred explanation was promissory reliance. 1A Arthur Corbin, Contracts: A Comprehensive Treatise on the Working Rules of Contracts Law § 207 (1950).

[2] Dan B. Dobbs, Paul T. Hayden, & Ellen M. Bublick, Hornbook on Torts 379 (2d ed. 2016),

Foundations of American Contract Law. James Gordley, Oxford University Press. © Oxford University Press 2023.
DOI: 10.1093/oso/9780197686089.003.0003

But that "relationship" was created by a promise, and indeed the action was in assumpsit for the breach of a promise. According to the *Second Restatement of Torts* a person whose conduct did not increase the risk of harm to another's property is under no duty to look after it, absent reliance by the owner:

> One who undertakes, gratuitously or for consideration, to render services to another which he should recognize as necessary for the protection of the other's person or things, is subject to liability to the other for physical harm resulting from his failure to exercise reasonable care to perform his undertaking, if:
>
> (a) his failure to exercise such care increases the risk of such harm, or
> (b) the harm is suffered because of the other's reliance upon the undertaking.[3]

According to this provision, to be liable to use care in performing services, a person must "undertake" to render them, presumably by making a promise. Borrowers or bailees who abandon property entrusted to them are liable if it is lost or destroyed, because they have "increased the risk of such harm" by breaking a promise to look after it. So we are back to contract principles.[4] The promise is the basis of the duty. Indeed, to ask whether "the harm is suffered because of the other's reliance upon the undertaking" is to rephrase the principle of promissory reliance. And that principle, as we have seen, does not explain liability.

We would do better to recognize that these are contractual relations that require special rules because they have special characteristics. Roman law recognized that they do. It distinguished a contract to loan money or fungibles gratuitously (*mutuum*), a contract to loan an object for the use of the borrower gratuitously (*commodatum*), and a contract to look after another's property gratuitously (*depositum*). These were "real" contracts (real as in real estate, not as in the real McCoys); they were binding when the object loaned or bailed (the *res*) was delivered.

In that respect, the result was the same as in common law. Such promises are not binding in advance of delivery. Once delivery has been made, a party who had consented to look after and return the property is obligated to do so.

These rules prevent a party who intended a favor to be costless from incurring a cost which that party did not expect. When a party reneges on a promise to do another a favor the reason is likely to be that circumstances have changed and the favor will not be costless. The promisor may wish to use the money or property

[3] RESTATEMENT (SECOND) OF TORTS § 323 (AM. LAW INST. 1964).

[4] I regret that I once took the opposite view. James Gordley, *Enforcing Promises*, 83 CALIF. L. REV. 547, 585–86 (1995).

for some unanticipated purpose or may no longer have extra space to store the other person's property.

Roman law developed special rules to govern the degree of care required of a person who looks after another's property. The standard of care depended on whether he was doing a favor or receiving one. A party who agreed to look after another's property without charge was liable only for gross negligence. A party who borrowed another's property for his own use without charge was liable for "the slightest negligence." It has been recognized since the Middle Ages that liability for "the slightest negligence" is really a form of strict liability.[5] A person is liable for negligence when they fail to take reasonable care. One cannot say that they were at fault for failing to take more care than was reasonable.

These rules were adopted by the common law. Explaining them is often left to writers on the law of torts. They look so strange that Dan Dobbs, Paul Hayden, and Ellen Burdick had trouble acknowledging their existence. They cited Thomas Cooley's 1879 treatise on torts[6] for "the supposed rule requiring extreme care, ordinary care or slight care depending on whether the bailment was for the benefit of the bailee, mutual benefit, or the benefit of the bailor only."[7] But one can cite any number of modern cases in support of these rules.

Hugo Grotius explained these rules by the principle that "in all contracts there should be equality."[8] In contracts of exchange, "equality requires that no more should be demanded by either party than what is just, which can scarcely have a place in gratuitous acts."[9]

> But it is to be noted that a certain equality is to be observed in gratuitous contracts, not, indeed, in every way as in contracts of exchange, but on the supposition that it may be said that one should not suffer harm by conferring a benefit. On this ground one who gratuitously undertakes a service for another (*mandatarius*) should be indemnified for the expense he incurs and the harm which he suffers in doing so. A gratuitous borrower (*commodarius*) is held to make compensation for the thing loaned if it perishes because he is obligated not only by reason of property, that is, by virtue of the lender's ownership, as any possessor is bound, as we said earlier, but also by reason of his acceptance of a favor. That is so unless the thing would have perished in the owner's custody. In that case the owner lost nothing by making the loan.[10]

[5] James Gordley, *Culpa Levissima and the Eclipse of Strict Liability*, 42 GROTIANA 5, 9–12 (2021).
[6] THOMAS M. COOLEY, THE LAW OF TORTS 628–33 (1879).
[7] DOBBS, HAYDEN, & BURDICK, *supra* note 2, at § 121, 379–80, 380 n.13.
[8] HUGO GROTIUS, DE BELLI AC PACIS LIBRI TRES II.xii.6–7 (1688).
[9] *Id.* at. II.xii.11.
[10] *Id.* at II.xii.13.1.

If the borrower did not compensate the owner, equality would be violated since he would have gained at the owner's expense.

The late scholastics used this same principle to criticize the Roman rules. Promises to do another a favor ought to be actionable by the promisee if the promisor so intended. But since the promisor intended the favor to be costless, he should not be obliged to keep his promise if he discovered that he could not perform it costlessly. If he found that he needed to use the property after he loaned it to another, he should be able to demand it back even if he had promised that the borrower could keep it for a certain length of time.[11] According to Roman law, he could not get it back before the time agreed.[12] The rule formulated by the late scholastics was later accepted in some civil law jurisdictions.[13] The late scholastics recognized that the other party might have relied on the lender's promise that he could keep the object borrowed. He might incur costs that he could have avoided if the promise had not been made. They answered that he assumed that risk since he knew that the lender intended to make the loan at no cost to himself.[14]

The Romans were correct that these are special transactions that call for special rules. In common law they are governed by special rules and that is why it is a mistake to try to explain these rules by the doctrines of consideration or promissory reliance. They are favors, intended to confer a benefit on the other party. Unlike promises to give away money or property, they are not intended to benefit one party at the other's expense. A problem arises when the promisor discovers that the promise cannot be performed costlessly, and yet the promisee will be hurt if the promisor does not perform it. At that point, one has to choose between two unforeseen consequences: a loss must be borne either by the promisor or by the promisee.

The common law solution is like that of Roman law. Promises to lend money or property or to look after it gratuitously are not binding in advance of delivery. Once delivery has been made, a party who had consented to look after and return the property received is obligated to do so. As in Roman law, the standard of care depends on which party is doing the other a favor.

A party who agreed to look after another's property without charge was liable only for gross negligence. A party who borrowed another's property for their own use without charge is held to a much stricter standard, one that approaches strict liability. A difference is that in Roman law, a promise to do a favor cannot be revoked, if the promisor had agreed that it would be binding for a certain

[11] 3 Ludovicus Molina, De iustitia et iure tractatus disp. 279, no. 10 (1614).

[12] Dig. 13.6.17.3.

[13] James Gordley ed., The Enforceability of Promises in European Contract Law 192 (2001).

[14] Molina, *supra* note 11, at disp. 279, no. 10.

term. In common law, this promise would lack consideration. Nevertheless, a promisee who was hurt by relying on it would be protected by the doctrine of promissory reliance. The common law solution is the result of historical accident. Nevertheless, it is a sensible solution even if it is not the only sensible solution.

II. Favors in a business context

In the situations we have discussed, one party was doing the other a favor, as the late scholastics said, out of liberality. In a business context, a party may promise to do a favor, not out of generosity, but to facilitate a contract of exchange between the parties. In the situations we have discussed, the favor was to lend money or property or to look after another's property gratuitously. The cases that arise in a business context typically concern another type of favor: one party had promised to do a service for the other which can be performed at no cost to itself.

Sometimes, the promise of such a favor was made after the parties had entered into a contract of exchange. For example, the seller of property promised to file papers to insure it.[15] A railway promised to help one of its customers obtain a rebate by filing papers with a government agency.[16] The holder of a security interest in property promised to insure it at the promisee's expense[17] or at their own expense for a short time.[18] In other cases, three parties were involved in a transaction, and one agreed to do something, not for the party who was paying him, but for the other party. For example, the senior creditor in a financing arrangement agreed to give notice of default to a junior creditor.[19] A general contractor agreed to write checks payable to his subcontractor's supplier rather than to his subcontractor alone.[20]

Since these promises do not have consideration, some scholars have said that the real reason for enforcing them is the reliance of the promisee.[21] Yet in the cases just described, courts have rarely required that the promisee prove that it changed its position. In some, the promisee could have done the act itself or

[15] Dalrymple v. Ed Shults Chevrolet, Inc., 380 N.Y.S.2d 189, 190 (App. Div. 1976), aff'd, 363 N.E.2d 587 (N.Y. 1977); *see also* Northern Commercial Co. v. United Airmotive, 101 F. Supp. 169 (D. Alaska 1951) (holding seller of airplane not liable on promise to keep it insured until buyer could get insurance, only because buyer did not exercise due diligence).

[16] Carr v. Maine Cent. R.R. Co., 102 A. 532 (N.H. 1917).

[17] East Providence Credit Union v. Geremia, 239 A.2d 725 (R.I. 1968).

[18] Siegel v. Spear & Co., 138 N.E. 414 (N.Y. 1923).

[19] Miles Homes Division of Insilco Corp. v. First State Bank, 782 S.W.2d 798 (Mo. Ct. App. 1990).

[20] United Elec. Corp. v. All Service Elec., Inc., 256 N.W.2d 92, 95–96 (Minn. 1977).

[21] *See* Benjamin F. Boyer, *Promissory Estoppel: Principle from Precedents* (pts. 1 & 2), 50 MICH. L. REV. 639, 665–74, 873–88 (1952); Warren A. Seavey, *Reliance upon Gratuitous Promises or Other Conduct*, 64 HARV. L. REV. 913, 926 (1951); Warren L. Shattuck, *Gratuitous Promises—A New Writ?*, 35 MICH. L. REV. 908, 918 (1937).

found someone else to do it: for example, it could have taken out its own insurance. But the promisee was not required to prove that it would have done so. In other cases, the promisee could not have done the act itself although, if the promisor refused, the promisee might have been able to exert pressure by threatening something within its legal rights. For example, in the three-party situations, the junior creditor could have told the senior creditor that it would not supply credit unless the senior creditor promised to give notice of default. Similarly, the subcontractor's supplier could have threatened to withhold materials unless it was paid directly by the general contractor. Nevertheless, in both of these cases, the promisee was not required to prove, or even allege, that it would have made the threat or that the threat would have been successful. Moreover, sometimes the promisee recovered even though there is nothing it could have done had the promisor refused to promise. The former customer of a railroad recovered when the railroad failed to send a government agency papers entitling it to a rebate, though it is not clear it could have somehow obtained the rebate had the railroad refused to cooperate from the beginning.[22] Moreover, as Yorio and Thel observed, courts have nearly always enforced the promise to its full extent instead of awarding compensation for the amount that the promisee was hurt through its reliance.[23]

In virtually all of these cases, either the cost of the performance to the promisor was obviously trivial, or one can assume it was trivial since otherwise the promisor would have been unlikely to make the promise in a commercial context. The same was true, or presumed to be true, in the case of the favors discussed earlier in which one party loaned money or property to another gratuitously or agreed to look after another's property gratuitously. Yet those promises are not enforceable in advance of performance.

A good reason for the difference is that in these instances, the favor was promised in connection with a preexisting contract. As we will see later on, each party to a contract of exchange has an implied duty to cooperate to effectuate the purposes for which the contract is made. For example, each is under a duty to take an action that is necessary for the other party to be able to perform[24] or for a condition to be fulfilled.[25] If a contractor cannot remodel a kitchen until an owner's cabinets are empty, or cannot build until the owner obtains a permit, the owner has a duty to empty the cabinets or apply for a permit even if the contract does not say so. As we will see, a party may be under an implied duty to take

[22] Carr v. Maine Cent. R.R., 102 A. 532 (N.H. 1917).

[23] Edward Yorio & Steve Thel, *The Promissory Basis of Section 90*, 101 YALE L.J. 111, 129–51 (1991).

[24] *E.g.*, Designer Direct, Inc. v. DeForest Redevelopment Authority, 313 F.3d 1036 (7th Cir. 2002) (failure to take steps to make contractor's performance possible constitutes a lack of good faith).

[25] Simon v. Etgen, 107 N.E. 1066 (N.Y. 1915) (when sale of a building is a condition to be fulfilled before payment was due, good faith requires sale within a reasonable time).

action even when it is not necessary, so long as it contributes to the purposes for which the contract and the cost is trivial. An express promise may make this duty concrete by specifying an action does contribute to these purposes and can be performed at a trivial cost.

In some instances, there were three parties. One agreed to do something, not for the other party to the contract, but for a third party. The senior creditor in a financing arrangement agreed to give notice of default to a junior creditor.[26] A general contractor agreed to write checks payable to its subcontractor's supplier rather than to his subcontractor alone.[27] It should not matter to which party the promise was made. In a three-party situation, A confers a benefit on B so that B may confer a benefit on C. If A can costlessly facilitate B's performance, it should not matter whether A's promise to do so was made to B or to C.

We saw in discussing gratuitous loans and bailments, that when a promise was intended to be costless, it should remain so. That consideration explains why, in some cases, courts have been reluctant to give relief when the promise of a favor was made in a commercial context. In some cases, the promisor's liability can be very large if it fails to perform. Although the performance may be almost costless, the exposure to liability is itself a significant cost. An example is a promise to help obtain insurance on the promisee's property. Some courts do not allow the promisee to recover.[28] The *Second Restatement* says that Section 90 should be "applied with caution to promises to procure insurance," noting that "[t]he appropriate remedy for breach of such a promise makes the promisor an insurer, and thus may result in a liability which is very large in relation to the value of the promised service."[29] In that event, as in a non-business context, the promisor should be liable only for conduct that such is such so seriously wrong and so easy to avoid that it would not be afraid of liability for breaching its duty inadvertently. It is like the rule in a non-business context that a party who gratuitously agrees to take care of another's property should be liable only for gross negligence.

26 Miles Homes Division of Insilco Corp. v. First State Bank, 782 S.W.2d 798 (Mo. Ct. App. 1990).

27 United Elec. Corp. v. All Service Elec., Inc., 256 N.W.2d 92, 95–96 (Minn. 1977).

28 *E.g.*, Hazlett v. First Fed. Sav. & Loan Ass'n, 127 P.2d 273, 276–77 (Wash. 1942) (holding mortgagee not liable on promise to secure insurance on mortgaged property); Comfort v. McCorkle, 268 N.Y.S. 192, 194–95 (Sup. Ct. 1933) (finding defendant not liable on promise to file insurance claim on plaintiff's behalf); Prescott v. Jones, 41 A. 352 (N.H. 1898) (declaring defendant not liable on promise to renew fire insurance on plaintiff's property).

29 RESTATEMENT (SECOND) OF CONTRACTS § 90 cmt. e (AM. LAW INST. 1981).

4

Promises to Make Gifts of Money or Property

I. Why such promises should be binding

The nineteenth-century will theorists were puzzled by the doctrine of consideration. They believed that, in principle, the law should enforce whatever obligations the parties willed to assume. Charles Fried defended a modernized version of the will theories in his book *Contract as Promise*. Yet he had to admit that the law should not enforce promises of "the more dubious and meretricious kinds of gifts in which strangers are promised the moon, to the prejudice of a spouse or children."[1] He was rediscovering the idea of liberality as it was understood by pre-nineteenth-century contracts theorists. When a promise is intended to enrich the promisee at the promisor's expense the law is concerned with whether it was made sensibly.

As we will see, that concern explains why the law provides safeguards to encourage the promisor to act sensibly. Nevertheless, what if the promisor has a change of heart? Why should the promise be binding?

As Hanoch Dagan and Michael Heller noted, some contemporary jurists have answered the question by formulating so-called "transfer theories."[2] The will of the promisor creates a legal right in the promisee to require that the promisor perform.[3] For the promisor to refuse to do so is unjust because it deprives the promisee of that right.[4]

According to Peter Benson:

[1] Charles Fried, Contract as Promise: A Theory of Contractual Obligation 38 (1981).

[2] Hanoch Dagan & Michael Heller, The Choice Theory of Contracts 33 (2017).

[3] *Id.* at 34.

[4] *See* Seana Valentine Shiffrin, *Promising, Intimate Relationships, and Conventionalism*, 117 Phil. Rev. 481, 507, 516 (2008) (explaining the effect of a promise is to create a moral obligation in the promisor and a "power" in the promisee to hold the promisor to the promise and how it is a "transfer of a party's power to change one's mind to the other party"); *see also* Arthur Ripstein, Force and Freedom: Kant's Legal and Political Philosophy 109 (2009). According to Arthur Ripstein, the will of the parties can transfer a preexisting right from one to the other. It can also "create new rights," including rights to things that need not exist as fully determinate antecedent to the transfer. *Id.* 109.

Foundations of American Contract Law. James Gordley, Oxford University Press. © Oxford University Press 2023.
DOI: 10.1093/oso/9780197686089.003.0004

> [One must] understand contract formation as itself effectuating between the parties a kind of *transactional acquisition* that vests in them exclusive entitlements with respect to what they have promised one another. And since the acquisition of each party is from the other, it is constituted by a transfer between them . . . [B]reach of contract can now plausibly be viewed as an injury to the rights already vested at formation. Breach becomes the equivalent of attempting to "take back" or "withhold" what, as a matter of rights, one has *already* given over to the other.[5]

Similarly, for Arthur Ripstein, the will of the parties can transfer a preexisting right from one to the other.[6] It can also "create new rights, including rights to things that need not exist as fully determinate prior to the transfer."[7] For Seana Shiffrin, "[A] promise by B [to A] creat[es] a moral obligation to A and the power in A to insist on or to release B from performance."[8] "[T]he power behind making promises . . . involves the transfer of a party's power to change one's mind to another party."[9]

These jurists, too, are rediscovering the teachings of pre-nineteenth-century contract theory. Benson correctly noted that his theory was proposed by "the great natural law writers in the continental civilian tradition, including Hugo Grotius [1583–1645] and Samuel Pufendorf [1632–1694]."[10] He quoted Grotius[11] who distinguished three statements we might make about what we intend to do in the future. We might be "setting forth the intention we now have." In that case, there is no promise. We might be making a "promise" without "giv[ing] another person a right of his own." In that case there is a promise but no commitment: the promisee has no right to hold the promisor to his promise. Or we might be "wanting to confer on another person a right of his own, which is called a perfect promise, and has an effect similar to the alienation of ownership."[12] There is a commitment in the sense of a promise that the promisee can enforce.

Grotius took this idea from the late scholastics. They were answering a question put by Cajetan (Tomasso di Vio) (1469–1534). Suppose that the promise was made sensibly, and that the promisor had broken it. The promisee is no worse off than if the promise had never been made. Commutative justice is violated only if one party is enriched at the other's expense. Therefore, it would seem, the promisee had no right to the promised performance as a matter of commutative

[5] Peter Benson, Justice in Transactions: A Theory of Contract Law 8 (2019).
[6] *See* Ripstein *supra* note 4, at 116.
[7] *Id.*
[8] Shiffrin, *supra* note 4, at 507.
[9] *Id.* at 516.
[10] Benson, *supra* note 5, at 10.
[11] *Id.*
[12] Hugo Grotius, De iure bellis ac pacis libri tres II.xi.1.6–2.1–4 (1688).

justice however disappointed he might be. He would have an action only if he had been harmed by changing his position in reliance on the promise.[13]

Luis de Molina (1535–1600) pointed out that if the donor had given something away and delivered it to the donee, it would belong to the donee.[14] Under the Roman law, the donor could not then take it back unless the donee was guilty of gross ingratitude.[15] But there is nothing magical about the moment of delivery. In principle, Molina argued, the donor ought to be able to transfer the right to a thing, or the right to claim it, in advance of delivery. If he did, then depriving him of that right by failing to perform violates commutative justice.[16] Leonard Lessius (1554–1623) agreed, Grotius followed Molina, and Pufendorf followed Grotius.[17]

But a question arises which neither the early jurists nor contemporary "transfer theorists" discussed. Why would a person who promises to give away money or property wish to give the promisee the right to enforce the promise?

This question was addressed by Melvin Eisenberg's "positive theory" of the enforceability of donative promises. According to Eisenberg, one reason a promisor might give up the right to change her mind is "to protect her present aspirations against defeat by a less worthy future self."[18] She believes that her decision to confer a benefit on the other party is likely to be a better decision than a later one to do otherwise. A second reason is that a promise might be subject to inchoate conditions under which the promisor's own needs trump those of the

13 *See* Cajetan (Tomasso di Vio), Commentaria to Thomas Aquinas, Summa theologica II–II, Q. 88, a. 1; Q. 113, a. 1 (1698).

14 *See* 3 Ludovicus Molina, De iustitia et iure tractatus disps. 272, 281 (1614).

15 The rule is described in Leonardus Lessius, De iustitia et iure, ceterisque virtutibus cardinalis libri quatuor lib. 2, cap. 18, dub. 8, no. 52 (1628), and Molina, *supra* note 14, at disps. 272, 281.

16 *See* Molina, *supra* note 14, at disp. 262.

17 *See* Lessius, *supra* note 15, at lib. 2, cap. 18, dub. 8, no. 52; Grotius, *supra* note 12, at II.xi.1.3–4 (1688); Samuel Pufendorf, De iure naturae libri octo III.v.5–7 (1688); Jean Barbeyrac, Le Droit de la guerre et de la Paix de Hugues Grotius n.2 to II.xi.1; n.1 to II.xi.3 (1729); Jean Barbeyrac, Le Droit de la nature et des gens . . . par le Baron de Pufendorf n.10 to III.v.9 (1734).

18 Melvin A. Eisenberg, Foundational Principles of Contract Law 109 (2018). In his inventory of the promisor's possible motives he mentioned three others: "to ensure performance by her estate if she dies without completing performance," "to increase the value of her performance," and "to permit the promisee to make reliable plans on the basis of the promise." *Id.* 109. The first would be a good reason for enforcing the promise only if she does not change her mind before she dies. The second would be a good reason, as Richard Posner said, only if the enforceability of the promise makes in it more valuable to the promisee by reducing the chance that she will break it. Richard A. Posner, *Gratuitous Promises in Economics and Law*, 6 J. Leg. Stud. 411 (1977). As Eisenberg noted, however, "[T]his argument is probably inapplicable in many or most cases because it depends on the promisor's forming a belief that the promisee thinks there is a significant likelihood that the promise will not be kept. . . . [A] donative promisor is unlikely to believe that the promisee so thinks, and often or usually the promisor would consider the promisee ungrateful for even entertaining such a thought." *Id.* 101 n.15. The last reason that Eisenberg mentioned is to permit reliance by the promisee, a possibility that we will discuss later on. For now, then, we are left with the reason described in the text.

promisee. Those conditions would be best known to the parties themselves and impossible to prove in court:

> All promises are subject to certain relatively well-specified moral (and legal) excuses, such as incapacity, but simple donative promises are likely to be subject to many additional and fluid moral excuses, such as "I find that I unexpectedly need a lot of new money in my business," or "for a retirement home," or "for my sick nephew," and on and on. In particular, the obligation created by a donative promise can be excused . . . by a change in the personal circumstances of the promisor that would make it improvident to keep the promise. If Uncle promises Nephew $50,000 in two years, . . . no one, not even Nephew, is likely to expect that Uncle remains morally obliged to keep his promise . . . if Uncle suffers a serious financial setback and is barely able to take care of the needs of his immediate family or if Uncle's wealth remains constant but his personal obligations significantly increase in an unexpected manner, as through marriage, the birth of children or illness, or perhaps even if Uncle's wealth and personal obligations both remain constant, but due to his miscalculation the gift would jeopardize his ability to maintain himself in the manner to which he is accustomed.[19]

Such matters are "often too subtle to be regulated by legal rules. . . . [M]any or most donative promises arise in an intimate context in which emotions, motives and cues are invariably complex and highly interrelated."[20]

It may be, however, that the promisor wishes the promisee to enjoy the same independence and security as if the money or property had already been transferred. It belongs to the promisee whose decision as to how to use the property can no longer be trumped by the needs of the promisor. If a parent gives a son and daughter-in-law a house or bonds, it is now theirs. They may treat it like anything else they own, using it as they see fit, without balancing their needs against those of the parent. If a parent allows a son and daughter-in-law to live in a house owned by the parent, it is not theirs. If a parent gives them the interest on bonds owned by the parent, it is not as though the son and daughter-in-law own the bonds. Parents can change their minds and weigh a child's needs against their own. The same is true if parents make a promise subject to the kind of inchoate conditions that Eisenberg described.

19 EISENBERG, *supra* note 18, at 99–100.
20 *Id.* at 100.

II. When such promises are enforceable

i. Formalities

In both civil and common law jurisdictions, a promise to make a gift of money or property can be made binding by using a legal formality. The formality makes it more likely that the promisor will deliberate and so act sensibly. It is also an indication of the promisor's intention to give the promisee the right to enforce the promise.

In civil law jurisdictions, the formality typically is notarization. The promisor subscribes to the promise before a notary, who, unlike the American notary public, is a member of the legal profession.

The traditional common law formality was the seal. It goes back to the Middle Ages when people of importance owned seals or signet rights which they used to make an impression in wax on a document. People today do not have seals or signet rings and are unfamiliar with their use. Consequently, some states have abolished the formality. Where it remains, the requirements for making a document under seal have become so liberalized that the requirement of a seal is a trap for the unwary. As the *Second Restatement* observed, "in most States in which the seal retains significance a seal may take the form of a written or printed seal, word, scrawl or other sign."[21]

Another way to make a promise to give money or property binding, which will still work in some states, is to make the promise in return for token ("nominal") consideration such as a peppercorn or a dollar. By the bargained-for-detriment formula, nominal consideration is not truly consideration. The promisee is giving up a legal right to the peppercorn or the dollar, but the promisor did not promise to induce the promisee to do so. The purpose of giving "nominal consideration" is to make the promise binding. Nevertheless, according to the *First Restatement of Contracts* a promise given for nominal consideration is binding.[22] According to the *Second Restatement*, as a general rule, it is not.[23] In this rare instance, the *Second Restatement* applied the bargained-for-detriment formula more consistently than the first.

Eisenberg claimed that the *Second Restatement* should have made an exception for donative promises. "A rule that nominal consideration makes a promise enforceable would enable donative promisors to make their promises enforceable if they have a specific intention to do so."[24] As we have noted, whether such

[21] Restatement (Second) of Contracts § 96(3) (Am. Law Inst. 1981).

[22] Restatement (First) of Contracts §84, illus. 1 (Am. Law Inst. 1932).

[23] Restatement (Second) of Contracts § 79 cmt. c (Am. Law Inst. 1981). There are exceptions for options and loan guarantees (*id.* at §§ 77–78) which will be discussed later.

[24] Eisenberg, supra note 18, at 112.

a promise should be enforceable depends on two considerations: whether the promise is made with deliberation, and whether the promisor intends to give the promisee a right to enforce the promise. The use of nominal consideration indicates that the promisor did wish to confer such a right, but it may be insufficient to ensure deliberation. It is like a promise that is made in a writing that states it is to be legally enforceable. Eisenberg observed that even a promise in writing may be "uncalculated rather than deliberative," and "made in an emotional state brought on by a surge of gratitude, an impulse of display, or some other intense but transitory emotion."[25] That is the same fear that led many states to abolish the legal effect of the seal once the formula had become trivialized.

Rather than make a contract, a would-be donor can commit to give away money or property by using an *inter vivos* document of transfer or a trust. In both cases, the law regards the transaction not as a promise as to what the party will do in the future, but as a present transfer of ownership. The effect, however, is like that of a promise made using a formality. A party giving away money or property is more likely to promise deliberately and to intend to confer a legal right on the other party.

A person makes an *inter vivos* document of transfer by executing a document declaring an immediate intention of making a gift, and naming the donor, the donee, and the object given. On receipt of the document, the transferee acquires a right to the property.

To confer such a right on the transferee at some future time, a person can use a trust. That person—the "settlor"—does so naming a "trustee" who holds the property in trust for the donee.[26] The trust is then irrevocable if the settlor so declares, and the intention to create an irrevocable trust will usually be presumed even absent such a declaration.[27] The terms of the trust may allow the settlor to continue to use the property or receive the income from the assets placed in trust for a period of time.[28] The property and money will then go to the person to whom the settlor wished to make a gift.

In practice, a layperson will not know how to make a deed of gift or establish a trust without the help of a lawyer. The requirement thus serves the same function in common law that notarization does in civil law jurisdictions. As mentioned, in those jurisdictions, typically, to make a promise to give money or property binding, the promisor must subscribe to the promise before a notary, who, unlike the American notary public, is a member of the legal profession. By doing so,

[25] *Id.* at 99.

[26] 1 Austin W. Scott & William F. Fratcher, The Law of Trusts 310–12, 312 n.4 (4th ed. 1987).

[27] *Id.* at 315.

[28] 1A *id.* at 188.

the promisor shows intention to be legally bound, is more likely to take time to deliberate, and may receive some good advice.

ii. Promises in prospect of marriage

As noted earlier, before the nineteenth-century jurists had identified consideration with bargain, the common law courts found consideration for promises to give money or property to children after they marry. Pollock claimed that these promises really were bargains. "Marrying the promisor's daughter" was "the price of the promise" and "all that [the promisor] bargained for."[29] Williston thought the enforceability of these promises could be explained by the doctrine of promissory reliance, but courts enforce them without proof of reliance. According to the *Second Restatement* proof of reliance is unnecessary. "A marriage settlement is binding . . . without proof that the promise induced action or forbearance."[30]

Edward Yorio and Steve Thel observed:

> [T]he most common explanation links the enforceability of these promises to social policies favoring . . . the institution of marriage. This rationale has an obvious ad hoc quality. For example, it fails to explain why the legal system would not enforce a promise to pay for a daughter's college expenses or for a son's medical operation in the absence of actual inducement given our strong social commitment to children, education, and health care.[31]

The question, however, is not whether it was good or wise or socially beneficial to promise to pay for a daughter's college expenses or for a son's medical operation. The question is whether the promisor wanted the promisee to enjoy the same independence and security as if the money or property had already been transferred. A parent may do so, as noted earlier, when he or she decides to give their children a house rather than allowing the children to live there, or to give the children bonds rather than periodically giving them the interest from the bonds. The children can then treat the house or bonds as their own. The parent may wish the children to be able to treat the promised money or property as their own as of the moment it is promised. If so, that promise is not made subject to the inchoate conditions that Eisenberg described. The German Civil Code

[29] Frederick Pollock, Principles of Contract at Law and in Equity, Being a Treatise on the General Principles Concerning the Validity of Agreements, with a Special View to the Comparison of Law and Equity, and with References to the Indian Contract Act, and Occasionally to Roman, American, and Continental Law 151–52 (1st ed. 1876).

[30] Restatement (Second) of Contracts § 90(2) (Am. Law Inst. 1981).

[31] Edward Yorio & Steve Thel, *The Promissory Basis of Section 90*, 101 Yale L.J. 111, 153–54 (1991).

also recognizes that a promise should be enforceable without the formality that is usually required when the promisor's motive is to confer independence on the married couple: as the Code puts it, when the promise is made "by the father or mother on account of marriage or obtaining an independent position in life, for founding or preserving the establishment of the position in life."[32]

In contrast, a promise to pay for a daughter's college expenses or for a son's medical operation is more likely to be subject to such inchoate conditions. Neither party may expect it to be kept if, to quote Eisenberg, the parent "suffers a serious financial setback and is barely able to take care of the needs of his immediate family or . . . his personal obligations significantly increase in an unexpected manner, as through marriage, the birth of children or illness, or . . . the gift would jeopardize his ability to maintain himself in the manner to which he is accustomed."[33]

iii. Promises to charitable institutions

As we have seen, American courts used the bargained-for-detriment formula to find consideration for promises to give money or property to charities. When that seemed artificial, they turned to the doctrine of promissory reliance. Yet many courts have not demanded proof of reliance. In deference to the case law, the *Second Restatement* provides that "a charitable subscription is binding without proof that the promise induced action or forbearance."[34]

As Yorio and Thel noted, the most common explanation "links the enforceability of these promises to social policies favoring the activities of organized charities."[35] E. Allan Farnsworth, the Reporter for the *Second Restatement*, said that the enforcement of promises to charities is "particularly desirable as a means of allowing decisions about the distribution of wealth to be made at the individual level."[36] Some courts have said the same,[37] for example, in *Salisbury v. Northwestern Bell Telephone*: "It is more logical to bind charitable subscriptions without a showing of consideration or promissory reliance." "Charitable subscriptions often serve the public interest by making possible projects which otherwise could never come about."[38]

[32] Bürgerlichesgesetzbuch (BGB) § 1624.

[33] Eisenberg, *supra* note 18, at 99–100, quoted *supra* note 19.

[34] Restatement (Second) of Contracts § 90(2) (Am. Law Inst. 1981).

[35] Yorio & Thel, *supra* note 31, at 153–54.

[36] E. Allan Farnsworth & William F. Young, Cases and Materials on Contracts 98 (4th ed. 1988).

[37] Some have not. In *In Re Morton Shoe Co.*, 40 B.R. 948 (Bankruptcy Ct., D. Mass., 1984), the court noted that to enforce such promise under the doctrines of consideration or reliance was flimsy and technical. Instead, the court said it would do so because that is what it had done in the past, leaving us in doubt as to why it had done so.

[38] 221 N.W. 2d 609 (Iowa 1974). See also cases cited in Eisenberg, *supra* note 18, at 116 n.51.

Eisenberg agreed that the reason for enforcing promises to charities, or, as he puts it, to "social service institutions" is not reliance. It is that "in a society such as ours which stresses the promotion of the general welfare through these decentralized institutions, there is an important social policy in favor of such giving."[39] Nevertheless, although aiding those in need may be a laudable goal, he objected that "the enforcement of donative promises would be a relatively trivial instrument for achieving that end."[40] "[I]t is also possible that less gifting would occur . . . some prospective donative promisors might refrain from promising in the first place if they knew the promise was legally enforceable."[41]

The reason such promises should be enforceable, however, does not depend on an analysis of what best serves social policy. Promises to give away money or property should be enforced when they are likely to be sensible, and when it is likely that the promisor wished to give the promisee the right to enforce them. The fact that a promise is made to a presumptively worthwhile cause suggests that it was made sensibly. Moreover, such promises are not made in what Eisenberg called "an intimate context." Promises to pay for a daughter's college expenses or a son's operation may be subject to a host of mutually understood implied conditions "too subtle to be regulated by legal rules." Any inchoate conditions to which a promise to a charitable institution are unlikely to be mutually understood, and consequently, less likely to have been implicitly imposed by the promisor.

These considerations explain why American courts enforce these promises. English courts do not. One could argue that they should not be enforced because the promisor's intentions are too speculative. If so, then English courts are right.

iv. The promisor-decedent

When the promisor dies without having second thoughts, there is no need to worry about whether the promise was made rashly or subject to one of the inchoate conditions just mentioned. Such a condition did not occur. A court could enforce the promise simply because the promisor died without disavowing the promise.[42]

Although no court has explained its decision that way, this consideration may have influenced the result in some well-known cases. *Hamer v. Sidway*[43] has often been used to illustrate the bargained-for-detriment formula for consideration.

39 EISENBERG, *supra* note 18, at 116.
40 *Id.* at 101.
41 *Id.*
42 *See* JOHN D. CALAMARI & JOSEPH M. PERILLO, THE LAW OF CONTRACTS 275 n.31 (3d ed. 1987).
43 27 N.E. 256 (N.Y. 1891).

An uncle promised to pay his nephew $5,000 if the nephew would not drink, smoke, swear, or gamble until he reached the age of 21. The nephew gave up his right to do so, and the uncle did promise, at least in part, to induce him to give up that right. The court held that there was consideration, but perhaps it should have been enforced because the uncle died before changing his mind.

Williston cited *Ricketts v. Scothorn*[44] in support of the doctrine of promissory reliance. A grandfather who had promised the plaintiff money so she could quit her job died after she quit but before he paid her. Perhaps the promise should have been enforced even if she had not relied upon it, since the grandfather died before changing his mind. In *Devecmon v. Shaw*,[45] a nephew traveled to Europe in reliance on an uncle' promise to pay for the trip. In *Sandoval v. Bucci* (*In re Estate of Bucci*),[46] the promisee relied by buying a house. In both cases, the promisor died without a change of heart.

There is a similar rule governing gifts of money or property. They are not effective unless delivery is actually made. Nevertheless, if the donor dies believing that that the conveyance was effective, a constructive trust may, in some cases, be imposed on the property for the benefit of the donee.[47]

v. Promissory reliance

We have seen that the doctrine of promissory reliance does not explain most of the cases that were cited in its support when it was formulated. The signal exception is *Ricketts v. Scothorn*.[48] Kathy Scothorn's grandfather had given her note for $2,000 so that she could quit her job, which she did. The court required his executors to pay the note on the ground that she quit work in reliance on the promise.[49] In his treatise in 1920, Williston cited the case to show that courts might be allowing reliance by the promisee to serve as a substitute for consideration.[50] He wrote this doctrine in the *First Restatement of Contracts*.

There is no ready parallel to this doctrine in civil law. As we have seen, according to Cajetan, a donative promise should be enforced only if the promisee had changed position in reliance upon it and would not be hurt if the promise were broken. His critics responded that if the promisor had given the promisee

[44] 77 N.W. 365 (Neb. 1898).

[45] 14 A. 464 (Md. 1888).

[46] 488 P.2d 216 (Colo. Ct. App. 1971).

[47] 1 Scott & Fratcher, *supra* note 26, at 350 (finding such trusts imposed where the donee was a "natural object" of the donor's bounty).

[48] Frederick Pollock, Principles of Contract at Law and in Equity 650 n.1 (Gustavus Wald & Samuel Williston, eds., 7th English ed., 3d American ed. 1906).

[49] 77 N.W. 365 (Neb. 1898).

[50] 1 Samuel Williston, The Law of Contracts 307–14 (1920).

the right to require performance, then the promisee would be hurt by being deprived of that right. Cajetan's suggestion that reliance by the promisee should matter was not pursued.

Reliance should matter. Suppose a promisor should later decide that a promise to give away money or property was made foolishly. Or suppose the promisor never wanted to give the promisee the right to enforce it. Absent reliance by the promisee, the promisor should remain free to reconsider how best to use the money or property. Absent reliance, the promisee will not be harmed. If, however, the promisee has relied and will be harmed if it is not kept, the promisor who disavows the promise does so at the promisee's expense. Part of the cost of pursuing what the promisor deems to be the best use of the money or property will be borne by the promisee. A promise to give money or property may be subject to inchoate conditions in which the promisor's needs can trump those of the promisee. But it would be unlikely that an inchoate condition would allow the promisor's needs to be met at the promisee's expense. An aunt might promise her niece $10,000 for a trip to Europe. If the aunt encounters serious financial setback or her personal obligations significantly increase in an unexpected manner, the niece may be expected to understand that the aunt need not keep her promise. If, however, the niece has already paid $2,000 for non-refundable tickets, the aunt who does not keep her promise is solving her own financial problems or meeting her personal obligations at her niece's expense. The aunt's promise to underwrite the niece's trip to Europe has left the niece paying for her aunt's bills.

Consequently, such a promise should not be enforceable to its full extent. The promisor should only be liable for the amount the promisee was harmed. The *Second Restatement* allows the court to award only that amount.[51]

This remedy resembles one in tort because the damages are the amount necessary to make the plaintiff as well off as they would have been if the promise had not been made. But the action is in contract because the defendant is liable for breaking a promise. The purpose of the promise was to benefit the promisee at the promisor's expense. The promisor may not be obligated to confer that benefit but should be liable if failing to keep the promise makes the promisee worse off.

This explanation steers a middle course between two alternatives. According to one, liability for the promisee's reliance is based on the principle of tort law that a person who is at fault must compensate whoever has been harmed. That explains why the remedy is compensation for the promisee's loss. According to the other explanation, liability is based on the principle of contract law that a person who makes a promise is liable for breaking it. That explains why the defendant is liable for breaking a promise. The better explanation, in our view, is that the action is in contract although the remedy is compensation for a loss.

[51] Restatement (Second) of Contracts § 90 cmt. d (Am. Law Inst. 1981).

Warren Shattuck suggested that the doctrine is based on tort principles in a thesis he wrote at Yale under Arthur Corbin's guidance.[52] A year later, Lon Fuller and William Perdue made the same suggestion in their famous article, *The Reliance Interest in Contract Damages*.[53] That view was endorsed in the 1950s in well-known articles by Warren Seavy[54] and Benjamin Boyer.[55] In his book *The Death of Contract* Grant Gilmore claimed that promissory reliance "has, in effect, swallowed up the bargain principle,"[56] and contract had merged into tort.

Although Melvin Eisenberg did not share Gilmore's concern about the imminent demise of the law of contract law, he also believed that the doctrine is based on tort principles:

> The promisor is at fault for making a promise and then breaking it. The fault caused a loss to the promisee, because the promise induced the promisee to incur costs that he would not otherwise have incurred on the reasonable assumption that the promise would be kept. Unlike the case of a simple donative promise, therefore, if a relied upon donative promise is broken, the promisee is worse off than he was before the promise was made . . . [A] relying promisee has suffered not merely disappointment, but an actual diminution of his wealth.[57]

Nevertheless, a promisor may have not have been at fault for failing to anticipate that the money promised would be needed for some other purpose such as their business, a retirement home, or to help a sick nephew. Yet the promisor should not be allowed to meet such unanticipated needs at the promisee's expense.

Eisenberg believed that the doctrine of promissory reliance is one application of a larger principle. A person is liable for words or actions that foreseeably may harm another:

> When one person, A, uses words or actions that he knows or should know would induce another, B, to reasonably believe that A is committed to take a certain course of action, and A knows or should know that B will incur costs if

[52] Warrren L. Shattuck, *Gratuitous Promises—A New Writ?*, 35 Mich. L. Rev. 908 (1937), 908. According to Shattuck, the idea was his own and not suggested by his thesis advisor at Yale Law School, Arthur Corbin. Telephone interview with Warren Shattuck (July 2, 1993).

[53] Lon L. Fuller & William R. Perdue, Jr., *The Reliance Interest in Contract Damages* (pts. 1 & 2), 46 Yale L.J. 52, 373 (1936).

[54] Warren A. Seavey, *Reliance Upon Gratuitous Promises or Other Conduct*, 64 Harv. L. Rev. 913, 928 (1951).

[55] Benjamin F. Boyer, *Promissory Estoppel: Principle from Precedents* (pts. 1 & 2), 50 Mich. L. Rev. 639, 873 (1952).

[56] Grant Gilmore, The Death of Contract 72 (1974).

[57] Eisenberg, *supra* note 18, at 117.

A doesn't take action, A should take steps to incur that if he doesn't take the action, B will not suffer a loss.[58]

The same view was expressed by T. M. Scanlon.[59]

Nevertheless, a person is not liable in tort for any negligent misrepresentation on which another person might foreseeably rely. Dan B. Dobbs, Paul T. Hayden, and Ellen M. Bublick have noted that a person who is liable must be "under a duty" to the plaintiff "typically based on a special relationship or affirmative undertaking."[60] As we will see, when an accounting firm negligently furnishes false information, it is liable only to its client and to third-party beneficiaries of its contract with its client. It is not liable to members of the public who relied on the information. A manufacturing company would not be liable if it announced that it would open a new factory in a certain town, or a real estate developer that it would build a residential, shopping, and cinema complex on a certain site, and then cancelled its plans to do so. It would not be liable even though it foresaw that the announcement would affect many people's decisions to buy or sell nearby land, and it made the announcement, or cancelled its plans, without weighing the costs to itself against those to others.

Randy Barnett and other scholars have taken the opposite position. The promise is enforced under the doctrine of promissory reliance, not because the promisee relied on it, but because the promisor intended to be bound. "Noncommercial promises" should be enforced if "the parties formally manifest their intention to be legally bound."[61] He claimed the support of a "new consensus" that had emerged in the 1980s and 1990s. He cited the work of Edward Yorio and Steve Thel, who maintained that "the basis of Section 90 in the courts is promise, not reliance."[62] Yorio and Thel believed that a promise should be binding when it was made with deliberation. "A promise will be fully enforced under the section if the promise is proven convincingly and is likely to have been

[58] Lon L. Fuller & Melvin Aron Eisenberg, Basic Contract Law 27 (8th ed. 1996). *See* Eisenberg, *supra* note 18, at 117.

[59] T.M. Scanlon, *Promises and Practices*, 19 Phil. & Pub. Affairs, 199, 202–03 (1990).

[60] Dan B. Dobbs, Paul T. Hayden, & Ellen M. Bublick, Hornbook on Torts 1123 (2d ed. 2016).

[61] Randy E. Barnett, *The Death of Reliance*, 46 J. Legal Educ. 518, 528 (1996).

[62] Yorio & Thel, *supra* note 31, at 113. Barnett also cited the work of Daniel Faber which concerned reliance on commercial promises. Daniel A. Farber and John H. Matheson, *Beyond Promissory Estoppel: Contract Law and the "Invisible Handshake,"* 52 U. Chi. L. Rev. 903 (1985). He cited others as well whose work is less in point; Jay Feimann, *The Last Promissory Estoppel Article*, 61 Fordham L. Rev. 303 (1992) (arguing that a "relational" approach could transcend the difference between the two views); Juliet P. Kostritsky, *A New Theory of Assent-Based Liability Emerging Under the Guise of Promissory Estoppel*, 33 Wayne L. Rev. 895 (1987) (discussing how successful the doctrine of promissory reliance has been); Michael B. Kelly, *The Phantom Reliance Interest in Contract Damages*, [1992] Wis. L. Rev. 1755 (discussing the use of reliance damages as a surrogate for expectation damages that are uncertain).

serious and well considered when it was made."[63] By this approach, reliance by the promisee matters only as evidence of the promisor's intention or of the deliberation with which the promise was made.

They concluded that sometimes a promise should be enforced even if the promisee did not rely on it. They observed that reliance does not explain why promises made formally are enforceable.[64] They noted that marriage settlement and charitable subscriptions are enforceable without reliance.[65] They also mentioned the cases we discussed earlier in which the promisee did rely, but the promisor died before disavowing the promise.[66]

Here, we have to be careful. It is not enough that a promise was made deliberately. A promisor might make a promise deliberately and still not wish to give the promisee the right to legally enforce it. Reliance matters, we have seen, because the promisor should not be able to have a change of heart at the promisee's expense.

These scholars claim that reliance matters because the expectation that the promisee will rely on the promise is evidence that the promisor intended to be legally bound. According to Yorio and Thel, "[s]o long as the *possibility* of definite and substantial action (or forbearance) by the promisee was conveyed to the promisor, the promise is likely to have been sufficiently well considered to justify enforcement."[67] Barnett said in an article with Mary Becker, "invited or observed reliance provides . . . some evidence that the promisor may have intended to make a reliable promise,"[68] meaning one that the promisee can enforce. If they are right, then the promisor should be bound to keep his promise however rash it appears in retrospect or whatever unanticipated needs have arisen. By the approach we have suggested, the promisor should not be bound to keep his promise, but to compensate the promisee for the amount that he was hurt by relying on it.

Moreover, it is implausible to think that because the promisor realized that the promisee might be hurt, the promisor intended to be legally bound. A person who promises rashly is one who disregards the consequences. A parent might act rashly by promising to leave children enough money that they would never

[63] Yorio & Thel, *supra* note 31, at 113.

[64] *Id.* at 165.

[65] *Id.* 1 at 53–54.

[66] Devecman v. Shaw, 14 A. 464 (Md. 1888); Sandoval v. Bucci (In re Estate of Bucci), 488 P.2d 216 (Colo. Ct. App. 1971). *See* Hamer v. Sidway, 27 N.E.256 (N.Y. 1891). *Hamer* is usually used to illustrate the doctrine of consideration, but some scholars believe the promise could have been enforced under the doctrine of promissory reliance. JOHN D. CALAMARI & JOSEPH M. PERILLO, THE LAW OF CONTRACTS 275 & 275 n.34 (3d ed. 1987).

[67] Yorio & Thel, *supra* note 31, at 152.

[68] Randy E. Barnett & Mary E. Becker, *Beyond Reliance: Promissory Estoppel, Contract Formalities, and Misrepresentations*, 15 HOFSTRA L. REV. 443, 455 (1987). *See* Barnett, *supra* note 61, at 528.

have to work for a living, particularly if the parent can foresee that the children would rely on it. A parent might act rashly if they promised a son a new sports car a week before a daughter is to take medical tests to see if she needs an operation. The severity of the consequences does not show that a promise was well considered but that it should have been.

5

Fair Exchange (*with* Hao Jiang)

I. Why promises to exchange are enforceable

Some modern jurists have explained why contracts of exchange are enforceable in terms of will, freedom, or autonomy, and some in terms of efficiency.[1] A better explanation, as we will see, is based on fairness or, as jurists once said, on equality in exchange.

The will theorists defined contract in terms of the will of the parties. No further explanation was thought necessary of why the parties were bound. As Valérie Ranouil observed of the French will theorists, the binding force of contract was taken for granted rather than justified.[2] She quoted Emmanuel Gounot's description of their view: "The contract is binding because it is the contract."[3]

Charles Fried developed a modernized will theory in which the reason that promises are binding is to give the greatest scope to the freedom of the will. "In order that I be as free as possible, that my will have the greatest possible range consistent with the similar will of others, it is necessary that there be a way in which I can commit myself."[4] The difficulty is that the promisor's later decision not to abide by an earlier commitment is also an act of liberty. One cannot say that a person who is bound by such a commitment is more free. There is no metric for comparing degrees of freedom.[5] As Melvin Eisenberg observed,

[1] This chapter is based on an article coauthored with Hao Jiang, *Contract as Voluntary Commutative Justice* Mich. St. L. Rev. 725 (2020).

[2] *See* Véronique Ranouil, L'Autonomie de la volonté: Naissance et Evolution d'un Concept 71–72 (1980).

[3] Emmanuel Gounot, Le Principe de l'Autonomie de la Volonté en Droit Privé: Contribution à l'étude Critique de l'individualisme Juridique 129 (Arthur Rousseau ed., 1912); *see* Ranouil, *supra* note 2, at 72 n.31.

[4] Charles Fried, Contract as Promise 13 (1981).

[5] Fried followed the approach John Rawls had taken in *A Theory of Justice* (at 7, 8). Rawls said that "each person is to have an equal right to the most extensive basic liberty compatible with similar liberty for others." John Rawls, A Theory of Justice 60 (1971). H.L.A. Hart objected that to speak of the extent of a person's liberty is "not only indefinite but unintelligible." H.L.A. Hart, *Rawls on Liberty and Its Priority*, 40 U. Chi. L. Rev. 534 (1973). One person's exercise of a liberty frequently limits that of another person. If I have the liberty to exclude others from trespassing on my land, they do not have the liberty to do so. There is no way to say whether the liberty granted in more or less extensive than the liberty abridged. With commendable intellectual honesty, Rawls admitted that Hart was right. John Rawls, Political Liberalism 289–91 (1993). Hart's objection that there is no metric by which amounts of liberty can be compared applies equally well to the theory that Fried based on the earlier work of Rawls.

Foundations of American Contract Law. James Gordley, Oxford University Press. © Oxford University Press 2023.
DOI: 10.1093/oso/9780197686089.003.0005

"Nothing in autonomy theory compels favoring earlier choices over later choices, and coercing a contracting party to take an action he now autonomously declines to take."[6] As Hanoch Dagan and Michael Heller noted, autonomy by itself does not answer the question, "why should free individuals not be able to change their minds without legal liability?"[7]

Theories based on efficiency are subject to a similar objection. Efficiency is defined in terms of preference satisfaction. A result is "efficient" when at least one person is better able to satisfy his preferences without anyone else becoming less able to do so. When the parties exchange, each of them expects to receive something of greater value than what they give in return. If they do, the result is efficient. Suppose, however, one of them does not. Eisenberg objected:

> The expressed preference of a promisor when he makes the contract is to keep his promise. The expressed preference of the promisor when the contract is sought to be enforced is to not keep his promise; otherwise, there would be no reason for the promisee to seek legal enforcement. Nothing in revealed-preference theory alone can tell us which of these two preferences the law [ought to] respect.[8]

Guido Calabresi made the same point in this article *The Pointlessness of Pareto: Carrying Coase Further.* A contract that makes both parties better off ex ante does not always make them better off ex post.[9] Ex ante, when they enter into a contract, both parties hope to be better off. Ex post, there will be winners, who are better off, and losers, who are not. As Calabresi noted, "all alleged improvements," that is, all changes that are allegedly Pareto optimal, "entail, at least ex ante, the possibility of losers."[10] Any time the law enforces a contract, it is against someone who made a bargain and lost, at least compared with some other bargain that the loser could have made.

In response to these difficulties, Peter Benson and other jurists formulated a "transfer theory." Benson pointed out that this theory was like that of Hugo Grotius, which, as we have seen, Grotius borrowed from the late scholastics. As Grotius said, a person may "promise" without "giv[ing] another person a right of his own." In that event, the promisee has no claim as a matter of justice if the promisor changes their mind. Or the promisor might "want . . . to confer on

[6] *See* Melvin A. Eisenberg, *Theory of Contracts*, *in* The Theory of Contract Law 206, 233 (Peter Benson ed., 2001).

[7] Hanock Dagan & Michael Heller, The Choice Theory of Contract 21 (2017).

[8] Melvin A. Eisenberg, Foundational Principles of Contract Law 39 (2018); *see also* Michael J. Trebilcock, The Limits of Freedom of Contract 244 (1993).

[9] *See generally* Guido Calabresi, *The Pointlessness of Pareto: Carrying Coase Further*, 100 Yale L.J. 1211 (1991).

[10] *Id.* at 1227.

another person a right of his own, which is called a perfect promise, and has an effect similar to the alienation of ownership."[11] The promisee then has a right to the performance of the promise which they can enforce. As we saw earlier, the theory is incomplete. It does not explain why a person would make one type of promise rather than another.

A reason that the parties to a contract of exchange would want it to be enforceable is that one party is compensating the other to assume a risk. For example, if a party buys fire insurance, the contract must be binding before either party knows whether the house will burn down. An aleatory contract such as insurance merely transfers a risk. A contract to exchange goods or services at a fixed price allocates the risk that a better or worse price might be obtainable in the future. Each of the parties gives up the chance of finding a more favorable bargain in order to avoid the risk that, if they wait, they will get one that is less favorable. If the item the parties are selling and buying has a market price, the seller will receive a less favorable bargain if the market price rises and the buyer will do so if it falls. If the item has no definite market price, such as a house or a painting, the seller who waits may not receive a better offer; the buyer may not find an equally desirable house or painting at as low a price. As Eisenberg said:

> making a forward contract for the sale of a differentiated commodity reflects a decision by the seller, embodied in a binding commitment, that her best bet is to take the buyer's present offer rather than to wait for a possible higher offer in the future. If the seller keeps searching for, or accepts, a higher offer, she is reneging on her bet.[12]

Similarly, if a party contracts to perform a service at a fixed price, each party is taking the risk that the cost of doing so will be greater or lesser than the amount estimated in advance. The party to perform the service loses if the cost is greater than anticipated, and loses if the cost is less.

For the parties to a contract of exchange to assign such risks, the parties must be able to commit themselves in advance. No one bets on a race that has already been run. By committing themselves in advance, the parties can place risks on the party who can bear them most easily. As economists say, most parties are risk averse. Unlike gamblers, who will pay to take risks, they will pay to avoid them. A risk is borne more easily by a party, who, like an insurance company, faces the same risk over and over and so can spread it across many transactions. It is borne most easily by the party who can best foresee it since risk is uncertainty

[11] Hugo Grotius, De iure bellis ac pacis libri tres II.xi.1.6–2.1–4 (1688).

[12] Melvin A. Eisenberg, *Actual and Virtual Specific Performance, the Theory of Efficient Breach, and the Indifference Principle in Contract Law*, 93 Calif. L. Rev. 975, 1009 (2005).

and a party who is less uncertain about the result can bear a risk more easily for the same reason that a card game is less risky for a player who peeks at another player's cards. A risk is borne most easily by the party who can most easily control it since there is less risk that a party who is liable for the consequences will neglect to take measures to avoid them. For any of these reasons, as economists say, it is efficient for the parties to a contract to place risks on the party who is best able to assume them and who receives an extra amount in compensation for doing so..[13]

Ex ante, both parties are better off. But efficiency does not explain why such a contract should be enforced. Ex post, one party is worse off, like a gambler who lost a bet. The reason the loser should pay is not that anyone will be better off in the long run if such contracts are enforced. It is that it would be unfair to allow a party who was compensated for assuming a risk to renege if the risk materializes. If an insurance company could so cleverly deny coverage of a legitimate claim that its refusal to pay would have no effect on the willingness of other persons to insure or on the amount that they would pay, its refusal would have no effect on efficiency. But it would be unfair. It would be unfair because the insurance company would be unjustly enriched at the expense of the party who paid it to assume the risk. It would be like allowing a party to keep the price for goods never delivered provided, or the fee for a service never performed. As the architects of the earlier theory of contracts would say, it would violate commutative justice. In the earlier theory of contract that we have described, a contract of exchange is an act of voluntary commutative justice. The parties must exchange performances of equal value. Otherwise, one party will be enriched at the other's expense. The same principle explains why it is fair that promises to exchange are binding.

II. Unconscionability

The same principle explains why a contract on unfair terms should not be enforced.

Since the nineteenth century, many jurists have had difficulty seeing how the terms of a contract can be unfair. Although courts of equity refused to enforce contracts that they deemed to be "unconscionable,"[14] as A. W. B. Simpson noted, the rationale changed. The courts claimed that they were refusing to enforce an

[13] On the first and last of these factors, *see* Richard A. Posner & Andrew M. Rosenfield, *Impossibility and Related Doctrines in Contract Law: An Economic Analysis*, 6 J. LEGAL STUD. 83, 90–91 (1977). On the second, *see* Guido Calabresi, THE COSTS OF ACCIDENTS: A LEGAL AND ECONOMIC ANALYSIS 135 (1970).

[14] *See* JAMES GORDLEY, THE PHILOSOPHICAL ORIGINS OF MODERN CONTRACT DOCTRINE 147–51 (1991).

"unconscionable" contract, not because the terms were unfair, but "because the harshness of the terms was evidence of fraud, not as an independent ground for relief."[15] As I have shown elsewhere, these were not cases in which the disadvantaged party alleged that he had been defrauded. The terms were simply too harsh.[16] Courts used other doctrines to strike down unfair contracts and to enforce fair ones without admitting that fairness should matter. Among them were the doctrines of consideration, impracticability, and offer and acceptance.

It is now recognized that the doctrine of unconscionability gives relief from unfair terms. In 1952, § 2-302 of the *Uniform Commercial Code* permitted relief for unconscionability in both law and equity.[17] In 1981, an equivalent provision was adopted in § 208 of the *Second Restatement of Contracts*.[18] It provides:

> If a contract or term thereof is unconscionable at the time the contract is made a court may refuse to enforce the contract, or may enforce the remainder of the contract without the unconscionable term, or may so limit the application of any unconscionable term as to avoid any unconscionable result.

Nevertheless, scholars still have difficulty explaining how the terms of a contract can be unfair. Charles Fried, as we have seen, believed that promises should be enforced because to do so maximizes the promisor's freedom. Yet Fried acknowledged that the freedom of the will does not explain why "some bargains, though they meet all the tests I have set out so far, seem just too hard to enforce."[19] The reason, according to Fried, is that a random event has caused the breakdown of what he calls a "functioning social system" or a "political system of social redistribution" within which exchange normally takes place.[20] The jurists who drew on Aristotle called it a system of distributive and commutative justice.

Dagan and Dorfman tried to explain unfairness in terms of autonomy. Autonomy means that the parties can "relate in a contract as equals either by assuming co-authorship of determining, or influencing the determination of, the terms of the interaction, or by satisfying reasonable expectations of typical

[15] A.W.B. Simpson, *Innovation in Nineteenth Century Contract Law*, 91 L.Q. Rev. 247, 269 (1975). Some scholars have taken these claims at face value. The bargains "vaguely condemned as unconscionable were almost invariably associated with some species of fraud, mistake, incapacity, or inadequacy of consideration." 1 Howard J. Alperin & Roland F. Chase, Consumer Law: Sales Practices and Credit Regulation 245 (1986); Note, *Unconscionable Contracts: The Uniform Commercial Code*, 45 Iowa L. Rev. 843, 846 (1960).

[16] *See* James Gordley, *Equality in Exchange*, 69 Calif. L. Rev. 1587, 1650–55 (1981).

[17] U.C.C. § 2-302 (Am. Law Inst. & Unif. L. Comm'n 1952).

[18] Restatement (Second) of Contracts § 208 (Am. Law Inst. 1981).

[19] Charles Fried, Contract as Promise: A Theory of Contractual Obligation 109 (1981).

[20] *Id.* at 109–10.

term-takers."[21] Terms are "substantive[ly] unconscionable" when they are "unreasonably favorable to the other party."[22] It is not clear, however, what the substantive fairness of terms has to do with the autonomy or freedom of the parties. Moreover, if terms were fair only if both parties are able to influence or determine them, the market price would not be fair since neither party can influence it. Yet if the market price is not fair, neither are the vast majority of contracts.

According to Peter Benson, "[j]ustice in transactions is a genuinely liberal conception of justice that . . . expresses itself in an appropriate view of parties as free and equal persons."[23] A contract at the market price is fair, not because the parties can influence or determine it, but precisely because they cannot. It is "the same for all and not decided by anyone in particular."[24] Therefore, it "embodies the very same kind of abstractly equal relational standpoint that contractual equality requires and that parties, as equal persons, may reasonably be presumed to accept when contracting with each other."[25] Their "presumed intention" is "an intention to give and receive equal value."[26] Benson is correct that the market price "is not decided by anyone in particular." But that does not explain why that price affirms the parties' status as "free and equal persons." It does not explain why parties trading at the market price "give and receive equal value." let alone why they would intend to do so. Suppose each of them has only their own interest in mind.

The doctrine of unconscionability compels us to consider what it means for the terms of a contract to be fair. In discussing why it is fair to enforce a contract of exchange, we saw that otherwise a party who was paid to assume a risk could escape responsibility when the risk materialized. That party would be enriched at the other party's expense. The principle that neither party should be enriched at the other's expense also explains how the terms of a contract can be unfair.

i. Inequality in the values exchanged

The price

The idea of equality of exchange was in disrepute when the common law first acquired a theory and a systematic body of doctrine in the nineteenth century. That idea had been a pillar of the earlier theory constructed by continental

[21] HANOCH DAGAN & AVIHAY DORFMAN, JUSTICE FOR CONTRACTS 47, 48 (2020) (internal emphasis omitted).
[22] *Id.* at 47.
[23] PETER BENSON, JUSTICE IN TRANSACTIONS: A THEORY OF CONTRACT LAW 11 (2019).
[24] *Id.* at 185.
[25] *Id.*
[26] Peter Benson, *The Unity of Contract Law*, *in* THE THEORY OF CONTRACT LAW: NEW ESSAYS 118, 188 (Peter Benson ed., 2001) (internal emphasis omitted).

jurists which had endured until the eighteenth century. They built this theory around the Aristotelian idea of voluntary commutative justice. The parties must exchange at a fair price which was a price that enriched neither of them at the other's expense.

For these earlier writers, the fair price was not an intrinsic or stable property of objects like their color. They identified the just price with the price on a competitive market,[27] which, they knew, fluctuates from day to day and place to place in response to need, scarcity, and cost.[28] When the parties exchange at this price, neither of them is richer or poorer at the moment of the transaction, although either might become richer or poorer the next day. The risk that the market price would change after the contract was made is an inherent risk of selling or buying property, just as the risk that property would be destroyed by fire is an inherent risk of ownership. As Domenico Soto and Leonard Lessius noted, a party who loses if prices fall would have gained if prices had risen.[29]

This explanation fits well with the account we have given of why contracts of exchange are enforceable. A contract to exchange goods or services at a fixed price allocates risk that a better or worse price could be obtained in the future. Each party gives up the chance of finding a more favorable bargain in order to avoid the risk of waiting and then getting a bargain that is less favorable. The seller will lose a better bargain if the market price rises, and the buyer will lose if it falls. If each party is compensated for assuming that risk, neither is enriched at the other's expense. The terms of the contract will be fair. Moreover, even though neither of the parties may have cared about whether the terms are fair, neither intended to enrich the other party by assuming a risk without receiving any compensation for doing so. Parities who exchange at a fair price achieve a result that they intended, which is to obtain something of greater value that what each gives in return, while avoiding a result neither wanted. Neither of them wished to enrich the other party at their own expense.

Indeed, if the chances that the market price will rise are equal to the chances that it will fall, the contract is fair in the same way as a fair bet. Ex ante, neither party gains or loses. Modern economics is often thought to conflict with the theory of the just price. Instead, it explains why the risk that market price will change is an inherent risk of buying and selling, and why the risk that it will rise is equal to the risk that it will fall.

27 As noted by JOHN NOONAN, THE SCHOLASTIC ANALYSIS OF USURY 82–88 (1957); Raymond de Roover, *The Concept of the Just Price and Economic Policy*, 18 J. ECON. HIST. 418 (1958).

28 *See* DOMENICUS SOTO, DE IUSTITIA ET IURE LIBRI DECEM lib. 6, q. 2, a. 3 (1553); 3 LUDOVICUS MOLINA, DE IUSTITIA ET IURE TRACTATUS disp. 348 (1614); LEONARDUS LESSIUS, DE IUSTITIA ET IURE, CETERISQUE VIRUTIBUS CARDINALIS lib. 2, cap. 21, dub. 4; (1628); HUGO GROTIUS, DE IURE BELLI AC PACIS LIBRI TRES II.xii.14 (1688).

29 SOTO, *supra* note 28, at lib. 6 q. 2 a. 3; LESSIUS, *supra* note 28, at lib. 2, cap. 21, dub. 4.

If prices were frozen, the supply for a good or service would no longer equal the demand for it. At a price below the one that the market would set, goods and services will not go to those who are willing to pay the most for them. They will go to whoever happens to be first in a line of would-be purchasers or to whoever happens to have friends who can make sure he gets them. At a higher price, goods and services will go unsold. One function of a competitive market, then, is to price ration goods and services. They go to whoever will pay most for them. Another function is to channel resources into the production of goods whose price rises and away from the production of goods whose price falls. To perform these functions, market prices must be allowed to change.

When the parties contract at a fixed price, each assumes a risk. Each will be better off for having contracted when they did if the market price moves in one direction and worse off if it moves in the other. That bet, however, is not like the ones that gamblers make in a casino. They are creating a risk that a person will win or lose that exists only because of the rules of the game that they play. They are not allocating a risk, like the risk that the market price will change, which must be borne by someone. As economists say, most people are risk averse. Risk-averse parties will not gamble. But they will allocate between them the risks that one party or the other must bear.

Although economists speak of efficiency rather than fairness, the tools of modern economics explain why an exchange at the market price is fair in the same way as a fair bet. If the market price were more likely to move in one direction than the other, it would already have done so. That, at least, is what economists call the "efficient market hypothesis."[30] Suppose that persons of superior insight could tell whether the market price at present is too low and will rise in the future. If there are a sufficient number of such persons, and they command enough money, the market price will constantly be corrected as they bid against each other. It cannot long remain above or below the level at which it is as likely to move up as it is to move down.

One might draw an analogy to players in a game of darts. The best player in the world could not beat the average of a thousand mediocre players if the thousand were given a single score computed by taking the average distance from the bull's-eye. For example, a miss by one player a foot to the left, and a miss by another player a foot to the right, are counted as two bull's-eyes. Similarly, among buyers and sellers trying to predict how the market price will change, some will guess high, some will guess low, but the average of their predictions should be on target.

[30] Eugene Fama first proposed the hypothesis. *See* Eugene F. Fama, *The Behavior of Stock-Market Prices*, 38 J. Bus. 34, 94 (1965); *see also generally* Paul A. Samuelson, *Proof That Properly Anticipated Prices Fluctuate Randomly*, 6 Indus. Mgmt. Rev. 41 (1965).

If the market price is as likely to move in one direction as to move in the other, each party is fairly compensated for the risk that they each assume. We can see, then, why, in the vast majority of cases, the law enforces a contract of exchange without any special examination of whether it is fair. Neither party may have given a thought to fairness, but although each person "intends only his own gain," to quote Adam Smith, "he is . . . led by an invisible hand to promote an end which was no part of his intention"—in this instance, to contract at a price that is fair to the other party.[31]

It may be fair to enforce the contract even if one party is better able than the other to predict in which direction the market may change. Even according to the efficient market hypothesis, a person who has information that others who are trading on the market do not is better able to make such a prediction. Yet a contract at the market price should be enforced even though it is made by a person who possesses this information and is therefore more likely to win than to lose.

One reason is that it may have cost money and time to acquire the information. The person who incurred the expense was betting that the information acquired would be worth the cost. It is fair that anyone who makes such a bet should profit if the bet pays off. Such efforts allow the current market price to reflect accurately the chances that it will change in the future. Consequently, such efforts should be rewarded.

In *Laidlaw v. Organ*, one party had learned of the signing of the Treaty of Ghent, ending the War of 1812, early on a Sunday morning.[32] Soon after sunrise, he called on the defendant with whom he had been negotiating and bought 111 hogsheads of tobacco. The defendant did not know about the treaty and had asked the plaintiff if he knew of any news that would affect its value, but the plaintiff remained silent. The news drove up the price of tobacco 30–50 percent. The United States Supreme Court refused to give relief. As plaintiff's counsel argued, there was "no circumvention or manoeuver by the vendee, unless rising earlier in the morning, and obtaining by superior diligence and alertness that intelligence by which the price of commodities was regulated, be such."[33]

There is another reason why it is fair to allow a person with such information to profit by it. Regardless of how the information was acquired, either the person who has it or someone else will benefit. If the information must be disclosed to the other party, that party will benefit by contracting at a more favorable price than everyone else trading on the market. There is no injustice allowing the

[31] Adam Smith, The Wealth of Nations bk. IV, ch. ii (1776).
[32] 15 U.S. 178, 182–83 (1817).
[33] *Id.* at 193.

person with advance information to take advantage of it rather than enabling another person to do so.

Another possibility is that the efficient market hypothesis is not true. If it is not, then some people, who have only the information generally available to other traders, have a skill that enables them to predict whether the market price will rise or fall. An exchange at the market price would still be fair and for the same two reasons. The party who profits has bet that the skill acquired is worth the time and money spent acquiring it or the money spent purchasing the advice of someone who has. Anyone who makes such a bet and wins should be allowed to profit. The efforts of skilled traders will lead the current market price to reflect more accurately the risks that it will rise or fall in the future. Moreover, as before, it would be absurd to require a person who has this skill to buy or sell at a less favorable price than others.

Yet another possibility is that there is no definite and easily ascertainable market price because the commodity traded is not fungible but unique. An example is the housing market. A house cannot be shown to all possible buyers all at once, nor can a buyer see, all at once, all of the houses offered for sale. The risk that each party takes is not simply that the housing market might rise or fall after the contract is made. The risk, for the seller, is losing the opportunity to obtain a better offer, and, for the buyer, missing out on a better house at a lower price. A party who does not wait longer or look longer assumes that risk.

If both parties were equally informed about the risk of committing themselves at once, rather than waiting, their contract would still be fair in the same way as a fair bet. Nevertheless, for the reasons just discussed, the contract may still be fair if they are not equally well informed. A party who does not seek further information concerning the chances of obtaining a better offer is taking the further risk that the information is not worth the cost of seeking it. A party who seeks further information is betting that to do so is worth the cost. If the bet pays off, again, it is fair that the winner should profit from it. Indeed, it is through this process that the prices of unique commodities adjust to supply and demand.

If a party contracts at a price that is less favorable than the market price, the reason must be either inability to use the market, or ignorance of the market price. Proponents of the idea of equality of exchange spoke of these two circumstances as "necessity" and "ignorance."[34]

In cases of necessity, a party is unable to use the market. An example is a ship in distress when the only ship that can rescue it charges a price equal to 99 percent of the value of the ship and its cargo.[35] Melvin Eisenberg's example is a geologist studying rock formations in the desert who finds a traveler, stranded

[34] *See* LESSIUS, *supra* note 28, at lib. 2, cap. 21, dub. 4.

[35] RICHARD A. POSNER, ECONOMIC ANALYSIS OF LAW 118 (7th ed. 2007).

without food and water after his car had broken down, and charges him a fortune for a ride to the nearest town.[36]

In these cases, if the rescuer were allowed to profit, it would not be because the parties allocated a risk between themselves, and he happened to win. It would not be because he spent extra time or money acquiring information that enabled him to profit—information, for example, about where a party in need of a rescue might be. Indeed, the risk in question is not one that must be borne by one party or the other, like the risk that the market price will change. The high price of a rescue, unlike a high market price, neither rations goods or services to those willing to pay the most for them, nor increases the supply of would-be rescuers searching the sea or the desert for people in need of rescue. Indeed, if each ship, or each traveler in the desert, were equally likely to sink or die without the other's help, and they could negotiate in advance, they would each agree not to take advantage of the other's need to extract a high price. Otherwise, they would be gambling on a chance event, and risk- averse people do not gamble.

The other reason that one party may contract at a price that is less favorable than the market price is ignorance of the market price. In such cases, courts of equity gave relief for unconscionability even before the doctrine was recognized in the *Uniform Commercial Code* and the *Second Restatement of Contracts*. A Kentucky court did so in 1892 in *Wollums v. Horsley*. A man who was 64 years old, disabled, living on a 200-acre isolated mountain farm, and out of touch with the world, sold the mineral rights to his land to a sophisticated businessman who was buying up mineral rights on thousands of acres in the locality. The mineral rights were then worth over thirty times the price to be paid.[37] Sellers in general knew the market price but the old man did not.

In *Wollums*, the seller was ignorant of the market price of his land. Under the unconscionability doctrine, courts have given relief to buyers who do not know the retail price of goods which they bought for several times that price from a door-to-door salesman.[38]

[36] *See* Melvin Aron Eisenberg, *The Bargain Principle and Its Limits*, 95 Harv. L. Rev. 741, 755 (1982).

[37] *See* Wollums v. Horsley, 20 S.W. 781, 781–82 (Ky. 1892). Similarly, a court of equity refused to enforce an exchange of land in Michigan worth $15,000 and subject to no mortgage for a parcel of land in Florida worth $25,000 but subject to a $25,000 mortgage. The owner of the Michigan parcel had not heard that the "Great (Florida) Boom" had collapsed and believed the Florida parcel to be worth $40,000. *See* Johnston Realty & Inv. Co. v. Grosvenor, 217 N.W. 20, 21 (Mich. 1928).

[38] *See* Jones v. Star Credit Corp., 298 N.Y.S.2d 264, 266–67 (Sup. Ct. 1969); Frostifresh Corp. v. Reynoso, 274 N.Y.S.2d 757, 759 (Sup. Ct. 1966), *rev'd on other grounds*, 281 N.Y.S.2d 964 (App. Div. 1967); Toker v. Westerman, 274 A.2d 78, 81 (N.J. Dist. Ct. 1970); Am. Home Improvement, Inc. v. MacIver, 201 A.2d 886, 889 (N.H. 1964) (discussing an instance of extravagant prices for windows and sidewalls); Unif. Consumer Credit Code § 5.108 cmt. 4 (Nat'l Conf. of Comm'rs on Unif. State L. 1974) ("[A] home solicitation sale of a set of cookware . . . for $375 in an area where a set of comparable quality is readily available . . . for $125 or less").

In such cases, the contract price was not a fair bet as to what the market price will be. They are not cases in which a party was able to charge more by exploiting knowledge or skill in predicting market prices that cost time or money to acquire. They are not sales of a unique commodity in which the parties each knew that they might receive a better offer if they waited. The advantaged party in *Wollums* was able to charge a higher price because he met someone who did not know the market price, and, indeed, in these cases, sought out such a person. The price he charged was not fair. It did not reflect any expenditure of time or money for which the advantaged party should be rewarded or any risk the disadvantaged party had assumed for which he had been compensated.

In all of these cases, there was a reason why the disadvantaged party did not receive the market price. In cases of necessity, there was no other party with whom to contract. In cases of ignorance, there was some reason why the disadvantaged party did not know the market price. In *Wollums*, he was old, disabled, solitary, and living on an isolated mountain farm. In the cases of the door-to-door sales, the salesman made his pitch in that party's home, which made it more difficult to do comparative shopping, and, for some people, difficult to tell the salesman to leave. Some scholars use the term "procedural unconscionability" to describe difficulties like these. They believe that both procedural and substantive unconscionability are necessary for courts to give relief. We discuss that claim later. For present purposes, all we need to note is that whether it is true or not, the evil remedied is substantive unfairness: a failure to receive the market price. Whatever their disadvantages in protecting themselves, if the old man in *Wollums* had been paid the market price of his land, or the customers of the door-to-door salesmen the market price of the goods, there would have been no wrong done for the courts to set right.

The auxiliary terms

The performance terms of a contract specify what each party is to give and to receive. In a sale, they are the object and the price. Some auxiliary terms allocate the risks and burdens of the exchange specified by the performance terms. Other auxiliary terms specify the procedure by which the rights of the parties are to be determined. Economists do not speak of fairness, but, again, their account of exchange helps to explain when both types of auxiliary terms are fair.

Terms that allocate risks and burdens

Terms that allocate risks and burdens are fair if they impose a risk on a party who is compensated for bearing it. As economists note, although the parties do not wish to gamble, they do wish to allocate risks that must fall on one party or the other. If the parties understand these risks, they will assign them to the party who can bear them at the lowest cost and adjust the contract price to compensate this party for doing so.[39] As Eric Posner said, "maximiz[ing] the ex ante value of the contract . . . usually means allocating obligations in a way that places the risk of any contingency on the party that can most cheaply bear it and that gives the parties proper incentives to breach, invest, and engage in related behavior."[40]

They will do so, according to Richard Posner, provided that the seller does not have a monopoly.[41] Actually, it should not matter if the seller has a monopoly as long as both parties fully understand the cost of bearing the risk. Suppose the seller would be willing to assume a risk for $100 that the buyer would not be willing to assume for less than $500. If the seller is a monopolist, it will be able to force the buyer to pay more than a competitive market price for its product. Yet the seller's liability for this risk is like any other amenity that is sold along with the product. If the seller were the sole producer of all the automobiles in the world, it would charge a high price for them. But it would still put in leather seats if buyers were willing to pay an additional amount that exceeds the cost of installing them. Similarly, the seller would assume a risk if buyers were willing to pay more than the cost of doing so.

Therefore, if the parties fully understand the cost of a risk imposed by a term of their contract, the terms will be fair in the same way as a fair bet. A party may lose, but he will have been compensated for taking the risk that he might lose. A contract is unfair if it places a risk or burden on a party without compensating him.

A contract would be fair if a party were compensated for bearing a risk even if the other party could bear it more cheaply. In that event, however, the other party would rather be the one to bear the risk. If it is clear that the terms of a contract placed a risk on the party who could not bear the risk most cheaply, it is unlikely that that party was compensated for bearing it.

An illustration is the well-known case of *Weaver v. American Oil Co.*[42] A poorly educated man leased a filling station from an oil company. The lease contained a clause that he would hold the oil company harmless for any damage caused by the negligence of its employees. The clause was buried among others in a form contract, and no one pointed out its significance to the lessee. The driver of one of the oil company's trucks negligently set fire to the lessee and the filling station. Applying the unconscionability doctrine, the court refused to enforce the clause.

As noted earlier, according to economists, which party is best able to bear a risk depends on three factors. In this case, each of them indicates that the oil company could bear the risk most cheaply. One factor is who can best foresee the magnitude of the risk. A risk is lower for the party who can best foresee it for

[39] *See* POSNER, *supra* note 35, at 116.

[40] Eric A. Posner, *A Theory of Contract Law Under Conditions of Radical Judicial Error*, 94 NW. U.L. REV. 749, 756 (2000).

[41] *See* POSNER, *supra* note 35, at 116.

[42] 276 N.E.2d 144, 145, 147 (Ind. 1971).

roughly the same reason that the risk of playing poker is lower for someone who can peek at the other players' cards. Another factor is who can take precautions to control the risk. Placing the risk on the party who can do so minimizes the further risk that these precautions will not be taken. A third factor is who can best spread the risk over similar transactions, whether by buying insurance or by self-insuring. The risk of a house catching fire is less for an insurance company than for a homeowner because it can spread that risk over the many houses it insures. A streak of bad luck is less risky for a casino than for an individual gambler.[43]

Here, the oil company could best foresee the probability that one of its drivers would be negligent, and it could best control that risk by taking care who it hires. It could best spread the risk that its drivers would cause harm to a lessee over its many leases. Yet the contract placed this risk on the lessee. Therefore, it is unlikely that the oil company fully compensated the lessee for bearing this risk. If the oil company could bear the risk more cheaply than the lessee, it would rather do so itself than fully compensate him. If, for example, Amoco would have been willing to bear the risk for $100 and Weaver for $500, Amoco would not have placed the risk on Weaver and also lowered his rent by $500. Since he was not compensated, to place the risk on him was unfair.[44]

It is also possible that even though a contract places the risk on the party who can most easily bear it, the contract is unfair because that party was not compensated for doing so. An example may be another well-known case, *Williams v. Walker-Thomas Furniture Co.*[45] A woman on welfare made a series of purchases from a store. The contract provided that all payments she made would be applied proportionately to all the items that she purchased, so that no item would be completely paid for until all were paid for. When she defaulted on a payment, the store sought to repossess everything she had purchased, although she had already paid an amount greater than the price of her earlier purchases.

Richard Posner and Richard Epstein both noted that these terms may have been of net benefit to the store's customers.[46] Because the store could repossess everything a customer had ever purchased, it ran less of a risk in selling him new items on credit. Therefore, it could have charged a lower price or a lower rate of interest. The difficulty with their argument is that there is no evidence that the store did so for Ms. Williams. If there were evidence, the store surely would have introduced it. So far as one can tell, she paid the same price and was charged the same rate of interest as a new customer with the same credit rating. Thus, even

43 On the first and last of these factors, *see* Posner & Rosenfield, *supra* note 13, at 90–91. On the second, *see* CALABRESI, *supra* note 13, at 135.

44 *See Weaver*, 276 N.E.2d at 145.

45 350 F.2d 445, 449 (D.C. Cir. 1965).

46 POSNER, *supra* note 35, at 117; Richard A. Epstein, *Unconscionability: A Critical Reappraisal*, 18 U. CHI. J.L. & ECON. 293, 306–08 (1975).

if the contract placed a risk on her that she could bear more easily, the store did not compensate her for bearing it. The contract was not fair in the same way as a fair bet.

In *Weaver* and in *Williams*, the courts stressed that the disadvantaged parties were unable to understand the terms on which they agreed. As mentioned earlier, according to some scholars, that inability made the agreement "procedurally unconscionable," which, in their view, is a prerequisite for relief. We will discuss that view later. Here, again, all that needs to be noted is that relief would not have been given if the term in question had not been substantively unfair despite their inability to understand the terms. We have seen why it was.

Terms that modify procedural rights

Sometimes the auxiliary terms of a contract specify the procedure by which the rights of the parties are to be determined. For example, they provide for arbitration or, as is often the case with an employment contract, an internal procedure for determining questions that would otherwise be decided by a court. These terms affect the burdens of determining what the parties' rights are and the risks of making an inaccurate determination.

The fairness of these terms depends on the considerations just described. They are fair if they do not increase the burdens or risks that fall on one party as compared with the other. An example would be a procedure that is cheaper for both parties and more likely to be accurate than litigation before a court. The terms are also fair if the procedure they create is more burdensome or risky for one party than for another provided that the disadvantaged party is compensated for bearing it.

The procedure may be more burdensome for one party even if it increases the cost to both parties of determining their rights by the same amount. One of the parties may be less likely to have the financial resources to bear the increased cost. The other party can then force them to accept an unfair settlement in order to avoid them.

The procedure may be riskier for one party even if it decreases the accuracy of the procedure in a manner that is unbiased so that neither party is more likely to prevail than if the case went to court. As mentioned earlier, a party who faces the same risk many times in similar transactions can bear it more easily. A party who is frequently involved in similar disputes might prefer a less expensive but less accurate procedure because their gains and losses will average out. The risk of inaccuracy will weigh more heavily on a party who may suffer greatly from a single loss and who may never be involved in a similar dispute.

The procedure provided by an auxiliary term will always be unfair if it is more expensive without any increase in accuracy, or less accurate without any decrease in cost. The only reason a party would insert an auxiliary term in a contract that provided for such a procedure is that the burden of the increased cost or the risk of decreased accuracy will weigh more lightly on them than on the other party for the reasons just described. The purpose of such a term would be to induce the other party to settle in order to escape the increased cost or to avoid the risk of losing. To compensate the other party fairly for assuming that burden and risk would defeat the very purpose of imposing it. One can safely assume that that party was not fairly compensated.

Another possibility is that the procedure is not only less accurate but biased, so that one party is more likely to win and the other to lose than if a court were to determine their rights. Here, again, one can safely assume that the disadvantaged party was not fairly compensated for bearing the risk of a biased procedure. To do so would defeat the purpose of inserting a term that created the bias.

ii. "Procedural" unconscionability

Although most scholars have accepted the unconscionability doctrine, they have modernized the will theories rather than leaving them behind. They believe that relief is given because a party did not autonomously choose the terms of the contract. Some scholars have said that the unconscionability doctrine does not or should not allow courts to decide when the terms of a contract are substantively unfair. The evil to be remedied is not the unfairness of the terms, but the process by which a contract was formed. According to Richard Epstein, the doctrine of unconscionability "should be used only . . . to police the process whereby private agreements are formed."[47]

Similarly, Stephen Smith correctly observed that when relief is given, there is usually present what he calls "cognitive asymmetry" between the parties. One party had "little education, low intelligence, lack of knowledge, [or] lack of independence." Or "the contract was difficult to understand, was in fine print, or dealt with difficult-to-estimate probabilities."[48] Smith concluded, incorrectly, that relief is not given because of substantive unfairness. Certainly, when there is cognitive asymmetry, contracts are more likely to be substantively unfair. According to Smith, however, cases of "cognitive asymmetry . . . are cases . . . in which courts have good reason to be concerned about fraud, undue influence, duress, or a simple failure to agree, but in which they lack direct evidence of the defect."[49] Fraud, duress, and undue influence are independent reasons for refusing to enforce a contract. They are cases in which one party lied to the other, threatened

[47] Epstein, *supra* note 46, at 294–95, 315.
[48] Stephen A. Smith, Contract Theory 344 (2004).
[49] *Id.* at 364.

the other party, or trusted the other party's judgment. Cases of "a simple failure to agree" are cases of mistake, which we will discuss later. The reason for giving a remedy is not cognitive asymmetry. A harsh bargain may be due to a party's lack of education, intelligence, or knowledge. But, in these cases, relief is only given when the bargain is harsh. Otherwise, a large number of people would be unable to enter into binding contracts.

The in-between position, taken by most scholars, is that although substantive unfairness matters, a contract must be both "substantively" and "procedurally" unconscionable for a court to give relief.[50] It is substantively unconscionable when the terms are unfair. Any sort of a "bargaining disadvantage" can constitute procedural unconscionability. The *Uniform Consumer Credit Code* lists examples like those mentioned by Smith: "inability . . . [to] reasonably [] protect his interests by reason of physical or mental infirmities, ignorance, illiteracy."[51] According to an Official Comment to the *Second Restatement*:

> Inadequacy of consideration does not of itself invalidate a bargain, but gross disparity in the values exchanged may be an important factor in a determination that a contract is unconscionable and may be sufficient ground, without more, for denying specific performance. Such a disparity may also corroborate indications of defects in the bargaining process, or may affect the remedy to be granted when there is a violation of a more specific rule. Theoretically it is possible for a contract to be oppressive taken as a whole, even though there is no weakness in the bargaining process and no single term which is in itself unconscionable. Ordinarily, however, an unconscionable contract involves other factors as well as overall imbalance.[52]

Hanoch Dagan explained in works coauthored by Michael Heller and Avihay Dorfman that in cases of procedural unconscionability, "[t]he weaker party suffers from 'physical or mental infirmities, ignorance, illiteracy or inability to understand the language of the agreement.' "[53] The vulnerable are often the "poor

[50] *See* Melissa T. Lonegrass, *Finding Room for Fairness in Formalism—The Sliding Scale Approach to Unconscionability*, 44 Loy. U. Chi. L.J. 1, 8–12 (2012)(describing the consideration of these two factors as the "conventional approach" and contrasting the "sliding scale approach" in which "*strong* evidence of both prongs is no longer required to justify relief"); *see also* Restatement of Consumer Contracts § 5 (Am. Law Inst., Tentative Draft, Apr. 18, 2019) ("In determining that a contract or a term is unconscionable, a greater degree of one [form of unconscionability may offset] a lesser degree of the other element," but "in appropriate circumstances a high degree of substantive unconscionability is sufficient to find that a standard contract term . . . is unconscionable"). Our point is not only that substantive unconscionability is sufficient. It is that procedural unconscionability should be relevant only as evidence of substantive unconscionability.

[51] *See* Unif. Consumer Credit Code § 5.108(e) (Nat'l Conf. of Comm'rs on Unif. State L. 1974).

[52] *Id.* cmt. c.

[53] *Id.* 48 (quoting Restatement (Second) of Contracts § 208 cmt. D).

or the weak, the foolish, and thoughtless."[54] Procedural unconscionability means an absence of "self-determination"[55] or "meaningful choice."[56]

No doubt, the party who accepts an unfair term was vulnerable. One who accepted a price less favorable than the market price was either unable to use the market or unaware of what the market price was. One who accepted liability for a risk and was not compensated for doing so, was, very likely, unaware of the risk. The factors mentioned by Smith and the *Uniform Credit Code* may explain why such parties were unable to protect themselves. Nevertheless, if the terms are unfair, why does it matter that the disadvantaged parties accepted them because they were vulnerable? No matter how vulnerable they were, they would not be given relief if the terms of the contract were fair. The evil to be remedied, then, is the unfairness of the terms, or, as it is sometimes expressed, their "substantive unconscionability." Vulnerability merely explains why a party accepted these terms.

If the evil to be remedied is substantive unfairness, one might well ask why procedural unconscionability should matter at all. One reason—though not a good one—is a belief that parties who can protect themselves should do so or suffer the consequences. But why deny relief to parties who could have protected themselves from an unfair contract but failed to do so?

The only good reason for taking a party's vulnerability into account is that it is more likely that the terms really were unfair. If an experienced businessman or businesswoman, familiar with an industry and the terms of contracts typically in use, were to negotiate a contract and later object to the fairness of its terms, that objection is likely to be unfounded.

Consequently, when the terms are clearly unfair, courts should give relief even if there is no sign of procedural unconscionability. As one might suspect, such cases will be rare. Nevertheless, sometimes, even before the doctrine of unconscionability was recognized by the *Uniform Commercial Code* and the *Second Restatement of Contracts*, courts of equity gave relief despite little or no evidence of procedural unconscionability. Relief was given to a physician who had exchanged property worth $11,800 for property worth $15,000 but subject to a $15,000 mortgage which he had agreed to pay;[57] to the operator of an automobile repair shop who acquired a house valued at $12,000 and sold it twelve days later to a machinist with a sixth grade education who had never owned property before;[58] when a trustee sold land for one-tenth of its value;[59] when the owner of

[54] HANOCH DAGAN & MICHAEL HELLER, THE CHOICE THEORY OF CONTRACTS 86–87 (2017) (internal quotation marks omitted).

[55] HANOCH DAGAN & AVIHAY DORFMAN, JUSTICE FOR CONTRACTS 47 (2020).

[56] DAGAN & HELLER, *supra* note 54, at 86–87 (internal quotation marks omitted).

[57] State Sec. & Realty Co. v. Shaffer, 142 N.W. 1058, 1060 (Mich. 1913).

[58] Miller v. Coffeen, 280 S.W.2d 100, 104 (Mo. 1955).

[59] Wright v. Wilson, 10 Tenn. 294, 295 (Ct. Err. & App. 1829).

a fruit farm parted with it for property worth little more than its mortgage, which he also assumed;[60] and when owner of a four-family flat exchanged it for a vacant lot in which he would have an equity worth less than half the equity he had given up.[61] Suppose that a used car dealer offered a customer a price for a used 2018 Mustang that the seller knew to be three times the *Kelley Blue Book* value for a car of that year and model. The customer agreed without consulting the *Blue Book*, which is an easily available listing of the price for which used cars are typically sold. The contract was unfair. The customer was careless, as the salesperson knew, but it is hard to see why the salesperson should be able to profit from it.

III. One-party commitments

The doctrine of unconscionability allows a court to examine directly whether the terms of an exchange are unfair. Nevertheless, a concern with the fairness of terms permeates the law of contract. It is reflected in the rules of consideration, promissory reliance, and offer and acceptance. Courts apply these rules to sophisticated persons and without any special inquiry into whether a party was vulnerable.

When only one party is committed, an agreement may or may not be unfair. Consider the following four cases:

1. Ann and Bert agree that, if he chooses, Bert can buy Ann's house any time within the next three years. A few months later Ann tells Bert she no longer wishes to sell.
2. Carla writes Don on Monday offering to sell him her house for $500,000. Don receives the letter on Wednesday and mails her a letter that evening accepting her offer. On Tuesday, having received a better offer from Emily, Carla writes to Fred that she is revoking her offer. Don receives that letter on Thursday.
3. Fay lists her house with George, a real estate agent and agrees that if he finds a purchaser who will buy it for more than $500,000, he will receive a 5 percent commission. After George spends considerable time and effort showing her property to prospective customers, he findsone who indicates he would like to meet with Fay to sign a contract for at least that amount. Fay then tells George she no longer wished to sell.
4. Helen offers to restore Ida's house for $95,000. She does so after having received an offer from Jack, a subcontractor, to do the tiling necessary for

[60] Koch v. Streuter, 83 N.E. 1072, 1077 (Ill. 1908).
[61] Linsell v. Halicki, 215 N.W. 315, 316 (Mich. 1927).

the job for $5,000. After Ida accepts Helen's offer, but before Helen accepts Jack's offer, Jack demands $7,000 for the tiling.

The first of these cases is governed by the doctrine of consideration. The second is governed by the rules of offer and acceptance in bilateral contracts. The third is governed by the rules governing the revocation of offers of unilateral contract. The fourth has been resolved by applying the doctrine of promissory reliance. Ann is not bound because the agreement lacks consideration. Carla is bound because an acceptance is effective when it is dispatched. Fay is bound because an offer of unilateral contract is irrevocable when the offeree either begins to perform or incurs significant costs preparing to do so. Jack is bound because Helen relied on his promise to do the work for $5000.

As we will see, in the first two cases, the rules governing contract formation have been used to prevent the unfairness that may arise when one party is bound and the other is not. In the last two, they have been used to modify to standard rules when it is fair for one party to be bound although the other is not.

i. Consideration

An option is an agreement that will become binding only if one of the parties so chooses. Under traditional doctrine, an option lacks consideration. For the option to have consideration, the party with the right to choose must pay something in return. Otherwise that party has not given up a legal right or promised to do so.

If a party pays nothing, the option may be unfair. Yet the doctrine of consideration is a blunt tool for invalidating unfair options. Some options are fair, even if they do not have consideration, and the doctrine invalidates them as well. Consequently, courts and legislatures have modified the doctrine.

An option may be unfair because it allows one party to speculate at the other's expense. An example is the case we just considered. Ann and Bert agree that, if he chooses, Bert can buy Ann's house any time within the next three years. The agreement is unfair since Bert can buy the house if its market value rises above $500,000 in the next three years and decline to do so if it does not.

Sometimes, however, an option is fair and serves a practical purpose. Suppose that Ann promises Bert that he can buy her house any time in the next week for $500,000. That amount is the current value of the house. Bert is willing to pay that amount, but he is unwilling to commit himself until he finds out whether he can raise the money from a lender or from his rich aunt. It is unlikely that Bert will take advantage of a fluctuation in the price of houses to speculate at Ann's expense. Moreover, in such cases, as the *Second Restatement* notes, "[t]he fact that the option is an appropriate preliminary step in the conclusion of a socially useful transaction provides a sufficient substantive basis for enforcement."[62]

The doctrine of consideration cannot accurately discriminate between options that are fair and those that are not because it does not examine fairness directly. The response of some courts[63] and of the *Second Restatement* is to enable the parties to make an option enforceable by paying nominal consideration if the option is likely to be fair.

As the *Second Restatement* recognized, nominal consideration is not genuine consideration. In the case of genuine consideration, a promise is made, at least in part, to induce the promisee to give up a legal right. In the case of nominal consideration, the promisee gives up a legal right—for example $1—but the reason is not to induce the promisor to give up a legal right but to make the commitment legally binding.

Although nominal consideration will not generally make a contract enforceable, the *Second Restatement* makes an exception for options if they are fair. It provides that an option is binding if it "is in writing and signed by the offeror, recites a purported consideration for the making of the offer, and proposes an exchange on fair terms within a reasonable time."[64] To enable the doctrine to discriminate between fair and unfair options, the *Restatement* recognized that it is necessary to take direct account of fairness.

The trouble with the way it does so is that whether a fair option is binding depends upon whether the parties use the right magic words. So long as a written document recites a purported consideration, the option is binding whether or not the purported consideration is ever actually paid. A fair option is enforceable if the document says "the offeror promises not to revoke in return for one dollar" but not if it only says "the offeror promises not to revoke this offer for a period of one week." Such a rule is most likely to protect those who are least likely to need protection: parties whose lawyers know the right magic words.

The "firm offer" rule of the *Uniform Commercial Code* eliminates the need to use magic words. It provides that, among merchants, a short-term option to buy or sell goods in a signed writing which is stated to be irrevocable does not require consideration. "[I]n no event may such period of irrevocability exceed three months."[65] The provision does not require the option to be on fair terms, but it is intended to prevent the unfairness that is most likely to arise with longer-term options. Although it makes no mention of fairness, "[e]very contract or

[62] Restatement (Second) of Contracts § 87 cmt. b (Am. Law Inst. 1981).

[63] 1464-Eight, Ltd. & Mills Management Corp. v. Joppich, 154 S.W.3d 101 (Tex. 2004) (adopting the rule of Restatement (Second) of Contracts § 87(a)); Board of Control of Eastern Michigan University v. Burgess, 206 N.W.2d 256 (Ct. App. Mich, 1973) (sixty-day option to purchase a house).

[64] Restatement (Second) of Contracts § 87(a) (Am. Law Inst. 1981).

[65] U.C.C. § 2-205 (Am. Law Inst. & Unif. L. Comm'n 1977).

duty within [the *Uniform Commercial Code*] imposes an obligation of good faith in its performance and enforcement."[66]

Sometimes a contract contains a condition which is under the control of one party. If the party can control whether the condition is realized at virtually no cost, the effect is the same as if that party had an option. The party will see to it that the condition is fulfilled only if the bargain proves to be favorable.

In *Scott v. Moragues*,[67] the court held that a contract had consideration even though whether it was binding depended on a condition that was under one party's control. Scott and Moragues agreed that if Scott purchased a certain ship, he would charter it to Moragues. Whether he would purchase it was left up to him.

Technically, the agreement had consideration. Scott gave up a legal right. He could not both buy the ship and refuse to charter it to Moragues. The agreement was unlikely to be unfair because of the circumstances. To accept a better offer from a prospective charterer, Scott would have to buy a different vessel. He would be unlikely to do so in order to charter it at a somewhat higher rate. In contrast, suppose A agreed to buy B's car for $20,000 if, in the next week, he decides to drive to a nearby town to visit his niece. A could look for a better offer, and, if he found one, escape his contract to buy B's car by postponing his visit. He would be using a condition that left a decision up to him to obtain an option that he did not pay for. That would be unfair, and yet, technically, the agreement would have consideration. He gave the legal right to visit his niece in the next week without buying the car.

As these examples show, the doctrine of consideration is a crude tool for preventing unfairness. In the case just described, a court would have the choice of upholding an unfair contract because the technical requirements of the doctrine had been fulfilled or refusing to enforce it anyway.

A subjective condition of satisfaction raises a similar problem. A condition of satisfaction allows a party who is not satisfied with the other's performance to reject it. If the condition is "objective," the party who is dissatisfied must accept the performance as long as a reasonable person would do so. An example is a condition that a builder will be paid only for work that meets the specifications of the contract. If the builder can prove that the work met the specifications, the condition is fulfilled. In contrast, if the condition cannot be met unless the other party is personally satisfied, it is "subjective." It does not matter if a reasonable person would have been satisfied as long as the party is not. The classic example is a contract to paint a portrait on condition that the client is satisfied. If the client does not like the portrait, it does not matter whether other people would.

66 *Id.* at § 1-304.
67 80 So. 394 (Ala. 1918).

Subjective conditions raise the possibility that the party who can escape by professing dissatisfaction is not bound de facto. Nevertheless, such a contract has been held to have consideration.[68] Technically it does because that party gave up a legal right: "good faith" allows only a party who is genuinely dissatisfied to reject the performance. The reason the contract may be fair, however, is because it may fairly allocate the risk that the party who is to receive a performance will be truly satisfied. One party or the other must bear the risk. A subjective condition places it on the party who is to perform. It may be hard to prove whether a party who claims to be dissatisfied is telling the truth. Nevertheless, it is fair to enforce the contract because the party to perform accepted that risk and would not have done so without compensation for assuming it.

ii. Offer and acceptance

A contract requires mutual assent and therefore is formed by an offer and an acceptance. According to the *Second Restatement*, "An agreement is a manifestation of mutual assent on the part of two or more persons."[69] "The manifestation of mutual assent to an exchange ordinarily takes the form of an offer or proposal by one party followed by an acceptance by the other party or parties."[70] The consent of each party is a *sine qua non* condition for the other party to be bound. We will deal with mutual consent in the next chapter.

Nevertheless, one purpose that the rules of offer and acceptance serve is not to ensure that consent is mutual, but to prevent the unfairness that can arise when one party is bound and the other is not. That will be our concern here.

The offer

What constitutes an offer

An offer proposes a contract on terms that become binding when it has been accepted by the other party. There may be an interval of time before the offeree accepts. In that interval, the offeror is not legally bound but is committed de facto. It would be unwise to contract with anyone else before the offeree accepts or rejects the offer. One purpose served by the rules that govern offers is to limit both the risk that this commitment places on the offeror and the opportunity it gives the offeree to speculate at the offeror's expense.

A party can avoid assuming this risk by soliciting an offer rather than making one, that is, by proposing terms that would be acceptable without making an

[68] Mattei v. Hopper, 330 P.2d 625 (Cal.1958).

[69] RESTATEMENT (SECOND) OF CONTRACTS § 3 (AM. LAW INST. 1981).

[70] *Id.* at § 22(1).

offer. If the other party makes an offer on these terms, that party assumes the risks of making a de facto commitment.

When it is unclear whether a party meant to make an offer or to solicit one, one factor to consider is the risk that making a de facto commitment would entail. In *Lonergan v. Skolnick*,[71] a communication was held not to be an offer, in part, because it said, "you will have to decide fast, as I expect to have a buyer in the next week or two." The would-be seller would not want to lose the chance to accept the offer of another buyer.

Advertisements are generally not considered to be offers for another reason: if a number of people accept, a seller may sell more goods than he owns. According to Eisenberg, the common law rule is wrong. "It should be implied in every offer that a reasonable quantity should be available and that the quantity will be allocated on a first-come first-served basis."[72] That is the rule in France where advertisements are considered to be offers.[73] But there is another reason for the traditional rule. It minimizes the length of time of the offeror's de facto commitment. To change the price, the offeror would have to readvertise. That would take time. During that time, the offeror would bear the risk that the price at which they advertised would prove unfavorable.

In exceptional cases, advertisements have been held to constitute offers. Sometimes, the issue has been whether the terms contained in the advertisement are part of an offer and hence binding on the parties. It is not whether a contract was formed. The plaintiff had bought and planted seed from the defendant, but it did not measure up to the claims made for it in an advertisement.[74] The plaintiff had purchased a certificate of deposit from a bank but was not paid the rate of interest it had advertised.[75] The buyer of a 1954 Ford did not have the right to a 1955 Ford as described in the car dealer's advertisement.[76] These courts could have reached the same result by holding that the terms described in the advertisement were incorporated by implication in the contract.

In other cases, the advertisement was used to "bait and switch" potential customers. A car was advertised at a price the car dealer never intended to sell to lure customers to his dealership.[77] The advertisement said that the first three customers to enter a store could buy a valuable fur coat at a token price. The customer who arrived first was told he could not do so.[78] The store owner never

71 276 P.2d 8 (Cal. App. 1954).
72 EISENBERG, *supra* note 8, at 423.
73 Cour de cassation, 28 Nov. 1968, JCP 15797 (1969).
74 Oliver v. Henley, 21 S.W.2d 576 (Tex. Civ. App., 1929).
75 Chang v. First Colonial Savings Bank, 410 S.E.2d 928 (Va. 1991).
76 Johnson v. Capital City Ford Co., 85 So.2d 75, 79 (La. App. 1955).
77 Izadi v. Machado (Gus) Ford, Inc., 550 So.2d 1135, 1139 (Fla. App., 1989).
78 Lefkowitz v. Great Minneapolis Surplus Store, Inc., 86 N.W.2d 698 (Minn. 1957).

intended to sell on the terms that he advertised. Holding that advertisement was an offer prevents him from using it to bait and switch.

Under Swiss law, the price tags placed on goods for sale in a store are considered offers.[79] Under common law they are not. The merit of the common law rule is that it recognizes the difficulty of revoking such an offer. The merchant would have to recheck his prices and relabel. Here, as in the case of advertisements, the common law rule limits the circumstances in which a party makes a de facto commitment.

The revocability of an offer

The common law rule allows the offeror to revoke an offer before acceptance even if he promised to keep it open.[80] Their promise not to revoke it lacks consideration. An irrevocable offer is, in effect, an option. As noted earlier, an option may be unfair because it allows one party to speculate at the other's expense. The offeror is committed while the offeree can take advantage of a change in the market price or to shop around for a better deal and so speculate at the offeror's expense.

Sometimes, however, an option is fair and serves a practical purpose. It may be unlikely that the offeree will speculate at the offeror's expense, and the offeree be unwilling to make a commitment before taking measures to ensure the contract will be beneficial, and unwilling to take these measures without a commitment from the offeror. The doctrine of consideration cannot discriminate between options that are fair and unfair. As we have seen, according to the *Second Restatement*, a firm offer will be irrevocable if it "proposes an exchange on fair terms within a reasonable time."[81] It will be irrevocable under the *Uniform Commercial Code* if it is made in writing between merchants and is binding for a maximum of three months.[82]

Eisenberg believes that all firm offers should be irrevocable:

> In considering whether to accept an offer an offeree may make an investment of time and, often, money. The offeree is more likely to make such an investment, or to make a greater investment, if he is sure that the offer will be held open while the investment is being made. The purpose of a firm offer is to induce the offeree to make such an investment so as to increase the probability that the offer will be accepted.[83]

79 Swiss Code of Obligations (*Obligationenrecht*) § 7(3).
80 Restatement (Second) of Contracts § 25, cmt. b (Am. Law Inst. 1981).
81 *Id.* at. § 87(a).
82 U.C.C. § 2-205 (Am. Law Inst. & Unif. L. Comm'n 1977).
83 Eisenberg, *supra* note 8, at 461.

His argument does not show that all firm offers should be irrevocable but only those that are made so that the promisee may make an investment of time or money knowing that the offer cannot be revoked. In that event, the offeror's promise not to revoke should be enforceable under the doctrine of promissory reliance. Indeed, courts were enforcing promises made for that purpose before the doctrine of promissory reliance was formulated. In 1880, in *The M. F. Parker*,[84] a man bought a ship for $315 after a carpenter had said repairs to the ship would cost $150. Although he did not commit himself to hire the carpenter if he bought the ship, when the carpenter later billed him $356 for making these repairs, the court held the carpenter could charge no more than $150.[85] In 1920, in *Wilson v. Spry*,[86] a court enforced the defendant's promise to hold an offer to sell his land open for forty-five days so that a prospective buyer could make a thorough examination of it at a significant cost to himself. To do so, the court, unconvincingly, construed the prospective buyer's opportunity to examine the property as an obligation to do so, and therefore as consideration for the prospective seller's promise to hold the offer open.

In his notes to Sir Frederick Pollock's treatise on contract law, Williston suggested that the result in *The M.F. Parker* could be explained by the principle of reliance.[87] He did not cite the case later in defense of the doctrine of promissory reliance when he served as Reporter for the *First Restatement*.[88] The reason may have been that it would have meant that the doctrine could be used, not only to enforce promises of gifts and promises, but promises made in a business context that are not supported by consideration. Since then, the use of the doctrine in that context has become common.

As mentioned earlier, the *Second Restatement* allows a court to give either of two remedies. It may enforce the promise in full, as it would if the promise had been supported by consideration. Or it may award damages that compensate the promisee for the loss suffered by relying on the promise. In discussing promises to give away money or property, we saw that the promisee should be able to recover only for the loss. The promisee is then no worse off than if the promise had never been made. In the case of a promise to hold an offer open, the remedy should be the same but for a different reason. The offeror is committed only to allow the offeree the opportunity to invest time or money deciding whether the

[84] 88 F. 853 (E.D. Va. 1880).

[85] *Id.* at 855. Though the court held the carpenter to the $150 estimate, it allowed him to collect an extra $60 for additional work not considered in the original estimate. *Id.* at 854–55.

[86] 223 S.W. 564 (Ark. 1920).

[87] Frederick Pollock, Principles of Contract at Law and in Equity 650 n.1 (Gustavus H. Wald & Samuel Williston eds., 7th English ed., 3d American ed. 1906).

[88] American Law Institute, Commentaries on Contracts: Restatement No. 2, at 20 (Commentaries (a), Mar. 9, 1926); Restatement of Contracts, Official Draft No. 1, § 90 explanatory notes, at 249–50 (1928).

offer is favorable. Even if it is, the offeree is not bound to accept the offer if another offer proves to be even more favorable. It would unfair if the offeror were bound when the offeree is not. It would also be unfair if the offeror could revoke the offer without compensating the offeree for the investment of time or money made in reliance on the offer. Therefore, provided the offeree is compensated, the offeror should not be bound.

It would be different if, by investing time or money, the offeree obtained information that allowed the offeror to make a more attractive offer to someone else. Suppose, for example, that the offeree paid for tests that show that there was a higher grade of oil or minerals on the offeror's land than the parties had expected. The offeror should be bound. Otherwise, the offeror would be speculating at the expense of the offeree, and the offeree would have no incentive to make the investment that provided the information.

The parties might agree, not simply that the offeror will hold the offer open, but that the offeree is bound to accept it if some condition is met. If so, there is consideration. Both parties are bound subject to a condition. That condition could be whether the offeree obtains information, whether or not through an investment of time or money, that makes the offer more attractive to him. The condition might be that tests show that land contains oil mineral of a certain grade. It could be that the offeree discovers that under applicable zoning laws the land could be used for a bed and breakfast. The condition could be that the offeree is satisfied with information obtained. That condition could be objective: for example, satisfaction that the land contains a certain quantity of board feet of timber. Or it could be subjective: for example, satisfaction with the leases on land to be purchased from the offeror for a shopping center.[89] As we have seen, there is consideration even if the condition of satisfaction is subjective.[90]

Justice Traynor applied the doctrine of promissory estoppel to make the offer of a subcontractor irrevocable in the leading case of *Drennan v. Star Paving Co.*[91] A subcontractor submitted a bid to do the paving work for a project on which the general contractor was bidding. After the general contractor's bid was accepted, the subcontractor refused to stand by its bid. Justice Traynor held that the subcontractor was bound under the doctrine of promissory reliance. The contractor had relied on the subcontractor's bid by using it to calculate its own. The result, as Traynor explained in a later decision,[92] and other courts have held,[93] is that although the subcontractor is bound by the bid he submitted if the general

[89] Mattei v. Hopper, 330 P.2d 625 (Cal.1958).

[90] p. 000.

[91] 333 P.2d 757 (Cal. 1958).

[92] Southern Calif. Acoustics Co. v. C.V. Holder, Inc., 456 P.2d 975 (Cal. 1969) (where, nevertheless, he held that the general contractor was bound because of the provisions of a California statute).

[93] Holman Erection Co. v. Orville E. Madsen & Sons, Inc., 330 N.W.2d 693 (Minn. 1983).

contractor uses it, the general contractor is not bound to that subcontractor. After receiving the contract, he may shop around to see if he can obtain a lower bid from someone else.

Traynor was not troubled by the possibility that the offeror would speculate at the offeree's expense. As he noted, the general contractor may have received the subcontractor's bid at the last moment before its own was due, as, in fact, happened in *Drennan*. The general contractor does not have time to see if he can obtain a more favorable bargain, nor may it be reasonable for it to do so, until it knows that its own bid has been accepted. In this situation, holding only one party bound equalizes their opportunities to shop for around.

The termination of an offer by lapse of time

An offeror can also obtain protection by specifying a time within which the offer may be accepted. If no time is specified, the offer must be accepted within a reasonable time.[94] As the *Second Restatement* explains, this rule "serves to limit" the "risk of commitment of the offeror during the period required for communication of the acceptance."[95]

> The more significant the risk, the greater is the need for limitation, and hence the shorter is the time which is reasonable. These considerations have their principal application in the sale of property which may be subject to rapid fluctuation in value, such as commodities, securities or land....
>
> The reasonable time for acceptance in a speculative transaction is brief not only because the offeror does not ordinarily intend to assume an extended risk without compensation but also because he does not intend to give the offeree an extended opportunity for speculation at the offeror's expense. If the offeree makes use for speculative purposes of time allowed for communication, there may be a lack of good faith, and an acceptance may not be timely even though it arrives within the time contemplated by the offeror.[96]

The *Second Restatement* provides two illustrations:

> 7. A sends B a telegraphic offer to sell oil which at the time is subject to rapid fluctuations in price. The offer is received near the close of business hours, and a telegraphic acceptance is sent the next day, after the offeree has learned of a sharp price rise. The acceptance is too late if a fixed price was offered, but may be timely if the price is market price at time of delivery.

94 Restatement (Second) of Contracts § 41 (Am. Law Inst. 1981).
95 *Id.* at cmt. f.
96 *Id.*

> 8. A sends B an offer by mail to sell at a fixed price corporate stock not listed on an exchange. B waits two days after receiving the offer and then sends a telegraphic acceptance after learning of a sharp rise in the price bid over-the-counter. The acceptance may be too late even though it arrives before a prompt acceptance by mail would have arrived.

The termination of an offer by a rejection

An offer is terminated when the offeree rejects it.

According to the *Second Restatement*, the reason is that "it is highly probable that the offeror will change his plans in reliance on the statement."[97]

> The reliance is likely to take such negative forms as failure to prepare or failure to send a notice of revocation, and hence is likely to be difficult or impossible to prove. To protect the offeror in such reliance, the power of acceptance is terminated without proof of reliance.[98]

Nevertheless, although the offeree did not say whether or not he would accept the offer in the future, the offeror will infer that the offeree is less likely to accept than the offeror expected when the offer was initially made. Because that expectation has changed, the offer should terminate whether or not it is "probable that the offeror will change his plans." As long as the offer is open, the offeror is committed de facto. He cannot contract with another party. The offeree is able to do. Although the offeror was willing to run the risk of making a de facto commitment before the offeree rejected his offer, one cannot assume that he would be willing to do so afterward. The risk is the same but the chances that taking the risk will pay off because the offeree will accept are much reduced.

The acceptance

What constitutes an acceptance

The offeree accepts by signifying a commitment to the proposal made by the offeror.

According to the common law rule, a counteroffer counts as a rejection.[99] Therefore it terminates the offer.

As we have seen, the reason that a rejection terminates an offer is that the offeror took a risk in extending it since the offer is binding de facto. We cannot assume the offeror is also willing to assume that risk after the offer has been

[97] *Id.* at § 38 cmt. a.
[98] *Id.*
[99] *Id.* at § 39.

declined. The same may be so if the offeree has made a counteroffer. Courts, however, have applied the so-called mirror image rule. If the response of the offeree varies in any respect from the offer, it is deemed not to be an acceptance, but a counteroffer, and consequently a rejection. That is so even though there is every prospect that the parties will reach agreement. It is so even if the parties evidently intended to conclude a contract.

The notorious example is "the battle of the forms": the parties each sign their own form contract but not that of the other, and the details of the forms conflict. They might exchange conflicting forms several times. For example, a seller might receive a "purchase order" which contained one set of terms, and, after sending back an "acceptance" that contained another, receive a "confirmation" which contained the same terms as the "purchase order." Each form counts as a rejection and a new offer. Which set of terms prevails depends on the "last shot fired." Eventually one party performs an act such as shipping goods or accepting a shipment that is deemed to be an implied acceptance of whatever offer was still open. Which offer was still open was largely a matter of chance.

In sales, this rule has been replaced by § 2-207 of the *Uniform Commercial Code*. This provision is so ill-conceived and poorly drafted that courts have not applied it by analogy to other contracts. We will consider those difficulties at a later point when we discuss mutual consent as a necessary element in contract formation. The source of the problem, however, is that courts had been applying the mirror image rule. It would be better if they had said that a counteroffer does not terminate an offer unless it indicates that the offeree is less likely to accept on the terms originally proposed by the offeror. Moreover, if the offeree's response indicates that he is willing to accept the terms originally proposed but would like them to be modified, it is not a counteroffer but a qualified acceptance. The question of which terms govern the contract if the offeree made a qualified acceptance will be considered when we discuss the difficulties that have arisen under § 2-207.

Acceptance by silence

As we have seen, doubts as to whether a party has made an offer should be resolved by considering whether that party would be willing to assume the risk of a one-sided commitment. Doubts about the meaning of the offeree's conduct should be resolved in a way that minimizes the ability to exploit the risk of the offeror's one-sided commitment. An offeree may be bound by an ambiguous response because otherwise there would be a prolonged period in which the offeror was committed de facto.

A prime illustration of ambiguous conduct is when the offeree was silent. Normally, a contract cannot be accepted by silence. One cannot know that the offeree is committed. Under some circumstances, however, the offeror could reasonably believe that the offeree who says nothing is committed. Doubts will be resolved against the offeree who need not have remained silent and, by doing so, could speculate at the offeror's expense.

For example, if the two parties have done business before, and they have treated the offeree's silence as signifying consent, it is reasonable for the offeror to put that same interpretation on their conduct in later transactions. The offeree has chosen that means of signifying assent should accept the risk of being misunderstood.

An example is a well-known but early Massachusetts case, *Hobbs v. Massasoit Whip Co.*[100] Without receiving any specific order for them, the plaintiff had shipped eel skins to the defendant on four or five occasions, and the defendant had paid. When the plaintiff made another shipment, the defendant kept the eel skins for four or five months without communicating with the plaintiff. When the eel skins were destroyed, he refused to pay for them. The court held that, in light of their previous course of dealing, the defendant's silence and retention of the eel skins could entitle the plaintiff to assume that he had accepted. Very likely, the plaintiff would have been justified in making that assumption. Be that as it may, a different result would have exposed the plaintiff to a risk for which he was never compensated. De facto, the defendant would have an option for which he was never paid: to remain silent if the deal remained favorable, and to reject the offer if it did not. The only way to prevent that kind of unfairness is to hold that he is bound by the terms of the offer.

It often happens that a potential buyer signs a form supplied by the seller which provides that no contract is made until there is an acceptance by the seller. If the seller does not notify the buyer that it accepts, it may be that a reasonable buyer would assume that acceptance is a formality which the seller had dispensed with. But if the seller has delayed acceptance unnecessarily, and events during the period of unnecessary delay have made the deal advantageous to the seller and disadvantageous to the buyer, it should not matter what the buyer reasonably thought. The unnecessary delay enabled the seller to speculate at the buyer's expense. The seller should not be allowed to do so.

For example, in *Cole-McIntyre-Norfleet v. Holloway*,[101] a retail merchant signed such a form to purchase fifty barrels of meal. The order was submitted on March 26, 1917, and he was not told that the seller would not accept it until May 26. In the meantime, prices rose by 50 percent, which was not surprising, since the United States entered World War I on April 2. The court said: "Delay in notifying the other party . . . amount[ed] to an acceptance. . . . Otherwise, [the offeree] could place his goods upon the market, and solicit orders, and yet hold

[100] 33 N.E. 495 (Mass. 1893).
[101] 214 S.W. 817 (Tenn. 1919).

the other party to the contract while he reserves time to himself to see if the contract will be profitable."[102]

In *Kukuska v. Home Mutual Hail-Tornado Insurance Co.*,[103] a farmer signed a similar order form to purchase hail insurance. He made a down payment and, if his order was accepted, the insurance was to cover his crop from the day that he had submitted his order. After months, the insurance company notified him that his order was not accepted. That afternoon, his crop was destroyed by hail. Since he had paid his deposit and the insurance policy was retroactive once accepted, it would have been difficult for him to find insurance elsewhere when the company delayed its approval. The reason the insurer should be liable is that its delay enabled it to wait to accept until it knew more about the chances of a hailstorm destroying the crops. It chose a mode of acceptance that took advantage of the farmer's de facto commitment or expose him to unnecessary risk.

The court acknowledged: "It is a well-established principle of the law of contracts that an offer does not ripen into a contract unless accepted; that, if the offeree within a reasonable time does not accept the offer, it may be treated as if rejected."[104] Yet:

> Does not the very nature of the transaction impose on the insurer a duty to act? . . . If the insurer is under such a duty and fails to perform that duty within a reasonable time and, as a consequence, the applicant sustains damage, it is not vastly important that the legal relationship be placed in a particular category. If we say it is contractual, that is, there is an implied agreement under the circumstances on the part of the insurer to act within a reasonable time, or, having a duty to act, the insurer negligently fails in the performance of that duty, or that the duty springs out of a consensual relationship, and is therefore in the nature of a quasi-contractual liability, is not vitally important. Each view finds some support in the cases. It seems to be more in accord with ordinary legal concepts to say that it is a quasi-contractual duty. The legal consequences may be somewhat different in each case, no doubt they would be widely variant under a system of pleading different than that which prevails here. The consequent liability to respond in damages is the same in each case.[105]

According to John Appleman, in such cases:

> A claim . . . is not based on a contract of insurance. Rather it is based upon the damages produced by the failure of the insurer to promptly perform the duty

[102] *Id.* at 818.
[103] 235 N.W. 403 (Wis. 1931).
[104] *Id.* at 404.
[105] *Id.* at 405.

> which the facts imposed upon it. The better rule is that the insurer has a duty either to accept or to reject an application within a reasonable time, and is liable if it delays unreasonably in acting thereon.[106]

It does matter whether "the legal relationship be placed in a particular category," despite what the court said in *Kukuska*. The claim is "based on a contract of insurance," despite Singleton's statement to the contrary. The amount the insured can recover, when he can recover, and the conditions that must be met for him to do so are those specified in the contract. Moreover, if the insurer were liable because, as in tort, it harmed the farmer by inducing him to expect a prompt consideration of his application, then, as in tort, its liability should be only for the harm he suffered as a consequence, for example, of not applying for insurance elsewhere. Yet the insurance company should be liable even if the farmer could not have obtained hail insurance from anyone else, or if everyone else delayed processing applications to gain the same unfair advantage as the insurer in *Kukuska*. The court suggested that the duty to consider the application promptly might rest on a "consensual relationship." But the reason for implying consent to do so promptly is that the insurance company chose a mode of acceptance that took advantage of the farmer's de facto commitment to expose him to unnecessary risk. That should be enough whether the company intended to consider the application promptly or the farmer though it had promised to do so.

Nothing is gained by calling the insurer's liability "quasi-contractual" rather than "contractual," as the court suggested in *Kukuska*. It is bound by the terms of the contract it proposed, just as if it had consented. This is not the only instance in which a person who did not consent is bound to a contract because the only alternative would be unfair to the other party. Earlier we saw that in the case of "bait and switch" advertising, the advertiser may be bound to a contract to which it never consented in order to prevent unfairness, albeit unfairness of a different kind. As we will see later on, sometimes a contract is binding whatever words the parties may have used, even though one party does not wish to be bound. For example, that party may have remained silent knowing that the other party believes that they have entered into a binding contract. The parties are also bound to many terms to which they did not consent but which the law reads into their contract because they are fair. In the situations we have just described, they are bound because the alternative would be unfair. But there is no more reason to call their liability "quasi-contractual."

[106] 12A John Alan Appleman, Insurance Law and Practice § 7216 (1981), quoted favorably by Eisenberg, *supra* note 8, at 138.

Late acceptance

A similar problem arises when an offeree fails to accept an offer on time. The offeree may not be aware that the acceptance was late or may hope that the offeror will not mind. The difficulty is that an offeror who does mind and does not say so right away may be in a position later to speculate at the offeree's expense by insisting on the deadline only if the contract becomes disadvantageous.

According to the traditional approach, if the offeree fails to accept on time, the offer lapses. There is nothing for the offeree to accept. Their purported acceptance is a new offer which the offeror can then accept or reject. That is the position of the *Second Restatement*. A Comment to the section on late acceptances explains:

> A purported acceptance conditional on a change of terms commonly has the effect of a counter-offer. In such cases the original offeror has not ordinarily given the original offeree reason to understand that silence will operate as an acceptance of a counter-offer. Moreover, although an acceptance would not call for a reply, a purported acceptance is not ordinarily a sufficient manifestation of assent to silence as acceptance of the counter-offer. Nor can the original offeror "waive" his right to reject, or at his election regard the counter-offer as an acceptance.

We can see the difficulties of this approach if we consider, first, a situation in which the offeree may reasonably believe that they have accepted on time, and then one in which the offeree knows or should know that the acceptance was late.

If the offer does not specify a time by which it must be accepted, it will lapse unless it is accepted in a reasonable time. The offeree might reasonably believe that the acceptance is timely even if it is not. The *Second Restatement* rejected the approach of courts which have held that the offeror who does not notify the offeree waives the right to object that the acceptance is late. In *Phillips v. Moor*, and early Maine case that is often cited for this rule, the court said:

> It is true that an offer, to be binding upon the party making it, must be accepted within a reasonable time; but if the party to whom it is made, makes known his acceptance of it to the party making it, within any period which he could fairly have supposed to be reasonable, good faith requires the maker, if he intends to retract on account of the delay, to make known that intention promptly. If he does not, he must be regarded as waiving any objection to the acceptance as being too late.[107]

[107] 71 Me. 78, 80 (1880).

We can see the difficulty of the *Second Restatement*'s approach if we examine the facts in *Phillips*, which it presents in one of its illustrations:

> A invites B to make an offer to buy hay in A's barn. On Friday B inspects the hay and mails A an offer which is received the following day. The following Thursday A mails B an acceptance which is received the following day, and B then employs a third party to haul the hay. There is a contract.[108]

The *Second Restatement* explained that "the failure of the original offeror to object to an acceptance and his subsequent preparations for performance may be evidence that the acceptance was made within a reasonable time."[109]

The *Second Restatement*'s illustration omitted the fact that in *Phillips*, "Sunday morning the hay was burnt in the barn."[110] It was then that the offeror announced that he was not bound by the contract. If he had been bound, under the law as it was then, he would have borne the risk of the loss of the hay. As the case illustrates, if the offeree responds within what they judge to be a reasonable time, and the offeror can wait to make their objection known, there will be an interval of time in which the risk that the contract will prove to be disadvantageous will fall on the offeree. If the contract becomes disadvantageous, as it did here when the hay burned, the offeror can object that the acceptance came too late. If it does not, the offeror need never raise that issue.

To say, as the *Second Restatement* does, that the offeror's silence is merely "evidence" that the offer was accepted in a reasonable time does not address the problem. The offeror can remain silent and later, to escape the contract, argue that there is better evidence to show that it was not.

If we say instead, as the court did in *Phillips*, that by remaining silent, the offeror has "waived" the right to demand an earlier acceptance, two different problems arise. First, it is odd to say that a right has been waived if the right-holder never communicated the intention to waive it. Second, the right-holder may not have intended to waive the right, intending, instead, to remain silent and see whether the contract would prove to be disadvantageous. The reason the offer should be bound is not "waiver" but to prevent speculation at the offeree's expense.

The problem seems to be different if the offeror set a deadline for acceptance, and the offeree knows or should have known that the acceptance was late. In one such case, *Sabo v. Fasano*, the offeree was a seller who claimed that no contract had been formed when he had accepted late. The court rejected the argument

[108] Restatement (Second) of Contracts § 70 illus. 2 (Am. Law Inst. 1981).
[109] *Id.* at cmt. b.
[110] 71 Me. at 79.

that to construe the buyer's silence as an acceptance "would leave the seller uncertain as to whether there is a contract because the buyer need not waive an untimely acceptance." It said that "[t]he simple answer to this argument is that the seller, who created his own dilemma by accepting late, can resolve any uncertainty by making an inquiry of the buyer."[111] That answer may be satisfactory in the case before the court in which the offeree was the one who claimed that no contract had been formed. Suppose, however, it had been the offeror. The offeree could, of course, contact him to see if he objected to the delay in acceptance. The offeree might assume, however, that unless he heard from the offeror, the delay did not matter. The offeror would again be in a position to decide whether to "waive" his objections after he decided whether the contract was disadvantageous.

If the offeror remained silent, one solution would be to examine other evidence of his intentions. The court did so in *Beirne v. Alaska Housing Authority*.[112] Nineteen days after a counteroffer terminated, the offeree wrote a letter to a third party explaining that he could not consider another offer because he had entered into a contract with the offeror. According to the court, "[t]his was evidence that [the offeree] was not going to insist upon the [deadline] . . . that the time limitation provision of the counteroffer had been waived." The court said that "a contract was formed" when the offeree accepted the offeror's check six days later.[113]

There can be no hard-and-fast rule. The realistic approach is to see whether it is likely that the offeror was speculating at the offeree's expense. If so, the offeree should be bound but it may be clear, because of the nature of the contract or the circumstances, that the offeree was not.

When an acceptance is effective: the mailbox rule

As we have seen, normally, the offeror may revoke the offer before the offeree accepts it. Suppose on Monday, Abe mails Barbara a letter offering to sell her his car for $25,000 which she receives on Wednesday. On Tuesday, he changes his mind and mails another letter withdrawing his offer which she receives on Thursday. On Wednesday, however, she mails a letter to Abe saying that she accepts his offer which he received on Friday. Do the parties have a contract?

According to the common law "mailbox rule" they do. An acceptance is effective when it is mailed, not when it is received. A withdrawal is effective when it is received, not when it is mailed. According to the *Second Restatement*:

[111] 201 Cal. Rptr. 270, 273 (Cal, App. 1984).
[112] 454 P.2d 262 (Alaska 1969).
[113] *Id.* at 265.

> Unless the offer provides otherwise,
>
> (a) an acceptance made in a manner and by a medium invited by an offer is operative and completes the manifestation of mutual assent as soon as put out of the offeree's possession, without regard to whether it ever reaches the offeror.[114]

It explains:

> The rule that an offer becomes irrevocable when an acceptance is mailed in effect imposes a risk of commitment on the offeror during the period required for communication of the acceptance, although during that period the offeror has no assurance that the bargain has been concluded.[115]

Christopher Columbus Langdell claimed that as matter of logic there cannot be a contract until the acceptance is received. Mutual assent requires communication. Communication requires the participation of both parties. If a party simply writes something down, they have not communicated anything until the other party reads it. Langdell noted that, according to some scholars, the common law rule better served the interests of the parties. "The true answer to this objection," he said, "is that it is irrelevant."[116] It was the age of conceptualism. One who knows the meaning of contract, mutual assent, and communication knows the right answer. There is no need to worry about the purposes that contracts serve.

Some scholars devised a tortuous explanation: the acceptance was received by the offeror at the moment that it was mailed.[117] Supposedly, by using the mail to send the offer, the offeror had appointed the post office as an agent for receiving an acceptance. The offeror need not have contemplated doing any such thing.

Here, as in other areas of law, the conceptualist approach has given way to one that asks about the purposes that a rule serves. The purpose of the mailbox rule is to protect the offeree. In our example, she is protected against the possibility that the offeror has already changed his mind and mailed a withdrawal that she had not received. She knows that even if it were so, a contract is concluded when she mails the acceptance.

Why the offeree should be protected has proven to be a harder question. According to the *Second Restatement*, "[a] better explanation of the rule that the acceptance takes effect on dispatch is that the offeree needs a dependable basis for his decision whether to accept."[118] That would be so if the offeree needed to

114 Restatement (Second) of Contracts § 63 (Am. Law Inst. 1981).
115 *Id.* at § 41 cmt. f.
116 Christopher Columbus Langdell, Summary of the Law of Contacts 20–21 (2d ed. 1880).
117 Criticized by Restatement (Second) of Contracts § 63 cmt. a (Am. Law Inst. 1981).
118 *Id.*

change his position with the assurance that he has a contract. But the mailbox rule applies even if the date of performance is far in the future or if the offeror must perform first.

A better explanation is that the mailbox rule minimizes the unfairness of a de facto commitment. When a contract is made by correspondence, one party must wait to hear from the other. The party who must wait, will be bound de facto while the other party is not. To accept a better deal from someone else would be to run the risk of buying or selling the same thing twice. Under the mailbox rule, the offeror must wait to see if the offer has been accepted. If an acceptance were effective only on receipt, the offeree would have to wait to see if the offer had been withdrawn before the acceptance arrived.

The unfairness is minimized by placing that burden on the offeror. The reason is that a person can choose whether to be an offeror. If, in our example, Abe anticipates that he will receive other offers and wishes to be free to accept them, he can write to Barbara that he will entertain an offer for $25,000. If Barbara writes back that she will buy his car for that price, then she is the offeror. He is free to accept any better offer he receives until he mails an acceptance of his offer. If Barbara does not want to run the risk missing the chance to buy a similar car at a lower price while she waits, she can write back suggesting that he make an offer at that price. The risk will end up on the party who is willing to accept it.

The mailbox rule also resolves a different problem: whether the offeree who has sent an acceptance can withdraw it before it reaches the offeror. Suppose on Monday, Abe mails an offer to Barbara which she receives Wednesday. She mails an acceptance on Wednesday which he receives on Friday. On Thursday, however, she changes her mind. She contacts Abe—in person, by telephone, or by putting a letter under his door—telling him that she does not wish to buy his car and that he should ignore the letter that he is about to receive. If a court applies the mailbox rule, a contract was formed when she mailed the acceptance on Wednesday. She cannot revoke her acceptance.

One might think that she should be allowed to do so, since changing her mind benefits her and cannot harm Abe. Nevertheless, according to the *Second Restatement*, the mailbox rule should also apply to this situation. "An attempt to revoke the acceptance by an overtaking communication is . . . ineffective, even though the revocation is received before the acceptance is received."[119] The reason is the one we have just mentioned: to minimize the unfairness that may arise when one party is bound and the other is not. If the mailbox rule does not apply, there will be an interval of time during which she can decide whether there will be a binding contract, and Abe cannot. The *Second Restatement* explains: "After mailing an acceptance of a revocable offer, the offeree is not

[119] *Id.* cmt. c.

permitted to speculate at the offeror's expense during the time required for the letter to arrive."[120]

This rationale explains why the offeree should not be able to accept a better offer after mailing the acceptance and before it arrives. It does not explain why the offeree should not be permitted to change her mind about whether what she is to receive is worth more to her than what she is to give. Perhaps the best solution would be to let the rule depend on the situation. The offeree is bound if she withdrew to accept a better offer but not if she merely changed her mind.

In a third situation, the offeree mails an acceptance that never reaches the offeror. Barbara writes an acceptance on Wednesday which is lost in the mail. Under the mailbox rule, Barbara's acceptance is effective as soon as it is sent. Therefore, she and Abe are bound. The *Second Restatement* provides that a contract is formed "without regard to whether [the acceptance] ever reaches the offeror."[121]

According to the *Second Restatement* although "[t]he convenience of the [mailbox] rule is less clear in such cases" than in those just discussed, it should be "[i]n the interest of simplicity and clarity." Nevertheless, it would be equally as simple and clear to provide that an acceptance that does not reach the offeror within a reasonable time is ineffective. Some scholars have suggested that the offeror should be bound because he knows that he sent an offer that has gone unanswered, and so is more likely to ask the offeree what happened than the offeree to ask whether the acceptance was received.[122] Perhaps. But another reason may be that, as before, a risk that must be borne by one of the parties ought to be borne by the offeror. He can decide whether to be an offeror, but the other party cannot decide whether to be an offeree.

"Unilateral" contracts

As we have seen, often it is unfair if one party is bound and the other is not. The party who is not can speculate at the first party's expense by shopping around for a better deal or taking advantage of a favorable movement in market prices. The first party cannot.

Nevertheless, sometimes it is fair for one party to be bound while the other is not. It may be fair when the parties are in doubt about whether one of them can perform successfully. Suppose that the victim of a robbery wishes to hire a detective to recover stolen jewels. It is uncertain whether the detective will succeed. The owner of the jewels does not want to pay the detective for the time spent looking for them, since the money will be wasted if the detective fails to

[120] *Id.*
[121] *Id.* at § 63.
[122] Eisenberg, *supra* note 8, at 451.

find them. The detective may be unable to find the jewels and so does not want to promise that he will succeed. The solution is a contract in which one side is bound and the other is not. The owner must pay if the detective finds the jewels, but the detective is free to decide what efforts to make and to quit any time.

Since the nineteenth century, common lawyers have described such an arrangement as a "unilateral contract." In a "bilateral contract" such as a sale, the promise of one party is given in return for the promise of another. In a "unilateral contract," the consideration for the offeror's promise is not a promise by the offeree but an actual performance. The offer cannot be accepted by making a promise but only by actually performing. The offeree, having made no promise, cannot be held liable for failing to perform. The offeree who does perform is entitled to the money that was promised by the offeror. That was the common lawyers explanation of why such a one-sided commitment is consistent with the doctrine of consideration.

The difficulty was that it would then seem that the promisor can revoke the promise at any time before the promisee performs. The unfairness of that result has often been illustrated by hypothetical cases in which the promisor offers a reward to the other party if he succeeds in climbing a cliff or crossing a bridge. Just before the promisee reaches the top of the cliff or the end of the bridge, the promisor calls out, "I revoke my offer." One legal scholar, who later repented "in sackcloth and ashes," claimed that the offeror could do so.[123]

By an excess of ingenuity, the drafters of the *First Restatement* escaped that result. They said that an offer of unilateral contract is irrevocable as soon as the other party begins to perform. This rule appears in § 45 of both the *First* and *Second Restatement*. The original logic was that the promisor had tacitly made a second promise not to revoke the first one. This second promise was itself an offer of unilateral contract which the promisee accepted tacitly when by starting to perform, for example, by beginning to climb the cliff or to cross the bridge.[124] The doctrine of consideration was thus satisfied by supposing that the parties made tacit offers and acceptances which they probably never envisioned.

There was still a difficulty. The promisor might revoke the promise after the promisee had incurred expenditure preparing to perform but before starting performance. That also seemed to be unfair. Consequently, the drafters of the *Second Restatement*, in their wisdom, retained § 45 and added § 87(2) which provides that the offer cannot be revoked if the offeree has made substantial preparations to perform. If the promisee were offered money for climbing the North America Wall, a famous cliff in Yosemite National Park, the promisor could not revoke

[123] Maurice Wormser, *The True Conception of Unilateral Contracts*, 26 YALE L.J. 136 (1916).
[124] EISENBERG, *supra* note 8, at 468.

after the promisee had flown to California to attempt the climb but had not yet started climbing.

The rule about substantial reliance under § 87(2) should not be confused with the rule about promissory reliance under § 90. Section 90 concerns when a promise is enforceable: if it is broken, the promisor is liable to a promisee who relied upon it. Section 87(2) concerns when an offer is irrevocable. If the promisee made substantial preparations to perform, the promisor cannot revoke the promise. The promisee who does not complete performance gets nothing.

The drafters had in mind such situations as promises to climb a cliff or cross a bridge. Their solution works less well in cases like that of the detective offered a reward for finding the owner's stolen jewels. A common situation is a promise of a fee to a real estate broker who succeeds in selling property for a certain price. It is difficult and perhaps meaningless to determine at one point the offeree begins to perform. Is it the moment when the detective begins to investigate or the broker lists the property? Or when the detective finds the first clue, or the broker the first prospect? Or when the detective or the broker are all but certain that they can find the jewels or sell the house? Or when the jewels are found or the house is sold? And, in any of these cases, is substantial reliance to be evaluated by how much time and money the promisee has expended, by whether the expenditure was reasonable given the prospects of success, or by how much the expenditure has enhanced those prospects?

The solution of the *Second Restatement* does not work well in another common situation in which a person offers to pay for the accomplishment of a certain result: a promise of a reward made to the general public. The owner might offer $1,000 for information leading to the recovery of their jewels in an advertisement in a newspaper. A banker's association might offer a reward to anyone who catches a bank robber. The promisor can revoke such an offer by another advertisement to that effect, if possible, in the same newspaper, or, if not, in one of similar circulation.[125] The question, however, is the right to revoke. If the *Second Restatement* is to be believed, the offer could not be revoked if one or more members of the general public have made substantial preparations to perform in reliance on the advertisement. That would be an odd result, and there is no legal authority to support it.

If there had been no doctrine of consideration, these problems might have been solved in a different and better way. We would not have developed a doctrine of unilateral contract in which the performance is said to be the acceptance of an offer. We could have said that the offer is binding without consideration. Whether it is revocable depends on whether a revocable offer would serve the purposes of the offeror as effectively as one that is irrevocable. If a specific

[125] E. Allan Farnsworth, Contracts 160–61 (3d ed., 1999).

detective is offered a reward for finding the stolen jewels or a broker is given the exclusive right to list a house, the purpose of the offer is to enlist special efforts by that detective or that broker. Those efforts are less likely to be forthcoming if the offeror can revoke for any reason or no reason. If the offer to find the jewels is made to the general public or the listing is non-exclusive, anyone who responds to it will know that others may do so as well and that their efforts will go to waste if others succeed before they do. The offeror may not expect anyone to make special efforts. The offer may have been made in hopes that someone happens to know where the jewels are, or with the expectation that brokers will include the house, almost costlessly, in a brochure that lists many others. The offeror's purposes could still be served if the offer is revocable. To adopt this approach, we must jettison the doctrine of unilateral contracts and start over. We would be well advised to do so.

IV. Open or indefinite terms

i. The quantity

A contract may leave the quantity of goods that one party is to buy or sell unspecified. In a "requirements contract," the quantity is to be partially or entirely to be determined by the buyer; in an "output contract," by the seller. The enforceability of these contracts is another instance in which the traditional doctrine of consideration prevented unfairness but proved to be too crude a tool.[126]

If the quantity to be bought or sold is left entirely to one of the parties, the agreement does not meet the technical requirements of the doctrine of consideration. That party is free not to buy or sell or to buy from or sell to someone else. Early cases held that there was no consideration if buyers agreed to take as much as they "would want to purchase"[127] or "may want or desire."[128] There was consideration if they agreed to purchase the amount that they needed[129] or required[130] or agreed "to deal exclusively in goods to be ordered from the seller."[131]

Supposedly, the doctrine of consideration has nothing to do with fairness. But courts themselves noted the unfairness that would result if the buyers' choice

[126] Civil law jurisdictions do not have a doctrine of consideration. Yet they will often refuse to enforce a severely unfair requirements contract. JAMES GORDLEY, ED., THE ENFORCEABILITY OF PROMISES IN EUROPEAN CONTRACT LAW 193–218 (2001).

[127] Wickham & Burton Coal Co. v. Farmer's Lumber Co., 179 N.W. 417, 419 (Iowa 1920).

[128] Cold Blast Transp. Co. v. Kansas City Bolt & Nut Co., 114 F. 77, 81 (8th Cir. 1902).

[129] Brawley v. U.S., 96 U.S. 168 (1877).

[130] Minnesota Lumber Co. v. Whitebreast Coal Co., 43 N.E. 774 (Ill. 1895).

[131] New York Cent. Ironworks Co. v. United States Radiator Co., 66 N.E. 967, 968 (N.Y. 1903).

depended, not on how much their business needs required, but on whether the market price had risen above the contract price. In *New York Central Ironworks Co. v. United States Radiator Co.*, the buyer agreed to purchase its "entire radiator needs for the year 1899." There was consideration. The court explained, however, that the buyer did not have:

> the right, under the contract, to order goods to any amount. Both parties in such a contract are bound to carry it out in a reasonable way. The obligation of good faith and fair dealing towards each other is implied in every contract of this character. The plaintiff could not use the contract for the purpose of speculation in a rising market, since that would be a plain abuse of the rights conferred.[132]

Sometimes, to prevent that unfairness, the doctrine of consideration was bent. In *Crane v. C. Crane & Co.*,[133] the court refused to uphold a contract in which the buyer agreed to purchase "all the dock oak that [they] would require for their trade in the Chicago market during the year 1897." Technically, there should have been consideration because the buyers had agreed not to purchase from anyone else. As the court noted, however, the buyers were "lumber merchants pure and simple— middlemen." Their business was to buy and sell whenever it was profitable to do so. Consequently, if the contract were upheld, they:

> would be held to occupy this advantageous situation: If the prices of dock oak lumber rose, they would, by that much, increase their ratio of profits, and probably, coming into a situation to outbid competitors, increase, also, the quantum of orders; if, on the other hand, prices fell below the range of profits, the orders could be wholly discontinued.[134]

In *American Cotton-Oil v. Kirk*,[135] the court refused to enforce a contract in which the buyers agreed to purchase 10,000 barrels of cotton-seed oil to be delivered "in such quantities per week as [the buyers] should desire."[136] Technically, there was consideration since the buyers were obligated to purchase 10,000 barrels regardless of how long they waited to place orders. Indeed, as the court noted, by the terms of the contract, the buyers might "order in such

[132] *Id.*
[133] 105 F. 869 (7th Cir. 1901).
[134] *Id.* at 872.
[135] 68 F. 791 (7th Cir. 1895).
[136] *Id.* at 791–92.

quantities as would require a hundred years to complete the delivery."[137] As a result:

> If the market price of oil should fall below the contract price, then, according to their contention as to the terms of the contract, the plaintiffs could purchase their supply of oil elsewhere, and at the lower price, resorting to the contract when, and only when, the price stated was lower than the market price – and this without respect to time.[138]

Thus, by requiring that a party act in "good faith,"[139] by construing a contract to limit the quantity to what a party actually needed, and by bending the doctrine of consideration, courts prevented the unfairness of allowing one party to speculate at another's expense. They did so even in the nineteenth and early twentieth centuries, when the courts were not supposed to consider the fairness of a contract.

The *Uniform Commercial Code* replaced the doctrine of consideration with a provision that looks directly at the reasonableness of the quantity bought or sold and at the good faith of the parties. According to § 2-306, in an output or requirements contract, the quantity must be "such actual output or requirements as may occur in good faith, except that no quantity unreasonably disproportionate to any stated estimate, or in the absence of a stated estimate to any normal or otherwise comparable prior output or requirements may be tendered or demanded." We will consider whether that provision solved the problem when discussing the topic of good faith.

ii. The price

If the parties have left the price to be determined in the future, there is consideration so long as and they have agreed upon how it is to be determined. They may agree that the price will be set by an arbitrator.[140] They may agree on a standard for setting the price: for example, that changes in the price will depend upon changes in the wholesale price index.

Sometimes the parties mention such a standard but provide that the price will be negotiated or agreed upon by themselves. If they do not reach agreement, the court must frustrate their intentions in either of two ways: by holding that they are not bound, or by setting a price by reference to a standard that they mentioned

[137] *Id.* at 792.
[138] *Id.* at 794.
[139] In addition to *New York Central Ironworks Co. v. United States Radiator Co.*, mentioned earlier, *see* Brawley v. U.S., 96 U.S. 168 (1877).
[140] 166 Mamaroneck Ave. Corp. v. 151 E. Post Rd. Corp., 575 N.E.2d 104 (N.Y. 1991).

despite their failure to agree. It is more consonant with their intentions for the court to set a price by reference to that standard. In these cases, the parties intended to be bound. If the courts set a price, it may not be the price on which the parties would otherwise have agreed. But the result will be closer to the result the parties intended than if one party is allowed to escape.

In *Toys, Inc. v. F.M. Burlington Co.*[141] a lease was to be renewed at a rent to "be renegotiated to the then prevailing rate within the [shopping] mall." Similarly, in *Oglebay Norton Co. v. Armco, Inc.*[142] iron ore was to be transported each season "at the regular net contract rate" recognized by the leading iron ore shippers. The contract provided that if there is no such rate, "the parties shall mutually agree upon a rate . . . taking into consideration the contract rate being charged for similar transportation by the leading independent vessel operators." In both cases, the court enforced the contract even though the parties were unable to agree.

The case is harder when the parties left the price to be determined by mutual agreement without mentioning any standard. For example, the parties leased premises for five years at a fixed rent, and their contract provided that the lease "lease shall be renewed for an additional five-year term at a rent to be agreed by the parties." At the end of the first five-year term, the parties could not agree on the rent. Courts have gone both ways. Some have enforced the lease as a rent fixed by the court,[143] thus frustrating the parties' intention that the rent should be one on which they agreed. Others have held the renewal clause is unenforceable, thus frustrating their intention that a party should have the option to renew.[144]

The alternative to an all-or-nothing rule would be to ask why the parties left the rent to be determined by mutual agreement. If they intended the renewal option to be binding, then they could not have intended to allow a party to name any rent he pleased and refuse to agree unless he received it. That party could then refuse to renew the lease for any reason or no reason by demanding an outrageous amount of rent. By looking at the circumstances in which the original lease was made, the court could try to determine the factors which, in the minds of the parties, would justify demanding a higher or lower rent. These factors might include economic considerations such as the general level or rents. They would not include non-economic factors that have nothing to do with the amount of the rent such as the lessors desire to lease to a cousin or a business associate. They would not include the lessor's ability to extract a higher rent because the lessee would have to relocate and would face substantial costs in doing

141 582 A.2d 123 (Vt. 1990).

142 556 N.E.2d 515 (Ohio, 1990).

143 Moolemaar v. Co-Build Companies, Inc., 354 F.Supp. 980 (D.Va. 1973).

144 Joseph Martin, Jr., Delicatessen, Inc. v. Schumacher, 417 N.E.2d 541 (N.Y. 1981); Walter v. Keith, 382 S.W.2d 198 (Ken. App. 1964); Deadwood Elks Lodge No. 508 v. Albert, 319 N.W.2d 823 (S.D. 1982).

so. They would not include an increase in the profitability of the rental location which was due, not to market conditions in general, but to the efforts of the lessee which the lessor now wishes to skim off. For example, if the lessee developed a popular restaurant, the landlord should not be able to demand a share of the profit by concealing it as a demand for higher rent.

If any of these factors are present, a party should not be able to turn down an offer to renew at a price that is fair in view of economic factors such as the general level of rents. If none of them are present, then, it would seem, a party is within his rights if they turn down what would appear to be a fair offer. The parties did not agree to renew at a fair rent or a rent set by a judge or an arbitrator. A party has the right to refuse a seeming fair offer provided that the reasons for doing so were of the kind envisioned by the parties when they provided that the lease could be renewed at a rent to be agreed.

Courts have taken such an approach when a contract provides that one party has the discretion to determine the price. The contract might so provide because the parties would like the price to depend on information they do not yet have, and one party trusts the other to make a fair determination based on that information. If so, the party entrusted with discretion is the judge of how that information or those circumstances should affect the price. Nevertheless, he must base the decision on that information and those circumstances, not on other factors which the parties did not have in mind when they left that determination to his discretion. In *Community Design Corp. v. Antonell*,[145] the defendant's president had promised a bonus to any employee at Christmastime if certain drawings were completed by that date. It was not likely that the amount of the bonus was left open because of doubt as to whether a bonus would be paid at all. It was left open, the court said because it was not known in advance how many employees would share in it. The court held that the contract was violated when the defendant did not pay any bonus.

The same approach should have been taken in *Baer v. Chase*.[146] Chase was the producer, writer, and director of the TV series the *Sopranos* which concerned organized crime. Baer helped him by introducing him to law enforcement officers who provided him with information, material, and stories about their own experiences. On a motion for summary judgment, Chase accepted Baer's claim that there was an oral agreement that "if the show succeeded" Chase would compensate Baer "in a manner commensurate with the true value of [his] services." Here, the determination was left up to Chase because the value of Baer's services was not yet known. Chase refused to pay anything at all. The court held for Chase on the grounds that the terms of the contract were indefinite. It would

[145] 459 So.2d 343 (Fl. App. 1984).
[146] 392 F.3d 609 (3rd Cir. 2004).

have been better to ask whether or not Chase refused to pay because he had determined that Baer's services were worthless, in which case his judgment should be respected even if it were erroneous, or because, as in *Community Design*, he did not wish to pay for what he had received.

iii. The performance

If the parties have left the performance to be made under the contract to be determined in the future, a contract has been formed so long as they agreed upon how that performance is to be determined. The parties may agree, for example, that the buyer of the offspring of a dog will have the pick of the litter.

Sometimes the parties have left the matter to be negotiated or agreed upon by themselves but with reference to a standard. If the parties fail to agree, as in the case of the price, the result will be closer to the parties' intent if the court specified the performance to be made by reference to that standard than if a party is allowed to escape. In *Lee v. Joseph E. Seagram & Sons, Inc.*,[147] when Seagram bought a wholesale liquor distributorship, Seagram agreed to provide the sellers with a Seagram distributorship in another city "whose price would require roughly an amount equal to the capital" that they obtained from the sale of their interests. The court enforced the contract.

When the parties have not specified a standard, there would seem to be no solution that does not violate the intentions of the parties. To refuse to enforce the agreement would violate their intention to be bound. For a court to specify the terms would violate their intention that the terms be specified by themselves.

As in the case of an indefinite price term, courts have often refused to enforce such an agreement. A better solution, however, would be to ask why the performance to be made was not more clearly specified in advance. In *Pyeatte v. Pyeatte*,[148] the plaintiff agreed with her then husband that she would put him through three years of law school, and when he finished, he would put her through her master's degree. She did so. They separated. He then refused to pay for her master's degree. The court refused to enforce the agreement on the grounds that "in order to be binding, an agreement must be definite and certain so that the liability of the parties may be exactly fixed." The parties had not agreed on where or when she would enroll or the amount of tuition. The court should have asked why these terms were not fixed in advance. The reason does not seem to be that the husband wanted his commitment to depend on the amount of the tuition or the school in which his wife enrolled. The reason was that she had not

[147] 552 F.2d 447 (2d Cir. 1977).
[148] 661 P.2d 196 (Ariz. 1983).

decided yet on where to enroll. Nor was the husband backing out because he was surprised at the amount of the tuition. He did not want to keep his commitment to pay.

In *Academy Chicago Publishers v. Cheever*,[149] the defendant, the widow of a widely published author, agreed to submit "the manuscript of the Work" containing a collection of her husband's unpublished stories to the plaintiff, and the plaintiff agreed to publish it. The court refused to enforce the agreement because it did not specify who would decide what stories would be included or how many or few stories or pages there would be. The court would have done better by asking why the parties had left these matters to be determined later on. The reason was that Mrs. Cheever did not yet know how many unpublished stories she could find. It was not because Mrs. Cheever did not know what a published edition would sell for, and that she wished to have the option to seek another publisher while locking the plaintiff in if she did not find one. As it happened, she found sixty stories, and also discovered that the paperback rights to them could be sold for $225,500, vastly more than she was to receive from the plaintiff.[150] Her reasons for trying to escape the contract had nothing to do with the question of whether a sufficient number of stories had been found to be worth publishing, or whether too many stories had been found to justify the cost of publishing them. By enforcing the contract, the court would have honored the parties' intentions to be bound without disrespecting their reasons for leaving the size of the publication to be determined later.

V. Unanticipated hardship

i. The doctrine of impracticability

If, at the time a contract is made, it imposes a risk on a party who is not compensated for bearing it, relief may be given under the doctrine of unconscionability. After the contract is made, a change of circumstances may make it more expensive for a party to perform. That party may not have been compensated for bearing that risk because it was not contemplated when the contract was made. If so, relief may be given under the doctrine of impracticability. In both cases, enforcing the contract would be unfair for the same reason: to do so would impose a risk on a party who was not compensated for bearing it.

[149] 578 N.E.2d 981 (Ill. 1991).

[150] Peter Kurth, book review (reviewing ANITA MILLER, UNCOLLECTING CHEEVER, THE FAMILY OF JOHN CHEEVER V. ACADEMY CHICAGO PUBLISHER, SALON (Nov. 25, 1998), quoted in LON L. FULLER, MELVIN ARON EISENBERG, & MARK P. GERGEN, BASIC CONTRACT LAW CONCISE EDITION 432 (10th ed. 2018)).

The doctrine of impracticability deals with a situation in which, because of a change of circumstances, a contract is unfair. As we will see, the doctrine of frustration of purpose deals with a situation in which, because of a change of circumstances, a performance is unwanted. Chapter 11 of the *Second Restatement of Contracts* treats the doctrines of "impracticability of performance and frustration of purpose" together. As the *Restatement* observes, both doctrines give relief for "changed and unforeseen circumstances." Nevertheless, they rest on different principles. In the case of frustration of purpose, the change of circumstances made a performance unsuitable for the purposes of the party who is to receive it. That change affects the voluntariness of an exchange. We will deal with it later. In the case of impracticability, the change of circumstances made it more expensive for one of the parties to perform. To enforce the contract as written would impose a risk upon him for which they were not compensated.

According to the *Second Restatement* and the *Uniform Commercial Code*, whether to give relief for impracticability depends on the "non-occurrence" of the event was "a basic assumption on which the contract was made."[151] That rule is not helpful. It is not clear what is meant by a "basic assumption." According to the Official Comments to the *Second Restatement*, the parties need not consciously have assumed anything: "The parties may have had such a 'basic assumption,' even though they were not conscious of alternatives."[152] Moreover, an "assumption" may be critical to the decision to contract and still not be "basic." "[M]arket conditions and the financial situation of the parties are ordinarily not such assumptions."[153] So we arrive at the curious rule that the parties must have made an assumption, whether or not they consciously assumed anything, and that the assumption must be basic, whether or not it is of great importance to them. One gets the impression that the drafters were not sure what the rule should be but could not think of a better one.

The doctrine of impracticability gives relief in situations in which a performance has become more costly. It may have become more costly because it has become physically more difficult, or because market prices have changed. We will take each situation in turn.

Hardship due to increased physical difficulty

In a classic California case, *Mineral Park Land Co. v. Howard*,[154] the defendants agreed to take all the gravel and earth from the plaintiff's land that they needed to

[151] U.C.C. § 2-615(a) (Am. Law Inst. & Unif. L. Comm'n 1977); Restatement (Second) of Contracts § 261 (Am. Law Inst. 1981).

[152] Restatement (Second) of Contracts § 152, cmt. b (Am. Law Inst. 1981). Section 152 deals with mistake, but, according to the *Second Restatement*, the term "basic assumption" has the same meaning in the rules governing that doctrine as in those governing changed circumstances.

[153] *Id.*

[154] 156 P. 458 (Cal. 1916).

build a bridge. Much of it proved to be under water, and it would have cost ten to twelve times the normal amount to excavate. The court held that the defendants were not bound.

The result was fair even though to give relief seems to contradict the very purpose of the kind of contract that the parties entered into. The contract was fixed price rather than cost plus. In a fixed price contract, a party agrees to perform for a price set in advance. The party makes a profit if the cost of performance is less than that price and suffers a loss if the cost is greater. In a cost-plus contract, the party to perform receives the amount it costs to perform plus an added amount, usually a percentage of the costs. By making one kind of contract rather than the other, the parties allocate the risk that a performance will be more expensive than anticipated. Provided that the price is adjusted to reflect that risk, either kind of contract can be fair in the same way as a fair bet.

In cost-plus contracts, there is no need for a special doctrine of impracticability to protect the party whose costs have risen. They were not hurt and may have profited. The doctrine only protects a party to a fixed price contract. The question arises: how can it be fair to give a party to a fixed price contract relief because the cost of performance was unexpectedly high? That would seem to be the very risk that the party was compensated to bear.

We can see an answer if we consider why the parties would enter into a fixed price contract rather than one that is cost plus. When a risk must be borne by either party, the parties will place it on whoever can bear it most cheaply. As noted earlier, there are three reasons why one party might be more easily able to bear a risk. That party might be best able to foresee the magnitude of the risk, best able to control the risk, or best able to spread the risk over similar transactions.

Accordingly, the reason for making a fixed price contract is not that the party making the performance is better able to assume all risks. Rather, they are better able to assume certain risks: those that he can better foresee, control, and spread across the other jobs he undertakes. Rightly, then, the law grants relief when the risk is one that he did not assume. As Skelly Wright said in *Transatlantic Financing Corp. v. United States*,[155] for relief to be given, "a contingency—something unexpected—must have occurred," and that "the risk of the unexpected occurrence must not have been allocated either by agreement or by custom." "Proof that the risk of a contingency's occurrence has been allocated may be expressed in or implied from the agreement." In *Transatlantic*, a shipper who had contracted for a fixed price to carry a full cargo of wheat from Galveston, Texas to Iran, was forced to sail around Africa, at a considerably increased cost, because, the Suez Canal had been closed due to a political crisis. While neither party could have

[155] 363 F.2d 312 (D.C. Cir. 1966).

controlled such an event, Skelly Wright said that the shipper could more easily have foreseen and insured against it. Although the nationalization of the Canal "did not necessarily indicate that the Canal would be blocked," "the surrounding circumstances do indicate . . . a willingness by Transatlantic to assume abnormal risks."[156]

> If anything, it is more reasonable to expect the owner-operators of vessels to insure against the hazards of war. They are in the best position to calculate the cost to performance by alternative routes (and therefore to estimate the amount of insurance required), and are undoubtedly sensitive to international troubles which uniquely affect the demand for and the cost of their services.[157]

Hardship due to a change in market price

A performance may become more costly, not because it is physically more difficult to perform, but because market prices have changed. There is an ongoing debate over whether relief should be given in that situation.

An American court has not yet done so. An Official Comment to the *Uniform Commercial Code* implies that it should:[158]

> Increased cost alone does not excuse performance unless the rise in cost is due to some unforeseen contingency which alters the essential nature of performance. Neither is a rise or a collapse in the market in itself a justification for that is exactly the type of business risk which business contracts made at fixed prices are intended to cover. But a severe shortage of raw materials or of supplies due to a contingency such as war, embargo, local crop failure, unforeseen shutdown of major sources of supply or the like, which either causes a market increase in cost or altogether prevents the seller from securing supplies necessary to his performance, is within the contemplation of this section.

One reason for thinking that the comment means what it says is that it was drafted by Karl Llewellyn who held a Swiss law degree and was thoroughly familiar with German law. It is hard for someone familiar with German law to read this Comment without thinking of the earliest cases in which the highest German court for civil matters gave relief for severe and unexpected changes in the market price. In one case, the outbreak of World War I caused the price of steam to soar.[159] In another in which the German collapse in 1918 caused a

[156] *Id.* at 318–19.
[157] *Id.* at 319.
[158] U.C.C. § 2-615, cmt. 4 (Am. Law Inst. & Unif. L. Comm'n 1977).
[159] RG Sept. 21, 1920, RGZ 100, 129.

huge increase in the price of iron wire.[160] Llewellyn's friend Stefan Riesenfeld was fond of recounting a conversation in which he asked Llewellyn whether he had drawn on German law in drafting Article 2. He answered, "Of course. But I left no evidence that I did,"[161] which was an understandable precaution in drafting an American model statute within a decade of the end of World War II.

Much of the debate in the United States over whether relief should be given has focused on the *Westinghouse* litigation.[162] Westinghouse had agreed to provide a continuing supply of uranium at a fixed price to fuel nuclear generators. The price of uranium then skyrocketed due to the Arab oil crisis. The case was settled before appeal.

As the Comment to § 2-615 itself suggests, relief should not be given when the change in market prices "is exactly the type of business risk which business contracts made at fixed prices are intended to cover." It does not follow that such a contract is made to allocate any risk that arises from a change in the market price.

When a party sells goods that they already own, parties allocate a risk that is inseparable from the ownership of goods. In a generic sale, however, the seller is obligated to deliver, not specific goods, but any goods that answer to a particular description, such as copper wire or uranium. Typically, the seller neither owns nor manufactures the goods. The buyer will need goods of a certain kind in the future and will be hurt if the price of them rises. As Paul Joskow noted, the seller insures the buyer against that risk.[163] The contract is one of insurance against price changes cast in the form of a contract of sale.

It does not follow, as Joskow thought, that the seller assumes the risk of a rise in price, however drastic.[164] In a conventional insurance policy, the amount the insurer can lose will be no greater that the loss that the insured could suffer. As noted earlier, if the parties are risk averse, there is no price for the extra insurance that is acceptable both to the owner and to the insurance company. In a generic sale, if the market price of the goods changes sufficiently, the difference between the market and the contract price may exceed any loss that the buyer may suffer, and consequently, it may exceed any loss against which the buyer would have been willing to insure. Recovery should be limited to what we would call, in a normal insurance contract, the "insurable interest": the amount of the loss the buyer might have suffered by purchasing the goods for its own use on the open market. If the price rose to the point that the buyer would make more by reselling

[160] RG Nov. 29, 1921 RGZ 103, 177.

[161] A story which Riesenfeld told the senior author several times while they were colleagues at Berkeley, 1978–99.

[162] *See generally* Paul L. Joskow, *Commercial Impossibility, the Uranium Market and the Westinghouse Case*, 6 J. Leg. Stud. 119 (1977).

[163] *Id.* at 162.

[164] *Id.*

the goods on the open market than by using them itself, it should not recover the excess.[165]

ii. The preexisting duty rule

According to traditional doctrine, performance of a preexisting duty could not serve as consideration for a promise. It did not matter whether the promise was made to a government official, a third party, or to the other party to a contract. The promisee who was already under an obligation was not giving up the legal right.

The modern approach is to distinguish these three situations. In the case of promises to a government official, the evil that the traditional doctrine served to remedy is corruption. If a victim of a jewel theft can promise $1,000 to a police officer if the officer succeeds in finding the stolen jewels, there is a danger that the police will serve the rich more zealously than the poor. As the *Second Restatement* observed, "there is often no direct sanction available to a member of the public to compel performance of the duty, and the danger of express or implied threats to withhold performance affects public as well as private interests." Such a promise "is therefore unenforceable as against public policy."[166] If so, one does not need the doctrine of consideration.

In the case of a promise by a third party, there is rarely any evil to be remedied. If a bankers' association promises $10,000 to whoever catches a bank robber, and a bank security guard does so in performance of his contractual duty to the bank, enforcing the promise does not harm the association, the guard, or the bank. The *Second Restatement* concluded that despite the traditional rule, the promise should be enforced because "there is less likelihood of economic coercion or unfair pressure." Therefore, "the tendency of the law has been simply to hold that the performance of contractual duty can be consideration."[167]

The third case is a promise made in return for a performance that the other contracting party has promised. According to the *Second Restatement* the purpose served by refusing to enforce the promise is to prevent unfairness. "[A]n unscrupulous promisor may threaten to breach in order to obtain such a bonus."[168] For example, in *Lingenfelder v. Wainwright Brewing Co*,[169] a builder demanded a higher price for finishing a brewery. The other party could not have

[165] James Gordley, Foundations of Private Law Property, Tort, Contract, Unjust Enrichment 350–51 (2006).

[166] Restatement (Second) of Contracts § 73 cmt. b (Am. Law Inst. & Unif. L. Comm'n 1977).

[167] *Id.* at cmt. d.

[168] *Id.* at cmt. c.

[169] 15 S.W. 844 (Mo. 1891).

hired a different builder to complete the job and still have the brewery finished on time.[170] When they contract, each party gives up the opportunity to obtain a better price to avoid the risk that he will have to accept one that is less favorable. Under normal circumstances, to demand more for one's performance than the amount agreed is to deprive the other party of that guarantee. The builder was acting unfairly in the same way as a person who reneges on a bet.

Nevertheless, the traditional doctrine of consideration is a crude way to prevent unfairness. The modification of the original terms might be fair because circumstances have changed. As we saw when we discussed the doctrine of impracticability, sometimes a performance becomes more expensive because of circumstances that were not anticipated at the time of the contract. The party who is to make the performance was not compensated for bearing this risk. If so, modifying the price is not unfair. The hard question is often whether the risk was anticipated.

Section 89(a) of the *Second Restatement* provides that a promise modifying a duty is binding "if the modification is fair and equitable in view of circumstances not anticipated by the promisor when the contract was made." In such a case, it is easier to determine whether the risk was unanticipated. If the promisor thought that the contract price compensated the promisee for bearing it, he would be unlikely to promise to pay more unless the promisee pressured him by threatening to break the contract.

An example is the result in *Angel v. Murray*.[171] A garbage collector had contracted to pick up all the town's garbage for a fixed yearly fee. Unexpectedly, a developer built a new tract of houses in the town, adding greatly to the garbage collector's expenses. The court enforced the town's promise to pay him an additional amount as compensation for his extra expenses. Again, because the doctrine of consideration is a crude tool for ensuring fairness, the *Second Restatement* and courts like the one in *Murray* modified it to take fairness directly into account.

[170] Civil law jurisdictions do not have a doctrine of consideration. Yet they will often refuse to enforce an unfair promise to pay more for a performance than was originally agreed. GORDLEY, *supra* note 126, at 219–38.

[171] 322 A.2d 630 (R.I. 1974).

6
Voluntary Exchange (*with* Hao Jiang)

I. "Subjective" and "objective" theories

The core idea that inspired contract theory before the nineteenth century was that a contract of exchange is an act of voluntary commutative justice.[1] The exchange is just when the parties each receive something equivalent in value to what they give.[2] It is voluntary when each receives something that each prefers what they give in return. As Aristotle said, the shoemaker does not exchange with the shoemaker but with the house builder.[3] Many features of American law are best explained as ways to promote equality in exchange. Others are best explained as ways to ensure that a contract is entered into voluntarily.

There is a long-standing controversy over whether a party who was mistaken acted voluntarily in entering into a contract. The Roman jurist Ulpian said: "It is obvious that there must be consent in contracts of sale. Therefore, a sale is invalid if there is dissent as to the fact of sale or the price."[4] There is no consent when copper is sold for gold, or when vinegar is sold for wine.[5] Before the nineteenth century, as Brian Simpson noted, courts had said little about the effect of mistake on consent.[6] In the nineteenth century, the common lawyers borrowed the doctrine that mistake vitiates consent from the civil law.[7]

Ulpian said that the reason that consent is lacking when copper is sold for gold or vinegar for wine is because they differ in "substance" (*substantia*) or "essence" (*ousia*).[8] "Substance" had many meanings in Greek philosophy but it is clear that Ulpian had no definite philosophical meaning in mind.[9] He was groping for a

[1] This chapter is based on an article coauthored with Hao Jiang, *Contract as Voluntary Commutative Justice*, MICH. ST. L REV. 725 (2020).

[2] ARISTOTLE, NICOMACHEAN ETHICS V.ii 1130b–1131a; V.i 1131b–1132b.

[3] *Id.* at V.v 1133a.

[4] DIG. 18.1.9.pr.

[5] *Id.*

[6] W.B. Simpson, *Innovation in Nineteenth Century Contract Law*, 91 L.Q. Rev. 247, 265–69 (1975). On how little was said in the early nineteenth century, *see* JAMES GORDLEY, THE PHILOSOPHICAL ORIGINS OF MODERN CONTRACT DOCTRINE 144–45 (1991),

[7] GORDLEY, *supra* note 6, at 146.

[8] DIG. 18.1.9.pr.

[9] He spoke interchangeably of *substantia* and *ousia* or essence. He said that when vinegar is sold as wine, whether the *ousia* remains the same depends upon whether the wine was prepared as vinegar (it does) or whether is soured into vinegar. No Greek philosopher would have used the words substance or essence in that way.

Foundations of American Contract Law. James Gordley, Oxford University Press. © Oxford University Press 2023.
DOI: 10.1093/oso/9780197686089.003.0006

word that vaguely indicated a difference in kind and could explain cases like copper sold for gold.

In the nineteenth century some common law courts borrowed the term: they said the validity of a contract depended on whether there was a mistake in substance.[10] Sir Frederick Pollock thought that this explanation was confused. He believed that the German jurist, Friedrich Karl von Savigny, had found the correct solution.[11] According to Savigny[12] (and Pollock),[13] a mistake, in and of itself, does not affect the validity of a contract. Nevertheless, by definition, contract is constituted by the declaration of the will of two or more parties. The declarations must be in accord with each other and with the will that they purport to declare. Relief is given when they are not in accord: a party declared something other than what they meant, or the declaration of one party does not match that of another.[14] Doubtless, the mismatch is due to a mistake of some sort. But the reason for giving relief is not the mistake itself. It is the absence of an element that is necessary, by definition, for a contract to be formed.

When the parties said different things, the case seemed to be easy. The declaration of will or intention of one party did not match the declaration of the other. For Pollock, as for Savigny, there is no contract.[15] We will see later that this case is not as easy as they supposed.

When the parties said the same thing but meant two physically different objects, the case also seemed to be easy. A contract was not formed because their "minds never met."[16] Pollock's illustration was *Raffles v. Wichelhaus*:[17] "a sale of 125 bales of Surat cotton, to arrive ex 'Peerless' from Bombay. "The defendants meant a ship called the 'Peerless' that sailed from Bombay in October, and . . . the plaintiff offered to deliver, not any cotton that arrived by that ship, but cotton that arrived by a different ship also called the 'Peerless' and that sailed to Bombay in December."[18]

The hard case is when the parties said the same thing and had the same physical thing in mind but were wrong about one of its qualities. An example is Ulpian's case in which copper was sold for gold. According to Savigny, the reason

10 Sherwood v. Walker, 33 N.W. 919, 923 (Mich. 1887).

11 Frederick Pollock, Principles of Contract at Law and in Equity, Being a Treatise on the General Principles Concerning the Validity of Agreements, with a Special View to the Comparison of Law and Equity, and with References to the Indian Contract Act, and Occasionally to Roman, American, and Continental Law (1st ed. 1876) 357.

12 3 Friedrich Carl von Savigny, System des heutigen Römischen Recht § 114 (1840).

13 Pollock, *supra* note 11, at 356 n. a, 357, 358.

14 Savigny, *supra* note 12, at § 135, 363–64.

15 Pollock, *supra* note 11, at 3–4, 371.

16 *Id.* at 373.

17 2 H. & C. 906; 33 L.J. Ex. 160.

18 Frederick Pollock, Principles of Contract: Being a Treatise on the General Principles Concerning the Validity of Agreements in the Law of England 429 (4th ed. 1885).

that sale is void is that some properties of an object are bound up with its identity. These are properties by which a thing is classified as a thing of a certain type "according to concepts dominant in actual commerce."[19] If a party who said that he would buy an object mistakenly believed that it had such a property, no contract was formed. The party did not will to buy that object.[20] Citing Savigny, Pollock said that the characteristic must be "such that according to the ordinary course of dealing and use of language the difference made by the absence of the quality wrongly supposed to exist amounts to a difference in kind."[21]

In this way, the idea that some characteristics are "essential," inasmuch as their presence or absence constitutes a difference in kind, crept back into the law governing mistake. Some nineteenth-century German jurists objected that Savigny's solution contradicted his own principles.[22] If the significance of a characteristic to a party did not matter, its significance according to "commercially dominant concepts" should not matter either.[23]

Pollock may have had his own doubts. At any rate, he also presented two other solutions that are not only different but conflicting.

In one, relief is given, not because there is an absence of consent, but because the mistake concerns an assumption on which the agreement was made. "There does exist a common intention, which however is founded on an assumption made by both parties as to some matter of fact essential to the agreement."[24]

In the other, the mistake must be mutual. "[T]he error must be common to both parties."[25] According to Pollock, in Ulpian's case, "the buyer thinks he is buying, and the seller that he is selling, a golden vessel."[26] "It must be shown that the object was in fact neither such as the vendor professed to sell nor such as the vendee intended to buy. And so in the case supposed the sale will not be

[19] SAVIGNY, *supra* note 12, at § 137.

[20] *Id.*

[21] POLLOCK, *supra* note 11, at 393. Note b cites 3 SAVIGNY, *supra* note 12, at § 137.

[22] Ernst Bekker, *Zur Lehre von der Willenserklärung: Einfluss von Zwang und Irrthum*, 3 KRITISCHE VIERTELJAHRESSCHRIFT FÜR GESETZGEBUNG UND RECHTSWISSENSCHAFT 180, 188–89 (1861) (reviewing A. Schliemann, *Die Lehre vom Zwange*); Achill Renaud, *Zur Lehre von Einflusse des Irrthums in der Sache auf die Gültigkeit der Kaufverträge mit Rücksicht auf v. Savigny: Der error in substantia*, 28 ARCHIV FÜR DIE CIVILISTISCHE PRAXIS 247, 247–54 (1846); M. Hesse, *Ein Revision der Lehre von Irrthum*, 15 IHERINGS JAHRBÜCHER FÜR DIE DOGMATIK DES HEUTIGEN RÖMISCHEN UND DEUTSCHEN PRIVATRECHTS 62, 101 (1877).

[23] Bernhard Windscheid accepted Savigny's solution despite the difficulty because, he admitted, he could not think of any other way to explain the Roman text concerning copper sold as gold. 1 BERNHARD WINDSCHEID, LEHRBUCH DES PANDEKTENRECHTS § 76a (7th ed. 1871). A version of it passed into § 119(2) of the GERMAN CIVIL CODE (*Bürgerlichesgesetzbuch*) which provides: "A mistake over those characteristics of a person or a thing that are regarded as essential in commerce counts as an error in the declaration."

[24] POLLOCK, *supra* note 11, at 373.

[25] *Id.* at 373, 393. This solution had been endorsed in *Smith v. Hughes* L.R. 6 Q.B. 597, 603, cited *id.* at 395 n. b.

[26] POLLOCK. *supra* note 11, at 393.

invalidated by the mistake of the buyer alone, if he thinks he is buying gold."[27] Citing Savigny,[28] he acknowledged that "[t]he somewhat refined distinction here taken does not seem to exist in the civil law . . . according to whom it makes no difference whether there be on the part of the vendor ignorance, passive knowledge, or even actual fraud: the sale being wholly void in any case."[29] Indeed, by Savigny's reasoning, it could not matter whether the error was common to both parties. There is no mutual consent as long as one party does not intend to be bound.

Pollock's solutions are still with us, and along with them, the difficulties of understanding them and also of reconciling them. They were accepted by Samuel Willison, even though he was a proponent of an "objective theory" of contract in contrast to Pollock and Savigny who held a "subjective theory" or will theory. In an objective theory, contract is defined as a set of obligations the law imposes on what the parties did or said whatever their intentions may have been.

The objective theory had been pioneered by Oliver Wendell Homes, whom Williston greatly admired. Holmes, unlike his friend Pollock, did not think it possible to explain relief for mistake by an absence of assent. Holmes noted, "[i]t is commonly said that the failure of a contract in such a case is due to the fact of a difference in kind between the actual subject-matter and that to which the intention of the parties was directed."[30] He claimed that the real reason for relief was that the parties' words and acts referred to different things, or there was no object to which these words or acts referred. In such cases, Williston agreed, "the acts of apparent assent, when their real meaning is discovered, do not in truth indicate assent."[31] Holmes's illustration was a hypothetical case in which "A agreed to buy, and B agreed to sell, 'these barrels of mackerel,' and . . . the barrels in question turn out to contain salt." The contract was void, Holmes said, because the words are contradictory: "these barrels" are not "mackerel" but "salt."[32] What if the parties had said "these barrels," falsely believing though not saying that they contained mackerel? Surely a court will still give relief. Holmes answered with a phrase he used more than once: "The distinctions of the law are founded on experience, not on logic."[33] In other words, Holmes's distinction was not logical.

In Williston's treatise, and in the *First Restatement of Contracts*, for which he served as Reporter, he adopted an objective theory. "The mental assent of the

[27] *Id.* at 394–95.
[28] *Id.* 395 note b, citing 3 SAVIGNY, *supra* note 12, at 293.
[29] *Id.*
[30] O.W. HOLMES, THE COMMON LAW 310 (1880).
[31] SAMUEL WILLISTON & GEORGE J. THOMPSON, TREATISE ON THE LAW OF CONTRACTS § 20 (rev. ed. 1938).
[32] HOLMES, *supra* note 30, at 310–11.
[33] *Id.* at 312.

parties is not requisite for the formation of the contracts."[34] That theory was accepted by the *Second Restatement*. It defines a promise as a "manifestation of intention."[35] "The phrase 'manifestation of intention' adopts an external or objective standard for interpreting conduct; it means the external expression of intention as distinguished from undisclosed intention."[36]

Nevertheless, he did not adopt Holmes's explanation of relief for mistake. He adopted the two alternatives suggested by Pollock. In his treatise, Willison said that a contract is voidable when the mistake is mutual and the parties were mistaken as to a "fundamental assumption.[37] These solutions passed in the *First Restatement of Contracts* and thence into the *Second*. According to the *First Restatement*, for relief to be given the mistake must be "mutual," and the parties must be mistaken "as to a fact assumed by them as the basis on which they entered into the transaction."[38] According to the *Second Restatement*, the mistake must be "mutual," and it must concern "a basic assumption on which the contract was made."[39]

Instead of trying to square these solutions with his objective theory, Williston claimed that in equity a contract may be voidable for mistake even though it is not void at common law. The objective theory explained why a contract is not void for mistake in law. Why it might be voidable in equity, according to Williston, is a different issue which the objective theory does not address.[40] He thus elevated technical distinctions between void and voidable, and remedies in law and equity, into a defense of the objective theory.

It was never clear why relief should be given only if a mistake is mutual. If, as Pollock thought, a contract requires mutual assent, the assent of only one party is not enough. If, as Williston thought, a contract does not require assent, it is not clear why mutual mistake should matter.

Nor is it clear what a basic assumption might be. As we have seen, according to the Official Comment in the *Second Restatement*, "[t]he parties may have had such a 'basic assumption' even though they were not conscious of alternatives." Moreover, even an assumption of crucial importance to a party may not be "basic": for example, "market conditions and the financial situation of the parties."[41] So the parties may have founded their contract on a basic assumption

[34] RESTATEMENT (FIRST) OF CONTRACTS § 71 cmt. a (AM. LAW INST. 1932). Similarly, "neither mental assent to the promises in the contract nor real or apparent intent that the contract shall be legally binding is essential." *Id.* at § 20.

[35] RESTATEMENT (SECOND) OF CONTRACTS § 2 (AM. LAW INST. 1981).

[36] *Id.* at cmt. b.

[37] WILLISTON & THOMPSON, *supra* note 31, at § 1544.

[38] RESTATEMENT (FIRST) OF CONTRACTS § 502 (AM. LAW INST. 1932).

[39] RESTATEMENT (SECOND) OF CONTRACTS § 152(1) (AM. LAW INST. 1981).

[40] WILLISTON & THOMPSON, *supra* note 31, at § 20; *see* HOLMES *supra* note 30, at 315.

[41] RESTATEMENT (SECOND) OF CONTRACTS § 152 cmt. b (AM. LAW INST. 1981).

even if they did not consciously assume anything, and the assumption may not be basic even if it is critical.

II. Mistake and frustration of purpose

A contract enables the parties to obtain something they value more than what they receive in return. The doctrines of mistake and frustration of purpose concern whether a party who does not do so can obtain relief. If the reason is an error at the time the contract was made, relief may be given for mistake. If the reason is a change of circumstances, relief may be given for frustration of purpose. In that respect, the two doctrines have the same relationship to each other as the doctrine of unconscionability to the doctrine of impracticability. As we have seen, the former concerns whether a contract is economically unfair when it was made, and the latter, whether it has become so thereafter.

A contract no longer serves the purpose for which one of the parties entered into it if, because of a mistake or a change of circumstances, that party no longer wishes to exchange. The only reason that party should be bound to a contract is that to refuse to enforce it might be unfair to the other party. It may be unfair in the sense described earlier. It is unfair to allow a party who was compensated for assuming a risk to escape liability. We have already seen that the reason why a contract of exchange should be enforceable is to prevent a party from doing so.

Whether it is unfair to allow a disappointed party to escape a contract typically depends on a distinction that is implicit in the decided cases although courts have not drawn it explicitly. A performance may be unsuitable for the purposes of buyers in general, or it may be unsuitable only for the purposes of the particular buyer. Normally, in the first case, to give relief is not unfair to the seller, and in the second case, it is.

In a contract of exchange, typically, each party gives up the chance of receiving a more favorable offer from another party to avoid the risk of receiving a less favorable one from someone else. Whether other parties are willing to purchase goods or services, and what they will pay depends on the purposes to which the goods or services are suited. If, because of a mistake, they are not suited to the purposes of other buyers, the seller has not given up the chance that they would be willing to pay a more favorable price. The contract should not be enforced because it allocates that risk. It would be fair to enforce it only if the parties were attempting to allocate a quite different risk—the risk of what purposes the goods or services in question will serve. In contrast, if the goods or services are unsuitable to the purposes of a particular buyer, but not to those of buyers in general, it would usually be unfair to give relief.

i. A performance unsuited for the purposes of buyers in general

One reason that goods or services may be unsuitable for the purposes of buyers in general is they cannot be used to accomplish it. In such cases, courts have given relief. A contract to sell land was set aside for mistake when "the sole purpose of the contract was to enable respondents to grow jojoba," and there was insufficient water to do so.[42] So was a contract to sell land when the parties believed that land was suitable for a building site, and legal restrictions prevented the buyer from building.[43] So was a contract to sell a rare coin which was of interest to collectors only if it was genuine when it turned out to be a fake.[44] Similarly, in *Griffith v. Brymer*, a contract was set aside for mistake when the defendants rented flats at a suitably enhanced price to view the coronation procession of King Edward VII and the parade had been cancelled because the king was sick.[45]

In *Griffith*, the parties contracted an hour after the decision had been made to operate on the king, which made the procession impossible. In *Krell v. Henry*, the parties entered into a similar contract before the decision to cancel the procession had been made.[46] The court gave relief for frustration of purpose. In a classic New York case, *Alfred Marks Realty Co. v. Hotel Hermitage Co.*, the court gave relief for frustration of purpose when the defendant agreed to place an advertisement in the program to be printed for an international yacht race to take place in September 1914.[47] The ad would have been useless because the races were cancelled due to the outbreak of World War I.

A second reason that goods or services may be unsuitable for the buyer's purposes is that, although they could be used to accomplish them, no buyer with only those purposes in mind and knowing the truth would have purchased them. They are more valuable for some other purpose. If the contract were enforced, the buyer would resell them. Unless they are uncertain about the purposes that the goods or services in question may serve, the parties do not enter into a contract to allocate this risk. The parties contract to avoid the risk of having to accept a less favorable price. In such case courts have given relief. In the famous case of *Sherwood v. Walker*, a cow of distinguished lineage, worth a large amount if she could breed, was sold for a small amount because she was thought to be sterile.[48] According to the majority opinion, the buyer wanted to butcher the cow for its meat. The cow was pregnant at the moment of sale. It would have been physically

[42] Renner v. Kehl, 722 P.2d 262, 265 (Ariz. 1986).

[43] Rancourt v. Verba, 678 A.2d 886, 886–87 (Vt. 1996); Gartner v. Eikill, 319 N.W.2d 397, 398, 400 (Minn. 1982).

[44] Beachcomber Coins, Inc. v. Boskett, 400 A.2d 78, 78–79 (N.J. App. Div. 1979).

[45] (1903) 19 T.L.R. 434 (KB Div.).

[46] Krell v. Henry (1903) 2 KB 740.

[47] 156 N.Y.S. 179, 179–80 (N.Y. App. Div. 1915).

[48] 33 N.W. 919, 923 (Mich.1887).

possible to butcher the cow, but no buyer would have purchased a fertile prize breeding cow for that purpose. The court gave relief for mistake.

It is the same when the parties were mistaken as to whether a jewel, an antique, a work of art, or a musical instrument is genuine. Physically, one can wear a ring, sit in a chair, decorate a wall with a painting, or play a piano whether or not the diamond in the ring is real, the chair is a Sheraton, the painting is a Rembrandt, or the piano is a Steinway. But if one's purpose could be served by an imitation, one would not pay the price of the genuine article. Courts have given relief when, for example, violins sold as a Stradivarius, a Guarnerius, and a Bernardel were imitations.[49]

In contrast, it is economically fair to enforce a contract when the parties were uncertain about the purposes that the goods or services in question would serve. Courts have denied relief for mistake when the parties entered into a contract despite that risk.[50] *Sherwood* was such a case according to a minority opinion, which said that the buyer understood that the cow might be sterile but bought it to see if it could be made to breed.[51] If so, the sale should have been upheld. Similarly, relief was denied when land was sold as is, when a rock of unknown composition turned out to be an uncut diamond, and when a locked safe was sold and later proved to contain cash.[52] Relief was denied when the parties who did not know what artist painted two works chose not to have them appraised, and when an appraiser expressed doubts as to the authenticity of an antique Parker A-1 shotgun, but the parties went ahead with the sale anyway.[53] Relief was also denied when a painting, which critics generally believed to have been the work of Albert Bierstadt, later proved to be the work of John Ross Key.[54] Parties who buy and sell art should recognize that attributions of art critics, even when widely accepted, are inherently uncertain. A party who buys or sells art assumes that risk.

When goods are unsuitable for the purposes of buyers in general, most likely, both parties will have been mistaken. Often, then, the result will be the same under the rule of the *Second Restatement* which requires that the mistake be mutual. But what matters is not whether the mistake is mutual but the unfairness to the seller of allowing the buyer to escape the contract.

49 Smith v. Zimbalist, 38 P.2d 170, 171 (Cal. App. 1934); Bentley v. Slavik, 663 F. Supp. 736, 742 (S.D. Ill. 1987).

50 Restatement (Second) of Contracts § 154(b) (Am. Law Inst. 1981) ("A party bears the risk of a mistake when . . . (b) he is aware, at the time the contract is made, that he has only limited knowledge with respect to the facts to which the mistake relates but treats his limited knowledge as sufficient").

51 33 N.W. at 924 (Sherwood, J., dissenting).

52 Lewanee Cnty. Bd. of Health v. Messerly, 331 N.W.2d 203, 210 (Mich. 1982); Wood v. Boynton, 25 N.W. 42, 44 (Wis. 1885); City of Everett v. Estate of Sumstad, 631 P.2d 366, 368 (Wash. 1981).

53 Estate of Nelson v. Rice, 12 P.3d 238, 241 (Ariz. Ct. App. 2000); Cydrus v. Houser, No. 98CA2425, 1999 Ohio App. LEXIS 5746, at *9 (Ohio Ct. App. Nov. 29, 1999).

54 Firestone & Parson, Inc. v. Union League of Phila., 672 F. Supp. 819, 821 (E.D. Pa. 1987).

ii. A performance unsuited for the purpose of a particular buyer

When goods or services are unsuitable only for the purpose of a particular buyer, the seller could have sold them to other buyers who do not want them for this particular purpose. If the buyer could withdraw, the seller would lose the guarantee the contract provides against receiving a less favorable price from another buyer. It would be fair to give relief if the seller had vouched for the suitability of the goods for the particular purpose of the buyer. The seller would have done so to induce the buyer to contract and so to avoid the risk of waiting for a better offer. To give relief would also be fair if the seller charged an extra amount for assuming the risk that the buyer would find the goods to be unsuitable. Otherwise, it would be unfair to the seller if the buyer could escape.

It is not surprising, then, that often relief for mistake has been denied when goods or services were suitable for the purposes of buyers in general but not for those of a particular buyer. A contract was upheld when a seller sold an antique armoire which the buyer discovered he could not use because it was too large to fit with his other furniture,[55] and when a seller sold a dredge designed to lay pipelines which the buyer later discovered could not be used for sweep dredging without modifications.[56] In the case of the dredge, the court denied relief because the plaintiff "alone was mistaken in assuming that the dredge was adapted, without modification, to the use he had in mind."[57]

The same is true of the doctrine of frustration of purpose. Relief was denied when an American buyer of lamb pelts from a Canadian seller could not ship them to the United States for resale, as he had planned, because of stricter import regulations. As the court noted, "the rest of the world was free to the buyer . . . as destination for the shipment."[58] The goods did not serve the purposes of this buyer, but they would have served the purposes of others. In these cases, to give relief would deprive the seller of a benefit they would have had if they had been dealing with buyers for whom the goods would have been suitable because they did not have a special purpose in mind.

Sometimes, however, the seller does not contract in order to avoid the risk of having to sell the same performance to someone else at a lower price. In such cases, courts have given relief for frustration of purpose even when the purpose frustrated was that of a single buyer, not that of buyers in general. In *La Cumbre Golf & Country Club v. Santa Barbara Hotel*, a hotel company entered into a contract with a golf and country club that allowed its guests to play on the club's golf

[55] Valiulis v. L'Atelier Wholesale Antiques, 519 So. 2d 312, 313 (La. Ct. App. 1988).
[56] Anderson Bros. v. O'Meara, 306 F.2d 672, 673 (5th Cir. 1962).
[57] *Id.* at 306 F.2d at 675.
[58] Swift Canadian Co. v. Banet, 224 F.2d 36, 38 (3d Cir. 1955).

course.[59] The hotel company did not have to pay when the hotel burned down, and there were no more guests. In *Chase Precast Corp. v. John J. Paonessa Co.*, the state of Massachusetts contracted with a construction firm to replace a grass median strip on a street with concrete barriers.[60] The contractor hired a subcontractor to produce the barriers. The project was cancelled after protests from angry residents. The contractor paid for all the barriers that the subcontractor had already produced. The court held that it did not have to pay for lost profits on those still to be produced under its contract. Neither the golf club nor the contractor was selling a performance which it now must resell to someone else who might pay a lower price.

Consequently, to give relief was not unfair to either of them.

iii. Mistakes as to collateral matters

Other mistakes concern, not the purpose for which a performance is suitable, but its value. They affect the price on which the parties agree.

Some mistakes concern market conditions. We considered them when we discussed unconscionability. In *Laidlaw v. Organ*, one party had learned of the signing of the Treaty of Ghent, ending the War of 1812, early on a Sunday morning.[61] Soon after sunrise, he called on the defendant with whom he had been negotiating, and bought 111 hogsheads of tobacco. We saw that the court was correct to deny relief. The buyer spent time and effort acquiring the information, as the court noted, "by rising earlier in the morning, and obtaining by superior diligence and alertness that intelligence by which the price of commodities was regulated."[62] Such efforts allow the current market price to reflect accurately the chances that it will change in the future. In contrast, even before the doctrine of unconscionability was revived in the late twentieth century, a court gave relief when an oil strike in the area had driven up land prices, and a sophisticated business bought mineral rights worth thirty times the contract price from a man who was 64 years old, disabled, living on a 200-acre isolated mountain farm, and was one of the few not to have heard the news. In that case the buyer's time and effort was spent not seeking information but seeking the ill-informed.

Other mistakes concern a characteristic of a performance that affects its value. We will consider them when we discuss warranties. If goods are warranted against defects, the proper remedy, as we shall see, depends on whether the buyer would have accepted the performance if the seller had offered a suitable discount

59 271 P. 476, 476 (Cal. 1928).
60 566 N.E.2d 603, 605 (Mass. 1991).
61 15 U.S. 178, 182–83 (1817).
62 *Id.* at 193.

in the price. If not, the contract should not be binding. If so, the buyer should be required to accept the goods despite the defect and receive the amount of the discount, That solution prevents the buyer from speculating at the seller's expense by using the defect as an excuse for repudiating a contract when the market price of the goods has fallen. It is not the law. The *Uniform Commercial Code* adopted a "perfect tender rule" which allows the buyer to refuse to accept whenever they fail to conform to the specifications of the contract. That rule has been much criticized, as we will see, for good reason.

The remedy should be the same when goods were priced at they were because the parties were mistaken about a characteristic of the goods that would affect their value to buyers in general. There is no reason that the seller should profit from the mistake. There is no reason that the buyer should be able to repudiate the contract if market prices have fallen using the mistake as an excuse.

III. Misrepresentation and fraud

i. Innocent misrepresentation

If a misrepresentation is made innocently, both parties are mistaken. The contract should be void if mistake affects the suitability of goods or services for the purposes of the buyer. Even if the purposes are those of the particular buyer rather than buyers in general, the misrepresentation was made, presumably, to induce the buyer to contract. Other mistakes concern a characteristic of a performance that affects its value. As mentioned, we will consider them when we discuss warranties. As we shall see, the contract should be voidable only if the buyer would not have agreed even if the seller had offered a suitable discount in the price. Otherwise, the buyer should be required to accept the goods despite the defect and receive the amount of the discount. That is not the rule under the *Uniform Commercial Code* but, as we will see, it should be.

Consequently, there is no reason to have a doctrine of innocent misrepresentation in addition to the doctrines of mistake and warranty. The doctrine of innocent misrepresentation is the unfortunate result of a historical accident.

According to conventional doctrine, if a misrepresentation made innocently is "material," a contract is not void but voidable. The *Restatement (Second) of Contracts* provides, "If a party's manifestation of assent is induced by either a fraudulent or a material misrepresentation by the other party upon which the recipient is justified in relying, the contract is voidable by the recipient."[63]

[63] RESTATEMENT (SECOND) OF CONTRACTS § 164(1) (AM. LAW INST. 1981).

This doctrine was developed in England by courts of equity and sometimes applied by courts of common law. Pollock noted:

> The rule given by the tendency of decisions and dicta in equity may be thus expressed . . . A contract . . . is voidable at the option of a party who has been induced to enter into it by a statement contrary to fact by the other party without reasonable grounds for believing it, though in fact he does believe it.[64]

Pollock disagreed with this doctrine. He described it as a "theory" which ought to be rejected.

He believed that relief given for misrepresentation could be better explained as relief given either because a condition of the contract had not been fulfilled or because a promise had been broken.[65] This theory "has always been more or less distinctly implied in the treatment of these matters by courts of common law."[66] He quoted Justice Stephen who said that, aside from cases of estoppel or criminal liability:

> every representation false when made or falsified by the event must operate [as] . . . a term of the contract, in which case its falsity will, according to the circumstances, either render the contract voidable, or render the person making the representation liable either to damages or to a decree that he or his representatives shall give effect to the representation.[67]

The misrepresentation might be a condition in which case the contract was not binding if it was unfulfilled. Or it might be a promise:

> To say that a man is answerable for the truth of statements made by him in good faith is to say that it is his legal duty to see that they are borne out or to make compensation for their not being borne out. Whence and of what nature is this duty? If the statement is of a fact, made as an inducement to another person to enter into a contract, the substance of the duty is no other than this, that the person making the statement undertakes that it is true. In that case must not his undertaking be a term of the contract? For if not, why should it bind him? . . .
>
> If . . . the statement is of something to be performed in the future, it must be a party's declaration of intention unless it a mere expression of opinion. But a

[64] Frederick Pollock, Principles of Contract: Being a Treatise on the General Principles Concerning the Validity of Agreements in the Law of England 483 (4th ed. 1885).

[65] *Id.* at 485.

[66] *Id.* at 483.

[67] Alderson v Madderson, 5 Ex. D. 293 cited by Pollock, *supra* note 64, at 484.

> declaration of intention made to another person in order to be acted on by that person is a promise or nothing.[68]

A warranty was a promise, and, if it was broken, the seller was liable in damages. It might be a condition as well in which case the buyer was not bound if the condition was not fulfilled. This distinction was preserved by the English *Sale of Goods Act of 1893*.[69]

In contrast, in the United States, both the *Uniform Sales Act* of 1906 and the *Uniform Commercial Code* treated every breach of warranty as though it were an unfulfilled condition: the buyer has the option of refusing to accept and pay for the goods. That is known as the "perfect tender rule." Yet, as we have seen, the *Second Restatement* adopted what Pollock called an alternative theory: misrepresentation is itself a ground for relief which made a contract "voidable at the option of a party who has been induced to enter into it by a statement contrary to fact." As a result, when a buyer misdescribes their goods, the situation is covered by overlapping doctrines: the buyer could avoid the contract for misrepresentation, or refuse to accept the goods for breach of warranty.

Although these remedies overlap, they are not quite the same. The perfect tender rule allows the buyer to reject the goods if they fail in any respect to conform to those the seller contracted to provide. That rule, as we will see, is subject to some rather peculiar exceptions. The rule adopted by the *Restatement Second* allows the buyer to avoid the contract only if a misrepresentation is "material."[70] For example:

> A, seeking to induce B to make a contract to buy a tract of land at a price of $1,000 an acre, tells B that the tract contains 100 acres. A is mistaken and does not know that the tract contains only 90 acres. Because the statement is not a fraudulent misrepresentation, the contract is voidable by B only if the misrepresentation is material.[71]

Yet if it were a sale of goods rather than a sale of land, the *Uniform Commercial Code* would allow the buyer to refuse delivery of oil if it was still usable but has sulfur content slightly less than the contract required.[72]

According to the *Second Restatement*, "A misrepresentation is material if it would be likely to induce a reasonable person to manifest his assent, or if the maker knows that it would be likely to induce the recipient to do so."[73] "A

68 *Id.* at 482.
69 SALE OF GOODS ACT, 1893, 56 & 57 Vict. Ch. 71, §§ 11(i)(a) & 11(i)(b).
70 RESTATEMENT (SECOND) OF CONTRACTS § 164(1) (AM. LAW INST. 1981).
71 *Id.* at § 164(1) illus. 2.
72 *See, e.g.*, T.W. Oil, Inc. v. Consolidated Edison Co., 443 N.E.2d 932 (N.Y. 1982).
73 RESTATEMENT (SECOND) OF CONTRACTS § 162(2) (AM. LAW INST. 1981).

misrepresentation induces a party's manifestation of assent if it substantially contributes to his decision to manifest his assent."[74] It would seem that anything that might affect the other party's decision substantially contributes to it. "It is not . . . necessary that [a party] would not have acted as he did had he not relied on the assertion."[75] Perhaps the drafters were trying to bring their rules on misrepresentation into closer harmony with the perfect tender rule: even a seemingly insignificant discrepancy matters. They did so, however, by saying that, contrary to both logic and language, a misrepresentation may substantially contribute to a decision that would have been made the same way had the truth been known. They also risked extending the perfect tender rule beyond contracts to sales to any contract in which a performance is not as "represented." Moreover, even if the doctrines perfectly overlapped, we would still have two doctrines which, for Pollock, presented as two different theories about how relief should be explained. We have adopted them both without reconciling them.

Pollock himself, however, never explained how to reconcile his theory with the doctrine of mistake. Whenever relief is given for mutual mistake, both parties believed that the performance has some characteristic which, in fact, it does not. Often the seller will have "represented" that the performance has this characteristic. In the Roman example, copper is sold as gold. Presumably, the seller represented it as such. Pollock himself used it as an example of when relief is given for mistake. Yet, in discussing misrepresentation, he claimed that relief was given because a representation is sometimes a condition. Again, two doctrines are competing for the same turf.

Indeed, nineteenth-century courts held that contracts were voidable for misrepresentation which could as easily have been held void under the doctrine of mistake. A contract could be avoided in equity "if one sells property to another who is particularly anxious to have the right of sporting over it, and it turns out that he cannot have the right of sporting because it belongs to somebody else,"[76] or if a variation in the quantity of land conveyed, though small, was important for the enjoyment of the whole.[77] The sale of a leasehold was held to be voidable at common law when it was subject to restrictions on the trades that could be carried on and only a few of these trades had been mentioned to the purchaser. The court held that there had been a "misdescription, although not proceeding from fraud." The purchaser was entitled to rescission because "it may reasonably be supposed that but for such misdescription the purchaser might never have entered into the contract at all." "Under such a state of facts the purchaser may be considered as not having purchased the thing which was really the subject of

[74] *Id.* at § 167.
[75] *Id.* at cmt. a.
[76] Earl of Durham v. Legard, 34 Beav. 611.
[77] Arnold v. Arnold (C.A.) 14 Ch. D. 270.

the sale." In these cases, the courts could equally well have given relief for mutual mistake and explained it in the same way. Yet if the same relief could be given when the parties are simply mistaken, there is no point in saying that their mistake must be the result of a misrepresentation.

The mystery of why there should be two doctrines governing similar factual situations has never been resolved. The *Second Restatement*, following the *First Restatement*, provides that a contract is void when a "mutual" mistake concerns "a basic assumption on which the contract was made."[78] As we have seen, it also provides that a contract is voidable by a party who relied on the other's "material" misrepresentation. When the misrepresentation is made innocently and relied upon by the other party, there will be a mutual mistake. Is the contract void for mistake but only if the mistake was one of a basic assumption, or it is voidable at the option of the party to which the misrepresentation was made provided the misrepresentation was material? The result should not turn on whether or not the mutual mistake was caused by an innocent misrepresentation.

When the contract is for a sale of goods, as we have seen, similar factual situations may be governed by three different doctrines: misrepresentation, mistake, and warranty. Liability for innocent misrepresentation in contract law parallels strict liability in tort for deceit. As Dan Dobbs, Paul Hayden, and Ellen Bublick noted "[m]ost cases impose strict liability for misrepresentations only in two special and limited cases": "when the plaintiff's suit is for recission or recission-limited damages," and "when the representation is construed to be a warranty."[79] Sometimes "when the plaintiff's suit if for recission or recission-limited damages" "the innocent misrepresentation is a special case of mutual mistake."[80] The result should be the same whichever doctrine is applied. Under the doctrine of mutual mistake, it does not matter which party caused the error by making an innocent misrepresentation. The contract is void, not voidable, at the option of whichever party happened to be the one to which the representation was made. Under the doctrine of misrepresentation, a party can avoid the contract whenever the fact misrepresented is material. As Dobbs, Hayden, and Bublick observed, such a rule "would, at least in theory, permit the plaintiff to overthrow a whole deal by rescission merely because of an erroneous statement about price or costs that could be remedied by a small damages award."[81] The same problem arises with the "perfect tender" rule. Any variation between the

[78] Restatement (Second) of Contracts § 152(1) (Am. Law Inst. 1981). *See* Restatement (First) of Contracts § 502 (Am. Law Inst. 1932).

[79] Dan B. Dobbs, Paul T. Hayden, & Ellen M. Bublick, Hornbook on Torts 1127 (2d ed. 2016).

[80] *Id.* at 1128.

[81] *Id.* at 1128–29.

goods contracted for and the goods delivered entitles the buyer to refuse to accept the goods and pay for them.

We have already discussed when relief should be given for mistake. The contract should be void if the mistake affects the suitability of a performance for buyers in general. If the mistake affects its suitability for the purposes of a particular buyer, it should be void only if the seller represented the goods as suitable for the buyer's particular purposes in order to induce him to contract. Otherwise, the seller will be exposed to the risk that he must enter into a less advantageous bargain with someone else, a risk against which the contract was supposed to protect him. That is the problem that Dobbs, Hayden, and Bublick noted with the doctrine of misrepresentation. If our analysis is correct, whether the mistake was caused by a misrepresentation should matter only in the case just mentioned: where the seller represented the goods as suitable for the buyer's particular purposes in order to induce him to contract.

When we consider warranty, like many other scholars, we will discuss why the perfect tender rule should be abandoned. In other contracts, a party cannot escape the bargain as long as the other has substantially performed, and the same should be true of a sale of goods. We will see that the doctrine of specific performance rests on the same considerations as the doctrine of mistake. Like the doctrine of mistake, it prevents one party from disavowing the contract in order to escape the risk that he assumed when he contracted: the risk of passing up a more favorable bargain.

ii. Fraud

The *Second Restatement* provides that a contract is voidable for "either a fraudulent or a material representation by the other party."[82] Fraud matters only because "a non-fraudulent misrepresentation does not make the contract voidable unless it is material, while materiality is not essential in the case of a fraudulent misrepresentation."[83]

The drafters did not arrive at this view by considering when fraud should matter. The relief given for a non-fraudulent misrepresentation had been stretched to the point where it was not clear when fraud should make a difference. The drafters of the *First Restatement of Contracts* faced the same problem. It provided that "[t]he difference between the effect of innocent and that of fraudulent misrepresentation in producing this result is twofold." One difference is that "the effect of innocent misrepresentation is destroyed if the facts subsequently

[82] Restatement (Second) of Contracts § 164(1) (Am. Law Inst. 1981).
[83] *Id.* at § 164 cmt. b.

accord with the representation" while the effect of a fraudulent one is not.[84] The other is that "materiality of the mistake induced by innocent misrepresentation is essential while materiality is not essential if a mistake induced by fraud produces the intended consequences."[85]

The *Second Restatement* wisely rejected the first distinction,[86] noting that if the facts become as the victim of fraud believed them to be, "there is ordinarily little likelihood of harm."[87] It accepted the second distinction but changed the definition of "material." According to the *First Restatement*, a representation is "material" "where the misrepresentation would be likely to affect the conduct of a reasonable man."[88] According to the *Second Restatement*, it is "material" "if it would be likely to induce a reasonable person to manifest his assent, or if the maker knows that it would be likely to induce the recipient to do so."[89] If so, then the fact that a misrepresentation is fraudulent matters if the misrepresentation is not likely to induce a reasonable person to assent, and the party committing fraud does not think it is likely to do so. To put it another way, a party is liable for a fraudulent misrepresentation even if it was not foreseeable that it would induce the other party to consent.

Although the drafters arrived at that strange sounding rule by a different route, it is actually an application of a more general principle: that a person is responsible for the unforeseeable consequences of a wrongful act. That principle is recognized in tort law.[90] Some courts have used it to explain, for example, why Ann is liable if she shoots at Bart and hits Carla whom she could not see even though she looked around carefully to be sure there were no witnesses. Other courts have spoken mysteriously of "transferred intent." Similarly, a party whose fraudulent misrepresentation induces the other party to consent should not be able to hold them to the contract even if they were unlikely to do so.

We will encounter this principle again when we discuss the rule in *Hadley v. Baxendale* which provides that a party who breaches a contract is liable only for harm that they could have foreseen at the time that the contract was made. This rule had been formulated by the French jurist Robert Pothier. He made an exception for fraud (*dol*). A party who willfully and wrongfully breached their contract was liable for unforeseeable damages as well.[91] Common law courts did

[84] Restatement (First) of Contracts § 476 cmt. b (Am. Law Inst. 1932).

[85] *Id.*

[86] Restatement (Second) of Contracts § 165 (Am. Law Inst. 1981). "This section . . . has been extended . . . to cover fraudulent as well as innocent misrepresentations." *Id.* Reporter's Note.

[87] *Id.* at cmt. a.

[88] Restatement (First) of Contracts § 470(2) (Am. Law Inst. 1932).

[89] Restatement (Second) of Contracts § 162(2) (Am. Law Inst. 1981).

[90] James Gordley, *Responsibility in Crime, Tort, and Contract for the Unforeseeable Consequences of an Intentional Wrong: A Once and Future Rule? in* The Law of Obligations Essays in Celebration of John Fleming 175 (P. Cane & J. Stapleton eds., 1998).

[91] Robert Pothier, Traité des obligations no. 166, *in* 2 Oeuvres de Pothier 497 (Bugnet ed., 2d ed. 1861).

not formally adopt that exception, but, as we will see, it can explain why they have sometimes allowed recovery of damages that the party in breach probably could not have foreseen.

Another reason that fraud should matter is because of a principle recognized by the law of torts: the negligence of the victim is not a defense to an intentional tort. If Ann shoots at Bart and wounds him, she cannot say it was his fault because he did not duck fast enough. This principle rarely comes into play because in cases of innocent misrepresentation it rarely matters whether a party was at fault for believing what he was told. As the *Second Restatement* provides: "A recipient's fault in not knowing or discovering the facts before making the contract does not make his reliance unjustified unless it amounts to a failure to act in good faith and in accordance with reasonable standards of fair dealing."[92]

Nevertheless, following conventional doctrine, the *Second Restatement* requires that a party's reliance on the misrepresentation be "justified," and here the issue of fault can creep back in. According to the *Second Restatement*: "If a party's manifestation of assent is induced by either a fraudulent or a material misrepresentation by the other party upon which the recipient is justified in relying, the contract is voidable by the recipient."[93] It observes:

> The most significant and troublesome applications of this principle occur in connection with assertions of opinion, assertions as to matters of law, assertions of intention, and fault. In other situations, the requirement of justification is usually met unless, for example, the fact to which the misrepresentation relates is of only peripheral importance to the transaction or is one as to which the maker's assertion would not be expected to be taken seriously.[94]

According to the *Second Restatement*, it does not matter whether a party was at fault for believing a misrepresentation. Nor does it matter whether the misrepresentation is a matter of fact or law.[95] Yet, the issue of fault is implicit in its treatment of assertions of opinion and intention.

A party who claims to have a certain opinion, may be telling the truth whether or not the opinion is correct. The other party may be at fault, however, in believing it to be correct and deciding, for example, not to investigate its truth. In contrast, a party who claims falsely to have a certain opinion is committing fraud. In that event, the other party's fault should not matter.

[92] Restatement (Second) of Contracts § 172 (Am. Law Inst. 1981).

[93] *Id.* at § 164(1).

[94] *Id.* at § 164 cmt. d.

[95] *Id.* at § 170 ("If an assertion is one as to a matter of law, the same rules that apply in the case of other assertions determine whether the recipient is justified in relying on it").

The *Second Restatement* provides that a statement of one's intentions is not an assertion when, under prevailing business mores, the other party would not be expected to believe it. Nevertheless, a party who knows that the other may believe the statement, is committing fraud. It should not matter whether the other party at fault for being credulous.

A party who contracts an obligation is assumed to intend to perform it. A party who does not intend to do so commits fraud. Again, it should not matter if the other party is at fault for being deceived.

Finally, a party who fraudulently misrepresents the terms of a contract is bound by the terms as they were understood by the other party, even if the other party failed to read or to understand the contract. When one party misled the other by redrafting a contract, the Seventh Circuit said:

> [t]he defendant was excused from not having read the new document because the general rule of being held responsible for contracts one signs, even if one has not read them, is not applicable when the neglect to read is not due to carelessness alone, but was induced by some stratagem, trick, or artifice on the part of the one seeking to enforce the contract.[96]

In that case, the plaintiff "carefully retyped the release in such a way that [the defendant's] agent would never expect that changes were made. The failure to read most definitely resulted from [the plaintiff's] clever scheme, and, accordingly, does not bar [the defendant] from challenging the validity of the fraudulent release."[97]

In such a case, the parties are bound to the terms as represented by the party committing the fraud. Consequently, as the *Second Restatement* provides, "[i]f a party's manifestation of assent is induced by the other party's fraudulent misrepresentation as to the contents or effect of a writing . . . the court . . . may reform the writing to express the terms of the agreement as asserted."[98] It adds, unfortunately, that the court should do so provided that "the recipient was justified in relying on the misrepresentation." To do so is to deny relief when the recipient was at fault for having done so.[99] The negligence of the victim should not be a defense against an intentional wrong.

We will encounter this principle again when we consider why, as the *Second Restatement* recognizes, a contract is formed even though the parties attach

[96] Hand v. Dayton-Hudson, 775 F.2d 757, 759–60 (6th Cir. 1985), *citing* Komraus Plumbing & Heating, Inc. v. Cadillac Sands Motel, Inc., 195 N.W.2d 865 (Mich, 1972), *citing in turn* International Transportation Ass'n v. Bylenga, 236 N.W. 771 (Mich. 1931).

[97] 775 F.2d at 760.

[98] Restatement (Second) of Contracts § 166 (Am. Law Inst. 1981).

[99] *Id.* at § 166(a).

different meanings to the words when one "party did not know of any different meaning attached by the first party, and the other knew of the meaning attached by the first party."[100] A party can commit fraud not only by lying but also by concealing the truth.[101] Therefore it does not matter that the first party was at fault or having attached a different meaning to the words of the contract.

IV. Duress

The basic rule is stated in the *Restatement (Second) of Contracts*: "If a party's manifestation of assent is induced by an improper threat by the other party that leaves the victim no reasonable alternative, the contract is voidable by the victim."[102] We will consider when a threat is improper, under what circumstances the victim has no reasonable alternative, and when a threat should be deemed to induce the other party's consent. We will see that sometimes the contract should be voidable and sometimes the terms should be adjusted so that they are fair.

i. The impropriety of a threat

To constitute duress, a threat must be improper. As the *Second Restatement* observes:

> An ordinary offer to make a contract commonly involves an implied threat by one party, the offeror, not to make the contract unless his terms are accepted by the other party, the offeree. Such threats are an accepted part of the bargaining process. A threat does not amount to duress unless it is so improper as to amount to an abuse of that process.[103]

Those remarks are true but misleading.

A threat is an abuse of the process by which a contract of exchange is made if it frustrates the purpose for which parties enter into such a contract. They do so, we have said, in order that they each may receive something that they value more than what they give in return. For a party to threaten "not to make the contract unless his terms are accepted by the other" is not merely an "accepted part of the

[100] *Id.* at § 201(2)(a).
[101] He has concealed the truth if, for example, he has painted a wall to conceal evidence of termites (De Joseph v. Zambelli, 139 A.2d 644 (Pa. 1958)).
[102] RESTATEMENT (SECOND) OF CONTRACTS § 175(1) (AM. LAW INST. 1981).
[103] *Id.* at § 176 cmt. a.

bargaining process." It is a *sine qua non* condition for a contract of exchange to serve this purpose.

A threat is an abuse of the process by which a contract of exchange is made if it frustrates the purpose for which parties enter into such a contract. The purpose, as we have said, is to enable each party to get something that values more than what he gives in return without enriching the other party at the other's expense. We have described a contract as "involuntary" if a party gets something that he values less than what he gives. We have described it as economically unfair if the exchange enriches the other party at his expense. For a party to threaten "not to make the contract unless his terms are accepted by the other" is not merely an "accepted part of the bargaining process." It is a *sine qua non* condition for a contract of exchange to serve this purpose.

An exchange is not involuntary if a party contracts to obtain a something that the other has the right to grant or withhold. It is involuntary if a party contracts to obtain something that the other party has no right to do or not to do.

A threat to commit a crime or a tort is improper.[104] The party who makes it is not selling anything to which the other party does not have a right.

That purpose, as we have said, is to enable each party to get something that values more than what he gives in return without enriching the other party at the other's expense. We have described a contract as "involuntary" if a party gets something that he values less than what he gives. We have described it as economically unfair if the exchange enriches the other party at his expense. A threat is improper when it renders an exchange involuntary or economically unfair.

An exchange is not involutary if a party contracts to obtain a something that the other has the right to grant or withhold. . It is involuntary if a party contracts to obtain something that the other party has no right to do or not to do.

A threat to commit a crime or a tort is improper.[105] The party who makes it is not selling anything to which the other party does not have a right. A stick-up man is not selling anything to which he has a right when he offers to spare a party's life in return for his money. Neither does a person who offers to sell her kidney in a jurisdiction in which it is illegal to do so.

A threat to bring a groundless lawsuit is improper.[106] It is an abuse of the civil process to bring one.

A threat of criminal proceedings is improper.[107] The person making that threat may have the right to give the authorities information that leads to criminal prosecution. But the purpose of that right is so that criminals may be caught and punished. It is not to enable blackmail.

[104] *Id.*at § 176(1)(a).
[105] *Id.*at § 176(1)(a).
[106] *Id.*at § 176(1)(c).
[107] *Id.* at § 176(1)(b).

In *Mayerson v. Washington Mfg. Co.*,[108] the plaintiff was told that if he did not agree to a series of modifications of his employment contract "he would be fired and 'blackballed in the industry as a trouble maker.'" The threat was improper. In return for these modifications the plaintiff received the assurance that he would not be blackballed which the defendant had no right to sell.[109]

In *Laemmar v. J. Walter Thompson Co.*,[110] the plaintiffs had purchased stock in the company that employed them subject to an option that the company could repurchase the stock if their employment were terminated for any reason. Officers of that company asked them to resell the stock to the company or to themselves in return for corporate notes payable over three years at 6.5 percent interest. The plaintiffs did so because they were told that otherwise they would be discharged. Presumably, the stock was worth more to the plaintiffs than the corporate notes that they received in return. Again, the threat was improper because it led them to accept a performance worth less to them than the one they made in return. The plaintiffs were at will employees, and the court assumed that the company had the right to discharge them. The court concluded correctly that "a threat to pursue an action to which one is legally entitled may constitute duress." As we will see, the right to discharge an employee at will must be exercised in accordance with the purpose for which it was conferred.[111] It was not conferred so that it could be sold to the plaintiffs in return for their stock.

The remedy, according to the *Second Restatement*, is that "[i]f a party's manifestation of assent is induced by an improper threat . . . the contract is voidable by the victim."[112] It should be voidable if as in *Laemmar*, because of the threat, victims accepted a performance worth less to them than the one they made in return. It is possible, however, that the victims would have contracted had the threat never been made. Consequently, they should have the right to affirm the contract. It Regrettably, they may use this option to speculate at the other party's expense. The extent to which they can do so is limited by the rule that they must choose whether to affirm the contract as soon as the threat is removed.[113] Nevertheless, if they do succeed in speculating at the other party's expense, the other party has only itself to blame since the threat was improper.

In other cases, a threat is improper because it is used to obtain terms that are unfair. If, absent the threat, the victim would have contracted anyway but on fair

[108] 58 F.R.D. 377 (E.D. Penn. 1972).

[109] Indeed, if he received nothing else, his promise would lack consideration. If blackballing the plaintiff constituted defamation, the threat would be improper for that reason.

[110] 435 F.2d 680 (7th Cir. 1970).

[111] *See* p. 000.

[112] RESTATEMENT (SECOND) OF CONTRACTS § 175(1) (AM. LAW INST. 1981).

[113] E. ALLAN FARNSWORTH, CONTRACTS 272 (3d ed. N.Y. 1999).

terms, the remedy should be different. The victim should not have the option to rescind the contract any more than when a contract is unconscionable but should be able to have the terms revised.

Indeed, the doctrine of economic duress was established before the doctrine of unconscionability was fully accepted. Once it was accepted, there was no longer a need to recognize an independent doctrine of economic duress.

In 1947, John Dawson described the situations in which relief for economic duress was given in a well-known article, *Economic Duress—An Essay in Perspective*:

> The direct conflict in decisions, on facts substantially identical, makes it likewise impossible to formulate any general proposition that could now achieve anything like universal acceptance. Nevertheless, it seems clear that many decisions have already shifted a considerable distance beyond the limits defined by conventional statements of doctrine and that further shifts are to be expected. The most that can be claimed is that change has been broadly toward acceptance of a general conclusion—that in the absence of specific countervailing factors of policy or administrative feasibility, restitution is required of any excessive gain that results, in a bargain transaction, from impaired bargaining power, whether the impairment consists of economic necessity, mental or physical disability, or a wide disparity in knowledge or experience.[114]

The considerations that Dawson mentions are the same as those to be taken into account when relief is given for unconscionability. One is "excessive gain" which is often described as "substantive unconscionability." The other an "impairment" of the disadvantaged party's ability to protect himself such as "economic necessity, mental or physical disability, or a wide disparity in knowledge or experience." It is often described as "procedural unconscionability." As we have seen, the evil to be remedied is the excessive gain. The weakness of the disadvantaged party explains why the advantaged party was able to obtain an excessive gain. So does a threat which leads a party to contract on unfair terms. The threat by one party and the weakness of the other should be relevant only as evidence, in a doubtful case, that the terms actually were unfair.

According to the *Second Restatement*, however, if the terms are unfair, a threat can be regarded as improper because it led the disadvantaged party to accept

[114] John P. Dawson, *Economic Duress—An Essay in Perspective*, 45 MICH. L. REV. 253, 289 (1947). His passage was quoted in *Capps v. Georgia Pac. Corp.*, 453 P.2d 935, 938 (Or.1969), which was praised by the *Second Restatement* for rejecting an older approach which was "contrary to the modern trend and inconsistent with the general principle of this Section." RESTATEMENT (SECOND) OF CONTRACTS § 175 cmt. b (AM. LAW INST. 1981).

them, even though, had the terms been fair, the threat would not have been improper at all. In response to "developing notions" of "economic duress" or "business compulsion," it provides that a threat is "improper" when "the impropriety consists of the threat in combination with resulting unfairness. Such a threat is not improper if it can be shown that the exchange is one on fair terms."[115] That formulation does describe the use some courts have made of the doctrine of economic duress. But it calls into question whether one needs such a doctrine.

In a Massachusetts case, *International Underwater Contractors, Inc. v. New England Tel. and Tel. Co.*,[116] the plaintiff was a contractor who had completed extra work not called for by the contract on defendant's assurance that he would be paid for it. Plaintiff claimed $811,816.73 but released his claim in return for $575,000 because, the plaintiff alleged, as "a result of the [defendant's] failure . . . to meet its commitments," "the bank had refused to extend any more credit and [its] cash position was overdrawn," and, had it not accepted the defendant's offer, "it would not have been able to survive the demands of [its] creditors."[117] The court held that these "allegations . . . if true, would make out a case for duress." They "raise a question . . . whether the plaintiff was forced because of such difficulties to accept a disproportionately small settlement which it would not otherwise have accepted."[118]

In *Cabot Corp. v. AVX Corp.*,[119] the Supreme Judicial Court of Massachusetts cited *International Underwater Contractors*[120] but held that the plaintiff had not made out a case for duress. The plaintiff alleged that the defendant had threatened to withhold a scarce product critical to its business unless it paid a high price. The court noted that the defendant was able to charge a high price because of "a worldwide shortage of the rare tantalum product, at a time when [it] was facing a rapidly growing demand from its customers for the type of capacitors it manufactured."[121] "Absent any legally cognizable restraint, [it] was free to drive whatever bargain the market would bear."[122]

In the first of these cases, the court would have had no objection if the defendant had threatened to pay no more than he owed. In the second, the court did not object when the defendant's threat was not to exchange unless the plaintiff paid the market price. Whether the threat constituted duress depended on whether the terms offered were unfair.

115 Restatement (Second) of Contracts § 176 cmt. a.
116 393 N.E.2d 968 (Mass. App. 1979).
117 *Id.* at 971.
118 *Id.*
119 448 Mass. 629, 863 N.E.2d 503 (2007).
120 *Id.* at 511.
121 *Id.* at 512.
122 *Id.*

In an 1885in *West Virginia Transportation Co. v. Sweetzer*, the West Virginia Supreme Court allowed a shipper to recover a freight overcharge saying:

> when the shipper was one whose business could not be successfully carried on without frequent use of this identical railroad for transportation purposes, then . . . in making over-payments for freight on the demand of the railroad company he should be regarded as making them under a species of moral duress."[123]

In 1989, in *Machinery Hauling, Inc. v. Steel of West Virginia*,[124] the same court cited *West Virginia Transportation Co.*, but held that there was no economic duress when the defendant signed an agreement to pay for work it had done because, the defendant said, "if I did not sign it, [the plaintiff] would sell me no more cranes, which would have put our company out of business." In dismissing the defendant's claim that the agreement was unconscionable, the court noted that the terms were not one-sided.

In the first of these cases, the court would have had no objection if the railroad had threatened to withhold service unless a customer paid a fair rate. In the second, the court did not object when the agreement was on fair terms.

The *Second Restatement* said, "An ordinary offer to make a contract commonly involves an implied threat by one party, the offeror, not to make the contract unless his terms are accepted by the other party, the offeree."[125] The threats in these cases were to refuse to settle a claim, to refuse to provide a service, or to refuse to sell goods. The result turned on whether those terms proposed were unfair. If what matters is unfairness, and not the character of the threat, then there is duress when one party refuses to contract except on terms that are unfair to the other. In that event, one cannot distinguish the scope of the doctrine of economic duress from that of unconscionability.

The drafters of the *Second Restatement* wished to avoid so broad a conception of economic duress. They said that a mere threat to refuse contract except on unfair terms is not improper. It would be improper only in three situations:

> A threat is improper if the resulting exchange is not on fair terms, and
>
> (a) the threatened act would harm the recipient and would not significantly benefit the party making the threat,
>
> (b) the effectiveness of the threat in inducing the manifestation of assent is significantly increased by prior unfair dealing by the party making the threat, or

123 West Virginia Transp. Co. v. Sweetzer, 25 W.Va. 434, 461 (1885).

124 384 S.E.2d 139 (W. Va.1989).

125 Restatement (Second) of Contracts § 176 cmt. a (Am. Law Inst. 1981).

(c) what is threatened is otherwise a use of power for illegitimate ends.[126]

As to the first rule, it is odd to think that a threat to refuse to contract except on unfair terms would be improper if the advantaged party gained little but proper if he gained a lot. The *Second Restatement*'s illustration of the second rule is a case in which "A, who has sold goods to B on several previous occasions, intentionally misleads B into thinking that he will supply the goods at the usual price and thereby causes B to delay in attempting to buy them elsewhere until it is too late to do so." A then refuses to sell unless B pays "a price greatly in excess of that charged previously."[127] A may have committed fraud. Be that as it may, if the decision in *West Virginia Transportation Co.* is correct, it should not matter that he misled B. It is enough that A took advantage of the fact that he is B's only possible supplier to charge an unfair price.

According to the third rule, "a threat is improper if the resulting exchange is not on fair terms, and . . . what is threatened is otherwise a use of power for illegitimate ends."[128] If it is illegitimate to seek unfair terms, there is duress whenever one party threatens not to contract unless his unfair terms are accepted. In their example of this rule, as in *West Virginia Transportation Co.*, a party took advantage of the fact that he was the only possible supplier to charge an unfair price:

> A, a municipal water company, seeking to induce B, a developer, to make a contract for the extension of water mains to his development at a price greatly in excess of that charged to those similarly situated, threatens to refuse to supply to B unless B makes the contract. B, having no reasonable alternative, makes the contract. Because the threat amounts to a use for illegitimate ends of A's power not to supply water, the contract is voidable by B.[129]

No one would agree to pay to pay one person an unreasonable price who knew that someone else would pay more. As noted earlier, anyone who pays more than the market price either cannot use the market or does not know what the market price is. Those are the situations in which a party can seek relief under the doctrine of unconscionability. Again, the question arises, what useful purpose is served by recognizing a separate doctrine of economic duress. It would be better to regard that doctrine as a stage through which the law passed on the way to recognizing unconscionability as a ground for relief in its own right.

[126] *Id.* at § 176(2).
[127] *Id.* at § 176 illus. 13.
[128] *Id.* at § 176(2)(c).
[129] *Id.* at § 176 illus. 16.

ii. The absence of a reasonable alternative

In Roman law, a party could claim duress unless the threat would have moved "a very firm man" (*homo constantissimus*).[130] Reinhard Zimmermann noted that this rule may have been inspired by Roman admiration of fortitude.[131] Blackstone adopted it, quoting Bracton.[132]

In the nineteenth century, as Allan Farnsworth noted, the standard became whether a threat was sufficient to overcome the will.[133] The reason was the rise of the will theories of contract. A contract was defined as an expression of the will of the parties. Duress interfered with the expression of a party's will.[134] That was not a good explanation. A party who agrees to pay to avoid some danger chooses among evils. A choice has been made whether the danger arises from storm at sea, as Aristotle noted,[135] or a life-threatening medical condition, or a stick-up man pointing a gun. Moreover, to ask whether a party's will was overcome is meaningless without some standard of what the party supposedly could have resisted.

The *Second Restatement* provides that the threat must be one that "leaves the victim no reasonable alternative." That standard is correct. The parties contract so that they each may receive something that they value more than what they give in return. A party who is threatened also takes into account the value of avoiding the consequences of the threat. The party who would not have contracted absent the threat had no reasonable alternative but to acquiesce by accepting the lesser of two evils.

The requirement that there be no reasonable alternative prevents the party who is threatened from speculating at the other's expense. It prevents a party who would have contracted anyway from escaping from the contract if it later proves to be unfavorable.

Sometimes, a party's alternative is to refuse to acquiesce and sue if the other party carries out the threat. Whether doing so is a reasonable alternative depends on whether the party who sues will be adequately compensated for the consequences of the breach. In *Austin Instrument Co. v. Loral Corp.*,[136] the plaintiff paid more than the contract price to a subcontractor who threatened that otherwise he would breach the contract. The court held rightly that bringing

130 DIG. 4.2.6.

131 REINHARD ZIMMERMANN, THE LAW OF OBLIGATIONS ROMAN FOUNDATIONS OF THE CIVILIAN TRADITION 653 (1990).

132 2 WILLIAM BLACKSTONE, COMMENTARIES ON THE LAWS OF ENGLAND 131 (1766).

133 FARNSWORTH, *supra* note 112, at 265.

134 JAMES GORDLEY, PHILOSOPHICAL ORIGINS OF MODERN CONTRACT DOCTRINE 183–84 (1991).

135 NICOMACHEAN ETHICS III.i.5.

136 272 N.E.2d 533 (N.Y. 1971).

a lawsuit if the subcontractor breached was not a reasonable alternative. If the plaintiff had not acquiesced, he would have defaulted on a contract with the Navy. He would not have been able to establish how much business he might lose in the future because he defaulted.

iii. Causation

The threat must have induced a party to contract. As Allan Farnsworth has said, the "[t]he requirement is simply one of causation." The same statement is made by Comment b to § 175 of the *Second Restatement*.[137] As we have seen, however, what matters is that a party who is induced to contract did not have a reasonable alternative.

Comment c to § 175 confuses the issue:

> In order to constitute duress, the improper threat must induce the making of the contract. The rule for causation in cases of misrepresentation stated in § 167 is also applied to analogous cases of duress. . . . A party's manifestation of assent is induced by duress if the duress substantially contributes to his decision to manifest his assent. . . . The test is subjective and the question is, did the threat actually induce assent on the part of the person claiming to be the victim of duress. Threats that would suffice to induce assent by one person may not suffice to induce assent by another. All attendant circumstances must be considered, including such matters as the age, background and relationship of the parties. Persons of a weak or cowardly nature are the very ones that need protection; the courageous can usually protect themselves. Timid and inexperienced persons are particularly subject to threats, and it does not lie in the mouths of the unscrupulous to excuse their imposition on such persons on the ground of their victims' infirmities.

The standard stated in § 167, which, according to Comment c, governs cases of duress, was drafted to deal with cases of misrepresentation. It is not helpful. It provides that "A misrepresentation induces a party's manifestation of assent if it substantially contributes to his decision to manifest his assent."[138] "It is not . . . necessary that [a party] would not have acted as he did had he not relied on the assertion."[139] It is confusing, and may be meaningless, to say that

[137] Restatement (Second) of Contracts § 175 cmt. b (Am. Law Inst. 1981) ("It is enough if the threat actually induces assent on the part of one who has no reasonable alternative").

[138] *Id.* at § 167.

[139] *Id.* at cmt. a.

a misrepresentation or a threat "substantially contributes" to a decision that a party would have made the same way anyway. Moreover, in the case of duress, a threat did substantially contribute to the decision of a party who had no reasonable alternative. A party who had a reasonable alternative cannot receive relief.

Section 167 has no clear relationship to the other considerations mentioned in Comment c which concern the threatened person's inexperience or timidity. To take these considerations into account might seem to resurrect the Roman idea which, according to Zimmermann, is that relief should not be given to a person of infirm character. Instead, as the *Second Restatement* suggests, we should be more willing to give relief to a timid person than to a brave one. To the timid, the consequences with which they are threatened will seem greater. So, then, will be value they place on avoiding the threat. Since they will lose more, in their eyes, if they acquiesce, it is more likely that they acquiesce because, in their eyes, there is no reasonable alternative. The brave person is more likely to have consented even if the threat had never been made. Perhaps that was the true rationale of the Roman rule that required that the threat be one that would influence even a most constant man. If all Romans were assumed to be constant, the Roman who contracted in the face of a lesser threat would probably have contracted anyway. He should not be allowed to escape from a contract that he would have entered into absent the threat.

In any event, these considerations concern whether a party who was threatened believed that defying the threat was a reasonable alternative. They do not call for a separate requirement that the threat induced the party to contract.

V. A contract for a performance no reasonable party could want

Sometimes parties are foolishly mistaken about the value to themselves of what they will receive. In our view, except in very rare cases, such contracts should be enforced anyway.

Nevertheless, contracts have sometimes been considered to be unconscionable when one party knew that the other would not benefit. According to a Comment to the *Second Restatement*:

> Factors which may contribute to a finding of unconscionability in the bargaining process include the following: belief by the stronger party that there is no reasonable probability that the weaker party will fully perform the contract; knowledge of the stronger party that the weaker party will be unable to receive substantial benefits from the contract.[140]

[140] *Id.* at § 208 cmt. d.

The *Uniform Consumer Credit Code* provides that relief will be given for "unconscionability" when there was "knowledge by the seller . . . at the time of the sale . . . of the inability of the consumer to receive substantial benefits from the property or services sold or leased."[141]

The *Uniform Consumer Credit Code* gave two illustrations of when relief should be given.[142] In one, a door-to-door salesman sold a vacuum cleaner to each of two poor people sharing the same apartment and the same rug. In the other, a door-to-door salesman sold a Hispanic laborer an English-language encyclopedia. He was a bachelor and only spoke Spanish.

According to another provision of the *Uniform Consumer Credit Code*, a contract may be held unconscionable when there was a "belief by the seller, lessor, or lender at the time a transaction is entered into that there is no reasonable probability of payment in full of the obligation by the consumer or debtor."[143] Mortgage loans violate both provisions when the lender knew that the borrower would have to pay a high fraction of a small income. Courts have given relief.[144] After the crash of 2008, many homeowners claimed that mortgage companies had lured them into taking loans they could not afford. In *Commonwealth v. Fremont Investment and Loan*, the Attorney General of Massachusetts brought an action claiming a number of subprime loans were "unfair" within the meaning of the *Consumer Protection Act* because the interest rate would jump within three years to more than 50 percent of the borrowers' income.[145] The lender argued that the loans made "in the expectation, reasonable at the time," that they could be refinanced because "housing prices would improve during the introductory loan term."[146] The Massachusetts Supreme Judicial Court said that "it was unreasonable, and unfair to the borrower, for [the lender] to structure its loans on such unsupportable optimism."[147]

One can sympathize with courts that give relief. Nevertheless, when the parties to these contracts entered into them, they thought that the performance was worth more to them than what they were to give in return. They were under no mistake as to the performance or the price. They were foolish to have agreed.

To give relief in such a case is dangerous. Sellers would not want to deal with anyone who could later claim that they acted foolishly. Courts would substitute

[141] Uniform. Consumer Credit Code § 5.108(4)(b) (Unif. L. Comm'n 1974).
[142] *Id.* at § 5.108(4)(b) cmt. 4.
[143] *Id.* at § 5.108(4)(a).
[144] Hughes v. Abell, 867 F. Supp. 2d 76, 82 (D.C. Cir. 2012) (explaining the borrower's monthly payment "amounted to approximately 46% of [his] monthly income of $3,511.83"); *see also* Williams v. First Gov't Mortg. & Invs., 225 F.3d 738, 743 (D.C. Cir. 2000) (stating the borrower had a seven-person household and "roughly $1,200 a month in disposable income, over half of which went to First Government to cover his $686 monthly payments").
[145] 897 N.E.2d 548, 550–51 (Mass. 2008).
[146] *Id.* at 558.
[147] *Id.*

their own judgment of the value a party should have placed on a performance for that of the party himself. It is quite different when a court gives relief from unfair terms. Anyone would prefer a more favorable price.

It is obvious that two poor people sharing one rug do not need two vacuum cleaners to keep it clean. Is it obvious that the Spanish-speaking laborer-bachelor cannot use the encyclopedia? If so, the court is telling him, "This encyclopedia is not for you. Whatever makes you think you can learn English well enough to read it?" It may seem obvious that the borrowers in *Hughes*, *Williams*, and *Fremont* would default. To give relief, however, is to say, "No matter how valuable owning your own home may seem to be to you, it is foolish of you to try when the odds are so much against your keeping it." All investors sometimes experience "unsupportable optimism." So do the students who enroll in four-year colleges and universities. An estimated 40 percent of them do not graduate within six years. "Even [ten] years after graduation, 32% of college graduates end up with jobs that [do not] require a college degree."[148] Should a court say, "Investing your own funds in the way you have chosen is too dangerous"? or "College is not for you. We do not think you can benefit from it"? There are occasions—drug laws are an example—when a person's right to choose is replaced by a right to act only as someone else thinks best. But to do so as a general principle of contract law is to infringe a freedom that is quite valuable: the freedom to bear the responsibility for one's own decisions, wise or foolish.[149]

VI. Offensive auxiliary terms

Parties make a contract of exchange so that each of them may receive something they value more than what they give in return. For the contract to serve this purpose, each party must understand what they are to get and what they are to give.

Generally, it is enough for the parties to understand the performance terms of the contract: the price and the object. Usually, it does not matter if they understand the auxiliary terms. What matters is whether these terms are fair. Sometimes, however, an auxiliary term is so offensive to a party as to affect the value of what he is to give or receive.

The law dealing with terms that are unwanted because they are offensive is poorly developed. With the exception of unconscionability, there is no general doctrine that can be used to give relief. The doctrine of unconscionability is rarely applied.

[148] Douglas Belkin, *Making the College Bet Pay Off*, WALL ST. J., Dec. 11, 2018, at A3.

[149] *See* James Gordley, *Morality and Contract: The Question of Paternalism*, 48 WM. & MARY L. REV. 1733, 1758 (2007).

Some situations are dealt with by special statutes. For example, some types of offensive behavior may violate statutory prohibitions on discrimination according to race or gender. One cannot include a term in a contract that violates these provisions. The difficulty is that an offensive term may not happen to violate a statute.

Other situations are dealt with as violations of public policy. The difficulty is that this approach only gives protection against terms that offend a person's dignity or moral principles when they also offend public policy. As the Illinois Supreme Court said, "public policy concerns what is right and just and what affects the citizens of the State collectively. It is to be found in the State's constitution and statutes and, when they are silent, in its judicial decisions."[150] "[M]atters that are the subject of public polic[y]" are distinct "from matters purely personal."[151] An offense to a person's sense of dignity or moral standards may be purely personal and may not affect the citizens of the state collectively.

Typically, violations of public policy are found when a party contract penalizes a party for refusing to violate a statute enacted for the benefit of others or requires a party to renounce the benefit of a statute enacted for that party's own benefit. For example, it is a violation of public policy to require an employee to commit perjury,[152] to engage in price-fixing,[153] to alter state-mandated pollution control reports,[154] to perform a medical procedure for which she was not licensed,[155] to violate consumer protection law,[156] or to conceal a violation of a statute prohibiting theft.[157] No doubt, the violation of public policy would violate the moral standards of a law-abiding citizen, and perhaps their sense of dignity as well, but only because their moral standards require them to be law-abiding and therefore to obey statutes that are concerned with the welfare of others. It is also a violation of public policy to require a party to renounce the benefit of laws that are intended to promote their own welfare. For example, an employer cannot prohibit a worker from joining a union or filing a claim for workers' compensation.[158] In such cases, the worker's moral standards and sense of dignity are violated only because they may regard it as immoral or servile to circumvent legislation designed for the worker's own protection.

150 Palmateer v. Int'l Harvester Co., 421 N.E.2d 876, 878 (Ill. 1981).

151 *Id.* at 878.

152 Petermann v. Int'l Brotherhood of Teamsters, Chauffeurs, Warehousemen & Helpers of Am., Local 396, 344 P.2d 25, 27 (Cal. Ct. App. 1959).

153 Tameny v. Atl. Richfield Co., 610 P.2d 1330, 1331, 1334 (Cal. 1980).

154 Trombetta v. Detroit, Toledo & Ironton R.R., 265 N.W.2d 385, 388 (Mich. Ct. App. 1978).

155 O'Sullivan v. Mallon, 390 A.2d 149, 149–50 (N.J. Super. Ct. 1978).

156 Harless v. First Nat'l Bank, 246 S.E.2d 270, 276 (W. Va. 1978).

157 Vermillion v. AAA Pro Moving & Storage, 704 P.2d 1360, 1361 (Ariz. Ct. App. 1985).

158 Glenn v. Clearman's Golden Cock Inn, 13 Cal. Rptr. 769, 771 (Ct. App. 1961); Frampton v. Cent. Ind. Gas Co., 297 N.E.2d 425, 427 (Ind. 1973).

Otherwise, a party to a contract must argue that an offensive term also happens to violate a public policy expressed in statutes or judicial decisions.[159] Some parties have succeeded, but the difficulties are illustrated by an Arizona case, *Wagenseller v. Scottsdale Memorial Hospital*.[160] A female hospital employee alleged that she had been fired because she offended her female supervisor by refusing to participate in a skit parodying the song *Moon River* that concluded with members of the group "mooning" the audience. The court held that to require her to expose her buttocks was a violation of public policy because a state statute prohibiting indecent exposure "establishes a clear policy that public exposure of one's anus or genitals is contrary to public standards of morality."[161]

By this reasoning, however, the limits of her employer's contractual right to fire her depend on the legislature's decision about what conduct to criminalize. The court gave itself some wiggle room by saying that it would reach the same result even if the employer had not violated the statute provided that the employer had violated the policy behind it.[162] Even this flexibility was taken away from the court by a subsequent Arizona law that provided that a violation of public policy must be a violation of statute.[163]

Suppose there had been no law prohibiting indecent exposure in Arizona. Suppose the skit required the plaintiff to strip down to whatever constituted the legal minimum of clothing that must be worn without violating the statute. Suppose that the plaintiff had been told to appear at a company beach event wearing a bikini or a two-piece bathing suit and had refused to do so, although other female employees might not have objected. The employer should not have the contractual right to require any type of behavior an employee regards as demeaning or morally offensive simply because the legislature failed to criminalize it. Moreover, as the example of the bikini illustrates, an employee's personal standard of dignity and morality may be violated even when that of other people would not.

A better approach would be to face the question squarely: when do incursions on personal standards of dignity or morality warrant relief on that ground alone? In such cases, a court might give relief because the term is unconscionable even though it is not economically unfair. It is helpful to distinguish cases in which an

159 Wagenseller v. Scottsdale Mem'l Hosp., 710 P.2d 1025, 1031 (Ariz. 1985).

160 *Id.* at 1035 (stating that "all of the onlookers were voyeurs and would not be offended").

161 *Id.*

162 *Id.*

163 Ariz. Rev. Stat. Ann. § 23-1501(A)(3) (2018) ("An employee has a claim against an employer for termination of employment only if one or more of the following circumstances have occurred . . . (b) The employer has terminated the employment relationship of an employee in violation of a statute of this state"). According to one Arizona court, "[t]he legislature in enacting A.R.S. § 23-1501 took express exception to the court's indication [in *Wagenseller*] that it rather than the legislature had the authority to define public policy." Galati v. Am. W. Airlines, Inc., 69 P.3d 1011, 1013 n.2 (Ariz. Ct. App. 2003).

incursion into those standards advances the interests of the other contracting party and cases, such as *Wagenseller*, in which it does not.

If the terms of the contract do advance the interests of the other party, the party who finds them offensive but should have known of them when entering into the contract should not receive relief unless there was no reasonable alternative but to accept. A sound general principle is provided by the *Second Restatement of Contracts*: "Where the other party has reason to believe that the party manifesting such assent would not do so if he knew that the writing contained a particular term, the term is not part of the agreement."[164] Conversely, a party manifesting assent who has reason to believe that the other party would not know a certain term would be offensive should ask whether the contract contains such a term.

Suppose a woman is hired to work in a jewelry store and signs a contract in which she agrees to comply with security procedures. Suppose one of the procedures requires her to walk through a metal detector that takes nude photographs that will be seen by a female employee.

So few enough women would object that the employer should not be required to draw her attention to that procedure before she is hired. If the photographs would be seen by male and female employees, enough women would object that the employer should be required to bring this provision to a future employee's attention.

As a further example, Stephen Curry, a star player of the 2017 NBA champion team Golden State Warriors, refused to visit the White House and meet with President Donald Trump on account of their political differences. Suppose that Curry, in his employment agreement with Warriors, was required to visit the White House and meet with the president. Suppose that term was buried among other terms, and so he would be unlikely to know of it unless it was explicitly pointed out. Had it been customary for NBA champions to visit the White House regardless of who was president, a professional basketball player such as Curry either should have known of the term or should have known enough to ask whether he would be obligated to do so. Had it not been customary, then if his employer knew that Curry might object, his employer should have told him that he would have to make the visit.

A person who knows of an offensive term may nevertheless have no reasonable alternative but to agree. There may be an emergency. Suppose a pregnant woman's water broke unexpectedly at 4:00 AM, and when she was rushed to the nearest hospital to have a Caesarean section, she signed an agreement which would allow the hospital to film the entire operation and show it to medical students for educational purposes. Because enough women would object to it, the hospital should call the term to her attention. Even if it did so, however,

164 Restatement (Second) of Contracts § 211(3) (Am. Law Inst. 1981).

the term should not be binding. The reason is not only that the woman found it offensive and had no reasonable alternative, but also that the hospital can adequately educate medical students by filming the childbirth of women who do not object.

Suppose an employee was informed when he was hired that he will be bound by a dress code that is established and periodically modified by an executive committee. Suppose that he is Jewish, and the committee forbids him to wear a yarmulke. If the job is in the service industry and requires daily contact with customers by employees with uniform headgear, the term serves an interest of the employer, who should be able to require him to dress like the other employees.[165] If the employer had reason to believe the employee would object, the employee should have been notified of this requirement in advance. If forbidding him to wear a yarmulke contributes nothing to his employer's business, the employer should not be able to forbid it.

This distinction was ignored in *Pierce v. Ortho Pharmaceutical Corp.*[166] The plaintiff, Dr. Grace Pierce, "was the only medical doctor on a project team developing loperamide, a liquid drug for treatment of diarrhea in infants, children, and elderly persons. The proposed formulation contained saccharin."[167] The "team agreed that the formula was unsuitable for children."[168] Dr. Pierce refused to work on the project when, in response to a directive from the company's marketing division, the decision was made to continue to develop the drug anyway. Although the company invited her to choose to work on another project, she resigned on the grounds that the new assignment amounted to a demotion and that she had been told that she would never be promoted because of an "inability to relate to the Marketing Personnel."[169] The court granted the company's motion for summary judgment.

By the approach we are suggesting that motion should have been denied, and Dr. Pierce should have prevailed at trial if she could prove that the company could have assigned her to another project, without impairing its interests, and without demoting her or diminishing her responsibilities or prospects of a promotion. Instead, the court dismissed her complaint on the grounds that since she had not been asked to violate a statute, her belief that she was violating her

[165] The Supreme Court drew a similar distinction in *Goldman v. Weinberger*, 475 U.S. 503 (1986), holding that the first amendment guarantee of freedom of religion was not violated when a rabbi serving in the Air Force was prohibited from wearing a yarmulke. The provision was not arbitrary, according to the court, because, in "[t]he considered professional judgment of the Air Force[,] ... the traditional outfitting of personnel in standardized uniforms encourages the subordination of personal preferences and identities in favor of the overall group mission." *Id.* 508.

[166] 417 A.2d 505, 513 (N.J. 1980).

[167] *Id.* at 506–07.

[168] *Id.* at 507.

[169] *Id.*

Hippocratic oath did not matter. Discharging her was not "contrary to a clear mandate of public policy."[170]

Suppose a secretary working for a law firm whose views are strongly pro-choice refuses to type a brief attacking the legality of abortion, or one whose views are strongly pro-life refuses to type one defending its legality. Since the firm can easily have that brief typed by another secretary who is not offended, it should do so. It should not be able to fire the secretary who refused.

Thus far, we have been discussing situations in which the term that one party finds offensive serves some interest of the other party. Some terms do not. To require compliance with such terms is arbitrary. In that event, the term should not be binding regardless of whether the party who finds it offensive could have expected it.

An example is *Wagenseller*. It did not advance the interest of the hospital to have its employees expose their buttocks. As another example, suppose that employees are required to attend an annual office event at which the CEO speaks in a way that is needlessly offensive. For example, the CEO habitually makes crude racial or sexual jokes. Those who find the jokes offensive should not be required to attend. That is so even if those who do not attend are not members of the race or gender that is ridiculed, and so cannot claim discrimination against themselves on the basis of race or sex.

Such terms should not be enforced because the performance required by the contract was unwanted. Although they are auxiliary terms, the performance they require should consciously be understood and accepted by the employees. In contrast, if terms are economically fair, as we have seen, they should be binding even if a party is not consciously aware of the terms.

[170] *Id.* at 513–14.

7
Commitment

I. Precontractual negotiations

In a fair exchange, the parties are each compensated for the risks that they assume. Contracts must be binding in advance of performance for the parties to allocate these risks. For them to become binding, each party must make a commitment.

A party cannot be bound before making a commitment. When an uncommitted party has been held liable during precontractual negotiations, it has been for some other reason. That party may have been unjustly enriched, or misappropriated information which the other party disclosed, or misrepresented something, or breached another contract that was already in force.

A party may have been unjustly enriched by the other party while negotiations were going on. An example is *Hill v. Waxberg*.[1] Hill asked Waxberg, a contractor, to help prepare for the construction of a building on Hill's property. It was understood that if the federal housing authority (FHA) would finance the project, Hill would give Waxberg the building contract. After Waxberg had put in considerable work and FHA financing was obtained, Hill and Waxberg were unable to agree on a contract and Hill hired another contractor. Waxberg nevertheless recovered for "the value of the benefit that was acquired" by Hill.

Similarly, in *Precision Testing Laboratories, Inc. v. Kenyon Corp.*,[2] while Ellis and Kenyon were negotiating a contract to develop emission systems for cars, Ellis provided labor and technical assistance bringing Kenyon's test car to certification level. Although no final contract was entered into, Ellis recovered the value to Kenyon of the services it had performed.

A party might have misappropriated information that was disclosed by the other party during precontractual negotiations. Even if one party was not enriched by the misappropriation, the other may have been harmed. For example, in *New England Insulation Co. v. General Dynamics Corp.*,[3] General Dynamics solicited bids, promising not to divulge engineering information they contained, and allegedly did so to a competing bidder as part of a kick-back

[1] 237 F.2d 936 (9th Cir. 1956), *cited in* E. Allan Farnsworth, Contracts 199–200 (3d ed. 1999).

[2] 644 F.Supp. 1327 (S.D.N.Y. 1986).

[3] 522 N.E.2d 997 (Mass. App. 1988).

Foundations of American Contract Law. James Gordley, Oxford University Press. © Oxford University Press 2023.
DOI: 10.1093/oso/9780197686089.003.0007

scheme. Although General Dynamics was held liable for violating its promise not to disclose, it should be liable for any harm its misuse of the information caused whether or not it made such a promise so long as that was the understanding concerning the information it received.

A party may be liable for misrepresentation or deceit. A party is liable if they deceived the other, for example, as to the intention to enter into a final contract. In *Markov v. ABC Transfer & Storage Co.*,[4] a lessee repeatedly urged a lessor to extend a lease, explaining that its business with its principal customer depended on the renewal. Its lessor assured it that the lease would be renewed but meanwhile was negotiating a sale to a third party. The lessor wanted to keep the possibility of renewal alive as a fallback if the sale fell through. The court held correctly that one who makes a promise without intending to keep it is liable for misrepresenting its intentions.

A party may be liable for breaching an existing contract while negotiating a new one. For example, in *Dixon v. Wells Fargo, N.A.*,[5] the Dixons owned a home on which Wells Fargo held a mortgage. While the parties were negotiating a modification of its terms, Wells Fargo told the Dixons that they should default on the payment due on their current mortgage as a step toward obtaining a new one. Wells Fargo then refused to agree to the new mortgage and began foreclosure proceedings under the old mortgage on the ground that the Dixons had defaulted. The court held that Wells Fargo could not do so. It said that because "the bank had taken advantage of their default status to initiate foreclosure proceedings" it was liable under the doctrine of promissory reliance, although it did not explain what promise the bank had broken. It would be more accurate to say that whether or not the bank made a promise, and whether or not a new mortgage was under negotiation, the bank could not foreclose under the old mortgage because it had waived the condition that payments under the old mortgage must be made on time.

II. Commitments to negotiate in good faith

Judge Level, in his often-quoted opinion in *Teachers Ins. & Annuity Ass'n of America v. Tribune Co.*, distinguished two types of agreements that the parties may make before they sign a formal contract.[6] In one type, the parties agree on all the terms of the contract. There is nothing left to negotiate. The purpose of the

[4] 457 P.2d 535 (Wash. 1969).
[5] 798 F.Supp. 2d 336 (D.Mass. 2011).
[6] Teachers Ins. & Annuity Ass'n of America v. Tribune Co., 670 F.Supp. 491 (S.D.N.Y. 1987) (Leval, D.J.).

formal contract is to memorialize the terms of their agreement. Such an agreement is enforceable.

In a second type, the parties commit themselves to the "major terms" and agree to negotiate the rest in good faith. The parties are then obligated to negotiate in good faith. Their contract is binding unless they fail to reach agreement on the remaining terms despite a good faith effort to do so.

Whether the parties entered into an agreement of the first type has traditionally been regarded as a question of intention. As Judge Embry said in 1894:

> [I]t is quite clear that, after all, the question is mainly one of intention. If the party sought to be charged intended to close a contract prior to the formal signing of a written draft, or if he signified such an intention to the other party, he will be bound to the contract actually made, though the signing of the written draft be omitted. If, on the other hand, such party neither had nor signified such an intention to close the contract until it was fully expressed in a written instrument and attested by signatures, then he will not be bound until the signatures are affixed.[7]

In *Teachers*, the parties clearly stated their intent. Their preliminary agreement was to be "a binding agreement between us" although contingent on preparation and execution of final documents satisfactory to the parties and "containing 'usual and customary' representations and warranties, closing conditions, other covenants, and events of default."[8]

Often, the parties do not clearly state whether they intend a memorandum to be legally binding. The reason is not necessarily that the parties were careless, or that each wished the other to believe the memorandum was binding while remaining free to break it. In the context of a negotiation, it can be awkward for a party to raise the issue. If one party suggests that the memorandum should not be binding, the other party may suspect them of insincerity. If one party suggests that it should, the other may suspect a trap.

In one situation, the parties agree that they will not negotiate with anyone else. If one party honors that agreement and the other party does not, the arrangement is unfair in the same way as an unfair option to contract. One party may speculate at the other's expense. An illustration is the leading case of *Channel Home Centers v. Grossman*.[9] The parties signed a letter of intent according to which Channel was to receive a lease in Grossman's shopping center and pay a specified rent. Neither party was to negotiate with anyone else. Grossman was

7 Mississippi & Dominion Steamship Co., v. Swift, 86 Me. 248, 258 (1894).
8 670 F.Supp. at 494.
9 795 F.2d 291 (3d Cir. 1986).

to "withdraw the Store from the rental market, and only negotiate the above described leasing transaction to completion." While Channel Home Centers honored its commitment, Grossman tried to find a better deal for himself. When he succeeded, he broke off negotiations. If he had not succeeded, he would have held Channel Homes to the terms to which it had agreed. The court correctly held that the agreement was enforceable. Otherwise, Grossman could have taken advantage of a situation in which Channel Holmes regarded itself as committed and Grossman did not.

This situation is different from one in which the parties do not agree to negotiate only with each other, but in which they set a deadline that makes it difficult for either to negotiate with anyone else. In *Cochran v. Norkunas*, the owner of a house signed a handwritten letter of intent with a potential buyer setting out the price, the down payment, the financing, and providing that a standard form Maryland Realtor's contract would be delivered to seller within twenty-eight hours with certain specified modifications in its terms. The court said that it was clear that the parties did not intend their preliminary agreement to be binding. Actually, all that was clear is that the final contract was to be executed very soon, presumably because neither party wanted to give the other much time to receive and consider other offers. But the preliminary agreement said nothing about the freedom of the parties to do so within that short time.

In a second situation, one party may incur expenses in the expectation that a final contract will be reached. The arrangement may be unfair if it is not clear that no commitment has been made. An illustration is *Budget Marketing, Inc. v. Centronics Corp.*[10] BMI signed a letter of intent covering the terms of its acquisition of Centronics. The letter said that it "shall not be construed as a binding agreement." Centronics alleged that BMI later promised that it could go ahead with the deal. Centronics then expanded operations, hired dealers, arranged for credit, and bought key man insurance. The court held that although the letter of intent was not binding, the later promise was. Any doubt as to whether the later promise superseded the earlier one was resolved against the party who knew that the other would incur expenses which it could only recoup if a final contract was made.

In the first situation, the parties enter into a preliminary agreement because they wish to lock in a favorable bargain. Neither is to negotiate with anyone else. In the second situation, they enter into a preliminary agreement to give one party an incentive to incur expenses in the expectation that a final agreement will be reached. It may be difficult to tell whether the purpose of a preliminary

10 927 F.2d 421 (8th Cir. 1991) (applying Iowa law).

agreement was to lock in a favorable bargain, as in the first situation, or to encourage a party to incur expenses, as in the second, or both.

An illustration is *Arcadian Phosphates, Inc. v. Arcadian Corp.*[11] The parties signed a memorandum of understanding describing the assets to be purchased, the purchase price, and an option which Arcadian would receive to buy up to 20 percent of the equity of API. They agreed "to cooperate fully and work judiciously in order to expedite the closing date and consummate the sale of the business."[12] Arcadian refused to proceed after a change in prices made the phosphate business much more profitable. The court said that the memorandum could not be intended as a commitment because it provided that "[a] binding sales agreement will be completed by December 31, 1986." It remanded on the ground that API might have a claim in promissory reliance for reliance damages "based on evidence that Arcadian knew and approved of API's expenditures and collateral contracts, but Arcadian suddenly demanded a majority interest in API when the phosphate business became 'dramatically' profitable." The decision may seem paradoxical. If the memorandum was not intended as a commitment, it is hard to see how it could be the basis of a claim in promissory reliance based, not on some additional promise, but on the knowledge that API would act in reliance. If the promise was intended as a commitment, then it would seem that Arcadian could not back out. The decision makes sense, however, if instead of asking whether or not the parties wished to commit themselves, we ask what commitment they wished to make. If the court was correct, they did not wish to lock in a favorable bargain. They did wish to guarantee Arcadian that it could incur expenses which would be reimbursed if a final agreement was not made.

In a third situation, one party did something that will benefit the other even if a final contract is not reached but did so without compensation expecting there to be a final contract. The arrangement may be unfair unless it is clear no commitment has been made and compensation for these expenses may never be paid. An example is *Brown v. Cara.*[13] The parties entered into a "memorandum of understanding" which stated their intention "to enter into a formal contract shortly," and in which they promised to "work together" on a real estate venture. Cara was to provide the land and Brown to cover building costs up to $175,000. The venture would be viable only if the property that they wished to develop could be rezoned. To obtain the rezoning, the developer had to draw up plans and hold hearings in advance of the final contract. The rezoning increased the value of Cara's land. If the memorandum were not binding, he could take advantage of

[11] 884 F.2d 69 (2nd Cir. 1989).
[12] *Id.* at 70–71.
[13] 420 F.3d 148 (2d Cir. 2005).

its increased value, which was due to Brown's efforts, and seek a better deal with someone else. The court held that he was bound.

Another example is *Channel Home Centers v. Grossman*,[14] in which, as the court emphasized, Channel had executed the memorandum so that Grossman could show it to lenders from which he could obtain financing.

[14] 795 F.2d 291 (3d Cir. 1986).

8
Enforcement by Third Parties

I. The problem

The modern discussion of when a promise made for the benefit of a third party is enforceable is the continuation of an ancient one. At Roman law, it was not. This rule was established for the formal contract of *stipulatio* in which, as we have seen, one party was asked "Do you promise such and such?" and responded, "I do promise." A formal promise to give or do something for a third party was not enforceable. Hence the rule "alteri stipulari nemo potest":[1] "no one can stipulate for another."

The Roman jurists generalized this rule to apply to all contracts.[2] There were exceptions. The contract was valid if the promisee had an "interest" in the promisor's performance: for example, when the promisor was liable to the third party for the performance of the promisor.[3] It did not follow, however, that in this situation the third party himself could enforce the promise. In post-classical law, if one party made a gift to the other with the proviso that the donee must pass the gift on to a third party, the third party had an action to enforce the agreement.[4]

The Roman texts thus provided a principle and some ways to wiggle around it. "However," as Reinhard Zimmermann noted, "the frontal attack on the 'alteri stipulari nemo potest' principle launched by the natural lawyers, led by Hugo Grotius." Grotius said:

> If a promise is made to me [to give something to another], then regardless of whether I have an interest, a consideration that was introduced by Roman law, it would seem that by the law of nature that I have the right to accept and that the right [to require performance] passes to the third party provided that he accepts.[5]

[1] DIG. 45.1.38.7.

[2] *Id.* 50.17.73.4.

[3] *Id.* 45.1.38.20. *See* REINHARD ZIMMERMANN, THE LAW OF OBLIGATIONS ROMAN FOUNDATIONS OF THE CIVILIAN TRADITION 35–37 (1999), 35–37.

[4] ZIMMERMANN, *supra* note 3, at 39–40.

[5] HUGO GROTIUS, DE IURE BELLI AC PACIS LIBRI TRES II.xi.18.1 (1688).

Foundations of American Contract Law. James Gordley, Oxford University Press. © Oxford University Press 2023.
DOI: 10.1093/oso/9780197686089.003.0008

That conclusion made sense in view of Grotius's account of why promises are enforceable. As we have seen, he believed in what some modern jurists have called a "transfer theory." The promisor was bound, not merely because he willed that his promise should be binding, but because he also willed to give the promisee the right to enforce it. There was no reason that the promisor could not give a third party the right to enforce it. As noted earlier, Grotius's transfer theory is incomplete. He did not explain why the promisor might choose to give a third party the right to enforce it.

Be that as it may, for a will theorist such as Friedrich Karl von Savigny, "good and accurate theory" required that such a conclusion be "rejected out of hand."[6] A contract or agreement (*Vertrag*) was constituted by the declarations of will of more than one party directed to altering the legal relationship between them.[7] By definition, it could not alter the legal relations between one of the parties and someone else. Sir Frederick Pollock defined "agreement" in the same way, observing in a footnote that he meant "*Vertrag*, as used by Savigny, whose analysis[8] we follow almost literally in this paragraph."[9] Paraphrasing Savigny, he said that the "intention of the parties" is "directed to legal consequences; and . . . those consequences must be such as to confer rights or impose duties on the parties themselves."[10] Citing Savigny, he explained:

> The original and simplest type of contract is an agreement between certain persons. The persons are ascertained by their descriptions as individuals. . . . And the person who become parties in the obligation created in the agreement are the persons who actually conclude the agreement in the first instance, and those only.[11]

Pollock's use of definitions was more pragmatic than that of Savigny. Pollock acknowledged that to an "extent, modern developments . . . have altered this primary type" of contract.[12] Thus the rule had exceptions:

> No third party can become entitled by the contract itself to demand performance of any duty under the contract.

[6] 2 Friedrich Carl von Savigny, Das Obligationenrecht als Theil des heutigen römischen Rechts 84 (Berlin, 1851–53).

[7] 3 Friedrich Carl von Savigny, System des heutigen Römischen Recht §104 (1840).

[8] *Citing* 3 *id.* at § 140.

[9] Frederick Pollock, Principles of Contract at Law and in Equity, Being a Treatise on the General Principles Concerning the Validity of Agreements, with a Special View to the Comparison of Law and Equity, and with References to the Indian Contract Act, and Occasionally to Roman, American, and Continental Law 1 note a (1876).

[10] *Id.* at 2.

[11] *Id.* at 170, citing Savigny, *supra* note 6, at § 53 (*id.* 170 note a).

[12] *Id.*

> *Exception.* Provisions contained in a settlement made upon or in consideration of marriage for the benefit of children to be borne of such marriage . . . may be enforced by the persons entitled to the benefit thereof.[13]

Nevertheless, the rule for Pollock was the same as for Savigny, and the exceptions, as the passage just quoted suggests, were few.

Samuel Williston in his annotated edition of Pollock's treatise made no comment on these passages.[14] In his own treatise, however, he sacrificed formal logic to practical concerns about purpose. He adopted a distinction between donee and creditor third-party beneficiaries[15] that the arch anti-formalist Arthur Corbin had proposed in an article published two years earlier.

In the case of a donee beneficiary, Corbin said, "the purpose of the promisee in securing a promise for the benefit of a third party is to confer a gratuitous benefit upon that third party." In contrast:

> [w]here the third party is a creditor of the promisee, or against him for some particular performance, the purpose with which the promisee contracts with the promisor may be to induce the latter to pay the debt or otherwise to discharge the third party's claim. In such case, performance will directly benefit both the third party (the creditor or claimant) and the promisee.[16]

Either type of beneficiary could sue directly to enforce the promise.

Corbin thus answered the question that Grotius had left unanswered. Why would a promisor choose to give a third party the right to enforce it? Corbin identified two purposes that a promisor might have. Grotius might well have agreed. As we have seen, Grotius, like other jurists before the rise of the will theories, identified two purposes that a party might have for making a contract or that the law might have for enforcing one. The party might wish to confer a benefit on another person gratuitously, or he might wish to receive a benefit in return for the one he conferred. In the case of a donee beneficiary, his purpose is to confer a gratuitous benefit on a third party. In the case of a creditor beneficiary, the promisor receives some benefit from the promisee in return for a promise that benefits the promisee by satisfying the claim of a third party. In either case, the reason for conferring the right to enforce the promise on the third party is

[13] *Id.* at 172.

[14] Frederick Pollock, Principles of Contract at Law and in Equity 220–22, 233 (additions and annotations, Gustavus H. Wald & Samuel Williston, 3rd American ed. from 7th English ed. 1906).

[15] Samuel Williston, The Law of Contracts 683–84, 685–86 (1920).

[16] Arthur L. Corbin, *Contracts for the Benefit of Third Persons*, 27 Yale L.J. 1008, 1011 (1918).

like the reason for conferring the right to enforce the promisee on the promisee in a two-party situation.

II. Benefits conferred gratuitously

A paradigm case of what came to be called a "donee beneficiary" is *Seaver v. Ransom*,[17] a "pivotal case"[18] decided by the New York Court of Appeals in 1918. Judge Beaman had drafted a will for his wife, who was about to die. It left a house she owned to him for life and, after his death, to a charity. She wished to change her will to leave the house to her niece Marion and was afraid that she would not last long enough for her husband to write another will. He promised that if she signed the will he had drafted, he would leave her niece enough in his own will to make up the difference. He did not do so before his death. Marion sued and recovered the amount that he had promised her aunt that he would leave her.

We will see why third parties should recover in such a situation and why, nevertheless, categorizing them as "donee" beneficiaries has been a source of confusion.

A third party should be permitted to enforce a promise if doing so better enables the promisee to confer a benefit gratuitously on the third party so long as no one except that party is enriched at another party's expense. Such a contract is fair and voluntary.

i. The paradigm situation

In *Seaver v. Ransom*, the promisee wanted her niece to be given a sum of money equal to the value of her house. She conferred a benefit on the promisor in return for his promise to pay the niece that amount. Allowing the niece to enforce that promise better enables her to accomplish that purpose. If the niece could not enforce the promise, the promisee's objective would be thwarted. The promisee (or, in this case, her estate) could not recover damages for breach of contract because she was not financially harmed. She or, rather, the estate, might recover in restitution but her objective would still be thwarted. Her objective was to confer a benefit on her niece. Moreover, if she or her estate did not recover, the promisor would be enriched by the amount intended for the niece.

Calling the niece a "donee beneficiary" causes no confusion as long as it means that the promisee contracted in order to confer a benefit on a third party

[17] 120 N.E. 639 (N.Y. 1918).

[18] Melvin A. Eisenberg, Foundational Principles of Contract Law 748 (2018).

"gratuitously"—or, in the language of the *First* and *Second Restatements*, so long as it means that the promisee contracted in order to make the third party a "gift."

The *First Restatement* confused matters by artificially extending the definition of "donee beneficiary" to include other cases in which the promisor did not wish to confer a benefit gratuitously. We will see how and why it did so later on.

The *Second Restatement* confused matters by providing that to recover, a third party must be an "intended beneficiary." According to Subsection § 302(1)(b), a third party is an "intended beneficiary" if "the circumstances indicate that the promisee intends to give the beneficiary the benefit of the promised performance."[19] If the circumstances so indicated, the beneficiary of a "gift promise . . . often referred to as a 'donee beneficiary' can recover."[20]

As Eisenberg objected, an "intent test" is largely empty without an explanation of how the promisee's intent is to be discerned.[21] According to the *Second Restatement*, one must ask whether "a gift promise" involves a manifestation of intention, by the promisee and promisor, sufficient, in a contractual setting, to make reliance by the beneficiary both reasonable and probable."[22] As Eisenberg noted, "presumably" the *Restatement* "does not require actual reliance." Therefore, the test is "whether reliance would have been reasonable if it had occurred." All this language does "is to shift from a largely empty intent test to a largely empty hypothetical reliance test."[23] Moreover, this test cannot be correct in principle. Whether it is reasonable for the beneficiary of a gift promise to rely depends (1) on whether the beneficiary believes that the promisee may have a change of heart and rescind the contract with the promisor and (2) on whether, if promisee does not, the promisor will be liable to the beneficiary. But however likely it may have been that the promisee would have a change of heart, the beneficiary should recover if the promisee does not. Moreover, if the promisee does not, whether the beneficiary can recover from the promisor is the very question that the test is supposed to answer.

According to Eisenberg, "a third party beneficiary should have the right to enforce a contract if . . . allowing the beneficiary to enforce the contract is a necessary or important means of effectuating the contracting parties' objectives, as manifested in the contract read in the light of surrounding circumstances."[24] Thus it is not surprising that Eisenberg's explanation of why a donee beneficiary should recover is like our own. In *Seaver v. Ransom*, allowing the niece

19 Restatement (Second) of Contracts § 302(1)(b) (Am. Law Inst. 1981).
20 *Id.* at § 302 cmt. c.
21 Eisenberg, *supra* note 17, at 752–53.
22 Restatement (Second) of Contracts § 302 cmt. d (Am. Law Inst. 1981).
23 Eisenberg, *supra* note 17, at 755.
24 *Id.*

"to enforce the contract was an important means of effectuating the contracting parties' objectives." Her estate could not recover expectation damages, and even if it could recover "for unjust enrichment . . . the suit would not effectuate the contracting parties' objectives" because the estate rather than the niece "would end up with the benefits. If the estate did not recover, the promisor would be "unjustly enriched."[25]

Eisenberg's analysis is equivalent to ours, not only in this case, but in others we are about to discuss. Often, we will merely show why it fits with our own approach.

ii. Would-be legatees

Suppose A hires B, a lawyer, to make a will naming C as a legatee. The will is invalid. In contrast to the paradigm situation, the benefit that A confers on B in return for his help in conferring the benefit on C is much smaller—one would hope—than the benefit that C will receive if B does his work properly.

That difference should not matter. As in the paradigm situation, A is better enabled to confer a benefit on C at his own expense if B keeps his promise. If B does not, he will be liable to C for more than he was paid by A, but C is not enriched at his expense. If he charges A his usual fee, it includes a premium to cover the possibility that he will make a mistake and be responsible in an action of malpractice for the consequences. A will pay a fee that includes that premium, but as Eisenberg points out, it is difficult to imagine that A would prefer to pay less so that B will not be liable if he botches the job.[26]

Whether the legatee should recover against the lawyer is analyzed as a tort problem in the *Restatement (Third) of Torts: Liability for Economic Harm*. It provides that in principle: "An actor has no general duty to avoid the unintentional infliction of economic loss on another." It recognizes seven specific exceptions, none of which are relevant here. It then recognizes that the plaintiff can recover for breach of "residual duties" in other situations, which include the one of concern to us:

> Lawyer prepares a will for Client. Lawyer negligently concludes that no witnesses are required to make the will effective so long as it is notarized. After Client's death, the will is found to be invalid because Client's signature lacked sufficient witnesses. Daughter, who would have inherited Client's entire estate

25 *Id.* at 759–80.
26 *Id.* at 762.

under the will, instead inherits 1/8 of it by intestate succession. Daughter sues Lawyer.[27]

Whether the plaintiff has a claim for breach of "residual duties" is a reference to the general reasons that explain why there is usually no liability for unintentional infliction of economic harm.[28] One reason is the danger of "[i]ndeterminate and disproportionate liability." "A single negligent utterance can cause economic loss to thousands of people who rely on it, those losses may produce additional losses to those who were relying on the first round of victims, and so on." Another is that the "[r]isks of economic loss tend to be especially well suited to allocation by contract." According to the *Restatement* these principles explain the result why Daughter should recover in Illustration 1. "Because Client has died, Lawyer may not be sufficiently answerable for his negligence by contract, and the scope of Lawyer's liability presents no special problems of clarity or proportionality."[29]

These reasons do not explain why the lawyer is liable. If they were all that mattered, he would be liable to anyone who suffered an economic loss because of his lack of skill, whether his client had paid him to benefit that person or not. Depending on how well he knew the family, the lawyer might have been able to foresee that if the will were invalid, a loss would be suffered by various family members who might have lived in the house or by a real estate agent or prospective purchaser if the house were put up for sale. The lawyer may have been able to foresee their losses, and these losses may have been as limited as the daughter's. Her father, however, did not pay the lawyer to draft a will for their benefit. If the lawyer is liable for his daughter's loss, the father achieves his objective, and the lawyer receives a fee that reflects not only the value of his services but the risk of liability for malpractice. The daughter should recover as a third-party beneficiary.

iii. Government contracts for the benefit of private citizens

In another situation, the government wishes to confer a benefit on a group of private citizens. It contracts with a private party who promises to confer this benefit. If the promise is broken, a member of the group should recover as a third-party beneficiary as long as (1) the purpose of the government was to confer a benefit on each of its members, (2) to allowing a member to recover helps effectuate this

[27] Restatement (Third) of Torts: Liability for Economic Harm, § 1 illus. 1 (Am. Law Inst. 2020).

[28] *Id.* at cmt. e.

[29] *Id.* at note to illus. 1.

purpose, and (3) no one is enriched at another's expense except the citizen on whom the government wishes to confer the benefit.

The paradigm case in which the citizens should recover is *Zigas v. Superior Court*.[30] The federal Department of Housing and Urban Development (HUD) contracted with Zigas as well as other developers to build housing for low-income people. HUD guaranteed the developers' mortgages so that they could borrow more cheaply. The developers agreed not to charge rents exceeding those on a prescribed rent schedule. When Zigas charged more than the prescribed rent, tenants sued for its violation of its contract with HUD. The tenants recovered damages.

That result is correct. Permitting the tenants to recover better enables the government to achieve its goal of providing them with lower-income housing. As Eisenberg pointed out, the government could have brought the suit itself but "it might well choose to allocate its limited litigation resources to matters with a higher priority."[31] If the government did not choose to sue, and the tenants were not permitted to do so, the developer would be enriched by keeping the benefits they received from the government without providing any to the tenants.

In contrast, there are three situations in which a citizen who was to benefit from such a contract should not recover. In one, the government contracts with a private entity such as a developer or caregiver to provide a benefit for which a class of citizens is eligible but which will not be provided to every member of the class. Suppose that Zigas had built fewer housing units than it was required to do, and so provided lower-cost housing to fewer people. None of the eligible citizens can recover by proving that, had the contract been kept, they would have had a better chance of being selected as a beneficiary.

It might seem that this case is like those which may arise among private parties in which the plaintiff can recover even though the contract did not guarantee them a benefit but only the chance of obtaining one. If the contract is broken, the plaintiff can recover for loss of the chance. An example is *Van Gulik v. Resource Development Council for Alaska*.[32] The promoter of a lottery had drawn the winning tickets in a way that violated its rules and so deprived the plaintiff of a 50 percent chance of winning $10,000. The court held that the plaintiff had the right to either $5,000 or to a redrawing involving only his ticket and one other. The difference is that here the goal of the government is to provide a benefit of certain kinds such as better housing, better healthcare, or the prevention of child abuse, not to provide the cash equivalent of any of those benefits. Its purpose is not furthered by allowing a party to recover who was eligible for such a

[30] 174 Cal. Rptr. 806 (Ct. App. 1981).
[31] EISENBERG, *supra* note 17, at 774.
[32] 695 P.2d 1071 (Alaska, 1985).

benefit but who was never selected. Liability to a third party would promote the government's objective only by imposing a cash penalty for breach of contract, and, unless the government chooses to do, one cannot assume that it would have sought its goal by that means.

In another situation, the private entity which has contracted to provide a benefit to citizens is paid by the government only for the benefits that it actually confers. An illustration is *Martinez v. Socoma Companies*.[33] The government paid manufacturers who agreed to train and employ, at minimum wage, for at least one year, a specified number of people certified by the government as disadvantaged. If they failed to do so, they were to return to the government a pro rata share of the money received for each job they failed to create. When Socoma Companies failed to create as many jobs as their contract provided, 2,017 people sued who had been certified as disadvantaged but had not been hired. The court held, rightly, that they could not recover as third-party beneficiaries.

One reason is the one just discussed. The contract did not obligate Socoma Companies to provide jobs for all 2,017 plaintiffs. Each was suing, then, for the loss of a chance of becoming employed. As Eisenberg pointed out, there is a second reason as well. "[M]anufacturers would be subject to a kind of double liability: they would have to pay both restitutionary damages (the refund to the government) and expectation damages (the expected lost wages)."[34] They would not become richer at another's expense but poorer.

In yet another situation, the government contracts with a private entity to provide benefits to citizens and to pay that entity in proportion to the benefits it provides. Nevertheless, the consequence if that entity breaches its contract will be far more severe for some beneficiaries than for others. An illustration is the well-known case of *Moch v. Rennselaer Water Co.*[35] A waterworks contracted with a city to provide water for hydrants for $42.50 for each hydrant. Because it did not supply as much water to the hydrants as its contract required, the plaintiff's warehouse was destroyed by fire. The New York Court of Appeals held correctly that the plaintiff could not recover as a third-party beneficiary. The *Second Restatement* approved of this result.[36]

The reason the warehouse owner cannot recover, according to Judge Cardozo, is that liability would impose a "crushing burden" on the waterworks. Therefore liability must have been beyond contemplation of the parties given the "trivial reward" to which it was entitled under the contract.[37] The liability, of course, would

[33] 521 P.2d 841 (Cal. 1974).

[34] Eisenberg, *supra* note 17, at 774.

[35] 159 N.E. 896 (N.Y. 1928).

[36] Restatement (Second) of Contracts § 313 illus. 2 (Am. Law Inst. 1988) (which is based on *Moch*).

[37] 159 N.E. at 897–98.

not be crushing if the waterworks operated like an insurance company, charging more per hydrant and paying for harm caused when a hydrant was unusable. There are two reasons it could not. First, as Cardozo noted, the company would be liable "if the whole city is laid low."[38] An insurance company with a broad enough market can spread the risk of widespread disaster caused by hurricanes and earthquakes. A local company cannot spread the risk of a local disaster. Second, the waterworks charged a certain amount per hydrant. The amount of harm that a property would suffer from fire varies from one owner to the next. The plaintiff in *Moch* who owned a warehouse would suffer far more than a homeowner. The waterworks would be insuring against its loss, and yet it would not be charged in proportion to how serious that loss would be.

For the same reason, a third party should not recover in the case described in the *Second Restatement*: Illustration 1 to the same section of the *Second Restatement*:

> B contracts with the United States to carry mail over a certain route. C, a member of the public, is injured by B's failure to perform his contract. B is under no contractual duty to C.[39]

The result is correct. B will pay the same postage as everyone else but C may suffer far greater harm if the letter or parcel is not delivered.

If B had contracted with a private company to deliver a package and he, rather than a third party, suffered consequential damages such as lost profits, a court would not deny recovery on the ground that the harm was "unforeseeable." That was the result in the leading case of *Hadley v. Baxendale*.[40] A mill owner was not allowed to recover for the profits he lost when the mill remained shut because of a shipper's delay in delivering a mill shaft. Later we will see that the result is best explained, not by foreseeability, but in the way suggested here. The harm the mill owner suffered by the shipper's delay was far more severe than that which most of the shipper's customers would have suffered. Yet it paid no more for the prompt delivery of its shaft.

III. Benefits conferred in exchange for other benefits

A paradigm case of what came to be called a "creditor beneficiary" is *Lawrence v. Fox*,[41] decided by the New York Court of Appeals in 1859. Holly owed $300 to

[38] *Id.*
[39] Restatement (Second) of Contracts § 313 illus. 1 (Am. Law Inst. 1988).
[40] 9 Exch. 341, 156 Eng. Rep. 145 (1854).
[41] 20 N.Y. 268 (1859).

Lawrence. He loaned $300 to Fox in return for Fox's promise to pay that debt. Fox failed to pay Lawrence. Lawrence recovered the amount of the debt from Fox.

We will see why third parties should recover in such a situation and why, nevertheless, categorizing them as "creditor" beneficiaries has been a source of confusion.

i. A three-party exchange: the simplest case

In a two-party exchange, each party contracts to confer a benefit on the other in return for the one received from the other party. We have seen that such a contract should be enforced if it is fair in the sense that neither party is enriched at the other's expense, and if it is voluntary, in the sense that each party puts a higher value on what they are to give than on what they are to receive.

In a three-party exchange, each party contracts to confer a benefit on another party in order to receive a benefit from a third party: A confers a benefit on B who confers a benefit on C who confers a benefit on A. In a three-party exchange, as in a two-party exchange, a promise to confer a benefit should be enforceable as long as no party is enriched at another's expense and each party puts a higher value on what they are to receive than on what they are to give.

These reasons are straightforward. Yet the case has caused confusion because the third party is neither a donee beneficiary in any ordinary sense nor a creditor beneficiary.

The problem is shown by an Illustration that appeared in the *First Restatement* and, with a change in wording, in the *Second*. To quote the *Second Restatement*:

> A, a corporation, contracts with B, an insurance company, that B shall pay to any future buyer of a car from A the loss he may suffer by the burning or theft of the car within one year after sale. Later A sells a car to C, telling C about the insurance. C is an intended beneficiary.[42]

C is not receiving a benefit gratuitously. He is paying a premium to B for the insurance coverage provided by A. Neither is he a "creditor beneficiary." B did not promise to pay a debt that A owed to C. Yet both *Restatements* agree that he should recover.

42 RESTATEMENT SECOND § 302 Illustration 11 (AM. LAW INST. 1988). It is like RESTATEMENT FIRST § 133 Illustration 3 (AM. LAW INST. 1932) ("A, a corporation, contracts with B, and insurance company, that that B shall pay to any future buyer of a motor car from A the loss he may suffer from the burning or theft of the car within one year after sale. Later a car is sold by A to C, who pays a price for which he receives from A the car with A's statement that the insurance has been effected. C is a donee beneficiary").

To explain that result, the *First Restatement* artificially expanded the definition of a "donee beneficiary." Section 133(1)(a) provided that a person is:

> a donee beneficiary if it appears from the terms of the promise in view of the accompanying circumstances that the purpose of the promisee in obtaining the promise of all or part of the performance is to make a gift to the beneficiary or to confer upon him a right against the promisor to some performance neither due nor supposed or asserted to be due from the promisee to the beneficiary.

The provision is "awkward," as Eisenberg said, because "the term *donee beneficiary* was used to describe donees, to whom the promisee intended to make a gift, and beneficiaries who could enforce the contract but were not true donees."[43] It is also of little help. It amounts to saying that the third party counts as a "donee beneficiary" whenever the promisee intended that party to be able to enforce the promise. Eisenberg asked: "How was a court to determine whether the relevant purpose was present? In the end, therefore, first *Restatement's* general principle was largely empty."[44]

The *Second Restatement* also found this case puzzling. The *Second Restatement* does not pretend that the car buyer is a "donee beneficiary." It allows him to recover as an "intended beneficiary" when "the circumstances indicate that the promisee intends to give the beneficiary the benefit of the promised performance."[45] Eisenberg noted, as we have pointed out, that the text is relentless in its focus on intent, and that the "intent test" is "largely empty" without some clue as to how the promise's intent can be discerned.[46]

Yet, as we have seen, the reasons that the third-party beneficiary should recover in a three-party exchange are straightforward. They are the same as the reasons a party should recover in a two-party exchange.

ii. The creditor beneficiary

In the paradigm case of a creditor beneficiary, A confers a benefit on B who promises to fulfill A's preexisting duty to C. In the leading case of *Lawrence v. Fox*,[47] Holly owed $300 to Lawrence. Holly loaned $300 to Fox who in return promised to pay $300 to Lawrence. In the three-party exchange just considered, A confers a benefit on B, who promises to benefit C, who confers a benefit on

[43] EISENBERG, *supra* note 17, at 750.
[44] *Id.* at 752.
[45] RESTATEMENT (SECOND) OF CONTRACTS § 302 (1)(b) (AM. LAW INST. 1988).
[46] EISENBERG, *supra* note 17, at 755.
[47] 20 N.Y. 268 (1859).

A. The only difference here is that the creditor beneficiary, C, has already benefited A, and A pays B to confer the benefit on C that A was supposed to give in return.

For the same reasons, then, the creditor beneficiary should be permitted to recover. Each party gives up something to get something that he values more in return, and no party is enriched at another's expense. Since B received a benefit from A, unless he keeps his promise he will be benefitted at the expense of either C or A. As Eisenberg noted, "if the promisee is not easily subject to suit—because, for example, he is outside the jurisdiction or has become incapacitated . . . [i]f . . . the creditor beneficiary cannot sue the promisor, the promisor would often be unjustly enriched."[48]

iii. Liability for information provided to third parties

Suppose A contracts with B, an accounting firm, to make a report on A's financial condition for the benefit of other parties. B breaches its contract with A by negligently providing incorrect information. The lenders or investors are harmed. Whether the firm should be liable, we will see, depends on whether the arrangement is a three-party exchange of the kind just discussed in which A, B, and the lender or investors are parties.

In *Ultra-Mares Corporation v. Touch*, recovery was denied when the accountants had negligently prepared a balance sheet which "they knew would be shown to banks, creditors, stockholder, purchasers and sellers."[49] Cardozo said that "[i]f liability for negligence exists, a thoughtless slip or blunder, the failure to detect a theft or forgery beneath the cover of deceptive entries, may expose accountants to a liability in an indeterminate amount for an indeterminate time to an indeterminate class."[50] This case and that reason have often been cited for the rule of tort law that "liability is generally not imposed upon strangers—those not in privity or near-privity—for negligent infliction of pure economic harm": that is, on "strangers . . . who negligently cause economic harm to the plaintiff without causing physical harm to the person or property of others."[51] The people to whom the balance sheet was to be shown were considered to be "strangers."

Yet lenders and investors have recovered when the financial report was prepared specifically for their use. In *White v. Guarente*,[52] an accounting firm was held liable for its negligence in preparing a report for limited partners. The court

[48] EISENBERG, *supra* note 17, at 761.

[49] 174 N.E 441 (N.Y. 1934).

[50] *Id.* at 444.

[51] DAN B. DOBBS, PAUL T. HAYDEN, & ELLEN M. BUBLICK, HORNBOOK ON TORTS 1068–69, 1071–72 (2d ed. 2016), citing Ultramares v. Touch 1072 n.82.

[52] 372 N.E. 2d 315 (N.Y. 1977).

distinguished *Ultramares*. That case "involved . . . an 'indeterminate class of persons who, presently or in the future, might deal with the [company] in reliance on the audit.'" In this one, the services of the accountant were not tied to a faceless or unresolved class of persons, but rather to a known group "possessed of vested rights." In *Credit Alliance Corp. v. Andersen & Co*,[53] the court decided two companion cases. In both, lenders sought to hold accountants liable for negligence in preparing financial statements on which they had relied. In the first case (*Credit Alliance*), the court dismissed the action because, although Smith, the lender, had relied on the statement, the accountants had not been "employed to prepare the report with the Smith loan in mind." In the second (*European American Bank & Trust v. Staubs & Kaye*), the court refused to do so because the accounting firm "was well aware that a primary if not the exclusive, end and aim of auditing its client . . . was to provide EAB [the lender] with the financial information it required."

Cardozo, as we have seen, spoke of the "crushing burden" of liability to a large class of people when he denied recovery in *Moch v. Rennselaer*. A warehouse owner whose house had been destroyed by fire could not recover against a waterworks that did not maintain proper pressure at its hydrants in violation of its contract with the municipality. There, we saw, what should matter is not simply that the potential liability was enormous. What should matter is that the harm suffered might vary greatly from one person to the next, and yet those who were more vulnerable did not pay more than others. The waterworks charged the same fee for each hydrant. Consequently, if the warehouse owner could recover as a third-party beneficiary of the contract between the waterworks and the municipality, he would obtain a benefit for which he did not pay, and the waterworks would assume a risk for which it was not compensated.

For the same reason, the limited partners in *White* and lender for whom the report was prepared in *European Bank & Trust* should recover as third-party beneficiaries. The clients paid the accountants to prepare information for the benefit of lenders or investors who would compensate the clients when and if they loaned or invested. It was a three-party exchange. In a three-party exchange, as in a two-party exchange, a promise to confer a benefit should be enforceable as long as no party is enriched at another's expense and the parties each put a higher value on what they are to receive than on what they are to give. In these two cases, if the accountants are liable for their negligence, they will be compensated by charging their client a higher fee, for which the client will be compensated by the investors or lenders for whom the financial information is prepared. It may not be certain that they will lend or invest even if the financial information is favorable. But the client believed that the chance of obtaining a loan or investment on favorable

[53] 483 N.E. 2d 110 (N.Y. 1985).

terms was worth paying the accountant's fee. He valued that chance more than the amount that he paid for it. Ex ante, no party is enriched at another's expense.

iv. Two-party contracts of exchange linking three or more parties

We have discussed cases in which there is a three-party exchange. A confers a benefit on B who confers a benefit on C who confers a benefit on A. We now turn to cases in which there is a series of two-party exchanges such that because A confers a benefit on B in order to receive a benefit in return, and B is then able to confer a benefit on C in order to receive a benefit in return. If A defaults, B may be unable to perform, and C may suffer.

Liability of those who furnish labor, parts, or materials

As a general rule, when A is to furnish B with labor, parts, or materials, and A defaults, B is unable to perform, and so C is hurt, C should not be able to recover against A as a third-party beneficiary of A's contract with B. In a hypothetical case put by Eisenberg:

> Diemaker contracts with Martial to supply it with dies to make toy soldiers, and then fails to provide them. Martial has to idle its plant. Consequently, Martial breaches its contract to sell the toy soldiers to Access, a toy distributor, which is then unable to realize its plan to resell them to Toys 'R We, a retailer. Martial purchases special paint for its soldiers from Color, and employs skilled workers on an hourly basis. Because Diemaker breaches, Martial cancels its order for paint and does not employ the workers.[54]

Eisenberg said, correctly, Diemaker should only be liable to Martial. Again, that result follows from the principle that no party should bear a risk for which he was not compensated. The price that Diemaker charged Martial would not have included a premium for bearing the risk of liability for the losses that third parties might suffer.

Eisenberg said that liability to third parties would conflict with "the interests of the contracting parties, Martial and Diemaker," but his underlying argument is similar:

> If upon breach, Diemaker would have been exposed to liability to third parties as well as liability to Martial, Diemaker would certainly have demanded a

[54] EISENBERG, *supra* note 17, at 751.

> higher price from Martial. Martial, however, would have almost certainly have been unwilling to pay that higher price, because it would receive little or no corresponding benefit in return.[55]

Indeed, Martial would have received no corresponding benefit for which Diemaker would have been willing to pay. The only possible benefit would be to compensate Martial if Martial were liable to Access. Whether Martial would be liable for Access's last profits will be discussed later. Supposing that it would be, however, Martial still would not be willing to pay Diemaker for assuming the risk of liability to Access because Martial could bear that risk better than Diemaker. The risk is whether the toy soldiers will sell and at what price. It may be that Diemaker makes dies for a variety of uses, and that it does not charge different amounts to different customers depending on the profits it may lose if it does not deliver the dies. The profits of a company that uses the dies to make toy soldiers may be quite different from those of a company that uses them to make jewelry or precision instruments. In any event, Martial or Access would be better able to estimate these profits than Diemaker. Consequently, there is no price that Martial could offer Diemaker that Diemaker would be willing to accept.

Suppose that Martial had already entered into contracts with the workers and with Colors which it was forced to breach when Diemaker breached. Again, Diemaker would be in a worse position than Martial to assume the risk of liability for their losses. Martial would not have paid for Diemaker to do so. So by the same argument, they should not be able to recover from Diemaker as third-party beneficiaries.

Liability of those who sell for resale

Thus far we have considered why the other parties affected by Diemaker's breach cannot recover their lost profits from Diemaker. Suppose, however, that Access had already contracted to sell the toy soldiers to Toys 'R We, and that it is forced to breach this contract because of Martial's breach. Can Toys 'R We recover from Martial as a third-party beneficiary of its contract with Access?

It cannot recover but for a different reason. As we will see, a party who breaches a contract to deliver goods which were sold for resale is liable to the buyer for lost profits. Like Martial, Access sold for resale. Toys 'R We can recover its lost profits from Access which can recover the amount it must pay Toys 'R We from Martial. Nevertheless, Toys 'R We should not be able to do so. The only reason it would need to do so is if Martial has become insolvent. The question then is who is in the best position to bear the risk of its insolvency? The answer must be that any

[55] *Id.* at 752.

party that chooses to do business with another bears the risk of the losses that party's insolvency will cause it to suffer. Even if Martial and Toys 'R We had the same knowledge of Martial's financial position, each was better able to estimate what it would lose if Martial defaulted and became insolvent. Each was better able to know what its opportunities were for minimizing or avoiding that risk, for example, by adjusting the terms of payment with Martial or seeking another distributor or supplier. Each was better able to decide how much it should charge to cover the risk that Martial would become insolvent.

Liability in construction contracts

Suits by owners against subcontractors

It might seem that an owner should not recover from a subcontractor for the same reasons that Access should not recover from Diemaker in the hypothetical case just considered. Diemaker defaulted on its contract to supply dies for making toy soldiers to Martial, and, as a result, Martial defaulted on its contract to Access. Similarly, a subcontractor responsible for plumbing might default on a contract with a general contractor causing it to default on a contract with the owner of the building to be renovated or constructed.

Some courts say the owner is a third-party beneficiary, some that the owner is not, and some allow recovery for negligence.[56] According to Eisenberg, the owner should not be able to recover. As he observed, normally, the general contractor is liable to the owner if the subcontractor defaults unless the general contractor can fix the problem that the subcontractor created and so avoid breaching itself.[57] Whether it can depends on the contractor's relationship with this subcontractor and others whom the contractor might hire. Therefore, the contractor is in a better position than the owner to assume the risk that a subcontractor might breach, which, by our approach, is what should matter.

The situation Eisenberg has in mind is one in which the subcontractor's work is incomplete or defective and can be fixed. If the owner were suing for losses suffered, for example, because a subcontractor's breach delayed completion of the project, as we have seen, the owner may not be able to recover those damages at all. As we have also seen, if the damages are disproportionately high, the subcontractor, rather than the general contractor, may be in the best position to bear that risk. In such situations, courts have denied recovery by saying that the damages were unforeseeable or uncertain, even when they actually were not. In situations where the owner can recover such damages from the general contractor, the owner still should not be able to do so from a subcontractor. The subcontractor who is to supply plumbing is in a worse position than the

[56] *Id.* at 768–69.
[57] *Id.* at 769.

general contractor to estimate the loss that the owner will suffer from a breach of contract and to adjust its bid to reflect that risk. It is in a position like that of Diemaker who is in a worse position to estimate the loss that will be caused if Martial cannot make toy soldiers.

Eisenberg made one exception. Suppose the subcontractor did defective work, and the defect is discovered only after the owner paid the general contractor the full contract price, and the general contractor became insolvent. The contractor's bankruptcy estate may not think it worthwhile to sue the subcontractor because it would be burdensome or because the recovery would be inconsequential. According to Eisenberg, the owner can recover as a matter of corrective justice if the general contractor's contract with the subcontractor limited damages by a liquidated damages clause or by excluding liability for consequential damages.[58]

What should matter is whether the subcontractor was paid to bear the risk that its own work would be defective. Presumably it was. While it may not be in the best position to estimate the loss that its breach might cause the owner if, for example, it delays completion of the project, it is in the best position to foresee and control the risk of a defect in its own work, and to spread the risk of fixing that defect over other contract it enters into, for example, for plumbing. If it is not held liable for a risk that it was paid to bear, then, as Eisenberg said, it will be unjustly enriched at another's expense.

Multi-prime contracts

In the hypothetical case considered earlier, Martial contracted with Diemaker to supply dies and Color to supply paints so that it could make toy soldiers. Diemaker's breach did not affect Color's ability to perform the contract, nor would a breach by Color affect Diemaker's ability. In contrast, when an owner undertaking a construction project hires a different prime contractor for different parts of the work instead of a general contractor, it often happens that a breach by one contractor causes another to default or to spend extra money to avoid breaching itself. The question arises whether that second contractor can sue the first as a third-party beneficiary of the first contractor's contract with the owner.

In such situations, most courts allow the second contractor to recover from the first. Eisenberg agreed.[59] He noted that if the first contractor breaches, the second contractor may have to incur extra costs to avoid breaching itself. The owner cannot recover the extra costs from the first contractor since it was not harmed by the first contractor's breach. Therefore, the second contractor

58 *Id.* at 769–70.
59 *Id.* at 767.

should recover as a third-party beneficiary of the owner's contract with the first contractor.

As Eisenberg noted, the first subcontractor will charge more if it is subject to the risk of liability to the second. The second subcontractor will charge less, however, if it does not bear the risk of incurring extra costs because of the first contractor's breach.[60] Again, risks should fall on the party who can bear them at the least cost, and it should be compensated for bearing them. Eisenberg's analysis explains why, by this approach, the second subcontractor should be liable.

There are circumstances, however, in which the second contractor is in a better position to run the risk of incurring these extra costs. It could be that a delay by the first contractor will cause a vast increase in the costs that the second contractor must incur. The second contractor may have been in a better position to anticipate and prevent them by a greater flexibility in its own planning or through contacts with possible subcontractors. The increased costs that another contractor will incur if the first contractor breaches may differ with each job the first contractor takes on. The costs the second contractor will incur if another party breaches may be similar from one job to another. For example, suppose that the first contractor is supposed to put a patch on the roof of a factory, and because it delays in doing so, the second contractor, who is installing machinery in the factory, must idle some very expensive equipment that could be damaged by rain. The cost of doing so is easier for the second contractor to anticipate and control. It is also a risk the second contractor will encounter whenever another contractor's breach delays installation. The risk of idling expensive machinery is not one that will frequently occur in the first contractor's other roofing contracts. Under these circumstances, the second contractor should not be able to recover.

Suits by subcontractors against the sureties of prime contractors

Another peculiarity of construction contracts is that the owner will often require that the general contractor obtain a performance or payment bond from a surety. A performance bond guarantees that the contract will be performed. A payment bond guarantees that the subcontractors will be paid. The question arises: can a subcontractor recover against the surety if the general contract becomes insolvent?

An owner who is a private person has a self-interested reason for requiring a payment bond. Subcontractors who are not paid will have a lien on the property if the general contractor becomes insolvent. In contrast, subcontractors often cannot have a lien against property owned by the government, and yet governments often require payment bonds. Some courts have concluded that a subcontractor should only be able to recover in public contracts. They have

[60] *Id.* at 767–78.

asked whether, in requiring a payment bond, the owner's intention is that the subcontractor be able to recover. In a public contract, it must be—they reason—because the subcontractor cannot acquire a lien against government property. In a private contract, the owner's intent is simply to prevent the subcontractor from acquiring a lien.[61]

Eisenberg's view is that the subcontractor should be able to recover in both public and private contracts. He has a good reason why such a rule would be in a government's self-interest.

Someone has to bear the risk that the contractor will not pay the subcontractors: either the subcontractors themselves or the surety. It is likely that the surety can do so more easily. It is likely to be better informed about the financial conditions of the general contractor. The surety can spread the risk that a general contractor will become insolvent over a larger number of general contractors than any subcontractor. Consequently, the owner will pay less by obtaining a payment bond that ensures the subcontractors will be paid than it would if the subcontractors increased their prices for fear they would not be paid.[62] If the surety is paid an additional amount for assuming that risk, then, by our approach, it should be liable to the subcontractors. The argument works equally well with private contractors.[63]

It may be that the owner required the general contractor to obtain a performance bond but not a payment bond, and the performance bond is silent as to whether the surety will be liable if the subcontractors are not paid. In that situation, as Eisenberg noted, it should not be liable to them. The owner required only a performance bond and not a payment bond instead of requiring both. Consequently, the owner did not pay for the surety to assume that risk.[64]

[61] *Id.* at 764–65.
[62] *Id.* at 765.
[63] *Id.*
[64] *Id.* at 766.

PART III

THE CONTENT OF A CONTRACT

9
Duties

I. "Subjective" and "objective" theories

As we saw in Part I, the nineteenth century was an age of will theories. Contract was defined in terms of the will or consent or promises of the parties. The idea that the parties enter into a contract by expressing their will or giving their consent was not new. The innovation was to think that the will of the parties is the source of all of their obligations.

One problem, as we have seen, is that sometimes the parties are not bound by terms to which they actually did agree. The terms are unfair. Another problem is that sometimes the parties are bound by many obligations which they did not actually intend. The language of their contract must be applied to situations they never consciously considered. For example, unless their contract provides otherwise, the parties to a sale or lease or partnership are bound by all the terms that the law of sale, lease, or partnership reads into their contract. As Samuel Williston pointed out, the source of these obligations could not be the parties' actual or "subjective" intent unless we assume that they knew the terms the law would read into their contract when they contracted. But "[t]o assume first that everybody knows the law, and, second, that everybody thereupon makes his contract with reference to it and adopts its provisions as terms of the agreement, is indeed to pile fiction upon fiction."[1]

One response was the formulation of "objective theories" of contract. The will of the parties does not matter. A contract is the legal effect that the law gives to their words and actions whatever their intentions have been. Oliver Wendell Holmes developed such a theory, and Williston accepted it. According to Williston, in interpreting the language of the contract "[t]he only meaning which is generally pertinent is the meaning of the language when judged by the standard adopted by the law." When the contract is silent, the obligations of the parties are those that the law reads into it whatever the parties intended.

The will theorists never answered Holmes's and Willison's objections. Charles Fried subscribed to a modernized will theory in which promises are binding because the promisor's freedom is thereby increased. He admitted that his theory could not explain the terms that a court reads into a contract. No one should

[1] 2 Samuel Williston, The Law of Contract § 615 (1920).

Foundations of American Contract Law. James Gordley, Oxford University Press. © Oxford University Press 2023.
DOI: 10.1093/oso/9780197686089.003.0009

make "the futile attempt to bring these cases under the promise principle."[2] If he is right, then, as his critics have pointed, the promise principle cannot explain most of contract law.[3] As Richard Craswell observed:

> Theories that explain the binding force of promises by pointing to the value of individual freedom . . . may well be valid answers to the question of why promises are binding. But . . . freedom can usually be served equally well by any background rule, so some other value must be introduced to explain why any one rule ought to be chosen over any other.[4]

Nevertheless, the objective theories were not a viable alternative. To say the meaning of the language of a contract depends on "the standard adopted by the law" or that the parties are bound by whatever obligations the law imposes does not answer the questions: What standards should the law adopt? What obligations should the law impose? As Craswell noted, "to endorse an objective approach is merely to identify one factor—the secret, subjective intention of either party—which should not be used as a reason for preferring one rule over another. It says nothing about which factors should be considered."[5]

Randy Barnett tried to find a middle ground between "an exclusively subjectivist conception of consent"[6] and objective theory. He claimed that a contract should be interpreted to conform to "the common-sense or conventional understanding of persons belonging to the parties' community of discourse."[7] To do so would "best reflect the subjective understanding actually shared by the parties" and "bring the enforcement of the parties' manifested consent into closer correspondence with their subjective intentions."[8] " 'Common sense,' " he said, "simply means the sense of things that most people share in common."[9] The difficulty, however, is that the parties may have no subjective understanding—common sense or otherwise—of how to deal with a contingency that they never considered. Distinctions may be important for achieving the purposes for which they contracted that are not be reflected in the "conventional understanding"

[2] CHARLES FRIED, CONTRACT AS PROMISE: A THEORY OF CONTRACTUAL OBLIGATION 60–61, 63, 69 (1981).

[3] *See* Melvin A. Eisenberg, *Theory of Contracts*, *in* THE THEORY OF CONTRACT LAW 206, 279 (Peter Benson ed., 2001). *See also* Conrad Johnson, *The Idea of Autonomy and the Foundations of Contractual Liability*, 2 L. & PHIL. 271, 300 (1983).

[4] Richard Craswell, *Contract Law, Default Rules, and the Philosophy of Promising*, 88 MICH. L. REV. 489, 528 (1989).

[5] *Id.*

[6] Randy E. Barnett, *The Sound of Silence: Default Rules and Contractual Consent*, 78 VA. L. REV. 821, 898 (1992).

[7] Randy E. Barnett, *Conflicting Visions: A Critique of Ian Macneil's Relational Theory of Contract*, 78 VA. L. REV. 1175, 1176 (1992).

[8] *Id.*

[9] *Id.* at 880.

of other "persons belonging to the parties' community of discourse." Moreover, "most people" other than lawyers do not have any clear idea what terms the law will read into sales, leases, partnerships, and so forth, to deal with matters the parties themselves did not consider.

These questions are commonly resolved in a way that appeals neither to "subjective" nor to "objective" theorists. Courts ask what the parties would have intended if they had considered a situation that has arisen but which they never actually considered. What they would have intended is called their "hypothetical intent" as distinguished from their "actual" intent which is what they really did consider. As David Cherney said:

> lawyers ask what would the parties have agreed to had they explicitly adverted to the issue? That is, the interpreter constructs a "hypothetical bargain": he determines how the parties would have bargained to treat the situation that has arisen had it been directly presented to them at the time they were forming the contract.[10]

For will theorists, whatever the parties "hypothetically" intend should not matter because they did not really intend it at all. Charney asked:

> Why are we bound by obligations to which we did not assent *explicitly*, but only hypothetically? It is by no means clear that individuals should be bound to hypothetical—as contrasted to actual—contracts, or even that it is appropriate to call such hypothetical contracts "contracts" at all.[11]

"[A]utonomy- or rights-based arguments for promissory obligation" like those of Fried "do not readily extend to merely hypothetical agreements."[12]For objective theorists, to speak of hypothetical intent is one more flawed attempt to explain contractual obligations by the intentions of the parties. Ian Macneil pointed out, however, that it is just as fictitious to claim, like the objective theorists, that the parties' obligations come from "the law" as to claim, like the subjective theorists, that they come from the will of the parties:

> [T]he limited extent to which it is possible for people to consent to all the terms of a transaction, even a relatively simple and very discrete one, soon forces the development of legal fictions expanding the scope of "consent" far beyond anything remotely close to what the parties ever had in mind. The greatest of these

10 David Charny, *Hypothetical Bargains: The Normative Structure of Contract Interpretation*, 89 MICH. L. REV. 1815, 1815–16 (1991).

11 *Id.* at 1817.

12 *Id.*

in American law is the objective theory of contract. The classical American contract is founded not upon *actual* consent but upon objective manifestations of intent. Moreover, in classical law manifestations of intent include whole masses of contract content one, or even both, parties did not know in fact.[13]

But that leaves us nowhere. As Eric Posner said:

> If Macneil is right, and courts cannot resolve contractual disputes by discovering initial contractual intentions on the basis of documents and other evidence, cannot use such intentions (even if they exist) to guide behavior late in the life of a relational contract . . . cannot fill in gaps by imagining the hypothetical bargain—then what should the courts do?[14]

We will first examine how courts can determine the parties' actual intention when the words they used do not indicate it clearly. We will then see how courts deal with situations which the parties themselves never considered. As Charny said, they often ask what the parties would have intended if they had done so. We will see why they should.

II. Actual intent

The parties may have been clear in their own minds about the terms on which they meant to contract but their language may have been imprecise. They used a term that was clear to themselves but not to the court.

To determine what they did have in mind, the court may look to the context in which a term was used, trade custom, prior dealing between the parties, negotiations between them, or the plausibility that a party would intend terms that did not answer to that party's purpose or were patently disadvantageous. According to the *Restatement (Second) of Contracts*, a court may consider "any relevant course of performance, course of dealing, or usage of trade."[15] It may consider "the principal purpose of the parties."[16] Here, we will only consider how these considerations can indicate what the parties actually had in mind, as

[13] Ian R. Macneil, *Contracts: Adjustment of Long-term Economic Relations Under Classical, Neoclassical, and Relational Contract Law*, 72 Nw. U. L. Rev. 854, 883–84 (1978). Macneil's views on consent are rather mysterious, but, as Barnett noted, in this passage he implies that actual consent is subjective consent. Barnett, *supra* note 7, at 1183.

[14] Eric A. Posner, *A Theory of Contract Law Under Conditions of Radical Judicial Error*, 94 Nw. U. L. Rev. 749, 751 (2000).

[15] Restatement (Second) of Contracts § 202(5) (Am. Law Inst. 1981).

[16] *Id.* at § 202(1).

opposed to what they might have intended had they dealt with a situation that they did not actually consider.

One consideration is the context in which a term was used. In *Davis v. Outboard Marine Corp.*,[17] the court said it was "absurd" to think that the contract was made in American dollars since it was an insurance contract in which the insurer and the named insured were "Canadian corporations with principal places of business in Canada." The court used the context to discover their actual intention: it is unlikely that they did not know whether they meant Canadian or American dollars.

Another consideration is trade custom and any prior dealings between the parties. In *Higgins v. California Petroleum & Asphalt Co.*,[18] the contract price was $0.50 for every ton of asphaltium mined. A "ton" can mean an ordinary ton of 2,000 pounds or a gross ton of 2,400 pounds. The court admitted evidence of custom and previous dealings to discover what they intended, meaning, again, their actual intent. It is unlikely that they did not know which sort of ton they had in mind.

The court considered prior negotiations between the parties in *Paul W. Abbott, Inc. v. Axel Newman Heating & Plumbing Co.*[19] A construction contract called for "all domestic water piping and rainwater piping installed above finished ceilings" to be insulated. The question was whether the piping to be insulated was only the rainwater piping or the domestic water piping as well. During negotiations and before submitting a bid, the contractor had asked about the extent of the job and was "advised . . . that insulation was to be installed on all domestic water piping, and on rainwater piping installed above finished ceilings." This evidence showed what the parties actually intended. It is unlikely that the parties would have agreed on a price for the job without knowing the extent of the work to be done.

Another consideration in determining the parties' actual intent is the purpose that the parties were trying to achieve. They are likely to have had in mind something that would serve that purpose. In *Udell v. Cohen*,[20] the seller of 10,000 single and approximately 10,000 double burner heaters "all in perfect condition" claimed that he only needed to deliver 1,756 of the one and 3,074 of the other since those were the only ones that he had that were in "perfect condition." It is unlikely that these words were put in the contract to save him the trouble of counting the number in perfect condition in advance. The court construed the term as a warranty: all 10,000 must be in perfect condition.

Another such consideration is whether a term is fair. It is unlikely that a party consciously intended to be bound by terms that are clearly disadvantageous to

17 415 N.W.2d 719 (Minn. App. 1987).
18 52 P. 1080 (Cal. 1898).
19 166 N.W.2d 323 (Minn. 1969).
20 122 N.Y.S.2d 552 (S.Ct. 1953) (per curiam).

them. In *Hardin v. Dimension Lumber Co.*,[21] a logger bought timber which he was to cut and remove for $1.25 per 1,000 feet. He claimed he needed to pay only $1,400 rather than over $4,000 because an unfortunately drafted clause in the contract said, "the entire sale and purchase price of said timber is $1400.00." It was followed by a provision that required the logger to pay that amount even if it amounted to more than $1.25 times the amount of timber he actually did cut and remove. It is understandable for the parties to agree that the logger would receive $1,400 however little timber he took. It is hard to understand why a seller would agree to pay him that amount for however much he took.

One obstacle to taking such considerations into account is the widely accepted "plain meaning" rule. According to the rule, if a word has a plain meaning, a court should not consider any evidence outside of the contract to see whether the parties used that word in any other sense. If a court had applied the plain meaning rule in the cases we have discussed, it would first have considered whether there might be a "plain meaning" to phrases such as "dollars," "tons, "all domestic water piping and rainwater piping installed above finished ceilings," and 10,000 burners" "all in perfect condition." If it thought so, it would ignore context, custom, prior dealings, and prior negotiations. It would not ask whether another meaning best served the parties' purposes or avoided a result that was clearly against the interests of one of them. The rule is an obstacle to determining what the parties actually intended. Later we will see that it is an obstacle to determining what they hypothetically intended.

III. Hypothetical intent

As noted earlier, when a situation arises that the parties did not actually consider, courts ask about their "hypothetical intention." What would they have intended if they had considered that situation? This approach is the right one, despite the objections discussed earlier.

To determine what the parties hypothetically intended, a court must ask what purpose they actually intended to accomplish when they contracted. They should then ask what means is most appropriate to effectuate that purpose. In scholastic vocabulary the distinction is between what a person "actually" intends and what a person "virtually" intends.

In ordinary speech we slip back and forth between the one meaning of intent and the other. If a person tells their travel agent to book them the next direct flight to Denver, and the travel agent books United Airlines Flight 296 to Denver leaving at 2:00, the travel agent has done what the client intended if that is the

[21] 13 P.2d 602 (Or. 1932).

next direct flight. The client did not actually intend United Flight 296. But the client did so "virtually" or "hypothetically." A client who wanted the next direct flight to Denver would have wanted Flight 296.

David Charney noted that there are two situations in which courts find it necessary to go beyond the actual intention of the parties: when "ambiguous" language in the contract must be applied to a "contingency . . . which they did not consciously envision," and when "there is a contingency that no language in the contract addresses."[22] We will consider them in turn.

i. Ambiguous language

Although the parties might have understood perfectly well how a term of their contract applies in one situation, a situation may then arise which is similar in some respects and different in others from the situation they had distinctly in mind. The language of their contract should be read to include this new situation if it is not different in any relevant respect from the one they consciously considered. "Relevant" means relevant given the purposes that they were trying to achieve when they used the term that they did.

For example, *Kirke La Shelle Co. v. Paul Armstrong Co.*[23] concerned the rights to a play, *Alias Jimmy Valentine*. One party was to have the right to approve any "contracts" made by the other for "the dramatic rights (exclusive of motion picture rights)" to the play "or the production of the said plays in New York City, 'on the road' or 'in stock.'"[24] After the contract was signed, talking motion pictures were invented. The court held, correctly, that the phrase "motion picture rights" did not apply to talking pictures. Since they were not yet invented, the parties could not have been using the phrase to include them. Nor were the purposes of the parties in excluding the right to silent pictures served by excluding the right to talking pictures.

In an English case,[25] an advertising agency contracted to fly an airplane towing a banner that read "Eat Batchelor's Peas" during a nine-month period. Due to an oversight, it flew on Armistice Day when crowds were observing two minutes of silence during memorial services, The agency was held liable for damages to Batchelor's public image. The language of the contract did not distinguish between a flight on Armistice Day and a flight on any other day during the nine-month period. The parties did not consciously consider whether there should be

[22] *Id.* at 816.
[23] 188 N.E. 163 (N.Y. 1933).
[24] *Id.* at 165.
[25] Aerial Advertising Co. v. Batchelor's Peas, [1938] 2 All E.R. 788 (K.B. 1938).

a flight on Armistice Day. But the distinction mattered in a contract to provide advertising.

The "plain meaning" rule is an obstacle to determining the hypothetical intent of the parties just as it is to determining their actual intent. According to this rule, if the words have a "plain meaning," a court should not consider other evidence of what the parties meant. The rule considers the meaning of a word in abstraction from the purposes of the particular parties. To do so can give the wrong result for it may be that a distinction that matters for their purposes does not matter when people ordinarily use the word.

An illustration is *Highly v. Phillips*.[26] The plaintiff sold all the "dirt" on a parcel of land for $500. The defendant removed 10,000 tons of sand of sufficiently high quality that it could be used for making concrete. It had a market value of $0.25 a ton. The court should have asked, did the parties consciously consider the possibility that the parcel might contain sand? If so, the buyer was entitled to as much as it contained. If not, then the parties never meant to sell or buy sand. The distinction mattered for the purposes of the parties because sand was worth much more than dirt. Instead, the court relied on the plain meaning rule: Words will be given their ordinary meaning when nothing appears to show that they are used in a different sense."[27] It quoted from the *New Standard Dictionary*, *Webster's New International Dictionary*, the *New Century Dictionary*, the *Winston Universal Reference Library*, and concluded: "the authorities generally treat the words 'dirt' and 'earth' as representing interchangeable terms; each of them signifying 'loose earth' as distinguished from the 'firm rock.'"[28] Therefore, when the contract referred to "dirt" it included "sand." One problem with this analysis is that all the dictionaries did show is that, in ordinary speech, it is common to distinguish both "dirt" and "earth" from "firm rock." They did not show whether or not it is common to distinguish "dirt" from "sand." Nevertheless, even it were uncommon, one could only conclude that for ordinary purposes the distinction between dirt and sand usually does not matter. It could matter when one is selling dirt or sand.

In *Lawrence v. Cain*,[29] the issue was whether a covenant not to compete by taking "school photographs" was violated by taking photographs at a college graduation. The court should have asked whether the reason the parties prohibited school photographs carried over to college photographs. If the distinction did not matter for their purposes, college photographs should be covered. Instead, the court applied the plain meaning rule. "[T]he word 'school' by common usage, is considered local school corporations and does not generally

[26] 5 A.2d 824 (Md. 1939).

[27] *Id.* at 829.

[28] *Id.* at 827–28.

[29] 245 N.E.2d 663 (Ind. App. 1969).

include higher seats of learning which are usually referred to as colleges or universities."[30] Therefore, the contract did not cover them. There are, indeed, many purposes for which it is useful to distinguish "schools" from "colleges or universities," and that is why common usage draws such a distinction. But what is important is whether the distinction mattered from the standpoint of the parties.

The plain meaning rule was defended by the proponents of the "objective theory" of contract which was described earlier. They believed that even the actual intention of the parties did not matter. They defined a contract as the consequences to be attached to the words the parties used regardless of their meaning to the parties themselves. According to Judge Learned Hand:

> It makes not the least difference whether a promisor actually intends that meaning which the law will impose upon his words. The whole House of Bishops might satisfy us that he had intended something else, and it would make not a particle of difference in his obligation. . . . Hence it follows that no declaration of the promisor as to his meaning when he used the words is of the slightest relevancy, however formally competent it may be as an admission. Indeed, if both parties severally declared that their meaning had been other than the natural meaning, and each declaration was similar, it would be irrelevant . . . [and w]hen the court came to assign the meaning to their words, it would disregard such declarations, because they related only to their state of mind when the contract was made, and that has nothing to do with their obligations.[31]

As we have seen, the objective theory does not explain why the law attaches the meaning to a contract that it does. Consequently, even if one grants that the parties are bound, not by what they intended, but to the legal effect of their words, the objective theory does not explain why the legal effect should depend on their plain meaning. Nor does it explain why the parties should be bound to consequences that they never intended.

One reason might be that one of the parties was misled. A party attached the "plain meaning" to a term in the contract which, to the other party, meant something else. This is a different problem and one to which we will return later. It is the problem of what a court should do when the actual intent of one party conflicts with that of another. Here, the problem is what to do if the parties' actual intent is the same but a situation arises which they did not consciously consider.

30 *Id.* at 666.

31 Eustis Mining Co. v. Beer, Sondheimer & Co., 239 F. 976, 984–85 (S.D.N.Y. 1917).

Eric Posner claimed that although "[l]iteral enforcement also produces error . . . at least this error would be predictable."[32] In the cases that we are considering, however, the errors produced by the plain meaning rule would not be predictable by the contracting parties. The problem is what to do with a situation they did not consider. They will not have considered the errors a literal reading of their contract might create, and, if they did, they would have resolved the problem themselves.

Some critics of the plain meaning rule have gone so far as to claim that words have no meaning aside from the one the parties attached to them in the particular context in which the words were used. Judge Alex Kozinski accused Judge Roger Traynor of doing so. Traynor said in *Pacific Gas & Electric Co. v. G.W. Thomas Drayage and Rigging Co.*:

> Words . . . do not have absolute and constant referents. . . . The meaning of particular words or groups of words varies with the "verbal context and surrounding circumstances and purposes in view of the linguistic education and experience of their users and their hearers or readers (not excluding judges). . . . A word has no meaning apart from these factors; much less does it have an objective meaning, one true meaning."[33]

The plain meaning rule "is a remnant of a primitive faith in the inherent potency and inherent meaning of words."[34]

According to Kozinski:

> [*Pacific Gas*] chips away at the foundation of our legal system. By giving credence to the idea that words are inadequate to express concepts, *Pacific Gas* undermines the basic principle that language provides a meaningful constraint on public and private conduct. If we are unwilling to say that parties, dealing face to face, can come up with language that binds them, how can we send anyone to jail for violating statutes consisting of mere words lacking "absolute and constant referents"? How can courts ever enforce decrees, not written in language understandable to all, but encoded in a dialect reflecting only the "linguistic background of the judge"? Can lower courts ever be faulted for failing to carry out the mandate of higher courts when "perfect verbal expression" is impossible? Are all attempts to develop the law in a reasoned and

[32] Posner, *supra* note 14, at 752.

[33] 442 P.2d 641, 644–45 (Cal. 1968), citing Arthur Corbin, *The Interpretation of Words and the Parol Evidence Rule*, 50 CORNELL L.Q. 161, 197 (1965).

[34] 442 P.2d at 643–44.

> principled fashion doomed to failure as "remnant[s] of a primitive faith in the inherent potency and inherent meaning of words"?[35]

Traynor is right that the meaning of a word depends on what the speaker was using it to convey, and that this meaning depends on the context. In the context of making a contract, however, the parties wish to convey their meaning to a third party, such as a judge, as, in Kozinski's examples, the drafters of criminal statutes wish to convey their meaning to those who are to obey and enforce them, and higher courts wish to convey their meaning to lower courts, among others. Their ability to do so does not presuppose "the inherent potency and the inherent meaning of words." Because the contracting parties do wish to convey their meaning to others, they will use language that they believe other people, such as judges, will understand. For that reason, the language they used is most often better evidence of what they meant than anything that extrinsic evidence can supply.

But it is only evidence of their intent. Since the words of a contract were written to be understood by others, it is likely that they meant what they seem to say. The trouble with the plain meaning rule is that sometimes they do not.

According to Kozinski, an advantage of the plain meaning rule is that it prevents the court from making an erroneous judgment about what the parties meant based on extrinsic evidence.

> Under *Pacific Gas*, it matters not how clearly a contract is written, nor how completely it is integrated, nor how carefully it is negotiated, nor how squarely it addresses the issue before the court: the contract cannot be rendered impervious to attack by parol evidence. If one side is willing to claim that the parties intended one thing but the agreement provides for another, the court must consider extrinsic evidence of possible ambiguity. If that evidence raises the specter of ambiguity where there was none before, the contract language is displaced and the intention of the parties must be divined from self-serving testimony offered by partisan witnesses whose recollection is hazy from passage of time and colored by their conflicting interests.[36]

Certainly, judges should attach more weight to the language of a clearly written, completely integrated, carefully negotiated contract and less weight to the self-serving testimony of witnesses who have dim memories or are biased by self-interest. In such a case, they should conclude that the parties meant what they said. In other cases, they will need to look further.

[35] Trident Center v. Connecticut General Life Ins. Co., 847 F.2d. 564, 569 (9th Cir. 1988).
[36] *Id.* at 569.

ii. Omitted terms

In the case of omitted terms, as in the case of ambiguous language, the law should ask about the hypothetical intent of the parties. What terms would they have chosen if they had considered such a contingency? The justification is the same as before. The terms that the parties would have chosen are those that are most appropriate for carrying out the purpose which they actually intended to achieve when they entered into a contract. Parties with that purpose would want to be bound by such terms.

The terms of a contract allocate risks and burdens to one party or the other. As economists say, and as we saw in Part I, parties who consider a risk in advance will place it on the party who can bear it most easily. They will then adjust the price to compensate that party for doing so. We saw in Part I that if a term in a contract does not place a risk on the party who can most easily do so, it is a sign that this party was not compensated for bearing that risk. The contract was unconscionable, and a court should give relief.

When the parties did not consider a risk, and so their contract does not contain a term to deal with it, a court should supply a term that places the risk on the party that can bear it at the lowest cost. That party may not have been compensated for bearing that risk since the parties did not consciously consider it. Even then, the risk will have been placed where it will cause the smaller loss. That is where the parties would have wished it to fall.

Moreover, the party who can best bear the risk may have been compensated for bearing it even though the parties did not have that specific risk in mind. As we saw in Part I, one reason a party may be best able to bear a risk is that he is best able to foresee it. A risk is lower for the party who can best foresee it for roughly the same reason that the risk of playing poker is lower for someone who can peek at the other players' cards. The party who can best foresee the risk may have taken it into account along with all the other risks they could foresee in setting his prices, although they did not contemplate them all when the contract was drafted.

A party who can best control a risk can bear it more easily. The costs that a party incurred to control that risk will be reflected in the contract price along with other costs although the party may not have been thinking of any one of them.

A party who encounters a risk repeatedly in similar transactions will also be able to bear it more easily by self-insuring or buying insurance against it. The cost of doing so may be reflected in the contract price even though at the time they contracted the parties did not consider that risk.

Much of the rest of this book will be concerned with which party can bear a risk most easily. That consideration is the key to understanding terms such as warranties that define the extent of the performance a party must make. The extent of the duty should depend upon which risks each party can best assume. It is the key to understanding a party's liability for failing to perform. The consequences of a failure to perform should be borne by the party that can bear that risk most easily. The two questions are inseparable.

Those who explain law in terms of economic efficiency also believe that when a contract is silent, risks should be placed on the party that can bear them most easily. As Eric Posner said:

> maximiz[ing] the ex ante value of the contract . . . usually means allocating obligations in a way that places the risk of any contingency on the party that can most cheaply bear it and that gives the parties proper incentives to breach, invest, and engage in related behavior.[37]

The difference is that economists are concerned with efficiency. They can explain why it is efficient ex ante for the parties to place a risk on whomever can most easily bear it. As we saw earlier, they cannot explain why it is efficient for a court to do so ex post. Ex post, a risk has materialized, a loss has been incurred, and the question is which party will bear it. Placing it on one party or the other does not affect efficiency unless, in anticipation of that loss, one of the parties is given an incentive to act differently in a way that will minimize the total costs that the parties incur. In and of itself, the fact that that one party will become richer or poorer ex post does not matter. It is neither efficient nor inefficient.

Some claim that to place risks ex post on the party who can most easily bear them is efficient because it will save drafting costs. Ex ante, the parties would place risks on that party, and therefore, if they are afraid that courts will not do so ex post, they will waste time ex ante negotiating and drafting terms themselves. According to Charles Goetz and Robert Scott, "gap filling" rules "serve the important purpose of saving most bargainers the cost of negotiating a tailor-made arrangement."[38] As Scott summarized this approach:

> One strategy is . . . to achieve ex ante efficiency. This strategy is designed to protect (and even improve) the utility of the set of contractual signals for future parties. . . . If so, the law ought to adopt the rule that the broadest number of parties would adopt were transactions costs low enough for negotiators to tailor-make their own rules. A legal rule mirroring what most parties would

[37] Posner, *supra* note 14, at 756.

[38] Charles J. Goetz & Robert E. Scott, *Principles of Relational Contracts*, 67 VA. L. REV. 1089, 1090 (1981).

adopt where transactions costs are low saves those parties the time, cost, and error inherent in negotiating contract terms and reducing them to writing.[39]

Charney objected that it is not "clear—from a consequentialist perspective—that a rule implying obligations to which transactors 'would have assented' generally will reduce, rather than increase, the costs of transacting."[40] Be that as it may, according to the economic explanation, there is only a gain in efficiency when a risk is so important that the parties would incur extra drafting costs to deal with it in advance. They would not do so if the risk and its consequences are sufficiently remote. In that event, it would not matter from the standpoint of efficiency how a court allocated the risk ex post. Moreover, if the economic explanation were correct, although vast amounts of money may be at stake in the court's decision, all that would matter is the possibility that parties might incur unnecessary drafting costs in future cases. The only reason for believing that all that matters is to avoid these costs is that, from an economic standpoint, it is all that could matter. That explanation could only appeal to a person deeply committed to the economic approach.

According to the *Restatement Second*, when a contract is silent, a court should consider not only the hypothetical intent of the parties but also whether a term to be supplied would be fair. It implies that these approaches are alternative, and that there is a conflict between them.

> Sometimes it is said that the search is for the term the parties would have agreed to if the question had been brought to their attention. . . . [T]he probability that a particular term would have been used if the question had been raised may be factors in determining what term is reasonable in the circumstances. But where there is in fact no agreement, the court should supply a term which comports with community standards of fairness and policy rather than analyze a hypothetical model of the bargaining process.[41]

This passage misconceives the way in which a court should "search for the term the parties would have agreed to if the question had been brought to their attention." The parties would have placed the risk on whomever could bear it most easily. To ask which party could do so is not to speculate on the outcome of a "hypothetical bargaining process." A term is fair when the party who bears the risk is compensated for doing so, or, at least, the risk is placed where the loss

[39] Robert E. Scott, *The Case for Formalism in Relational Contract*, 94 Nw. U. L. Rev. 847, 850 (2000).

[40] David Charny, *Hypothetical Bargains: The Normative Structure of Contract Interpretation*, 89 Mich. L. Rev. 1815, 1817 (1991).

[41] Restatement (Second) of Contracts § 204 cmt. d (Am. Law Inst. 1981).

will be the smallest. The reason it is fair is not because it reflects "community standards." In any event, the *Restatement*'s appeal to "community standards" is like Barnett's appeal to the "common sense" of "most people." Neither the community nor most people are likely to have any clear idea about how risks that the parties themselves did not consider should be fairly allocated.

Peter Gerhart agreed that a court should supply terms that are fair. He observed correctly that when "performance obligations" are "unaddressed" by the parties, "the goal . . . is to preserve the ex ante balance of benefits and burdens that each party bargained for in the exchange, the ex ante exchange equilibrium." He has a different idea, however, of what terms preserve the ex ante equilibrium and why the parties would want to adopt them. According to Gerhart, equilibrium is created and preserved by "other-regarding or values-balancing reasoning" in which each party "appreciate[s] both parties' private projects but d[oes] not know which private project would be favored by the reconciliation of values."[42] "The other regarding person does this by means of the thought process behind the veil of ignorance, a process that ensures that the appraisal of conflicting values is neutral."[43] "The veil of ignorance [i]s the core concept that other-regarding persons will undertake when they have made promises."[44]

The "veil of ignorance," for Gerhart as for John Rawls, is a metaphor that means a fair solution is neutral: no party's concerns are given more weight than any other's. The question, however, is what terms are neutral. The answer is to be found, not by asking what they would do behind a veil of ignorance, but by asking who could bear a risk at the lowest cost. That is where the parties themselves would have placed the risk even if they were not particularly concerned about fairness. They need not be "other regarding people" or be put behind a veil of ignorance to arrive at a fair result.

IV. The duty to perform in good faith

i. The doctrine and its purposes

According to the *Second Restatement*: "Every contract imposes upon each party a duty of good faith and fair dealing in its performance and its enforcement."[45] In virtually every state, a contract is deemed to include an implied covenant of good faith and fair dealing.

[42] Peter M. Gerhart, Contract Law and Social Morality 69 (2021).
[43] *Id.*
[44] *Id.* at 65.
[45] Restatement (Second) of Contracts § 503 (Am. Law Inst. 1981).

This implied duty serves the same purpose as the other terms that are read into a contract. Supplying such a term is the most appropriate means for accomplishing the end for which the parties contracted.

In one respect, however, recognizing that the parties are under a duty to act in good faith is different than supplying the other terms that we have considered. Those terms could have been provided by the parties themselves if they had considered a question in advance. The most puzzling applications of the doctrine of good faith are in situations in which the parties could not have done so.

In one situation, the parties would not have wanted to provide all the terms of the contract in advance because they wished their obligations to be more flexible. To provide flexibility, they wished to confer discretion on one of the parties to decide later on what some terms of the contract would be.

In another situation, to achieve the benefits for which they contracted, the parties must cooperate, and cooperate in ways that they cannot specify in advance. It would not be possible to describe in advance all things that each party must do or refrain from doing if they are to cooperate successfully.

We will examine how the duty to cooperate in good faith serves each of these purposes: to provide flexibility and to enable cooperation.

Providing flexibility

There are two ways to make a commitment more flexible by conferring discretion on one of the parties. A party can be required to exercise discretion according to a standard to be applied, not mechanically, but according to that party's best judgment. An example is an output or requirements contract in which one party determines the quantity to be bought or sold, and the standard is what that party produces or needs.

The other way is to allow a party to exercise discretion without regard to any such standard. An example is an option which a party can exercise only if it is advantageous. We will take them in turn.

Discretion to be exercised according to a standard

In *Feld v. Levy & Sons*,[46] the defendant agreed to sell all the breadcrumbs it produced. The contract could be terminated on six months' notice. When the seller found it "uneconomical" to produce breadcrumbs, and the buyer refused to pay a penny a pound more than the contract price, it shut down production and sold the raw material to an animal feed producer.

In the sale of a definite quantity of goods yet to be produced at a fixed price, the seller assumes two risks. One is that he could have sold the goods to someone else for a better price if he had waited. The other is that the goods will cost him

[46] 335 N.E.2d 320 (N.Y. 2009).

more to produce that he estimated. If he did not wish to assume either of these risks, his contract would not be an output contract but an option. If he did not wish to assume the second, he would have contracted to be paid cost-plus rather than fixed price. In *Feld*, the seller tried to escape the risk that a party selling at a fixed price normally assumes and which he was compensated to bear. The court held correctly that he did not act in good faith. Peter Gerhart observed that the seller should have prevailed if he "lowered the price of breadcrumbs in order to buy the freedom to terminate the contract without notice."[47]But, then, in return for lowering his price, he would have entered into an option rather than an output contract or a contract cost-plus rather than fixed price.[48]

In an output or requirements contract, unlike an option, the seller or buyer must exercise discretion according to a standard. That requirement predates the *Uniform Commercial Code* (*UCC*).[49] According to the *UCC*, the quantity supplied or ordered must be:

> such actual output or requirements as may occur in good faith, except that no quantity unreasonably disproportionate to any stated estimate, or in the absence of a stated estimate to any normal or otherwise comparable prior output or requirements may be tendered or demanded.[50]

Nevertheless, in an output or requirements contract all that is necessary is that there be a standard. A party who supplies or orders an amount that is not proportionate to a stated estimate or its normal output or requirements may still be acting in good faith.

In *Feld v. Levy & Sons*,[51] the defendant agreed to sell all the breadcrumbs it produced. As the court noted, breadcrumbs are "a manufactured item, starting with stale or imperfectly appearing loaves and followed by removal of labels, processing through two grinders, the second of which effects a finer granulation, insertion into a drum in an oven for toasting and, finally, bagging of the finished product."[52] Consequently, the standard was not its "normal or . . . prior output" but the number of stale and imperfect loaves available to produce them.

In *New York Central Ironworks Co. v. United States Radiator Co.*,[53] the court upheld the contract even though the buyer required 100,000 "feet of radiation"

[47] GERHART, *supra* note 42, at 140-41..

[48] Also, for the reason just explained, it is unlikely that he did. If so, Gerhart said, "the seller is likely to have evidence to that effect available." *Id.* at 141. That evidence would have to be convincing indeed..

[49] Brawley v. United States, 96 U.S. 168 (1877); New York Central Ironworks Co. v. United States Radiator Co., 66 N.E. 967, 968 (N.Y. 1903).

[50] U.C.C. § 2–306 (AM. LAW INST. & UNIF. L. COMM'N 1977).

[51] 335 N.E.2d 320 (N.Y. 2009).

[52] *Id.* at 321.

[53] 66 N.E. 967, 968 (N.Y. 1903).

and the most it had ever required before was 48,000 feet. "After the execution of the contract there was a large advance" in the price of "radiation." There was no evidence, however, that the buyer increased the quantity he purchased, not because his needs increased, but rather to take advantage of the rise in prices.[54] That was so, even though the buyer may have needed more because the price of his own product had risen and so it became advantageous to him to produce more. He profited from a change in the market price, but he was not ordering more simply because the market price had changed.

So long as there is a standard, a party whose output or needs are disproportionate to a "stated estimate" may still be acting in good faith. In the early case of *Brawley v. United States*,[55] the plaintiff agreed to supply Fort Pembina in Dakota Territory with 880 cords of oak wood "more or less, as shall be determined to be necessary, by the post-commander." The post-commander determined that only forty cords were needed. The court held that as 880 was "only an estimate of the probable amount," the army could take only forty.[56] "[S]o long as [it] acts in good faith," in both making the estimate and in determining how many cords were needed, the buyer could take only what it needed.[57]

Rather than leave the quantity to be determined according to some standard, the parties may do so with the price. As with an output or requirements contract, a party who deviates from that standard acts in bad faith.

Neither the standard that should govern determination of the price nor the duty to act in good faith needs to be set out in the contract. In *Best v. United States National Bank of Oregon*,[58] a depositor claimed that a bank had abused its authority to set fees for checks drawn on insufficient funds (NSF fees) by charging far more than its costs plus a reasonable profit. According to the court, the Bank did not act in good faith if the depositors "reasonably expected that the Bank's NSF fees would be priced . . . to cover the Bank's NSF check processing costs plus an allowance for overhead costs plus the Bank's ordinary profit margin on checking account services."[59]

There is an ongoing controversy as to whether the duty of good faith can be violated only by one who acts dishonestly, that is, by one who knowingly does what is wrong.[60] As Robert Summers said, "[m]any theorists have been tempted

54 *Id.* at 968.

55 96 U.S. 168 (1877).

56 *Id.* at 771.

57 *Id.* at 172.

58 739 P.2d 554 (Or. 1987).

59 *Id.* at 555–56.

60 *E.g.*, Thomas A. Diamond & Howard Foss, *Proposed Standards for Evaluating When the Covenant of Good Faith and Fair Dealing Has Been Violated: A Framework for Resolving the Mystery*, 47 HASTINGS L.J. 585, 602, 614. (1996)(distinguishing two types of bad faith: "commercial unreasonableness" which does not require "dishonesty," and "dishonesty" or "causing contractual injury through deceptive or disingenuous means"); Teri J. Dobbins, *Losing Faith: Extracting the Implied*

to try to conceptualize . . . bad faith, partly in terms of some necessary or singular 'mental element,' such as a 'bad motive.'"[61] Some courts have recognized that when discretion must be exercised according to a standard, then that element should not be necessary. What matters to the other party is whether the standard was not observed, not why it was not.

An example is *Best*. All that mattered was that the bank charged higher fees than those to which it was entitled to according to the standard the depositors expected it to observe. The court said:

> It is . . . not necessarily sufficient, as the Bank contends, that the Bank acted honestly in setting its NSF fees. . . . Undoubtedly, parties to a contract always expect that the other party will perform the contract honestly and, where the performance of a commercial enterprise is at issue, ordinarily expect that it will do so in a commercially reasonable manner. But the reasonable expectations of the parties need not be so limited.[62]

In *Best*, the defendant was liable for deviating from the proper standard intentionally but not dishonestly. A defendant may also be liable when the deviation was not intentional but negligent. In *Miller v. Othello Packers, Inc.*,[63] one party agreed to plant and grow a crop of lima beans, and the other to harvest the crop and process it by freezing. Payment was according to tonnage and grading to be determined by the processor as the beans went through its plant. The processor's sampling, grading, and record keeping was done so negligently that its figures could not be used to determine the compensation due to the grower. The processor awarded the market value of the crop at the time of harvesting. The Washington Supreme Court held that the processor had violated the implied covenant of good faith and fair dealing.[64]

Discretion which is not subject to a standard

Sometimes there is no standard or criterion by which a party's discretion is to be exercised. Nevertheless, the discretion was given to the party for a purpose, and good faith requires that it be exercised in accordance with that purpose.

Covenant of Good Faith from (Some) Contracts, 84 Or. L. Rev. 227, 270 (2005)(arguing that "motive should be irrelevant"); Restatement (Second) of Contracts (1978) § 205, cmt. d (1978) ("Subterfuges and evasions violate the obligation of good faith in performance even though the actor believes his conduct to be justified").

[61] Robert S. Summers, *The General Duty of Good Faith—Its Recognition and Conceptualization*, 67 Cornell L. Rev. 810, 820 (1982).

[62] 739 P.2d at 558.

[63] 410 P.2d 33 (Wash. 1966).

[64] *Id.* at 34.

An example is an option. In *Market Street Associates v. Frey*,[65] the purpose of the option was to allocate various risks concerning the future value of property and the financing of improvements. Judge Posner held correctly that the option could not be used to take advantage of the other party's momentary inattention to the terms of the contract. J. C. Penney Company had sold property to General Electric Pension Trust and leased it back with an option to repurchase for twice the purchase price. It could exercise the option only if, after J. C. Penney requested the Trust to consider refinancing improvements on the premises, the parties failed to reach agreement. J. C. Penney assigned the lease to Market Street Associates. The general partner of Market Street Associates contacted the Trust about financing improvements on the property. He did not mention the option, and when the Trust indicated that it was not interested, he tried to exercise it. According to Posner, he took "deliberate advantage of an oversight by [his] contract partner concerning his rights under the contract."[66] As Peter Gerhart recognized, what mattered was the purpose of the option. Its "function was to put a cost on the developer's failure to negotiate in good faith," not on "remembering that the forfeiture provisions was there."[67]

As noted earlier, another situation in which a party is given discretion without a standard by which it must be exercised is when a contract contains a "subjective" condition of satisfaction. A party whose dissatisfaction is genuine has acted in good faith. Such conditions are common when the condition concerns aesthetics or business judgment. An artist may agree to paint a portrait for a client who will pay only if satisfied. In *Mattei v. Hopper*,[68] a developer agreed to buy a parcel of land for a shopping center but only if he was satisfied with the leases that he could enter into with third parties. In *Western Hills v. Pfau*,[69] a purchaser agreed to buy land subject to his ability "to negotiate with the City of McMinnville as to planned development satisfactory" to both parties. In these cases, the standard is the party's own satisfaction, not whether a reasonable person would have been satisfied. Yet the standard is not whether the contract will be advantageous. If it were, the contract would give the party an option. A client may not back out in order to patronize a different artist or developer in order to buy a less expensive but equally suitable piece of land. The discretion must be exercised according to the purpose for which it is conferred by the contract.

A condition that a party must be genuinely satisfied need not be explicit. In *Locke v. Warner Brothers*, Inc.,[70] Warner had a right of first refusal on Locke's

[65] 941 F.2d 588 (7th Cir. 1991) (Posner, J.).
[66] Market Street Associates v. Frey, 941 F.2d 588, 594 (7th Cir. 1991).
[67] GERHART, *supra* note 42, at 142.
[68] 330 P.2d 625 (Cal.1958).
[69] 508 P.2d 201 (Or. 1973).
[70] 66 Cal. Rptr. 2d 921 (Cal. App. 1997).

proposals for film productions and the discretion to accept or reject them. The plaintiff claimed that "the . . . deal was a sham, that Warner never intended to make any films with her, and that Warner's sole motivation in entering into the agreement" was to do a favor for the star Clint Eastwood by helping him to settle litigation with Locke.[71] The court held that although Warner had the "right to make a subjective creative decision, which is not reviewable for reasonableness," its "dissatisfaction [must] be bona fide or genuine."[72] Teri Dobbins criticized the court for "read[ing] into the contract a 'satisfaction' requirement that was not included in the language of the contract itself."[73] Warner was given discretion, however, and, as with a subjective condition of satisfaction, the question is whether it exercised this discretion in accordance with the purpose for which it was given. Doubtless, Locke ran the risk that her proposals would be turned down, but the provision would have been pointless if Warner did not need to consider them.

In another situation, a contract gives a party the discretion to determine the price without prescribing a standard that the party must follow in doing so. The question again is whether this discretion was exercised in accordance with the purpose for which it was conferred. In *Wilson v. Amerada Hess Corp.*,[74] Hess marketed gasoline through independent franchise dealers and through Hess-run "cooperative" dealers. The prices at which it sold were to be "determined by Hess."[75] Plaintiffs alleged "that Hess knowingly sets its . . . prices at a level that will not allow the dealers to cover operating expenses and achieve profit."[76] It did so, they alleged, in order to drive out independent dealers so that Hess could replace them with its own cooperative stations. If so, Hess acted in bad faith, as the court correctly held. The purpose of giving Hess discretion to determine the price was not so that it could drive them out of business. They were not compensated for assuming the risk that it would exercise its discretion to do so.

In *Amoco Oil Co. v. Ervin*,[77] the contract allowed Amoco to set the prices and rent that it charged dealer-lessees according to a formula which it was to devise. Its formula for rent charged twice for the value of service bays. The court held that Amoco acted in bad faith. "The dealers were justified in expecting that . . . Amoco would not charge double for any one element of the calculation" and "they presumably would not have signed the agreements had they known" that it would.[78]

[71] *Id.* at 922.
[72] *Id.* at 925.
[73] Dobbins, supra note 60, at 248.
[74] 773 A.2d 1121 (N.J. 2001).
[75] *Id.*
[76] *Id.* at 1125.
[77] 908 P.2d 493 (Colo. 1995).
[78] *Id.* at 499.

A recurring situation is a clause allowing a party to terminate a contract at will. Whether a party acted in good faith depends, again, on whether that right was exercised in accordance with the purpose for which it was conferred.

In an employment contract, it has been held to be bad faith for a company to terminate a contract with an employee[79] or other agent[80] to avoid paying a commission or giving a stock option[81] to which they would otherwise be entitled. As the *Restatement (Second) of Agency* correctly provides:

> An agent to whom the principal has made a revocable offer of compensation if he accomplishes a specified result is entitled to the promised amount if the principal, in order to avoid payment of it, revokes the offer and thereafter the result is accomplished as the result of the agent's prior efforts.[82]

The employer acts in bad faith if he uses his discretion to deprive a party of the extra amount he was to receive if he were successful. It was a part of his compensation. He did not assume the risk that if he were successful, the employer would take that amount away.

Similarly, a franchisor, licensor, or wholesale distributor cannot use a termination clause to appropriate an increase in the value of the business in which the other party is engaged. Courts have sometimes applied this principle without acknowledging that they are doing do. They have relied instead on the phrasing of the parties' contract. In *Atlantic Richfield Co. v. Razumic*,[83] the franchisor refused to renew a franchise because it wished to replace the franchisee with someone else. If it were able to do so, it could appropriate the value of the franchise. The Pennsylvania Supreme Court held that it could not. In *Amoco Oil Co. v. Burns*,[84] the franchisor wished to terminate the franchise and sell off the property that it had leased to the franchisee. It was not appropriating the franchisee's business but cutting its losses. The same court held that it could terminate. The reason for the difference in result, according to the court in *Amoco* was that "unlike *Razumic*, the right to terminate the relationship without cause was reserved by the parties in their written agreement."[85] It was not. The contract in *Razumic* contained no provision governing the right to renew.

79 Fortune v. Nat'l Cash Register Co., 364 N.E.2d 1251 (Mass. 1977).
80 RLM Assocs. v. Carter Mfg. Corp., 248 N.E.2d 646 (Mass. 1969).
81 Lemmon v. Cedar Point, Inc., 406 F.2d 94 (6th Cir. 1969).
82 Restatement (Second) of Agency § 454 (Am. Law Inst. 1958).
83 390 A.2d 736 (Pa. 1978).
84 437 A.2d 381 (Pa. 1981).
85 *Id.* at 383.

The same principle limits a landlord's right to refuse consent to an assignment or sublease. The modern rule, in the words of the California Supreme Court, is that the landlord cannot refuse without "a good faith reasonable objection."[86] According to the *Restatement Second of Property*:

> A restraint on alienation without the consent of the landlord of a tenant's interest in leased property is valid, but the landlord's consent to an alienation by the tenant cannot be withheld unreasonably, unless a freely negotiated provision in the lease gives the landlord an absolute right to withhold consent.[87]

As the Supreme Court of California said, to refuse consent, "in order [to] charge a higher rent than originally contracted for" fails "the tests of good faith and reasonableness."[88]

Again, the question is the purpose for which the landlord was given the right to consent. Normally, a lease allocates risks in the same way as a sale: the lessor avoids the risk that if they wait or lease for a shorter term, the market value of the leasehold may fall, and the lessee avoids the risk that it may rise. A lessee who wished to move out before the end of the term, for example, because someone else can operate a business there more profitably, would continue to pay the rent specified in the original lease if the rental value of the property had fallen. It should be the same if the rental value had risen.

Promoting cooperation

In other situations, the issue of good faith arises because the parties must cooperate in ways that cannot easily be specified in advance. Whether there is a duty to do so depends on the risks and burdens each party has been compensated to assume. A party is under a duty to cooperate when it is possible to do so without assuming any additional risk or burden, and a failure to cooperate exposes the other party to risks or burdens that party was not compensated to bear. For example, one party's failure to cooperate may deprive the other party of the compensation that induced that party to contract. As Gerhart said, sometimes "a party will accept some burdens on behalf of the counterparty in order to provide the counterparty with the rewards that the counterparty bargained for." "It is part of the obligation that maintains the ex ante equilibrium."[89]

[86] Kendall v. Ernest Pestana, Inc., 709 P.2d 837, 842 (Cal. 1985), *quoting* Cohen v. Ratinoff, 195 Cal. Rptr. 84 (Cal. App. 1983).

[87] Restatement (Second) of Property, § 15.2(2) (Am. Law Inst. 1977).

[88] Kendall v. Ernest Pestana, Inc., 709 P.2d 837, 842 (Cal. 1985), *quoting* Schweiso v. Williams, 198 Cal.Rptr. 238 (Cal. App. 1984).

[89] Gerhart, *supra* note 42, at 139.

Positive duties of cooperation

Sometimes cooperation requires a positive act without which the other party's performance cannot be made[90] or without which a condition cannot be fulfilled.[91] If an owner must empty the kitchen cabinets before a contractor can remodel or must seek a permit before a contractor can begin work, the owner must make a good faith effort to do so.

A good faith effort is not necessarily the same as "best efforts." In *Beraha v. Baxter Health Care Corp.*,[92] the court held that the licensee of the rights to a biopsy needle did not have a duty to use best efforts to develop a market even though the licensor was to be paid a percentage that depended on the success of its efforts. "Especially . . . when an inventor grants a license to patented technology, the application of which is unknown, a commitment on the part of the licensee to devote best efforts to the development of the technology is a substantial commitment which should not be automatically inferred."[93] But the defendant was under a duty "to exercise reasonably its discretion in developing and marketing the Beraha needle." If, in its "business judgment," development of the needle was unwise, it acted in good faith "even if it exerted no efforts at all to develop" it.[94]

Negative duties of cooperation

In contrast, sometimes a party's duty to cooperate is negative rather than positive. A party must not obstruct the other from receiving a benefit which induced that party to contract. The issue of good faith arises because it is difficult to specify in advance all the actions that a party should not take.

Unfortunately, many courts say that a duty to act in good faith can only be implied from a duty or condition that is set out in the contract. All the negative duties to cooperate cannot be set out in advance. There is no limit to the ways in which, by failing to act, one party could obstruct the other's opportunity to receive a benefit that was anticipated by both parties and induced that party to contract.

The benefits that a party anticipated may be part of the compensation the party was supposed to receive under the contract. Or there may be additional benefits such as the opportunity to make advantageous bargains with others. We will discuss each situation in turn.

[90] *E.g.*, Designer Direct, Inc. v. DeForest Redevelopment Authority, 313 F.3d 1036 (7th Cir. 2002) (failure take steps to make contractor's performance possible constitutes a lack of good faith).

[91] Simon v. Etgen, 107 N.E. 1066 (N.Y. 1915) (when sale of a building is a condition to be fulfilled before payment was due, good faith requires sale within a reasonable time).

[92] 956 F.2d 1436 (7th Cir. 1992).

[93] *Id.* at 1442–43.

[94] *Id.* at 1445.

In *Seidenberg v. Summit Bank*,[95] the benefits that the plaintiffs expected were part of the compensation they were supposed to receive. In return for selling stock in a corporation to Summit Bank, they were to retain their position as its executives and to be placed in charge of the daily operations of other insurance businesses that Summit acquired. They alleged that Summit's obstructive conduct showed that it "never had any intention to perform to begin with," and that "from the start [it] never [was] committed to developing the business with [plaintiffs], but rather simply wanted to acquire the business and seek out their own broker to run it or grow it."[96] If so, the court held, the defendant acted in bad faith. In this case, the court implied the duty to act in good faith from an express provision in the contract: "Summit and [plaintiffs] shall work together to formulate joint marketing programs."[97]

Sometimes the compensation a party is to receive depends on the extent to which the other party uses or profits from the goods or services he provides. In *Ryder Truck Rental, Inc. v. Central Packing Co.*,[98] the rent charged for truck trailers to transport frozen food depended on how many miles the trucks were driven. There was no minimum rental and no requirement that the trailers be driven a minimum number of miles. The lessee's assignee did not use them at all. The court held that he had acted in bad faith by "interfer[ing] with the right of the other to the fruits of its bargain."[99] The court was correct. The risk that the lessor assumed by charging by the mile was that not that the lessee would acquire a back-up fleet and pay nothing for it.

Unfortunately, instead of simply asking what risks the parties assumed, the court felt compelled to imply a duty of good faith from an express clause in the lease. The lease said that the lessee would "use and operate the motor vehicle equipment . . . in the normal and ordinary conduct of its business."[100] That clause had nothing to do with the non-use of the trailers, a problem the drafters never considered. By reading the clause as though it did, the court reached the right result while claiming it had not "impl[ied] an additional covenant enlarging [the] terms" of a "seemingly complete" agreement.[101] This is dangerous line of argument. It suggests that if the lease had not happened to mention "use," the result would be different.

That line of argument led to the wrong result in *Mutual Life Insurance Co. of New York v. Tailored Woman, Inc.*[102] The plaintiff leased three floors fronting 5th

95 791 A.2d 1068 (N.J. Super., 2002).
96 *Id.* at 1073.
97 *Id.* at 1072.
98 341 F.2d 321 (10th Cir. 1965).
99 *Id.* at 323.
100 *Id.* at 322.
101 *Id.* at 323.
102 128 N.E.2d 401 (N.Y. 1955).

Avenue to the defendant, a women's clothing store, in return for 4 percent of all sales made "on, in, and from the demised premises." Six years later, it leased the defendant part of the fifth floor for a fixed rent. The defendant connected this space to the other floors by installing an elevator, and moved its fur department, which sold its most expensive clothes, to the fifth floor. The court said that it accepted "the good old rule that there is in every contract an implied covenant of fair dealing."[103] Yet it found for the defendant because it thought it had to tease an answer out of words in the original lease "on, in, and from the demised premises." These words were drafted before the possibility of moving the fur department had arisen. Yet the court did not ask why the defendant moved the fur department. If the reason was not to increase sales but to lower the amount of its rent, it should have been held to have acted in bad faith. The rent in the original lease had not increased to compensate the lessor for the risk that the lessee would sell his most expensive goods from a floor yet to be rented.

Sometimes, the benefit of which a party has been deprived was not part of the compensation due under the contract. It was an opportunity that the contract provides to enter into profitable bargains with others, which was reflected in the contract price. To deprive that party of this opportunity would be to act in bad faith.

An example is *Sanders v. FedEx Ground Package Sys., Inc.*[104] FedEx recruited Sanders to be an independent contractor charged with making pick-ups and deliveries along a specified route. Sanders claimed that FedEx told him that he would have the ability to grow his business by buying routes from other contractors as they became available. FedEx obstructed his efforts to do so for reasons that had nothing to do with his qualifications to operate the routes. The lower court reached the wrong result by the line of reasoning just described. "[T]he implied covenant of good faith and fair dealing must be tied to a specific clause or term of the contract."[105] On appeal, its decision was reversed. The implied covenant of good faith "prohibit[s] one party from obstructing the other party's benefit, whether that benefit is express or implied."[106] FedEx had charged Sanders an amount that reflected the benefit Sanders expected from buying additional routes. FedEx could no more deprive him of that benefit than of the amount of money promised him in the contract.

In *Olympus Hills Shopping Center, Ltd. v. Smith's Food & Drug Centers, Inc.*,[107] the lessee in a shopping center frustrated the lessor's expectations concerning the use it would make of the premises. Those expectations had enabled the lessee

103 *Id.* at 403.
104 188 P.3d 1200 (N.M. 2008).
105 *Id.* at 1203–04.
106 *Id.* at 1203.
107 889 P.2d 445 (Utah 1994).

to obtain more favorable terms. The premises were leased for a grocery store for any "lawful retail selling business not directly in conflict or competition with another major tenant." The lessee opened a grocery store nearby and used the space it had leased as a "box store" which, the shopping center claimed, was "a sham operation designed to improperly 'freeze' the space in Olympus Hills and to force customers to its new location." The court correctly held that the lessee had violated the shopping center owner's "justified expectations."[108] The lessee's "minimum rent was below the break-even point for the shopping center's operating costs" because it was "the anchor tenant at the center, generating significant customer traffic, necessary to the financial health and operation of the shopping center."[109]

Yet ten years later, on similar facts, the same court reached the opposite result. It did so by employing the line of argument we have criticized. It tried to extract an answer from the language of a contract that was never meant to deal with the question. In *Oakwood Village, L.L.C. v. Albertsons, Inc.*,[110] a shopping center leased space to the lessee for a supermarket and guaranteed that it would be the only supermarket in the center. It expected the lessee "to function as the center's anchor tenant."[111] "[A]fter perceiving a better opportunity in a new shopping center across the street, [it] . . . moved one block south to become the anchor tenant in the Marketplace," another shopping center. After it relocated, [it] 'went dark' at its [old] location . . . while continuing to pay the monthly rent on the now vacant building." Its counsel admitted at trial that it "intentionally kept the old building unoccupied in order to restrict competition with its new store."[112] It is hard to imagine that the shopping center assumed the risk it would do so in return for an increase in rent. Yet the court held that the lessee was entitled to act like a "dog in the manger."[113] It said that the doctrine of good faith "cannot be read to establish new, independent rights or duties to which the parties did not agree ex ante."[114] The court distinguished *Olympus Hills Shopping Center* on the grounds that there, "the lease contained an express covenant of continuous operation and a restriction on the nature of operations."[115] That is an odd way to characterize the clause in *Olympus Hills* that said that the lessee can operate any "lawful retail selling business not directly in conflict or competition with another major tenant." Again, this line of reasoning led to the wrong result.

108 *Id.* at 452.
109 *Id.*
110 104 P.3d 1226 (Utah 2004).
111 *Id.* at 1229.
112 *Id.* at 1230.
113 *Id.* at 1241.
114 *Id.* at 1240.
115 *Id.* at 1241.

ii. Other conceptions of good faith

Scholars have failed to agree on the meaning of good faith. Robert Summers claimed that the phrase cannot be defined positively but only negatively, as what he calls an "excluder." According to other scholars, the doctrine is pernicious because it conflicts with standard methods of contract interpretation. Some say it is unnecessary because it merely recapitulates them. Some say that the doctrine ensures fairness but their conception of fairness borders on altruism. Some say the doctrine promotes economic efficiency. Our approach is different but, as we will see, it captures the element of truth in each of the others.

Good faith as an "excluder"

In a seminal article, Robert Summers claimed that one cannot define "good faith." "[G]ood faith is an 'excluder.' It is a phrase without general meaning (or meanings) of its own and serves to exclude a wide range of heterogeneous forms of bad faith."[116] According to Robert Braucher, who then served as Reporter, Summers's approach influenced that of the *Second Restatement of Contracts*. The *Second Restatement* does not define good faith. It provides: "Every contract imposes upon each party a duty of good faith and fair dealing in its performance and its enforcement."[117] According to Braucher:

> [T]he trouble with this section, of course, is that it's very general, very abstract, and it needs specification in the worst way, and specification is not to be had. I am indebted for its formulation here in the comments—formulations in the comments—to Professor Summers.[118]

He was referring primarily to Comment a: "Meanings of 'good faith' ":

> The phrase "good faith" is used in a variety of contexts, and its meaning varies somewhat with the context. Good faith performance or enforcement of a contract emphasizes faithfulness to an agreed common purpose and consistency with the justified expectations of the other party; it excludes a variety of types of conduct characterized as involving "bad faith" because they violate community standards of decency, fairness or reasonableness. The appropriate remedy for a breach of the duty of good faith also varies with the circumstances.

[116] Robert S. Summers, *"Good Faith" in General Contract Law and the Sales Provision of the Uniform Commercial Code*, 54 Va. L. Rev. 195, 201 (1968).

[117] Restatement (Second) of Contracts § 205 (Am. Law Inst. 1981).

[118] 47 ALI Proceedings 489 (1970).

The comment neither refers to "good faith" an excluder nor says that a definition is impossible. Nevertheless, it does not provide the "specification" which, according to Braucher, the section "needs in the worst way." The reason, presumably, is that Braucher agreed with Summers: it "is not to be had."

The term "good faith" has no one meaning since it has been used in heterogeneous situations. One definition will not fit all of them, but that does not mean the term is undefinable. In a follow-up article, Summers enumerated these situations. They concern the doctrine of consideration ("conjuring up a pretended dispute in order . . . to lay a basis for a settlement"), the fairness of the modification of the terms of a contract ("taking advantage of another's necessitous circumstances to secure a favorable modification"), the general problem of how to interpret the language of a contract ("asserting an overreaching or 'weaseling' interpretation or construction of contract language"), and problems of conditions and remedies ("willful rendering of only substantial performance"; making harassing demands for assurances of performance; wrongfully refusing to accept performance; and "willfully failing to mitigate damages").[119] In each of those contexts, "good faith" has a different meaning. It has a different meaning in the two situations we have discussed: those in which the duty to act in good faith is needed to provide flexibility or to ensure cooperation. No description of good faith will fit all of those situations. Nevertheless, we have described its meaning in those two situations.

Good faith, like other legal concepts, should be defined with reference to the purposes that the law serves. The conceptualists of the nineteenth century have been criticized for defining concepts without regard to purposes.[120] We have explained the duty of good faith in terms of the purposes of permitting flexibility and promoting cooperation. Summers described six "different methods of conceptualization," one of which is to use a concept as an excluder. He argued that good faith must be an "excluder" since its meaning cannot be captured by the other five. The source of the difficulty, however, is that none of the six define a concept in terms of its purposes.

The first "method of conceptualization" is the one common in the nineteenth century:

> 1. Conceptualization by formal definition—e.g., resort to necessary and sufficient conditions for the use of a word or phrase.[121]

[119] Robert S. Summers, *The General Duty of Good Faith -- Its Recognition and Conceptualization*, 67 Cornell L. Rev. 810, 812–13 (1982).
[120] James Gordley, The Jurists A Critical History 276–77 (2013).
[121] Summers, *supra* note 119, at 817.

The element of truth in Summers's approach is that legal concepts cannot be defined in this way. If they could, the dream of the nineteenth-century jurists could be realized. When a new case arose, one would simply ask whether the necessary and sufficient conditions for using a term have been satisfied.

Summers then described four methods which attempt to define a concept without a "formal definition":

> 2. Conceptualization by synonymous paraphrase of the word or phrase in question (including contrastive paraphrase).
> 3. Conceptualization by paradigmatic sample, specifying what is required for the use of the word or phrase.
> 4. Conceptualization mainly by recital or representative examples illustrating the application of the word or phrase.
> 5. Conceptualization by specification of family resemblances that run through diverse uses of the word or phrase.[122]

As Summers recognized, none of these methods can provide an adequate, usable definition of good faith. He is right.

To explain one term by a paraphrase or synonym (method 2) sidesteps the question of how to define the synonym or the terms used in the paraphrase. To explain a term by a paradigm (method 3) or representative examples (method 4) sidesteps the question of what makes the paradigm paradigmatic or the examples representative.

The idea of using family resemblances (method 4), as Summers recognized, was borrowed from Wittgenstein[123] whose illustration was the term "game." If parents asked a babysitter to teach their children a game, and the babysitter taught the children to duel with kitchen knives, the parents would say, "That's not the kind of game I meant." The example is supposed to show that one can only explain what a game is in terms of resemblances between different instances of what we call games. What it actually shows is that words should be understood in terms of their purposes. The parents used the term "game" with one purpose in mind: to provide diversion for their children. Where the purpose is different, as in athletic competitions or games of chance, what counts as a "game" will be different.

Since these five methods are inadequate to define good faith, Summers concluded that one must use a sixth:

[122] *Id.* at 818.

[123] Ludwig Wittgenstein, Philosophical Investigations (G. Anscombe trans., 1958), *cited id.* at n.33.

6. Conceptualization by way of "excluder" analysis.[124]

He took this idea from John Austin,[125] and applied it to a much different problem. Austin was trying to solve the problem of Cartesian doubt: how do I know that everything I take to be real is not a hallucination or a dream? Austin's answer was that the word "real" is an excluder: it is defined as that which is not unreal such as a dream or a hallucination. The Aristotelian view, challenged by the philosophy of Descartes, was the opposite. Reality a first principle of human reason. It is what the mind grasps before it grasps anything else, and it the basis for any conclusions that reason can reach about what it real.

Be that as it may, Austin's approach is only helpful if one knows what is being "excluded." If one knows what a dream or a hallucination is, one can say: "reality is not that." For the term "good faith" to function as an excluder, one would have to know what is meant by "bad faith." But how is one to know? Perhaps in the way that the *Restatement Second* suggests: " 'bad faith' . . . violate[s] community standards of decency, fairness or reasonableness." But, if so, why say, that good faith is an excluder? Why not define it as conformity to "community standards of decency, fairness or reasonableness"? If that definition is too vague to mean anything, then how is one to know what "bad faith" means? Summers illustrates the meaning of bad faith by giving as series of examples and claiming that no definition of good faith can explain them all. But that would seem to be "conceptualization" by representative examples, a method, he said, which cannot be used to understand the meaning of "good faith." Why, then, can it be used to understand "bad faith"?

Good faith as a violation of fundamental principles of interpretation

According to Terri Dobbins, "in many contracts, the implied covenant of good faith is not capable or worthy of being saved from the chaos that currently surrounds it."[126] It is based on construing the parties' duties according to their expectations. But "the parties' agreement should take precedence over the parties' expectations, to the extent that the two do not coincide."[127] The "parties may not share the same expectations and one party may be ignorant of the expectations of the other."[128]

The element of truth is that the duties to which the parties are held should be based on their expectations. The confusion is that Dobbins uses the term "expectations" too loosely. The parties' duties should be based on their expectations

124 Summers, *supra* note 120, at 818.

125 John Austin, Sense and Sensibilia 70–71 (G. Warnock ed., 1962), *quoted id.* at 819.

126 Dobbins, *supra* note 60, at 231–32.

127 *Id.* at 230.

128 *Id.*

concerning the performance that each will receive and the risks and burdens that each will bear. Other expectations do not matter. The party who was compensated for bearing a risk may have expected to win.

Good faith as a recapitulation of fundamental principles of interpretation

In contrast, Jay Feinman claimed that "[g]ood faith is simply another embodiment of the basic principle of contract law—the protection of reasonable expectations."[129] Similarly, according to Harold Dubroff, the difficulties of "defin[ing] good faith . . . would be eliminated if cases that are really about contract interpretation were approached that way without regard to the issue of good faith."[130] Contracts should be interpreted in accordance with "the actual intentions and expectations of the parties, although they may have been expressed imperfectly."[131]

The element of truth in this approach is that the doctrine of good faith, as we have seen, is based on the same principles as those that that explain why other terms are read into a contract to govern situations that the parties did not anticipate. Nevertheless, as we have also seen, the doctrine applies when the parties could not have provided a term to resolve an issue in advance and still provide flexibility and promote cooperation. In that situation, questions arise that require a distinct doctrine to resolve them.

Good faith as altruism

Other scholars do regard the doctrine as based on fairness to the other party. But they conceive of fairness in such a general way that it is little different from a concern for the other party's interest or welfare, a concern without any limiting principle.

According to Robert Scott, when there is a "gap in the agreement or risk allocation" some scholars believe that "courts should fill such gaps by creating contract terms that are fair ex post."[132] They should do so "by imposing an equitable adjustment that takes all of the relational and contextual factors into account as they appear at the time of adjudication."[133] There seems to be no limit to what those factors might be. According to Scott, "[t]his has been the solution most frequently suggested by the law-and-society branch of relational contract."[134] He cited the work of Ian Macneil and Richard Speidel.

[129] Jay M. Feinman, *Good Faith and Reasonable Expectations*, 67 Ark. L. Rev. 525, 526 (2014).

[130] Harold Dubroff, *The Implied Covenant of Good Faith in Contract Interpretation and Gap-Filling: Reviling a Revered Relic*, 80 St. John's L. Rev. 559, 563–64 (2006).

[131] *Id.* at 569.

[132] Robert E. Scott, *The Case for Formalism in Relational Contract*, 94 Nw. U. L. Rev. 847, 851 (2000).

[133] *Id.* at 850.

[134] *Id.*

Macneil developed a "relational theory" of contract law. "[E]very transaction is embedded in complex relations." "[E]ffective analysis of any transaction requires recognition and consideration of all essential elements of its enveloping relations that might affect the transaction significantly."[135] These relations are fluid. One cannot determine the parties' obligations by asking about their intentions, real or hypothetical, at the time that they contracted. As Eric Posner said, by this approach "the parties . . . cannot expect the court to enforce contractual obligations on the basis of the initial contract, given that the initial contract will most likely have nothing to say about events occurring many years later."[136]

Certainly, every contract, like every crime, tort, and the exercise of every private right is embedded in a set of circumstances, including relationships with others, without which it cannot be fully understood. But it is hard to turn this insight into a theory. Macneil himself said:

> Upon starting down th[is] road . . . it did not occur to me consciously that I might be developing a theory. Rather, I was simply exploring and trying to make sense of reality, the reality of what people are actually doing in the real-life world of exchange.[137]

What, then, are the legal implications of understanding "what people are actually doing in the real-life world of exchange"? Macneil admonished those who look for such implications:

> I challenge to a duel anyone who, after this notice, persists in converting my descriptions of relational contract law into prescriptions of what the law should be, particularly prescriptions of some universal application of relational contract law.[138]

According to Speidel, the implications are that the doctrine of good faith should be given much greater scope. He commended a provision of the *UNIDROIT Principles of International Commercial Contracts* that deals with the problem of impracticability due to changed circumstances.[139] It provides that

[135] Ian R. Macneil, *Relational Contract Theory: Challenges and Queries*, 94 NW. U. L. REV. 877, 881 (2000).

[136] Posner, *supra* note 14, at 751.

[137] Macneil, *supra* note 135, at 879.

[138] *Id.* at 899. He qualified that remark. "Notwithstanding the challenge just offered, in my work I have gone beyond observation and included two types of prescription respecting relational contract law." One, he said "is entirely personal to my perceptions of the good life." *Id.* at 900. It concerned "excessive bureaucratization of modern life." *Id.* at 900 n.81. The other is "a general idea that relational contract law should generally track the relational behavior and norms found in the relations to which it applies." *Id.* at 900.

[139] *Id.* at 841.

one party can require the other to negotiate, and, if negotiations break down, the court should "adjust the contract."[140] Speidel suggested that American courts expand the doctrine of good faith to impose a similar requirement when an issue was not resolved when the parties contracted.[141] The negotiations, however, would be based on the parties' expectations of how a court would "adjust the contract" if negotiations broke down. Speidel is no clearer than Macneil about how a court should do so.

Charles Goetz and Robert Scott explained that "[i]f the basic risk allocation provided by a legal rule fails to suit the purposes of particular parties, then bargainers are free to negotiate an alternative allocation of risks."[142] Nevertheless, in "relational" contracts, "the future contingencies are peculiarly intricate or uncertain, practical difficulties arise that impede the contracting parties' efforts to allocate optimally all risks at the time of contracting."[143] The question again arises, what a court should do then.

Since, by hypothesis, the court cannot look to the way the parties allocated the risks at the time of contracting, it must look to what appears to be fair ex post. The implication is that courts would be empowered to do what is fair with no standard of what fairness entails. Perhaps the implication is that there should be no winners or losers, or, at least, that no one should be hurt too badly. Teri Dobbins objected that if the court imposes "a result that the court believes to be fair . . . the implied covenant of good faith makes every party a guarantor of the other party's satisfaction with the outcome of the bargain."[144] Scott said that the consequences to one party will be deemed to be unfair if they are severe.[145]

The fear that courts will do so has haunted discussions of the doctrine of good faith. Robert Braucher, who served as Reporter for the *Second Restatement*, said of the section on good faith: "I have been asked about [this] Section . . . Isn't this an attempt . . . to write the Sermon on the Mount into the Restatement of Contracts?"[146]

As Judge Posner observed, "even after you have signed a contract, you are not obliged to become an altruist toward the other party and relax the terms if he gets into trouble in performing his side of the bargain."[147] That point was made

[140] UNIDROIT PRINCIPLES OF INTERNATIONAL COMMERCIAL CONTRACTS § 6.2.3(1).

[141] Richard E. Speidel, *The Characteristics and Challenges of Relational Contracts*, 94 NW. U. L. REV. 823, 840–41 (2000).

[142] Charles J. Goetz & Robert E. Scott, *Principles of Relational Contracts*, 67 VA. L. REV. 1089, 1090 (1981).

[143] *Id.*

[144] Dobbins, *supra* note 60, at 232.

[145] Scott, *supra* note 132, at 851.

[146] 47 ALI PROCEEDINGS 489–91 (1970).

[147] Market Street Associates v. Frey, 941 F.2d 588, 594 (7th Cir. 1991).

in another Seventh Circuit opinion in *Kham & Nate's Shoes No. 2, Inc. v. First Bank of Whiting*.[148] The lower court held that a bank had behaved inequitably in terminating a line of credit. It "was fully aware of the Debtor's plight, and its reliance upon the line of credit, and disregarded the consequences for the Debtor and its creditors."[149] The Seventh Circuit reversed the decision. Judge Easterbrook observed, "Debtor and Bank signed a contract expressly allowing the Bank to cease making further advances."[150] "Although Bank's decision left Debtor scratching for other sources of credit, Bank did not create Debtor's need for funds."[151] " 'Good faith' " is a compact reference to an implied undertaking not to take opportunistic advantage in a way that could not have been contemplated at the time of drafting."[152] It "does not imply a general duty of 'kindness' in performance."[153]

Similarly, in *Martin v. Hamilton State Bank*,[154] a bank loaned the defendant $2.7 million. When he failed to make several payments, the bank sued to recover the loan. The defendant claimed that it had not acted in good faith because the parties were unable to agree on a plan by which "the indebtedness might be restructured."[155] The court held that it had not acted improperly, whatever its motivation might have been. It had loaned the money and was entitled to be repaid.

The element of truth in this approach is that it recognizes the critical role of fairness in explaining good faith. But fairness does not mean reaching a result ex post that commends itself to both of the parties. Fairness means reaching a result ex post that corresponds to how risks were assigned by the parties ex ante.

Good faith as efficiency

There is also an element of truth in the approach of scholars who explain the doctrine of good faith in terms of efficiency: they recognize the importance of considering how risks were assigned ex ante. According to Steven Burton, "[b]ad faith performance occurs precisely when discretion is used to recapture opportunities forgone upon contracting—when the discretion-exercising party refuses to pay the expected cost of performance."[156]

148 908 F.2d 1351 (7th Cir. 1990).
149 *Id.* at 1354.
150 *Id.* at 1357.
151 *Id.* at 1358.
152 *Id.* at 1357.
153 *Id.*
154 723 S.E.2d 726 (Ga. Ct. App. 2012).
155 *Id.* at 334–35.
156 Steven J. Burton, *Breach of Contract and the Common Law Duty to Perform in Good Faith*, 94 Harv. L. Rev. 369, 373 (1980).

Dubroff objected that this description of good faith is too broad. Any breach of contract is an attempt to recapture foregone opportunities:

> Clearly, parties who enter into contracts forgo their opportunities to act in specified and unspecified ways. The very nature of a bilateral contract is to create obligations in exchange for rights. Thus, if I promise to cut my neighbor's lawn in exchange for her promise to pay me $10, I have forgone the opportunities that might have been available to me by not cutting her lawn.

That is true. The difference, however, is that one does not have to consider what opportunities were foregone to determine whether I breached a contract by breaking my promise to cut a neighbor's lawn. One must do so to determine whether I breached a contract by violating my duty to act in good faith. In the case of the neighbor's lawn, each party gave up opportunities. The neighbor gave up her chance of getting it cut for less than $10, and I gave up my chance of cutting someone else's lawn for more. One can determine whether there has been a breach of contract by asking whether I cut the lawn and whether she paid me $10. Sometimes, one has to ask what opportunities were foregone in order to determine whether there was a breach of contract. In those cases, courts speak of "good faith."

The element of truth in Burton's approach is that it is a violation of good faith to try to recapture a foregone opportunity. The difference is that he and others committed to economic analysis which tries to explain good faith in terms of efficiency rather than fairness. According to Burton, to require a party to act in good faith:

> enhance[s] economic efficiency by reducing the costs of contracting. The costs of exchange include the costs of gathering information with which to choose one's contract partners, negotiating and drafting contracts, and risk taking with respect to the future. The good faith performance doctrine reduces all three kinds of costs by allowing parties to rely on the law in place of incurring some of these costs.[157]

In *Market Street Associates v. Frey*,[158] Judge Posner, citing Burton, took the same approach:

> The office of the doctrine of good faith is to forbid the kinds of opportunistic behavior that a mutually dependent, cooperative relationship might enable

[157] *Id.* at 393.
[158] 941 F.2d 588 (7th Cir. 1991).

> in the absence of a rule. "Good faith" is a compact reference to an implied undertaking not to take opportunistic advantage in a way that could not have been contemplated at the time of drafting, and which therefore was not resolved explicitly by the parties.[159]
>
> ...
>
> [T]he overriding purpose of contract law, which is to give the parties what they would have stipulated for expressly if at the time of making the contract they had had complete knowledge of the future and the costs of negotiating and adding provisions to the contract had been zero.[160]

Posner, like Burton, did not say that taking opportunistic advantage is unfair. He said:

> Such taking advantage . . . [l]ike theft . . . has no social product, and also like theft it induces costly defensive expenditures, in the form of overelaborate disclaimers or investigations into the trustworthiness of a prospective contract partner, just as the prospect of theft induces expenditures on locks.[161]

Economic analysis is concerned with what is efficient, not what is fair. A transaction is efficient if at least one party is better off, and no one is worth off. Theft makes one party worse off. Therefore it is not efficient. It "has no social product." Indeed, it is inefficient because "the prospect of theft induces expenditures on locks." Taking opportunistic advantage is inefficient because "it induces costly defensive expenditures, in the form of overelaborate disclaimers or investigations into the trustworthiness of a prospective contract partner." It increases "the costs of gathering information with which to choose one's contract partners, negotiating and drafting contracts."[162]

Is that all? Suppose a party took opportunistic advantage in a way that was so unanticipated that it would not increase these costs? Can it really be that the reason a party should be prevented from acting in bad faith is to prevent others from overinvesting in defensive measures? Consider Posner's analogy to theft. Most people would say it is unjust to steal, or, for that matter, to take opportunistic advantage of another contracting party. I suspect that only a disciple of economic analysis would think the real problem is to optimize money spent on locks or on negotiating and drafting.

[159] *Citing* Kham & Nate's Shoes No. 2, Inc. v. First Bank of Whiting, 908 F.2d 1351, 1357 (7th Cir. 1990).

[160] 941 F.2d at 595–66.

[161] *Id.* at 594.

[162] Burton, *supra* note 156, at 393.

It is a particularly poor explanation of the duty to act in good faith. As we have seen, this duty is implied in situations in which an appropriate term could not be supplied in advance if drafting a contract were costless. If discretion is conferred on a party to make the terms of a contract more flexible, it is impossible to specify in advance how that discretion should be used. It is impossible to specify everything that each party must do or refrain from doing for the other to obtain the benefit for which they contracted, then a drafter could never succeed in doing so. The reason for implying a duty to act in good faith cannot be to save "future parties" the time, cost, and error inherent in negotiating contract terms and reducing them to writing."[163]

[163] Scott, *supra* note 39, at 850.

10
Conditions

I. The conventional approach to non-fulfillment

In the words of the *Second Restatement*:

> A condition is an event, not certain to occur, which must occur, unless its non-occurrence is excused, before performance under a contract becomes due.[1]

A party who fails to perform a duty is liable for breach of contract. In contrast, if a condition is not fulfilled, a party is not under a duty to perform.

i. The rule of perfect fulfillment

According to standard doctrine, a condition must be exactly or "perfectly" fulfilled.[2] Conditions, unlike duties, are not governed by the substantial performance doctrine.

Doubtless, there are some conditions that must be perfectly fulfilled. It is not correct that this rule applies or should apply to all conditions or to conditions in general.

The rule is a legacy of the conceptualism of the nineteenth and early twentieth centuries. By definition a party cannot be under a duty to perform if a condition is not fulfilled. Therefore it must be perfectly fulfilled. To hold otherwise would be to disregard what the parties said that they intended. According to Williston:

> Since an express condition . . . depends for its validity on the manifested intention of the parties, it has the same sanctity as the promise itself. Though the court may regret the harshness of such a condition, as it may regret the harshness of a promise, it must, nevertheless, generally enforce the will of the parties unless to do so will violate public policy.[3]

[1] Restatement (Second) of Contracts § 224 (Am. Law Inst. 1981).
[2] Restatement (Second) of Contracts § 227 (Am. Law Inst. 1981).
[3] 5 Samuel Williston, The Law of Contract § 669 (1920).

Foundations of American Contract Law. James Gordley, Oxford University Press. © Oxford University Press 2023.
DOI: 10.1093/oso/9780197686089.003.0010

An illustration of the perfect fulfillment rule is *Jungmann & Co. v. Atterbury Bros.*,[4] decided by the New York Court of Appeals in 1928 in one of the most illustrious periods of its history. The opinion was written by Judge Lehman with Cardozo, Pound, Andrews, Kellogg, and O'Brien concurring. The parties had entered into "a written contract for the sale of 30 tons of casein." The contract provided: "Advice of shipment to be made by cable immediately goods are dispatched." The plaintiff shipped the first 15 tons without notice to the defendant, who rejected the shipment. He then shipped the remaining 15 tons to the defendant, but again failed to provide notice by cable and instead sent two letters. The defendant rejected that shipment as well. According to the court, it did not matter whether the failure to give notice by cable prejudiced the defendant or not.

> It is said that since the defendant received notice when the steamship Magnolia sailed with 15 tons that upon its arrival the plaintiff would tender to the defendant the entire 30 tons, the defendant is in no worse position than if it had received the stipulated "advice of shipment by cable immediately the goods are dispatched." Even if that be true, the fact remains that the plaintiff was obligated under its contract to see that defendant obtained advice of shipment by cable. That it failed to do. It may be that the defendant would have been satisfied to enter into a contract which required the plaintiff only to notify the defendant of intention to make delivery a definite time before actual delivery. It stipulated for another kind of notice. It may have believed that certainty of delivery would be greater if it received advice of actual shipment by cable. We may not weigh the benefit it might receive from other notice. The plaintiff may not recover upon its contract without proof that it has performed all conditions precedent required of it.[5]

The court cited Williston in support.[6] Williston, as we have seen, held an objective theory of contract. Yet, as we have seen, he claimed that the requirement of perfect fulfillment rested on the principle that a court must "enforce the will of the parties." He defended his objective theory by pointing that it is a fiction to believe that the terms that the law reads into a contract are the will of the parties.[7] Yet he thought that a harsh condition of a harsh bargain is willed by the parties when it is found in a document to which the parties subscribed. He did not ask why both parties would have willed to be bound by a term that is harsh to

[4] 249 N.E. 123 (N.Y. 1928).
[5] *Id.* at 123–24.
[6] WILLISTON, note 3, at §§ 674, 675, *cited id.* 124.
[7] *Id.* at § 615.

only one of them. He did not believe that it is a fiction to assume that each party understands all of the terms contained in the document, and their legal effects, let alone wills to be bound by them. As Eisenberg pointed out:

> Most persons are likely to be unaware of the legal distinction between the substantial but imperfect performance of promises and the substantial but imperfect performance of express conditions, and the potentially draconian consequences of failure to perfectly fulfill an express condition. Furthermore, because the parties normally expect to fulfill conditions, the consequences of less-than-perfect fulfillment will seem remote at the time that the contract was made. As a result, the parties are likely to view the costs of fully deliberating on the operation of an express condition as unduly high.[8]

Nevertheless, the *Second Restatement* still maintains that the requirement of perfect fulfillment rests on the principle of freedom of contract. According to an Official Comment to § 227:

> The non-occurrence of a condition of an obligor's duty may cause the obligee to lose his right to the agreed exchange after he has relied substantially on the expectation of that exchange, as by preparation or performance. The word "forfeiture" is used in this Restatement to refer to the denial of compensation that results in such a case. The policy favoring freedom of contract requires that, within broad limits the agreement of the parties should be honored even though forfeiture results.[9]

ii. Excuse for disproportionate forfeiture

An escape route

According to standard doctrine, there is an escape route. The rule of perfect fulfillment need not be followed when it would result in disproportionate forfeiture. According to § 229 of the *Second Restatement*:

> To the extent that the non-occurrence of a condition would cause disproportionate forfeiture, a court may excuse the non-occurrence of that condition unless its occurrence was a material part of the agreed exchange.[10]

[8] Melvin A. Eisenberg, Foundational Principles of Contract Law 117 (2018).
[9] Restatement (Second) of Contracts § 227 cmt. b (Am. Law Inst. 1981).
[10] *Id.* at § 229.

One suspects that, again, the *Second Restatement* has formulated a doctrine in a way that nineteenth- and early twentieth-century jurists would have accepted and then made an exception which conflicts with that formulation and which no one understands. As we have seen, it did so with the doctrine of consideration. Section 79 of the *Restatement* provides: "If the requirement of consideration is met, there is no additional requirement of . . . equivalence in the values exchanged." Section 208 then gives a remedy for "unconscionability." An Official Comment to § 229 on forfeiture explained that "both this Section and § 208, on unconscionable contract or term, limit freedom of contract."[11] Just as § 208 fails to explain what is meant by an "unconscionable" term, so § 229 fails to explain what is meant by a "disproportionate forfeiture," other than one for which the law will give relief despite the principle of freedom of contract. Neither do the Comments explain what that principle means, what principle justifies relief for unconscionability or disproportionate forfeiture, or how these principles are related. The old idea of freedom of contract has not been rejected, yet its implications are no longer accepted, and we have little explanation as to why.

We should reconsider the idea that a condition must be exactly or "perfectly" fulfilled.

The meaning of "forfeiture"

Before we do so, however, we should note an anomaly in the way "forfeiture" is customarily defined. It is taken to mean that a party lost property or money or incurred expense in reliance on a contract. According to an Official Comment in the *Second Restatement*:

> The non-occurrence of a condition of an obligor's duty may cause the obligee to lose his right to the agreed exchange after he has relied substantially on the expectation of that exchange, as by preparation or performance. The word "forfeiture" is used in this Restatement to refer to the denial of compensation that results in such a case.[12]

As we have seen, the *Second Restatement* uses the term "forfeiture" in the same sense in discussing substantial performance. In his treatise, Allan Farnsworth explained that the term "forfeiture" is used to refer to the "loss of reliance interest" when "the obligee has relied on the expected exchange by, for example, performing or preparing to perform."[13] "As the term *forfeiture* suggest, the

[11] *Id.* at § 229 cmt. a.
[12] *Id.* at § 227 cmt. b.
[13] E. Allan Farnsworth, Contracts 533 (4th ed. 2004).

obligee's loss of the reliance interest is regarded as more serious than the obligee's loss of the expectation interest."[14]

Nevertheless, as we saw in our discussion of substantial performance, if a party who was compensated for bearing a risk were allowed to escape, the other party would forfeit the right to the benefit of the bargain. That may be the greater loss. The difficulty is illustrated by a case that has been called "a poster-child for the perfect-fulfillment rule,"[15] *Oppenheimer & Co. v. Oppenheim, Appel, Dixon & Co.*[16] The plaintiff, who held a lease on the thirty-third floor of One New York Plaza agreed to sublease the floor to the defendant, which already held a lease on the twenty-ninth floor and wanted more space. A condition of the lease was that by February 28, the plaintiff's landlord would give written consent to the installation of a telephone communication linkage system between the twenty-ninth and the thirty-third floors. By that day, the plaintiff had not received the landlord's written consent but, as they informed the defendant, they had received oral consent. The next day the defendant told the plaintiff that the sublease was null and void. The landlord provided written consent three weeks later. The jury awarded damages of $1.2 million dollars for breach of contract. The trial court vacated the verdict on the ground that conditions must be strictly fulfilled. The Appellate Division reversed, and the Court of Appeals reinstated the trial court's decision.

According to the Court of Appeals, "plaintiff has not suffered a forfeiture."[17] To induce the plaintiff the move to the World Financial Center, its prospective landlord there had promised to indemnify the plaintiff for any loss it suffered if it failed to sublease its premises in One New York Plaza. Therefore "the critical concern of forfeiture . . . is simply not present in this case."[18]

What about the $1.2 million? Presumably, it represented the difference between the rent that the defendant had agreed to pay and the rent the plaintiff owed its landlord. To ignore it violates the principle that each party should be responsible for risks it was compensated to assume. In a sale, by agreeing on a contract price, each party gives up the opportunity to obtain a more favorable price to avoid the chance of receiving a less favorable one. In a lease, each party gives up the opportunity to obtain a more favorable rent in return to avoid the chance of obtaining a less favorable one. A delay in receiving the landlord's written consent, after the parties had received his oral consent, should not allow the defendant to escape a bargain that had become a less favorable bargain than he had hoped.

[14] *Id.* at 533–34.
[15] EISENBERG, *supra* note 8, at 720.
[16] 660 N.E.2d 415 (N.Y. 1995).
[17] *Id.* at 419.
[18] *Id.*

The same unfortunate result was reached in *enXco Development Corp. v. Northern States Power Co.*,[19] which cited the *Restatement*'s definition of "forfeiture." The plaintiff agreed to construct a wind energy generation project for the defendant, a gas and electric company. The plaintiff "owned the Project's real estate and assets until completion," and then the defendant "would essentially purchase the Project's real estate and assets for $15 million."[20]

The project could not proceed without the permission of the North Dakota Public Service Commission, and the contract was conditional on obtaining its permission by a certain date. Permission was not obtained by that date because the hearing before the Commission was postponed by a snowstorm; a hearing was then held in the wrong county contrary to North Dakota law, and the Commission refused to waive a twenty-day notice requirement before a new hearing could be held. Permission was granted but after the date specified in the contract had passed. The defendant terminated the contract.

The Eighth Circuit Court of Appeals, applying Minnesota law, held that the defendant could do so because there had been no forfeiture.

> Here, [the plaintiff] parted with nothing. It still maintained possession and ownership of the Project assets and real estate. [The plaintiff] transferred the Project's physical capital for use in other projects, and it hopes to employ the real property associated with the Project in the future. [The defendant] did not obtain ownership of any property as a result of termination. [The defendant] therefore did not receive something for little or nothing.[21]

Nevertheless, the plaintiff "suffered several million dollars in losses."[22] As the court acknowledged:

> From execution of the contracts in October 2008 until their termination in April 2011, wind-energy-generation profit prospects declined such that [the defendant] stood to lose significant amounts of money should it proceed with the Project. Apparently the market for wind turbines dried up significantly during this time. As a result, [the defendant] had the economic incentive to avoid the contract.[23]

Each party to a sale assumes that risk that the goods or services purchased may turn out to be worth less or more than the contract price. Here the defendant was

19 758 F.3d 940 (8th Cir. 2014).
20 *Id.* at 942.
21 *Id.* at 947.
22 *Id.* at 941.
23 *Id.* at 943.

allowed to renege when the assets proved to be worth a great deal less. It escaped liability for a risk that it had been compensated to assume.

If one party imperfectly performed a duty, the other party could not escape from the bargain as long as the duty had been substantially performed. It would be liable for the contract price minus whatever cost it had incurred. The rule should be the same when a condition is imperfectly fulfilled.

II. Non-fulfillment and the purpose of a condition

Whether non-fulfillment of a condition should allow a party to terminate the contract should depend on the principles of voluntariness and fairness which we have described. On the one hand, a party who would never have agreed to the contract without the right to insist on perfect fulfillment should be allowed to do so. On the other hand, a party who would have agreed should not be able to escape from a disadvantageous contract.

According to Eisenberg:

> the governing principle should be as follows: the imperfect fulfillment of an express condition should trigger a right to terminate the contract only if the nonfulfillment is significant and it is likely that the parties would have agreed that the sanction of termination could be exercised in the circumstances that actually arose.[24]

What the parties are likely to have agreed depends on the purpose of the condition.

i. A condition that makes a performance possible

In considering what constitutes forfeiture, we discussed two cases, *Oppenheimer & Co. v. Oppenheim, Appel, Dixon & Co.*[25] and *enXco Development Corp. v. Northern States Power Co.*[26] In both cases, a performance could not have been made without the approval of a third party: in *Oppenheimer*, the landlord of the prospective sublessor, in *enXco*, the North Dakota Public Utilities Commission. In *Oppenheimer*, the contract was conditional on receipt of approval in writing by a certain date, and by that date, only oral approval had been received. In *enXco*,

[24] EISENBERG, *supra* note 8, at 718.
[25] 660 N.E.2d 415 (N.Y. 1995).
[26] 758 F.3d 940 (8th Cir. 2014).

it was conditional on approval of the Commission by a certain date and approval by that date could not be obtained due to a snowstorm, a procedural mistake in holding a first hearing, and the Commission's refusal to waive a twenty-day notice period for a second hearing.

One can see that neither party should be bound to the contract if the performance is impossible. Indeed, the impossibility doctrine operates like a condition and relieves a party of the duty to perform absent an express term in the contract. As we have seen, in a contract to accomplish a certain result, the inability to do so is not an excuse. Yet, the reason a party agrees to such a contract is not that they are best able to bear all risks of non-performance but some of them—those which they can control, foresee, or spread across similar transactions—better than the other party. If a risk is not one a party could best bear and consequently would have assumed, the impossibility doctrine relieves that party of the duty to perform. In these two cases, the risk that performance would be impossible because approval was not obtained was one that neither party could better foresee, control, or spread across similar transactions. One can see why the parties made it a condition.

But why should a party be relieved of their duty to perform because approval was given orally or late? The reason for specifying that it be given in writing was to be sure the landlord was bound. The reason for specifying that it be given by a certain date many months later was to give concreteness to the parties' need for timely notice that they could proceed. But neither party was greatly harmed when the oral notice was followed by written notice or the hearings to obtain approval were delayed by chance events. As we mentioned in discussing those cases, by agreeing on a price, each party gave up the opportunity to obtain a more favorable price in order to avoid the chance of obtaining a less favorable one. The risk each party assumed was that a bargain at the contract price would later prove less advantageous to himself and more advantageous to the other party. One cannot see why the parties to such a contract would agree that one or the other could renege if an event occurred which had little effect on whether the bargain had proved to be favorable or unfavorable. It would be like agreeing to flip a coin and call off the bargain if the coin landed heads. Parties who are risk averse, in the technical economic sense of the term, do not gamble.

In *Red River Commodities, Inc. v. Eidsness*,[27] the court reached the correct result. A grain dealer contracted with a farmer to buy a certain quantity of sunflowers. The contract contained a condition that if performance of the promise became impossible, the farmer would notify the dealer by certified mail.

[27] 459 N.W.2d 805 (N.D 1990).

He gave oral notice instead. The court held the contract was binding because the purpose of the notice requirement had been fulfilled.

ii. A condition that specifies or defines a performance

Specification of the performance

A condition may specify the performance that the other party is to make.

An example is the famous case of *Jacob & Youngs v. Kent*.[28] It was a "condition" of a contract to build a country house that the contractor use "pipe of Cohoes rather than Reading manufacture." Cardozo, speaking for the court, said that the condition was excused even though the contractor used Reading pipe because "the difference in value would be either nominal or nothing." The *Second Restatement* used the facts of *Jacobs* to illustrate the principle that a condition can be excused when its "importance to the obligor" is outweighed by "the extent of the forfeiture."[29]

Because the condition concerns what a party is to receive, the consequences when it is imperfectly fulfilled concern not only fairness but voluntariness. As we will see, both considerations matter in applying the doctrine of substantial performance. Imperfect fulfillment of this sort of condition should be treated in exactly the same way as failure to perform perfectly. The underlying considerations are the same. On the one hand, a party should not be bound to accept a partial or defective performance at a price to which he never would have agreed. On the other, it would be unfair to allow him to escape from a disadvantageous bargain on the excuse that the performance was partial or defective.

Otherwise, a party could escape the doctrine of substantial performance by making perfect performance a "condition" for the other party to be paid. It is not surprising, then, that commentators have used *Jacob & Youngs v. Kent*, as we will do later, to illustrate the doctrine of substantial performance.

Aleatory contracts

An aleatory contract is one in which the performance to which one of the parties is obligated is to assume a particular risk. A condition may define that risk.

An example is an option contract. One party must exchange on certain terms if the option holder so chooses by a certain date. The option holder pays for that commitment. Farnsworth noted that in such cases, courts have held that the right must be exercised by that date. "Any delay is fatal."[30] The reason, he

28 129 N.E. 889 (N.Y. 1921).

29 RESTATEMENT (SECOND) OF CONTRACTS § 229 cmt. b & illus. 1 (AM. LAW INST. 1981).

30 FARNSWORTH, *supra* note 13, at 549.

correctly observed, is that "the option holder has paid for an option that is good for a stated period, during which the option holder has paid for the opportunity to speculate on market changes at the expense of the owner. It would be unfair to allow the holder to prolong this period by delay."[31]

Another example of an aleatory contract is a contract of insurance. Sometimes conditions in insurance contracts specify the date by which some auxiliary duty is to be performed, such as giving notice of an accident, and then we will see that they need not be perfectly fulfilled. Sometimes, however, they define the risk which the insurer assumes. An example is a condition in a life insurance contract that the insured party must die before the insurer is liable. But a condition also defines the risk that an insurer assumes when it concerns the risks the insured is running. When the condition was that the insured take a blood test, the insurance company was not liable when they died in an automobile accident before doing so.[32] When the condition was that the insured does not commit suicide within two years, the company was not liable when they did so thirty-four days before that date.[33]

Some insurance policies contain a condition that a claim be made and reported to the insurer within the period of coverage. One might think that such a condition is an auxiliary one like giving notice of an accident by a certain date. The Wisconsin Supreme Court held that it defines the risk the insurer runs. Such conditions are common in professional liability policies to avoid "long-tail exposure" which is the risk created by the time elapsed "between the date of the error and the time the claim is made."[34]

> Long tail exposure prevents insurance companies from making a precise calculation of premiums based upon the cost of the risks assumed.... [B]ecause claims-made-and-reported policies are advantageous to insurance companies, they apparently result in lower premiums for the insured.[35]

The reason a condition in an aleatory contract must be perfectly fulfilled is that it defines the risk that the insurer has assumed. As Farnsworth said, for the stated period, "the option holder has paid for the opportunity to speculate on market changes at the expense of the owner. It would be unfair to allow the holder to prolong this period by delay."[36] Suppose, however, that during the option period it becomes clear to both parties that the option has become valuable indeed. There

31 *Id.*
32 Fox v. Catholic Knights Ins. Soc., 665 N.W.2d 181, 188 (Wisc. 2003).
33 Officer v. Chase Ins. Life & Annuity Co., 541 F.3d 713 (7th Cir. 2008).
34 Anderson v. Aul, 62 N.W.2d 304, 312 (Wisc. 2015).
35 *Id.*
36 Farnsworth, *supra* note 13, at 549.

is no doubt that to exercise it will be advantageous to the option holder and correspondingly disadvantageous to the other party. The option holder has taken a risk and won. It is not unfair to the other party for the option to be exercised if the option holder accidentally misses the deadline. The option holder did not use the extra time to speculate at that party's expense. Indeed, it is unfair for the other party to escape a losing bargain by insisting on the deadline. The purpose of the deadline was to define the risk that each party was running, not to take away the gain a party made who successfully took that risk.

An example is the celebrated case of *Holiday Inns of America, Inc. v. Knight*.[37] Knight granted Holiday Inns an option to purchase certain real estate for $198,633. Holiday Inns was required to make an initial payment of $10,000 and, to keep the option alive, additional payments of $10,000 on July 1 each of the next four years. On June 30, 1966, Holiday Inns mailed a check for $10,000 which Knight received on July 2, and which he returned with notice that the option was terminated because the payment was late. By that time, the land had increased substantially in value and was clearly worth more than the option price.

The California Supreme Court held that Knight could not terminate the option because to do so would result in a forfeiture. "[I]t is clear that each payment of the $10,000 installment was partially for an option to buy the land during the year and partially for a renewal of the option for another year up to a total of five years." "With the passage of time, the plaintiffs have paid more and more for the right to renew, and that right would be forfeited by requiring payment strictly on time."[38] Moreover, the land had increased in value in part because Holiday Inns had at great expense developed a residential and commercial center on adjacent land.

This result was approved by the *Second Restatement* in illustration 4 to § 297, in which the facts are the same as in *Holiday Inns*. Yet, the *Second Restatement* maintained that the condition would not be excused if, at the end of the five-year period, the option holder were a day late exercising the option to purchase the property.

> The facts being otherwise as in Illustration 4, [the option holder] makes the payments on June 30 of each of the four succeeding years, but does not exercise the option by tendering the $200,000 until July 1, following the June 30 expiration date. [A] court may not decide that the non-occurrence of the . . . condition is excused to the extent of one day because that would give

[37] 450 P.2d 42 (Cal. 1969).
[38] *Id.* at 45.

[the option holder] a more extensive option than that on which the parties agreed.

Technically, yes. As a practical matter, no. The only reason the extra day would advantage the option holder or disadvantage the property owner is if something could happen that day that would affect whether the option was worth exercising. In *Holiday Inn*, the chances of that happening were insignificant. Suppose the option were worth $1,000,000 above the exercise price, and the odds that the option holder would by mistake miss the deadline by a day were 1 in 10,000. Risk-averse parties would never bet on whether the option holder would miss the deadline. The property owner would be unwilling to pay the option holder more than $100 to do so, and the option holder would be unwilling to accept less. The risk of being a day late in exercising an option that clearly is valuable is not one a party would be compensated for bearing.

Another difficulty with the *Restatement* illustrations, and with the *Holiday Inns* decision, is that they both regard forfeiture as a loss of costs incurred. The option holder had lost the value of its previous payments of $10,000 and, perhaps, some of the value of its expenses developing neighboring property. Suppose that Holiday Inns had missed its first renewal payment by one day, before it spent money developing adjacent property, but after Knight's property had doubled in value. Holiday Inn would have taken a risk and won. As discussed earlier, there is no reason why taking away its gain should be treated differently than taking away the value of expenses it had already incurred.

iii. A condition that protects against the increased cost of a performance

One risk the parties allocate when they contract is that a performance may cost more or less than estimated. When they make a contract at a fixed price, the party to perform assumes the risk of a cost overrun. The party receiving the performance assumes the risk that the job could be done more cheaply.

Farnsworth noted that a condition may operate in the same way as the doctrine of impracticability. There is no breach of contract, the party protected by the doctrine need not perform, but the consequence is that the other party is not obliged to do so.[39] As we have seen, in a fixed price contract a party will not assume all the risks that a performance will be more expensive than anticipated but only those that the party can better foresee, control, or spread among similar transactions. The doctrine of impracticability protects a party who has not

[39] FARNSWORTH, *supra* note 13, at 519.

assumed a risk against liability for its consequences. Some conditions either give concreteness to the doctrine of impracticability or extend it. In either case, as with the doctrine of impracticability, the party who need not perform never assumed the risk that the performance would cost so much.

As we saw earlier, the doctrine of impracticability excused performance in *Mineral Park Land v. Howard* where gravel could only be extracted at ten to twelve times the normal cost due to an unforeseen condition: the gravel was under water. The party who agreed to extract it could have limited his risks still further by a condition that he would only extract gravel that could be removed at less than 4 cents a cubic yard. If so, he would not be required to extract gravel that cost 4.1 cents. Farnworth noted that "[i]f the purchaser's duty to close the deal is conditioned on the bank's approval of an eight and one-half percent mortgage, the condition has not occurred if the bank approves and eight and three-quarters percent mortgage."[40] In *Slack v. Munson*,[41] a sale was conditioned on the buyer receiving a $10,000 loan at an anticipated 4.5 percent. He did not have to accept a $9,000 loan plus a $1,000 second mortgage at a higher rate.

Farnworth concluded that a condition must be fulfilled even if the deviation is not "of great moment." He is right, so long as the deviation makes performance more costly for the party protected by the condition. It is as though after the parties had contracted at one price, the buyer wished to give slightly less, or the seller wished to be paid slightly more. The condition has the same effect as the price term. It specifies what a party is to give for what they are to get.

It may be however that the condition is not perfectly fulfilled, and yet the cost of performance of the party it protects will be no greater than if it were. Farnsworth cited *Luttinger v. Rosen*,[42] in which the court held that a buyer did not have to accept an 8.75 percent loan when purchase was conditioned on obtaining a loan of 8.5 percent "from a bank or other lending institution." The purchaser offered to make up the difference "by a funding arrangement, the exact terms of which were not defined."[43] The court held the condition was not fulfilled because in *Luttinger*, the purchaser did not receive a loan for 8.5 percent "from a bank or other lending institution." The purchaser's offer would have left him worse off: he would have been committed to pay 8.75 percent to the bank and trust that the buyer would pay the additional 0.5 percent. He would have been no worse off, however, if the purchaser, rather than a lending institution, had agreed to loan him the full amount at 8.5 percent.

40 *Id.* at 526.
41 61 So.2d 618 (La. App. 1952).
42 316 A.2d 757 (Conn. 1972).
43 *Id.* at 758.

In *Antonini v. Thrifty-Nifty Homes*,[44] a sale was conditioned on receiving a $6,250 loan on the customary terms. The bank would lend the buyer only $4,000. The court held that the buyer did not have to accept the seller's offer to lend him the difference on worse terms: 8 percent repayable in a year and a half. The court said that "neither of the parties at the time of the confecting of the agreement entertained any idea whatsoever of carrying out the financing of the sale wholly or partly between the seller and purchaser."[45] Suppose that the seller had offered to lend him the full $6,250 on the same terms he had anticipated receiving from a bank?

In *Holst v. Guynn*,[46] the contract was conditioned on obtaining a loan from the Veterans' Administration (VA) which the VA approved conditional on no change in the buyer's income. The VA then disapproved the loan when the buyer lost his job. The seller claimed he should have sought a loan elsewhere. The court held he did not need to do so because "the contract language . . . expressly provided that the earnest money would be refunded if the [buyers] did not obtain a V.A. loan." The court noted, however, that the buyer had unsuccessfully sought financing elsewhere, and that "it is doubtful that [he] could have obtained financing from any source while he was unemployed."[47] Suppose he has received financing elsewhere on the same terms as the VA loan. Could he have refused to go ahead because "the contract language expressly provided" that he receive a loan from the VA?

In an illustration in the *Second Restatement*, A sells good to B "conditional on B obtaining from X Bank" on certain terms.[48] What if X bank turned him down, but the same terms were offered to him by Y Bank or by the seller himself?

As long as imperfect fulfillment does not leave the party protected by the condition financially worse off, it should not matter. Otherwise the condition does not shift a risk to the party who can best bear it. It creates a risk that only exists because of the phrasing of the condition. The party protected by the condition would be as well protected if the condition were phrased differently so that it did not require the loan be made by a lending institution or the VA or the X bank. When the parties agree to buy and sell at a set price, they allocate a risk that must fall on one party or the other, and each is compensated for the risk that they take. Each assumes the risk that they might receive a better offer to avoid the risk of receiving a worse one. Parties who are risk averse in the technical economic sense of the term would no more allow the enforceability of that bargain to depend on

[44] 76 So.2d 564 (La.App. 1955).

[45] *Id.* at 565.

[46] 696 P.2d 632 (Wyo. 1985).

[47] *Id.* at 634.

[48] RESTATEMENT (SECOND) OF CONTRACTS § 224, illus. 1 (AM. LAW INST. 1981).

an event that does not affect its value to either party than they would allow it to turn on the flip of a coin.

Were it otherwise, a great deal would turn on accidents of phrasing. In *Anaheim Co. v. Holcombe*,[49] the buyer agreed to purchase a house for $45,000 contingent on obtaining a loan for $25,000. The seller offered to loan him that amount on the same terms after he was denied a loan by a savings and loan association. The court held that he must accept the seller's offer of financing and go ahead with the sale. In *Bilman v. Hensel*,[50] the sale was conditional on the buyer's ability to obtain a $35,000 loan. He informed the seller that he needed an extra $5,000 to obtain such a loan. The court held that he could not back out after the seller agreed to cut the price by $5,000. A slight difference in phrasing and the conditions in both contracts would not have been perfectly fulfilled. That difference should not affect the result.

Supposing that the non-fulfillment of a condition does increase the costs of performance to one of the parties, it still may be that the party whom the condition protects would have been willing to compensate the other party for this added security given the consequences to him of terminating the contract. In *Varel v. Banc One Capital Partners Inc.*,[51] a borrower transferred stock as security for a loan subject to a right of first refusal if the lender were to sell it. The transaction was conditional on several loan guarantees, one of which lapsed when the borrower dissolved the corporate guarantor. The court held since that guarantor's assets were worth only $3,000, the loss of security was far outweighed by the loss of the right of first refusal:

> [T]he penalty facing Varel [the borrower] is extreme when measured against the purpose of the default provision. Varel, the eighty-two-year-old founder of Varel Manufacturing, has always wished to keep control of the company within the family. He argues that without his right of first refusal . . . regaining control over his company is placed beyond his financial grasp.[52]

In reaching this conclusion, the court proceeded just as it should, according to an Official Comment of the *Restatement Second* explaining when a condition is excused by forfeiture. A court must "weigh the extent of the forfeiture by the obligee against the importance to the obligor of the risk from which he sought to be protected and the degree to which that protection will be lost if the non-occurrence of the condition is excused to the extent required to prevent forfeiture."[53] In *Varel*, the adverse effect of non-fulfillment was outweighed by

[49] 426 P.2d 743 (Or. 1967).

[50] 391 N.E.2d 671 (Ind. App. 1979).

[51] 55 F.3d 1016 (5th Cir. 1995) (applying Texas law).

[52] *Id.* at 1018.

[53] Restatement (Second) of Contracts § 229 cmt. b (Am. Law Inst. 1981).

the harm that termination of the contract would cause the other party. That approach is correct. As we have said, if the risk or burden of placing the condition on one party is greater than if it were placed on the other, it should fall on the party who can bear it most easily. If it falls on the party who can bear it least easily, they surely would not be compensated for bearing it.

iv. A condition that safeguards the expected benefits of a performance

Other conditions reduce the risk that the performance will not provide the benefit that the recipient hoped to receive. As we have seen, in some situations, even without such a condition, the recipient would be protected by the doctrine of frustration of purpose. Farnsworth, who noted that conditions may operate like the doctrine of impracticability, also noted that they may operate like the doctrine of frustration of purpose. They give concreteness to the doctrine, or they extend it.

An example is a hypothetical case in the *Second Restatement*:

> A, as the result of financial reverses, sells B a valuable painting for $1,000,000, but reserves a right to repurchase it by tendering the same price on or before August 18 if he again finds himself in such a financial condition that he can keep it for his personal enjoyment. A's tender of $1,000,000 by August 18 and his being in such financial condition that he can keep the painting for his personal enjoyment are cumulative conditions and redelivery of the painting does not become due unless both of them occur.[54]

The benefit A wants from the contract is to part with the painting for $1,000,000 if he must but only if he must. The condition assures him of that benefit. Absent the condition, the doctrine of frustration of purpose would not allow him to avoid the sale if, unexpectedly, he inherited so much money that his own purpose in selling the painting was frustrated. As we have seen, that doctrine applies only when the purpose of buyers or sellers in general would be frustrated, not just the purpose of a particular party. An example is the coronation cases in which the postponement of the king's coronation frustrated the purpose of anyone who had rented a flat overlooking the route of the procession.

It may be that the condition is not perfectly fulfilled. An example is *Burger King v. Family Dining, Inc.*,[55] which the *Second Restatement* commended for its

[54] *Id.* at § 224, illus. 5 (1979).
[55] 426 F.Supp. 485 (E.D.Penn. 1977).

"excellent discussion" of the issue.[56] Family Dining promised to open or have under active construction one new restaurant in each of the first ten years of the contract. Burger King would grant a year of exclusivity for each new restaurant followed by an additional eighty years of exclusivity if all the restaurants were built on time. Exclusivity meant the exclusive right to operate a restaurant in a given territory. Family Dining did build ten restaurants but not on time, and Burger King tried to take away its right to exclusivity. The court construed timely construction of the restaurants by Family Dining as a condition for it to receive the right to exclusivity. It acknowledged that the condition had not been fulfilled. It held that, nevertheless, that Burger King could not take away this right. The right was far more valuable to Family Dining than the exact fulfillment of the condition to Burger King:

> In arguing that by termination Family Dining will lose nothing that it earned, Burger King overlooks the risks assumed and the efforts expended by Family Dining . . . in making the venture successful in the exclusive territory. While it is true that Family Dining realized a return on its investment, certainly part of this return was the prospect of continued exclusivity. . . .
>
> Assuming all ten were built on time Burger King would have been able to expect some definable level of revenue, a percentage of which it lost due to the delay. . . . In any event if Family Dining were forced to forfeit the right of exclusivity it would lose something of incalculable value based on its investment of time and money developing the area, the significant risks assumed and the fact that there remains some 76 years of exclusivity under the Territorial Agreement. Such a loss would be without any commensurate breach on its part since the injury caused to Burger King by the delay is relatively modest and within definable limits.[57]

The Reporter's Note to the section of the *Second Restatement all the way through* on the excuse of conditions commended the opinion in *Burger King* for its "excellent discussion of the principle on which this Section is based."[58] A court must "weigh the extent of the forfeiture by the obligee against the importance to the obligor of the risk from which he sought to be protected and the degree to which that protection will be lost if the non-occurrence of the condition is excused to the extent required to prevent forfeiture."[59] As we have seen, that is exactly how a court should proceed.

56 Restatement (Second) of Contracts § 229 cmt. a (Am. Law Inst. 1981).
57 426 F.Supp. at 494–95.
58 Restatement (Second) of Contracts § 229 cmt. a (Am. Law Inst. 1981).
59 *Id.* at cmt. b.

v. A condition that facilitates the determination of whether a duty has been performed or a performance is due

A party can put a condition in the contract that makes it easier to tell whether a duty has been performed or a performance is due.

A condition may do so by giving concreteness to an ancillary duty. For example, a person owing a performance has an ancillary duty to complete it within a reasonable time. A condition may make that duty more specific and so make it easier to tell if the duty has been fulfilled. It may provide that performance must be completed by a particular date.

The *Restatement Second* suggests that if the delay is small, the condition should be excused. According to an illustration in the section on excuse for forfeiture:

> A contracts to make repairs on B's house, in return for which B agrees to pay \$10,000 "on condition that the repairs are completed by October 1." The repairs are not completed until October 2. A court may decide that there are two cumulative conditions, repair of the house and completion of the repairs by October 1, and that the non-occurrence of the second condition is excused to the extent of one day.[60]

The *Restatement* is correct. A party who must perform perfectly and fails to do so can recover for benefits conferred on the other party but not for lost profit or costs incurred. Those amount may be much larger than the amount cost of the imperfection in performance to the other party. In the *Restatement* example, the loss to A if he cannot recover \$10,000 may be larger than the loss B will suffer if the repairs are a day late. If so, it is unlikely that B would have been willing to compensate A for running the risk of finishing a day late. To require perfect fulfillment would impose a risk on A for which he was not compensated.

It is true that if performance is delayed, the party for whom it was made may have trouble proving the amount of his damages. The solution, as we will see, is for the parties to include a liquidated damages clause in their contract estimating in advance what these damages are likely to be. As we will also see, however, courts will enforce such a clause only if it is a reasonable estimate of the harm a party is likely to suffer. They will not enforce a penalty, that is, a clause in which the party in breach is liable for an amount that bears no relationship to this harm. In that respect, the burden imposed by a requirement of perfect fulfillment is like a penalty clause. Parties who are risk averse in the technical economic sense of the term would not agree either to a penalty clause or to a requirement of perfect fulfillment.

[60] *Id.* at § 239 illus. 3.

A condition may also make it easier to determine whether the other party has a duty to perform. An example is a time limit for giving notice of a potential claim or providing information about it so that the party who may be liable has a better opportunity to investigate. A time limit may be set to the duty of a contractor who fires a subcontractor to give notice, before he hires someone to take their place, to the surety who guaranteed the agent's performance. A time limit may be set to the duty of a company that discovers it has been defrauded by its agent to provide evidence to the surety who guaranteed the agent's fidelity. A time limit may be set to the duty of an insured to provide the insurer with evidence of a claim.

The purpose of these provisions is to facilitate investigation of a claim by a party who may be liable. The additional uncertainty caused by the delay in notice concerns whether that party owes anything at all. As before, the loss which that party suffers from the delay may be small compared with the loss the other party will suffer by losing the benefit of the bargain. Yet it is harder to tell.

Consequently, it is not surprising then that courts are divided on the effect of such a condition. Even in insurance cases, some courts insist on strict compliance.[61] Others give effect to the condition only if the insurer was prejudiced.[62] Some of these courts do not require proof of prejudice if the insured failed to give notice for an unduly long time. Courts have said that strict compliance is required with the notice provisions of conditions of performance and fidelity bonds in cases in which it did not matter because, again, notice was not given for an unduly long time.[63] There cannot be a general rule. All a court can do is to compare the prejudice to the one party of losing the opportunity to better investigate with the loss to the other party of losing the benefit of the contract. It should ask whether prejudice to the one party is so great that it would be willing to compensate the other for the risk of losing that benefit by a failure to strictly comply.

vi. A condition that avoids litigation

If a duty is violated, the non-breaching party has an action against the party in breach but not if a condition is unfulfilled. A party may wish to insert a condition in a contract to avoid having to sue the other party for failing to perform.

[61] Remarkably, the Massachusetts Supreme Judicial Court applied this rule in the case in which it repudiated it, on the grounds that the new rule, which requires prejudice, should be applied only prospectively.

[62] Clementi v. Nationwide Mut. Fire Ins. Co., 16 P.3d 223 (Colo. 2001).

[63] Hunt Const. Group, Inc. v. National Wrecking Corp., 587 F.3d 1119 (D.C. Cir. 2009). (performance bond); U.S. Shipping Board Merchant Fleet Corporation, to Use of U.S. v. Aetna Casualty & Surety Co., 98 F.2d 238 (D.C. App. 1938) (fidelity bond).

For example, it may be a condition of the seller's agreement that before closing the contract, the buyer put funds in escrow or otherwise demonstrate they are available.[64] It may be a condition that before closing the buyer provide title insurance.[65] It may be a condition that the seller receive a deposit to be kept if the buyer defaults.[66] In such cases, courts have held correctly that the seller is not bound unless the condition is fulfilled. The alternative would be to require the seller who is not paid or does not receive good title to litigate, and that is the result that the condition is meant to avoid.

Other conditions require a party to give notice of a claim before bringing suit so that the other party will have a chance, not only to investigate, but to decide whether to settle and so avoid the cost of litigation. In *Soltani v. Western & Southern Life Insurance Co.*,[67] the Ninth Circuit, applying California law, refused to enforce such a condition in an employment contract. In *Inman v. Clyde Hall Drilling Co.*, the Supreme Court of Alaska reached the opposite result.[68] *Inman* is cited by Farnsworth as an example of the perfect compliance rule. Nevertheless, neither case concerned the doctrine of excuse by forfeiture. Both courts applied the doctrine of unconscionability. The reason that the outcomes differed is that the Ninth Circuit, correctly, paid attention to whether the term was substantively unconscionable. The Supreme Court of Alaska, incorrectly, insisted that the term had to be procedurally unconscionable as well. That view, as we saw earlier, is mistaken. Procedural unconscionability should be relevant only as evidence of substantive unconscionability.

In *Soltani*, a provision in an employment contract held that the employee must give notice of a claim within ten days. The court said:

> we can discern little justification for the short ten-day notice provision. . . . Ten days is simply not enough time for the company to investigate the factual basis of a claim, to attempt to settle claims without litigation or consider fiscal implications of potential litigation, or to take corrective action to prevent other such claims.[69]

In *Inman*, a derrickman claimed that he had been wrongfully discharged. His contract provided that it is a "condition precedent" to any claim that he give notice of it within thirty days after the claim rises and that he cannot sue within six months thereafter. He brought a suit within thirty days. The court said that

[64] Edelman Arts, Inc. v. Art Intern. (UK) Ltd., 841 F.Supp.2d 810 (S.D.N.Y. 2012).
[65] Merritt Hill Vineyards Inc. v. Windy Heights Vineyard, Inc., 460 N.E.2d 1077 (N.Y. 1984).
[66] Silver Air v. Aeronautic Development Corp. Ltd., 656 F.Supp. 170, 175 (S.D.N.Y. 1987).
[67] 258 F.3d 1038 (9th Cir. 2001).
[68] 369 P.2d 498 (Ala. 1962).
[69] 258 F.3d at 1046.

the "purpose [of the condition] is not disclosed." It "may have been intended to afford the Company timely opportunity to rectify the basis for a just claim." But "whatever the objective was," the term "was not unfair, unfair without any examination of the burden to the employee of forfeiting his claim if he did not comply versus the advantage to the company if he did."[70] The reason supposedly was that the employee understood the term, and the employer did not insert it to set a trap for him. In short, because there was no evidence of procedural unconscionability, the court believed that it did not have to examine whether the provision was substantively unfair. As we maintained earlier, what matters is substantive unfairness. "Procedural unconscionability" matters only because, the easier it is to take advantage of a party, the more likely it is that advantage was taken. The court said that for it "[t]o hold otherwise would be to simply ignore an explicit provision of the contract and say that it had no meaning."[71] In the first place, that is the usual result of holding that a term is unconscionable which is the question the court claimed to be addressing. In the second, the employer could have asked that the employee's suit be dismissed without prejudice to give it time to consider his claim.

III. Conditions of satisfaction

A condition of satisfaction may serve various purposes. Such a condition is not met unless someone—a party or a third person—is satisfied that the event on which the contract is conditioned has occurred.

i. "Subjective" conditions of satisfaction

As noted earlier, if a condition of satisfaction is "subjective," a party who is genuinely dissatisfied is not bound. Sometimes the reason for including such a condition in the contract is that a performance is only valuable to a recipient who is genuinely satisfied with it. An artist may agree to paint a portrait for a client who will pay only if satisfied. Such a condition could be a term of any contract in which the object is a party's gratification or enjoyment or sense of security or well-being. It could be a contract in which I agree to rent a vacation house as long as, upon inspection, I am satisfied with the accommodation, or to hire a nanny whom, after a trial period, I am satisfied I can trust.

70 369 P.2d at 500.
71 *Id.* at 501.

Sometimes, the reason for including such a condition is that a party wants to make a judgment based on further information before making a commitment. In *Mattei v. Hopper*,[72] a developer agreed to buy a parcel of land for a shopping center but only if he was satisfied with the leases that he could enter into. In *Western Hills v. Pfau*,[73] a condition was held to be subjective in which the purchaser agreed to buy land subject to his ability "to negotiate with the City of McMinnville as to planned development satisfactory" to both parties. Since the purpose of the condition is to make the commitment contingent on a party's judgment, the condition, again is "subjective." The contract is binding only if that party is genuinely satisfied.

ii. "Objective" conditions of satisfaction

To be distinguished are cases in which a party uses a condition of satisfaction to ensure that the other party's performance is made correctly. For example, the contract may provide that the contractor will be paid only if the recipient or a third party is satisfied that the work has been completed according to the specifications of the contract. Such a condition is "objective" in the sense that there is a standard other than the recipient's personal satisfaction for determining whether the performance is the one the recipient contracted to receive. The question is what to do if the recipient or the third party is not satisfied but their dissatisfaction is unreasonable.

The satisfaction of the party to whom performance is due

As with a subjective condition, the dissatisfaction of the party who is to receive the performance must be genuine. The recipient must honestly believe that the performance is not as it should have been. Otherwise, a court will set such condition aside.[74]

It may be, however, that the recipient's dissatisfaction is honest but unreasonable. For example, a person with the requisite qualifications—an architect or engineer—would conclude that the performance conformed to the specifications in the contract. One might conclude from this evidence that the recipient who claims to be dissatisfied is not being honest. The question, however, is what to do if that claim is honest but unreasonable.

[72] 330 P.2d 625 (Cal.1958).

[73] 508 P.2d 201 (Or. 1973).

[74] Grobarchik v. Nasa Mtg. & Inv. Co., 186 A. 433 (N.J. Sup. 1936). Although the court construed the contract to call for "calling for actual satisfaction, as distinguished from reasonable satisfaction," the condition was that the work be done "in a good, workmanlike and substantial manner." *Id.* at 434.

The answer should depend on whether the other party was compensated for bearing the risk that the recipient would be unreasonably dissatisfied. That is an unlikely possibility. Suppose the recipient were to explain:

> I want you to understand that you are assuming the risk that you will not be paid, not only if I am reasonably dissatisfied with your performance but also if I am unreasonably satisfied. That additional risk is significant, or I would not have assigned it to you in the contract. For that reason, I am paying you an extra amount to bear it, an extra amount which, by the way, you will not receive if I am unreasonably dissatisfied with your work.

The larger that risk seems to be, the less likely it is that the party to perform would be willing to bear it in return for an extra amount of money that may never be paid.

Consequently, even if it cannot be shown that a party's dissatisfaction was insincere, most courts have refused to enforce the condition when it can be shown that it was unreasonable. According to the *Second Restatement*:

> When it is a condition of an obligor's duty that he be satisfied with respect to the obligee's performance or with respect to something else, and it is practicable to determine whether a reasonable person in the position of the obligor would be satisfied, an interpretation is preferred under which the condition occurs if such a reasonable person in the position of the obligor would be satisfied.[75]

According to an Official Comment, "it will not usually be supposed that the obligee has assumed the risk of the obligor's unreasonable, even if honest, dissatisfaction."[76]

To show that the obligor was unreasonably dissatisfied, it must, of course, be "practicable to determine whether a reasonable person in the position of the obligor would be satisfied." Nevertheless, whether it is practicable is a different issue that whether the condition should be enforced if the obligator's dissatisfaction is unreasonable. Sometimes, as we have seen, the reason for including such a condition in the contract is that a performance is only valuable to a recipient who is genuinely satisfied, like the client who commissions a portrait. The *Restatement*'s illustrations obscured this distinction by suggesting that in such cases, the reason

[75] RESTATEMENT (SECOND) OF CONTRACTS § 228 (AM. LAW INST. 1981).
[76] *Id.* at cmt. b.

that the condition is enforced is if the impracticability of determining whether a party's dissatisfaction was unreasonable. For example:

> A contracts with B to paint a portrait of B's daughter, for which B promises to pay $5,000 "if entirely satisfied." A paints the portrait, but B honestly states that he is not satisfied with it and refuses to pay the $5,000. B gives no reason except that the portrait does not please him, and according to experts in the field the portrait is an admirable work of art. A has no claim against B since it is not practicable to apply an objective test to the painting.[77]

The reason is not that one cannot apply an objective test to the painting. The reason is that it does not matter whether A was unreasonably dissatisfied.

Similarly:

> A contracts to have B furnish a four-piece band to play in A's inn for six months, with a provision, "If band proves unsatisfactory to A contract is subject to two weeks' notice." A occasionally objects when B is absent and a guitar is substituted for B's string bass. After two months, A gives notice of termination, stating that he is dissatisfied for this reason. B has no claim against A since it is not practicable to apply an objective test to the band's performance.[78]

Again, the reason is not that one cannot apply an objective test to the band's performance. If A had been hiring the band to perform at his wedding, the case would be like that of the portrait: it does not matter whether he is unreasonably dissatisfied. But the same is true when he is hiring the band to play at his inn. Whether it will be profitable to employ them is a matter of business judgment on which he has the final say, like the quality of the leases in *Mattei.*

For the *Second Restatement*, the issue is how to interpret a condition that is ambiguous. It would enforce the condition if its meaning is clear. According to an Official Comment: "If the agreement leaves no doubt that it is only honest satisfaction that is meant and no more, it will be so interpreted, and the condition does not occur if the obligor is honestly, even though unreasonably, dissatisfied."[79]

Nevertheless, such a condition should not be enforced for reasons we considered in discussing when a term of a is unconscionable and when a condition should be excused. A party who was not compensated for assuming a risk should not be held responsible if it materializes. According to the *Restatement*, "it will not usually be supposed that the obligee has assumed the risk of the obligor's

[77] *Id.* at illus. 4.
[78] *Id.* at illus. 5.
[79] *Id.* at cmt. a.

unreasonable, even if honest, dissatisfaction."[80] Why should it be supposed, then, that the obligee not only assumed that risk but was compensated for doing so when the language is clear? If not, then the provision should not be enforced even if the language is clear. Otherwise, so long as the language is clear, no term would be held unconscionable, and no condition would be excused.

The problem is illustrated by one of Judge Posner's noteworthy opinions, *Morin Building Products, Co. v. Baystone Construction, Inc.*[81] General Motors hired Baystone to build an addition to its plant. Baystone hired Morin to construct the aluminum walls. The contract provided that:

> all work shall be done subject to the approval of [General Motor's] authorized agent, and his decision in matters relating to artistic effect shall be final. . . . [S]hould any dispute arise with regard to the quality or fitness of materials or workmanship, the decision as to its acceptability shall rest strictly with [General Motors].[82]

General Motors' authorized agent rejected the work because "[v]iewed in bright sunlight from an acute angle, the exterior siding did not give the impression of a uniform finish."[83] Judge Posner noted that "aesthetic considerations were entirely secondary to considerations of function and cost."[84] He observed:

> It is unlikely that Morin intended to bind itself to a higher and perhaps unattainable standard of achieving whatever perfection of matching that General Motors's agent would have insisted upon. . . . Morin would have been running a considerable risk of rejection if it had to agree to such a condition, and it therefore could have been expected to demand a compensating increase in the contract price. This would have required General Motors to pay a premium to obtain a freedom of action that it could not have thought terribly important, since its objective was not aesthetic.[85]

In short there was every reason to believe that Morin was not compensated for the risk that it was assuming. For Posner, that was not enough. Although the language of the condition seems perfectly clear, he cast doubt on whether the parties would have intended it to cover such a case. He then applied the rule of the *Restatement* regarding unclear conditions.

80 *Id.* at cmt. b.
81 717 F.2d 413 (7th Cir. 1983).
82 *Id.* at 414.
83 *Id.*
84 *Id.* at 415.
85 *Id.* at 416.

> Lest this conclusion be thought to strike at the foundations of freedom of contract, we repeat that if it appeared from the language or circumstances of the contract that the parties really intended General Motors to have the right to reject Morin's work for failure to satisfy the private aesthetic taste of General Motors' representative, the rejection would have been proper even if unreasonable. But the contract is ambiguous.[86]

As noted earlier, in discussing unconscionability, parties with their eyes open would never put a term in a contract that imposed a burden or risk on one party without compensating them for bearing it. Posner's hypothetical case in which General Motors and Morin genuinely agreed to impose a risk on Morin for which General Motors would be unwilling to compensate it is a phantom. It is a mistake to think that the reason for refusing to enforce such a term is respect for the intention of the parties who, in this hypothetical case, would not have agreed to it. The reason is fairness.

Satisfaction of a third party

New York courts regard contracts conditioned on the satisfaction of a third party as subject to the same rule as those conditioned on the satisfaction of one of the parties. The condition is not enforced if the third party is genuinely but unreasonably dissatisfied. In *Arc Electric Construction Co. v. George A. Fuller Co.*,[87] the contract was conditioned on an architect's satisfaction that the work had been completed. The court held that condition need not be fulfilled when there was no evidence of "any defects in performance which could have justified the architect's failure to approve."[88] The court cited an old New York case, *Nolan v. Whitney*,[89] in which, again, payment of a builder was conditioned on obtaining an architect's certificate. According to the court, as "he had substantially performed his contract, the architect was bound to give him the certificate, and his refusal to give it was unreasonable." "An unreasonable refusal on the part of an architect in such a case to give the certificate dispenses with its necessity."[90]

It might seem that it should not matter whether the recipient or a third party is unreasonably dissatisfied with the performance. It would seem that the other party is as unlikely to have been compensated for bearing the one risk as for bearing the other. The difference is that the condition that a third party be satisfied may be put in the contract for the legitimate purpose of avoiding litigation. Of course, the same purpose might be served by a condition that the

[86] *Id.* at 417.
[87] 247 N.E.2d 111 (N.Y. 1969).
[88] *Id.* at 114.
[89] 88 N.Y. 648 (1882).
[90] *Id.* at 650.

other party themself be satisfied, but it would not do so as well. To leave the matter to a third party is as expeditious, more likely to be accurate, less subject to bias, and less likely to cause litigation over whether that party was honestly dissatisfied.

Such a condition changes the procedure for answering the question whether the performance was as it should have been. It is answered by a third party rather than by a judge or jury. Earlier, we discussed the fairness of an auxiliary term that modifies the procedure by which the rights of the parties are determined. Such a modification is fair if it does not increase the burden or risks that fall on one party rather than the other. An example is a procedure which is cheaper for both parties or more accurate than litigation. If the parties leave the issue to be determined by a neutral and qualified third party, the procedure is certainly cheaper than litigation and may be more accurate. It is less likely to be biased than if the issue were left to one of the parties.

In *Brant Const. Co., Inc. v. Metropolitan Water Reclamation Dist. of Greater Chicago*,[91] the 7th Circuit upheld the decision of a third party which was challenged as unreasonable, noting that the parties might prefer to leave the decision to him rather than to a jury. A contractor disputed the decision of a chief engineer, based on the suitability of the soil, concerning the amount that the contractor was obliged to excavate. According to a condition of the contract, "[t]o prevent all disputes and litigation, it is further agreed . . . that the engineer shall in all cases decide every question of an engineering character which may arise relevant to the execution of the work under this contract on the part of the contractor, and his decision shall be final and conclusive on both parties hereto."[92] Commendably, in denying that the decision of the engineer could be challenged, the court did not merely point to the language. It explained the purpose the condition served. "A jury is not the appropriate arbiter of soil suitability where the contract explicitly delegates that task to the Reclamation District's chief engineer."[93]

That result is endorsed by the *Second Restatement* in one of its illustrations.

> A contracts with B to repair B's building for $20,000, payment to be made "on the satisfaction of C, B's architect, and the issuance of his certificate." A makes the repairs, but C refuses to issue his certificate, and explains why he is not satisfied. Other experts in the field consider A's performance to be satisfactory and disagree with C's explanation. A has no claim against B. . . . If C is honestly

[91] 967 F.2d 244 (7th Cir. 1992).
[92] *Id.* at 247–48.
[93] *Id.* at 248.

> not satisfied, B is under no duty to pay A, and it makes no difference if his dissatisfaction was not reasonable.[94]

Once, again, however, the third party must be genuinely dissatisfied. Moreover, it is widely accepted that the condition will not be enforced if that party is not merely mistaken but grossly mistaken. In another illustration from the *Second Restatement*, the facts are the same as those in the one just described except:

> C does not make a proper inspection of the work and gives no reasons for his dissatisfaction. A has a claim against B for $20,000. In using the quoted language, A and B assumed that C would exercise an honest judgment and by failing to make a proper inspection, C did not exercise such a judgment. Since the parties have omitted an essential term to cover this situation, the court will supply a term (see §204) requiring A to pay B if C ought reasonably to have been satisfied.[95]

The *Restatement* is correct that the parties assumed that C would make a proper inspection. Parties who are risk averse in the economic sense of the term would not have agreed to be bound by his opinion regardless of whether he does so. If he does not, his decision is random, like the result of flipping a coin. And, as we have seen, risk-averse parties do not gamble. Neither party would be willing to compensate the other for bearing such a risk. Therefore, it would be unfair to enforce the condition. It is awkward to say that the reason is that the parties "omitted an essential term" by failing to say that the architect must make a proper inspection, and this omission will be filled by supplying a term as provided by applying § 204. Section 204 says that a court will supply "a term which is reasonable," and an Official Comment to that section explain that a reasonable term is one that "comports with community standards of fairness."[96] Which "community" is not made clear, but as long as this hypothetical community believes it is unfair for a party to bear a risk for which they were not compensated, the answer comes out the same.

[94] Restatement (Second) of Contracts § 229 illus. 5 (Am. Law Inst. 1981).
[95] *Id.* at illus. 7.
[96] *Id.* § 204 cmt. d.

11

Conflicts in the Expression of Assent

I. Conflicts between expression and intent

i. "Subjective" and "objective" theories

One of the great debates in the nineteenth and early twentieth centuries was over which of two theories of contract formation is correct: the "subjective" or the "objective" theory. As we have seen, critics of the subjective or will theory claimed that it cannot explain why the parties are sometimes bound by terms which they did not envision, let alone intend. They also claimed that it cannot explain why relief was given for mistake.

Yet another problem, according to critics, is that the will theories cannot explain why a party is sometimes bound by what they said even though it was not what they meant. The solution, they claimed, was an "objective theory": contract is defined as the effect that the law gave to what the parties did or said regardless of what they meant. According to Williston, in interpreting the language of the contract "[t]he only meaning which is generally pertinent is the meaning of the language when judged by the standard adopted by the law."

Williston acknowledged:

> In most instances it would make little practical difference whether it was said that the mental assent of the parties was the vital element in the formation of contract, and that their words or acts proved their mental attitude, or whether it was said that their words and acts were the only essential matters in the formation of a contract.[1]

Nevertheless, according to Williston, mental assent does not matter. Otherwise a party who said one thing and meant another would only be bound because of the effect on the other party. "[T]he consequences would properly follow . . . that unless the other party has altered his position in reliance on the mistaken manifestation, there would be no obligation, and even if there were such alteration of position, the obligation would be based on estoppel rather than

[1] Samuel Williston & George J. Thompson, Treatise on the Law of Contracts 20 (rev. ed. 1938).

Foundations of American Contract Law. James Gordley, Oxford University Press. © Oxford University Press 2023.
DOI: 10.1093/oso/9780197686089.003.0011

on contract."[2] The party who misspoke would be liable only if the other party acted in reliance. There was no solid support for such a doctrine in the case law.[3]

As we have seen, Williston wrote his objective theory into the *First Restatement*: "The mental assent of the parties is not requisite for the formation of the contracts."[4] It was then accepted by the *Second Restatement*. The *Second Restatement* defines a promise as a "manifestation of intention."[5] "The phrase 'manifestation of intention' adopts an external or objective standard for interpreting conduct; it means the external expression of intention as distinguished from undisclosed intention."[6] Allan Farnsworth, the Reporter for the *Second Restatement*, wrote in 2004 that the objective theory had triumphed. "By the end of the 19th century the objective theory had become ascendant and courts universally accept it today."[7]

Nevertheless, Melvin Eisenberg had observed twenty years earlier that the rules of the *Second Restatement* conflict with the objective theory. The *Second Restatement* "stands the position of the [objective] school on its head by giving primacy to mutually held subjective intent."[8] As we will see, Eisenberg was right. Amazing as it seems after the long-standing debate between proponents of subjective and objective theories, the makers of the *Second Restatement* abandoned the objective theory without realizing that they had done so.

Part of the explanation lies in the maneuvers that Williston had performed in the *First Restatement* to prevent his objective theory from colliding with common sense and case law. One, described earlier, was to sidestep cases in which the relief given for mistake conflicted with the objective theory. Relief was given in courts of equity, and therefore, supposedly, it did not need to be explained by the objective theory. A second was to grant that the parties were bound by what one party intended if the other knew that his intention differed from the meaning of the words in the contract.[9] According to the *First Restatement*, a party's "intention is material." "only" in that "exceptional case."[10] A third was to provide that the parties' mental assent did matter if their words or acts were

[2] *Id.*

[3] *Id.*

[4] RESTATEMENT (FIRST) OF CONTRACTS § 71 cmt. a (AM L. INST. 1932). Similarly, "neither mental assent to the promises in the contract nor real or apparent intent that the contract shall be legally binding is essential." *Id.* at § 20.

[5] RESTATEMENT (SECOND) OF CONTRACTS § 2 (AM. LAW INST. 1981).

[6] *Id.* at cmt. b.

[7] E. ALLAN FARNSWORTH, CONTRACTS 117 (4th ed. 2004).

[8] Melvin A. Eisenberg, *The Responsive Model of Contract Law*, 36 STAN. L. REV. 1107, 1126 (1984).

[9] RESTATEMENT (FIRST) OF CONTRACTS § 71(c) (AM. LAW INST. 1932).

[10] *Id.* at § 71, cmt. a. Actually, there was another case as well: according to the *Restatement*, a party was not bound if, without negligence, he indicated his assent to a contract when he did not intend to any such thing: for example, he signed a promise to settle a claim which he believed to be a receipt. *Id.* § 70, illus. 1; *see id.* at § 20, illus. 4 (offer mailed "absent-mindedly"); WILLISTON & THOMPSON, *supra* note 1, at § 95a.

"uncertain or ambiguous." If both parties attached the same meaning to these ambiguous words or acts, they were bound by that meaning. If they attached different meanings, no contract was formed unless one party had reason to know the meaning attached to the words or acts of the other. If so, the party who knew was bound by the meaning that the other party attached to them.[11] Williston was adjusting his objective theory pragmatically. He did not explain why mental assent should matter when words or acts are ambiguous. By an objective theory, it would seem, mental assent should not matter at all.

In the *Second Restatement*, these exceptions became the rule. It dropped the requirement that mental intent only prevails when the words or acts are ambiguous. According to § 201(1), "Where the parties have attached the same meaning to a promise or agreement or to a term thereof, it is interpreted in accordance with that meaning." According to § 201(2)–(3), no contract is formed "where the parties have attached different meanings" with two exceptions: (a) when one "party did not know of any different meaning attached by the other, and the other knew of the meaning attached by the first party," and (b) when one party "had no reason to know of the meaning attached by the other, and the other had reason to know the meaning attached by the first party."

The objective theory had been implicitly discarded. A contract is formed when both parties attach the same meaning to their words, whether or not the words correspond to that meaning. With the two exceptions just noted, it is not formed when the parties attached different meanings whatever words they may have used. As Eisenberg observed, the *Second Restatement* "squarely reverses the strict objectivism of classical contract law, under which the subjective intention of the parties was irrelevant even if it mutually held. . . . [T]he objectivists had it wrong."[12]

According to Eisenberg, the passing of the objective theory is for the best. Yet the objectivists were correct that sometimes mental assent does not matter. We need to reconsider why.

ii. When expression prevails over intent

When one party's words do not correspond to their intent, the words may matter because the other party was misled. The difficulty, as Williston and Eisenberg noted, is that it would then seem that the party who was misled should not be able to hold the other party to the contract but should only be entitled to

[11] Restatement (First) of Contracts § 71 (Am. Law Inst. 1932).

[12] Lon L. Fuller, Melvin Aron Eisenberg & Mark F. Gergen, Basic Contract Law 347 (9th concise ed. 2013).

compensation for any damages they suffered through being misled. As Eisenberg noted, "the difficult question in such cases is not liability but damages. Since the addressor is held liable as a principled matter only because he has used language carelessly, the issue is whether he should be liable in tort for the addressee's costs, or in contract for the addressee's expectation."[13]

Eisenberg's argument for liability in contract rests on what one might call the Eisenberg Uncertainty Principle:

> Reliance [can] become extremely difficult to measure, particularly since it is likely to consist of forgone opportunities or abstinence from considering alternative courses of action. If a defendant, by convincing the factfinder that his subjective intent varied from the reasonable meaning of his expression, could both avoid expectation damages and put the burden on the plaintiff to establish the existence and extent of any costs, contracts might be rendered unduly insecure and private planning might be unduly jeopardized.[14]

If this argument were correct, we would not hold the defendant to the contract if we were certain about the defendant's intent and the costs that the plaintiff incurred in reliance. In that event, one would expect courts to be much more concerned than they are about how difficult it is to establish the defendant's intent and the plaintiff's costs.

A party is intentionally misled

According to the *Second Restatement*, when the parties attach different meanings to the words they use, a contract is formed when one "party did not know of any different meaning attached by the first party, and the other knew of the meaning attached by the first party."[15]

To see why such a contract is binding, one does not need an objective theory of contract. One needs no more than two well-established principles of the law governing fraud. They are principles to be found in the *Second Restatement* itself.

The first concerns when non-disclosure constitutes fraud. According to § 159 of the *Second Restatement*: "A misrepresentation is an assertion that is not in accord with the facts." According to § 161:

> A person's non-disclosure of a fact that is known to him is equivalent to an assertion . . .

[13] Melvin A. Eisenberg, *The Responsive Model of Contract Law*, 36 Stan. L. Rev. 1107, 1120 (1984).
[14] *Id.* at 1121.
[15] Restatement (Second) of Contracts § 201(2)(a) (Am. Law Inst. 1981).

> (c) where he knows that disclosure of a fact would correct a mistake of the other party as to the contents or effect of a writing, evidencing or embodying the agreement in whole or in part.

Suppose that one "party did not know of any different meaning attached by the other, and the other knew of the meaning attached by the first party." Disclosure "would correct a mistake of the other party as to the contents or effect of a writing." Non-disclosure would constitute fraud.

The second principle concerns the effect of fraud. Fraud makes a contract not void but voidable. The defrauded party can enforce it if they choose. Section §164 of the *Second Restatement* provides:

> If a party's manifestation of assent is induced by . . . a fraudulent . . . misrepresentation by the other party upon which the recipient is justified in relying, the contract is voidable by the recipient.

These principles have nothing to do with the merits of an objective or a subjective theory of contract. A non-disclosure of the effect of a writing is fraudulent for the same reason as other fraudulent non-disclosures: for example, the non-disclosure by "a seller of real or personal property" of "a known latent defect of quality or title that is of such a character as would probably prevent the buyer from buying at the contract price."[16] The defrauded party, if they wish, may hold the other party to the contract.

This principle explains cases in which contracts have been upheld even though the court never mentioned the word "fraud." Eisenberg discussed one such case: *Embry v. Hargadine, McKittrick Dry Goods Co.*[17] An employee's one-year contract of employment had expired. He told his employer that if it were not renewed for another year, he would stop work and look for another job. He was told, "Go ahead, you're all right. Get your men out, and don't let that worry you." The court held that a reasonable person would have understood the employer's language to mean that the contract was renewed, and consequently a contract was formed, whether the employer so intended or not. Eisenberg cited the case as authority for the proposition that "a mutually held subjective interpretation is determinative even if it is objectively unreasonable."[18] Very likely, however, the employer did not intend to renew the contract.[19] He merely wished the employee

[16] See *id.* § 161 cmt. d.

[17] 105 S.W. 777 (Mo. App. 1907).

[18] Eisenberg, *supra* note 8, at 125.

[19] The court said:

> We hold that, though McKittrick may not have intended to employ Embry by what transpired between them according to the latter's testimony, yet if what McKittrick said

to think that the contract was renewed. The employer should be bound because he intentionally, and therefore fraudulently, let the employee think that it was.

A party is unintentionally misled

According to the *Second Restatement*, a contract is formed when one party "had no reason to know of the meaning attached by the other, and the other had reason to know the meaning attached by the first party."[20] The party with reason to know mislead the other party unintentionally although perhaps negligently.

Eisenberg assumed that the party with reason to know was negligent for using language "carelessly."[21] If so, on tort principles, that party should be liable for any harm the other party suffered. The difficulty is that then, as in tort, liability should be limited to the harm that a party has suffered, for example, by reliance on the promise. As we have seen, Eisenberg tried to avoid that conclusion by what we called his Uncertainty Principle: it may be hard to prove subjective intent and the other party's reliance damages. If Eisenberg were right, courts should not award expectation damages when these matters can be proven easily.

Nevertheless, there is a different reason enforcing a contract when only one party had reason to know that the parties attach different meanings to their agreement. The other party believed that a contract had been formed. The first party could escape by proving that the parties attached a different meaning to their words, and, most likely, is in a unique position to prove that they did. The contract will not be binding if that party chooses to come forward with this proof. Otherwise, it will be. The first party will be in a position to speculate at the other party's expense. A party who promised to sell the other party their "cow" for $2,000 but really meant "horse," could reveal the truth and escape the contract if someone else offered $2,500 for the cow the next day. If $2,000 was still the best offer, that party could remain silent.

An example is *Lucy v. Zehmer*,[22] a case often cited in support of the objective theory. Zehmer and his wife had signed a document which said that they sold Lucy a farm for $50,000. Zehmer claimed that he meant the entire transaction as a joke. The court did not believe him. It held, however, that even if he were joking, "[n]ot only did Lucy believe, but the evidence shows that he was warranted in believing, that the contract represented a serious business transaction." It held

> would have been taken by a reasonable man to be an employment, and Embry so understood it, it constituted a valid contract of employment for the ensuing year.
>
> (*Embry*, 105 S.W. at 779)

[20] Restatement (Second) of Contracts § 201(2)(b) (Am. Law Inst. 1981).
[21] Eisenberg, *supra* note 8, at 120.
[22] 84 S.E.2d 516 (Va. 1954).

him liable on an objective theory of contract: "The mental assent of the parties is not requisite for the formation of a contract."

Whether he should be held liable depends upon which version of their story one believes. After the document was signed, Lucy offered Zehmer $5 to bind the bargain. According to Lucy's testimony, Zehmer refused to take it, saying "You don't need to give me any money, you got the agreement right there signed by both of us." According to Zehmer, however, he then realized for the first time that Lucy did not realize that he had been joking. He refused the money, saying, "Hell no. That is beer and liquor talking. I am not going to sell you the farm."

After their meeting on December 20, Lucy hired a lawyer to see that title was satisfactory, and on learning that it was, wrote Zehmer on January 2 to make arrangements for closing. On January 13, Zehmer wrote back that he had never intended to sell. If Lucy's testimony is to be believed, only then did Lucy learn that Zehmer claimed the transaction was a joke. If so, Zehmer should be bound whether or not he was negligent in leading Lucy to believe that the transaction was seriously meant. The reason is not the one Eisenberg proposed: the difficulties of proving reliance which "is likely to consist of forgone opportunities."[23] Lucy did not forego any opportunities and the cost of reliance was the amount he paid the lawyer. The reason Zehmer should be bound is that between December 20 and January 13, Lucy thought he was bound; consequently Zehmer should not be free to repudiate the transaction by proving that he meant it as a joke. Otherwise, he would have been free during the interval to change his mind or to look for a better offer. That is a sufficient reason for enforcing the contract even if Zehmer was not negligent in bringing the situation about.

Suppose, however, that Zehmer was telling the truth, and that he had informed Lucy that he meant the transaction as a joke when Lucy offered him the $5 binder. If so, and Lucy believed him, there was never a moment when Lucy thought that the parties' minds had met while Zehmer knew that they had not. Suppose one party offered to sell their cow for $2000, the other party accepted, and then the first party immediately said, "Oh, I'm sorry. I meant my horse." If the second party believes them, then there is never a moment when the second party thought that their minds had met on the sale of the cow. It is hard to see any reason for holding the first party or Zehmer to a contract he never intended to make. One purpose of contract law is to enable the parties each to receive something which they believe to be of more value to them that what they give in exchange. This purpose is defeated if they sell something they never intended to sell.

[23] Eisenberg, *supra* note 8, at 1121.

iii. When intent prevails over expression

Mechanical errors and so-called unilateral mistakes

Courts have spoken of "unilateral mistake" when a party misstated, or miscalculated the price at which they wish to be bound. They said or wrote one price when they meant another. They incorrectly added a column of figures in preparing a bid. In such cases, since only one party was mistaken, courts have spoken of "unilateral mistake." As Melvin Eisenberg has said, it is better to speak of a mechanical error. As he noted, "virtually all cases that are categorized as involving unilateral mistakes are mechanical error cases."[24] Most of them concern a mistake as to the price.

The rule toward which courts are tending is that the party who made a mechanical error is not bound when the other party is not made worse off by the mistake. That is as it should be. As we have seen, the purpose of making a binding contract would be defeated if the mistake concerns which is more valuable to a party—the price or the object. That purpose is not defeated by giving relief for a mechanical error. On the contrary, it is furthered, since parties who make such an error have never decided that, in a sale at that price, what they give is worth more to them than what they receive.

Courts have tended toward this rule by a circuitous path. Samuel Williston was committed to an objective theory of contract in which what matters is what a party said, not what he meant. It seemed to follow that a party who proposed a certain price was bound by what they said even if they had meant a different price. That rule was written into the *First Restatement* for which Williston served as Reporter. There was one exception. If "one party knows that the other does not intend what his words or other acts express" "this knowledge prevents such words or acts from being operative."[25] This rule passed into the *Second Restatement*.[26]

Some courts have taken this approach. For example, an ex-wife was not bound when she signed a settlement for a figure based on a mistaken calculation, and her ex-husband knew of the mistake.[27] A company was not bound by a post-trial settlement offer in which it had neglected to reduce the amount by the fraction of the total for which the jury held that it was liable and opposing counsel should have known of the mistake.[28] A bidder was not bound when the amount of his bid was so different than that of others that the other party must have known he had made a mistake.[29]

[24] Lon L. Fuller & Melvin Aron Eisenberg, Basic Contract Law 715 (8th ed. 2006).
[25] Restatement (First) of Contracts § 71(c) (Am L. Inst. 1932).
[26] Restatement (Second) of Contracts § 153(b) (Am. Law Inst. 1981).
[27] Stare v. Tate, 98 Cal. Rptr. 264 (Cal. App. 1971).
[28] Sumerel v. Goodyear Tire & Rubber Co., 232 P.3d 128 (Col. App. 2009).
[29] M. F. Kemper Const. Co. v. City of Los Angeles, 235 P.2d 7 (Cal. 1951).

By Williston's approach, the reason that relief is given in these cases is that one party knew that the other had made a mistake. His approach does not explain why the mistake must concern a mechanical error. Even if a person knows that the contractor they wish to hire has underbid or that the home a person wishes to buy is underpriced, a court will not give relief where the mistake was one in judgment. Williston's approach does not distinguish between enforcing a contract despite errors in judgment, which serves the purposes of contract law, and enforcing one despite mechanical errors, which does not. Neither does the *Second Restatement*. It provides that a contract is voidable for the mistake of one party when "the other party had reason to know of the mistake."[30]

Some courts now give relief when a party made a mechanical error even if the other party did not know of it, provided that the party was not harmed by the mistake. For example, a contract was rescinded when a dealer, who had purchased a Jaguar for $35,000 mistakenly offered to sell it for $25,995, and the offer was accepted by a customer who did not know a mistake had been made.[31] A contract was rescinded when a contractor had prepared an erroneous bid for an agency which he assured the agency was correct, and the agency had accepted it without knowling of the mistake.[32]

According to the *Second Restatement*, if the other party did not know of the mistake, relief may be given:

> Where a mistake of one party at the time a contract was made as to a basic assumption on which he made the contract has a material effect on the agreed exchange of performances that is adverse to him, the contract is voidable if . . .
> (a) the effect of the mistake is such that the enforcement of the contract would be unconscionable.[33]

Once again, the rule is off target. It does not distinguish between mechanical errors and errors in judgment even though, as Eisenberg noted, virtually all if the cases of "unilateral mistake," the error was mechanical.[34] Moreover, the rule is framed using words of doubtful meaning and relevance. If a party has misadded a column of figures in submitting a bid, it hard to see the point in asking whether their mistake is "material," "unconscionable," and made as to a "basic assumption." If the mistake is one in price, all three terms seem to only that it must be big

30 Restatement (Second) of Contracts § 153 (Am. Law Inst. 1981).
31 Donovan v. RRL Corp., 27 P.3d 702 (Cal. 2001).
32 Elsinore Union School District v. Kastorff, 353 P.2d 713 (Cal. 1960).
33 Restatement (Second) of Contracts § 153 (Am. Law Inst. 1981).
34 Fuller & Eisenberg, *supra* note 24, at 715.

enough to matter. It that is all that should matter, the use of these terms is unfortunate, since it suggests that something else does.

According to the *Second Restatement*[35] and the decisions just cited, the mistaken party can be given relief even if they were negligent in making the mistake as long as they acted in good faith and with no intention to deceive. That conclusion is correct when the other party has not been harmed by the mistake. As in tort law, if they have not been harmed, there is no reason that the other party's negligence should matter. As discussed elsewhere, the extent to which that principle applies to intentional misconduct is less clear.

Whether the other party has been harmed has sometimes been construed too strictly. Relief should still be given as long as the harm can be undone by awarding reliance damages. As Eisenberg observed:

> It is sometimes said that relief for unilateral mistake will not be granted unless the parties "can be placed in status quo in the equity sense, i.e. rescission must not result in prejudice to the other party except for the loss of his bargain."[36] Taken literally, this would preclude relief when there has been *any* reliance by the nonmistaken party. Such a rule would be unnecessary to serve the purposes intended, and expressions like that [one] should be read to mean that relief will not be granted unless the other party has either not relied or cannot be restored to his precontractual position by the award of reliance damages.[37]

Reformation of the contract

Thus far we have considered situations in which the parties did not agree on a term of the contract. In another situation, they did agree but they said or wrote something other than what they meant. In this situation, they did consent, and, despite the objective theory, they are bound by what they meant and not by what they said. If the parties agreed to an insurance policy that would pay the insured $500 per year after age 65, and by mistake the policy said that the insured would be paid $500 per month, they receive $500 per year.[38] If the parties agreed that the amount of a loan would be $25,000 and, due to a scrivener's mistake, the amount of the loan was written as $15,000, the loan is for $25,000. The court will a grant a remedy called "reformation." It will rewrite the contract to conform to the parties' understanding.[39]

35 Restatement (Second) of Contracts § 157 (Am. Law Inst. 1981).

36 *Citing* James T. Taylor & Son, Inc. v. Arlington Independent School District, 335 S.W.2d 371 (Tex. 1960).

37 Fuller & Eisenberg, *supra* note 24, at 728.

38 Travelers Ins. Co. v. Bailey, 197 A.2d 813 (Vt. 1964).

39 Restatement (Second) of Contracts § 155 (Am. Law Inst. 1981).

In *Stare v. Tate*, the court went further. An ex-wife signed a settlement for a figure based on a mistaken calculation which favored her ex-husband.[40] He knew of the mistake. The court held, not only that she was not bound by the smaller figure, but that he was bound by the larger one, and granted reformation. Since he knew of the mistake and remained silent, he was estopped from claiming that he would have settled for some other amount. There is poetic justice in the court's decision, but a requirement for any sort of estoppel—promissory estoppel, equitable estoppel, estoppel in päis—is a change of position by the other party. Here the ex-wife intended one amount and the ex-husband never made up his mind. Absent a change of position on her part, there is no reason why he should be bound.

II. Conflicts between expressions of intent

i. Conflicts between offer and acceptance: the battle of the forms

To form a contract, the parties must agree on the performance terms. They specify what each party is to give and receive. In a sale, they identify the object sold and the price. Auxiliary terms determine the details and allocate the risks and burdens incident to the transaction specified by the performance terms. The parties need not expressly agree on the auxiliary terms. If they do not, the law will supply these terms.

Suppose that the auxiliary terms specified by one party differ from those specified by another. That problem often arises when the parties exchange form contracts, and neither party signs the other party's form. As we have seen, the traditional common law rule held that no contract was formed. The acceptance must be a "mirror image" of the offer. Section 2-207 of the *Uniform Commercial Code* (*UCC*) provides that a contract may be formed anyway. That result is correct, but § 2-207 is such an inept solution that courts have found ways around it.

We have seen that if the parties were fully aware of the risks and burdens incident to the transaction, they would place them on the party who could bear them the most cheaply and compensate them for doing so. If the parties have done so, the terms of the contract will be fair. Normally, the parties will be assumed to have done so when a term of their contact expressly allocates a risk or burden. In exceptional cases, when such a term imposes a risk on a party which they were not compensated for bearing, a court will hold the term to be unconscionable.

40 98 Cal. Rptr. 264 (Cal. App. 1971).

We have also seen that when the parties did not consider a risk, and so their contract does not contain a term to deal with it, a court should supply a term that places the risk on the party that can bear it at the lowest cost. Because the parties did not consider that risk, that party may not have been compensated for bearing it. Even then, the risk will have been placed where it will cause the smaller loss. That is where the parties would have wished it to fall. Moreover, as we have seen, a party may have been compensated for bearing a risk even if the parties did not consider that specific risk when the contract was drafted.

When an auxiliary term specified by one party differs from one specified by another, that term may be so important that neither party would have been willing to be bound unless the other assented to the term that they proposed. Commonly, however, the parties would have wished to be bound despite the discrepancy. The question is which party should assume the burden or risk in question. The answer should be, once again, that a court should place that risk on the party best able to bear it, just as it would if the parties had agreed on no such term. The only difference is that the court has an extra piece of information. It can see the terms that each party proposed. The fact that a party proposed a term is some evidence of which party is best able to bear it.

The common law "mirror image rule" frustrates the intention of the parties if they wish to enter into a contract despite the discrepancy. It also can produce arbitrary results. In a common situation, the parties exchange printed forms specifying different auxiliary terms. Under the mirror image rule, each document that conflicts with the last is construed as a rejection of the other party's offer and a new counteroffer. If a party is bound by the other's terms if they received such a counteroffer and then behaved as if a contract has been formed, for example, by shipping goods or accepting them, they will be deemed to have accepted it. They are deemed to have accepted the last form sent, and which party sent the last form may be a matter of chance. The party who wins is whoever "fired the last shot."

Karl Llewellyn, recognizing the difficulties of the mirror image rule, drafted an alternative which became § 2-207 of the *UCC*. It provides:

> (1) A definite and seasonable expression of acceptance or a written confirmation which is sent within a reasonable time operates as an acceptance even though it states terms additional to or different from those offered and agreed upon, unless acceptance is expressly made conditional on assent to the additional or different terms.
>
> (2) The additional terms are to be construed as proposals for addition to the contract. Between merchants such terms become part of the contract unless:
>
> (a) the offer expressly limits acceptance to the terms of the offer;
>
> (b) they materially alter it; or

(c) notification of objection to them has already been given or is given within a reasonable time after notice of them is received.

(3) Conduct by both parties which recognizes the existence of a contract is sufficient to establish a contract for sale although the writings of the parties do not otherwise establish a contract. In such case the terms of the particular contract consist of those terms on which the writings of the parties agree, together with any supplementary terms incorporated under any other provisions of this Act.

Llewellyn was so bright that it is hard to believe he wrote a provision so dim. Bruce Frier and James White have suggested that he focused on only one problem: preventing a party who has found a better deal from escaping a contract because the terms of the offer and acceptance do not quite match.[41] That problem is solved by paragraph 1 which provides that a contract is formed despite the discrepancy. Lewellyn dealt less ably with the question that then arises: what are the terms of this contract?

According to paragraph 1, a contract is formed by a "definite and seasonable expression of acceptance . . . even though it states terms additional to or different from those offered." An offeree's response is a "definite and seasonable expression of acceptance" if it indicates that the offeree wishes to accept despite the variation in terms. Courts have held that no contract is formed if the response contains a difference in performance terms, such as the number of vehicles to be sold.[42] No contract is formed if the parties have been negotiating over a term contained in the response,[43] since, if they are negotiating, neither party is likely to wish to be bound before the issue is settled. Otherwise, a contract will be concluded despite the variation in terms even if it is material.

Yet paragraph 1 seems to allow an offeree to reintroduce the mirror image rule. The offeree can prevent the offer from forming a contract by providing that his "acceptance is expressly made conditional on assent to the additional or different terms." Suppose then the offeror behaves as if there were a contract, for example, by shipping goods or accepting a shipment from the offeree. If the offeror is deemed to have accepted the terms of the offeree, then the offeree is in the same position as if they had fired the last shot under the mirror image rule. The offeree gets its way. As we will see, courts have twisted the language of the provision to avoid that conclusion.

According to paragraph 2, although a contract has been formed, an "additional term" will not become part of a contract if it is "material." One might think that

41 Bruce W. Frier & James J. White, The Modern Law of Contracts 183–84 (3d ed. 2012).

42 Columbia Hyundai, Inc. v. Carll Hyundai, Inc., 484 S.E.2d 468 (S.C. 1997).

43 Koehring v. Glowacki, 253 N.W.2d 64 (Wis. 1977) (parties negotiating over whether sale would be "F.O.B." or "as is, where is").

any term of economic significance would be "material." According to the Official Comment to § 2-207, however, to be "material" a term must "result in surprise or hardship if incorporated without express awareness by the other party." Examples are "a clause negating such standard warranties as merchantability or fitness for a particular purpose . . . [or] a clause requiring that complaints be made in a time materially shorter than is customary or reasonable."[44] Examples of terms that are not material are:

> a clause setting forth and perhaps enlarging slightly on the seller's exemption due to supervening clauses beyond his control or . . . a clause fixing a reasonable time for complaints within customary limits . . . a clause providing for interest on overdue invoices . . . a clause limiting the right of rejection for defects that fall within the customary trade tolerances for acceptance "with adjustment" or otherwise limiting remedies in a reasonable manner.[45]

Judge Posner has sensibly observed that "the doctrine of material alteration is an aid to interpretation rather than an ironclad rule." Consequently, although one can infer from the Official Comment that terms that are material do cause hardship and surprise, the test of whether a term is material is whether the one party can presume that the other party would consent to it. That being so, even if a term is material, it can still become part of the contract if the offeree can show "that the offeror in fact consented to the alteration—whether (i) expressly or (ii) by silence against the background of a course of dealings."[46]

The difficulty with paragraph 2, as is often observed, is that it contradicts one of the basic purposes of § 2-207 which is to escape the arbitrariness of the mirror image rule. Under that rule, as we have seen, the terms that govern the contract depend on which party's document happened to be sent last. Its terms govern, although the order in which the forms were sent may be a matter of chance. It would seem, however, that under paragraph 2, the order in which they were sent still matters. The first document sent is now an "offer" and the second document an "acceptance." The acceptance forms a contract but it if adds "material terms," they do not become part of the contract. Thus the party who sends the first document will get its way except when an additional term is not material. As we will see, courts have twisted the language of paragraph 2 to avoid that result.

Paragraph 3 contains what is called a "knock-out" rule. When terms conflict, they are ignored. The parties are bound by the terms they have provided that do not conflict. Gaps are filled by "supplementary terms incorporated under any

[44] U.C.C. § 2-207 cmt. 4 (Am. Law Inst. & Unif. L. Comm'n 1977).
[45] *Id.* at cmt. 5.
[46] Union Carbide Corp. v. Oscar Mayer Food Corp., 947 F.2d 1333 (7th Cir. 1991).

other provisions of this Act." This rule favors neither party. It does not depend on which document was sent first or last.

From the language of § 2-207, it is difficult to tell when paragraph 3 would apply. If the parties exchanged documents that conflict, the second was either a "definite or seasonable expression of acceptance" or it was not. If it was, a contract is formed and, it would seem, the conflict is resolved by paragraph 2. If it was not, no contract was formed, there is no conflict to resolve. By its terms, paragraph 3 applies when the parties act as though they had a contract but the "writings of the parties do not . . . establish a contract." But what does that mean? If one of the writings was a "definite and seasonable expression of acceptance," then, it seems, we would never get to paragraph 3. A contract would be formed under paragraph 1 and conflicts in terms would then be resolved under paragraph 2. So, it would seem, paragraph 3 would apply only if the parties had entered into a contract by their conduct rather than by an exchange of writings, and the writings had been meant to state the terms of a contract that had already been made. Official Comment 6 suggests that this is the situation paragraph 3 was supposed to govern:

> Where clauses on confirming forms sent by both parties conflict each party must be assumed to object to a clause of the other conflicting with one on the confirmation sent by himself. . . . The contract then consists of the terms originally expressly agreed to, the terms on which the confirmations agree, and terms supplied by this act.

It would seem, then, that paragraph 3 applies only to "confirming forms" sent to confirm a contract that has already been made. Nevertheless, the "knock-out" rule of paragraph 3 contains the only solution that avoids the arbitrariness of the mirror image rule that § 2-207 was supposed to prevent. Consequently, courts have twisted the meaning of the rest of § 2-207 in order to apply paragraph 3. The result is that all paths now seem to lead to paragraph 3 whereas, by the language of § 2-207, nearly all paths seem to lead away from it.

The first obstacle to be overcome was the provision of paragraph 1 allowing the offeree to provide that "acceptance is expressly made conditional on assent to the additional or different terms." To avoid applying this provision, some courts have said that "it is not enough that acceptance is expressly conditional on different or additional terms; rather, an acceptance must be *expressly* conditional on the offeror's *assent* to those terms."[47] It is not enough, for example, to say that it is "strictly understood that these terms and conditions become part of this order"[48]

[47] Dorton v. Collins & Aikman Corp., 453 F.2d 1161 (6th Cir. 1972).
[48] Gardner Zemke Co. v. Dunham Bush, Inc., 850 P.2d 319 (N.M. 1993).

or even that "this order expressly limits acceptance to the terms stated herein. Any additional or different terms proposed by the seller are rejected unless expressly agreed to in writing."[49] Some courts have said that language alone is not enough to make an acceptance conditional. A court must make a factual inquiry to determine if a party was actually willing to go ahead without the other party's assent.[50]

Supposing, however, that an offeree's document does make acceptance expressly conditional on the offeror's assent to its terms, then it still matters in which order the documents are received, as it did under the mirror image rule. The last document contains the conditional acceptance. To escape this problem, some courts have held that if the effect of a conditional acceptance is to allow the offeree to refuse to be bound by the contract unless the offeror expressly assents to the offeree's terms. If, instead, the offeror merely proceeds as though the parties had a contract, the offeror will not be deemed to have assented. The court will apply the knock-out rule of paragraph 3. The conflicting terms will cancel out, and the parties will be bound by the terms on which their documents do agree plus those supplied by the *UCC*.[51]

The second obstacle to be overcome was the provision of paragraph 2 which states that "additional terms... become part of the contract unless... they materially alter it." The problem was how to avoid applying this provision, which is as arbitrary as the mirror image rule, and to apply the knock-out rule of paragraph 3 instead. Some but not all[52] courts have said that paragraph 2 applies to terms that are "material" but paragraph 3 to those that are "different." They have noted that, although paragraph 1 speaks of "terms additional to or different from those offered and agreed upon," paragraph 2 speaks only of "additional terms." They have concluded that paragraph 2 only applies to "additional terms." Since § 2-207 does not say what to do about conflicts in terms that are "different" but not "additional," these conflicts are to be resolved by the knock-out rule of paragraph 3.[53] Proponents of this solution sometimes cite Comment 6, quoted earlier, although, as we have seen, that comment deals with "confirmation forms" which presumably confirm a contract already entered into. Proponents dismiss Comment 3 which expressly provides that "[w]hether not additional or different terms will become part of the agreement depends upon the provisions of Subsection (2)."

By this interpretation, paragraph 2 applies to terms that are "additional" and paragraph 3 to those that are "different." There is no good way to answer the question whether a term is "additional" or whether it is "different." One cannot look

[49] Brown Machine, Inc. v. Hercules, Inc., 770 S.W.2d 416 (Mo. App. 1989).

[50] *Gardner Zemke*, 850 P.2d 319.

[51] Diamond Fruit Growers, Inc. v. Krack Corp., 794 F.2d 1440 (9th Cir. 1986); C. Itoh & Co. (America), Inc. v. Jordan International Co., 552 F.2d 1228 (7th Cir. 1977).

[52] Steiner v. Mobil Oil Corp., 569 P.2d 751 (Cal. 1977); Air Products & Chemicals, Inc. v. Fairbanks Morse, Inc., 206 N.W.2d 414 (Wis. 1973).

[53] *Gardner Zemke*. 850 P.2d 319; Diatom, Inc. v. Pennwalt Corp., 741 F.2d 1569 (10th Cir. 1984).

to the purpose of the statute since, as we have seen, the drafters did not draw this distinction. One cannot look to the purpose of the courts since their purpose is to escape paragraph 2 in order to arrive at paragraph 3. That purpose is served only so long as a term is "different." According to the ordinary use of language, it might seem that a "different" term conflicts with a term in the offer while an "additional" one concerns an issue that the offer does not mention. But that interpretation leads to a paradox. Suppose a term in the acceptance conflicts with a term that was expressly stated in the offer but which the law would read into a contract absent agreement by the parties. It would seem that such a term is "different." The result would be that the conflicting terms would be knocked out by paragraph 3, and the result will be a contract on the terms that the law would have supplied had the parties been silent. It seems odd that this result would be reached because one party happened to state expressly a term that the law would read in anyway. But suppose that the terms were deemed to be different if an implied term of one document—one which the law would read in anyway—conflicts with an express term of another. Then any deviation in one party's document from the terms that the law would read absent agreement would be considered a different term. Terms would never be additional, and the terms of the contract would always be those the law would read in if the parties were silent.

Since there is no good solution, in practice, courts may decide that a term is "different" whenever they think that the fairer solution is to apply the knock-out rule of paragraph 3. That rule does, indeed, seem fairer than the alternative provided in paragraph 2. We began by noting that the proper approach, when auxiliary terms conflict but the parties would wish to be bound despite the discrepancy, is to place the risk or burden on the party best able to bear it. That is what the terms read into a contract absent the parties' agreement ought to do.

The problem with the knock-out rule, however, is that after conflicting terms are cancelled out, the parties are bound by "those terms on which the writings of the parties agree, together with any supplementary terms incorporated under any other provisions of this Act." As noted earlier, however, when one or both of the parties proposed a term that the law would not read in absent their agreement, the situation is not the same as it is when they were silent. The fact that a party proposed such a term is evidence as to which of the parties may be best able to bear the risk in this particular situation, regardless of what the normal situation may be. Such a party may quite reasonably wish to be bound by a different term. Yet under paragraph 3, it is difficult for this party to avoid being bound.

Suppose the seller wishes to disclaim a warranty. If the other party makes sure that their document contains a warranty (or if conflict with an implied warranty triggers the knock-out rule), then the disclaimer does not become part of the contract. The result may be unfair. Most often, the seller is in the best position to bear the risk that the goods are defective. They can best foresee and control that risk. As long as the loss that the buyers of defective goods will suffer is roughly the same, they can self-insure against that risk by raising the price for all buyers by an amount sufficient to compensate those who buy defective goods and suffer that loss. Suppose, however, that the losses that some buyers of defective goods may suffer are much greater than those of others. The buyer might be in the best position to know and control that risk. Moreover, if the seller were to raise the price for all buyers by an amount sufficient to compensate those who suffer the greater losses, the result would not be fair. Every buyer would pay more to compensate some buyers for a risk that the others do not face.

For example, suppose the seller markets an adhesive, and that the purpose for which it is ordinarily purchased is to provide an airtight seal to protect perishable commodities. If the harm caused by a broken seal varies greatly from one buyer to another, the buyer might be in the best position to know and control the risk of harm and to spread it across the transactions in which they use the adhesive. In the notorious case of *Rotolith, Ltd. v. F.P. Barker & Co.*,[54] the manufacturer of such an adhesive used a form which disclaimed the warranty. A warranty was included in the form of his customer. The court held for the seller on the ground that "a response which states a condition materially altering the obligation solely to the disadvantage of the offeror" falls within the "expressly conditional" language of paragraph 1. Courts and scholars have criticized the opinion vigorously for frustrating the purpose of § 2-207 by, in effect, reinstating the mirror image rule. Nevertheless, if, as more recent decisions suggest, all paths lead to paragraph 3, the seller of the adhesive would be hard put to disclaim the warranty as long as it conflicted with the buyer's form. The disclaimer would be knocked out and replaced by the warranty provision of the *Code*. Yet, in situations like *Rotolith*, the disclaimer may be fairer and more reasonable than a warranty under the *UCC*.

Another problem is that under the knock-out rule, the parties may be bound by terms contained in neither of their forms. One form might provide for a warranty that is limited to repair and replacement of the product sold if a defect is detected within six months; the other might provide for one that is general but limited to harm that occurs within one year. Under the knock-out rule, the parties would be bound by a general warranty with no time limitation, since that is the term supplied by the *UCC*.

When a party uses a form that provides a different term, they are claiming, in effect, that their situation is different than that of the typical buyer and seller. That claim becomes more credible if his form contains a few differences from the provisions of the *UCC* which are reasonably related to differences between his situation and that of the typical buyer or seller. The court should enforce them if

[54] 297 F.2d 497 (1st Cir. 1962).

it believes that, for a party in their situation, they do place the risk or burden on the party who can most easily bear it.

ii. Conflicts between preliminary and final expressions: the parol evidence rule

When one party wishes to introduce evidence extrinsic of terms that supplement or change the meaning of a written agreement, there is a natural concern about what force to give this extrinsic evidence. There may be doubts about its credibility, and these doubts may arise simply because these terms were not included in the written agreement.

This problem of credibility is addressed by the parol evidence rule—misnamed because it concerns evidence of extrinsic terms whether the evidence is written or oral. If the parties intended their written contract to be a final statement of every term of their agreement, it is said to be "completely integrated." No extrinsic evidence of a term that supplements or contradicts it can be considered. If they intended their agreement to be a final statement of some of the terms, it is said to be "partially integrated." No extrinsic evidence of a term that is inconsistent with it can be considered.

In the words of the *Second Restatement*:

> § 209. Integrated Agreements
>
> (1) An integrated agreement is a writing or writings constituting a final expression of one or more terms of an agreement.
>
> . . .
>
> § 210. Completely and Partially Integrated Agreements
>
> (1) A completely integrated agreement is an integrated agreement adopted by the parties as a complete and exclusive statement of the terms of their agreement.
>
> (2) A partially integrated agreement is an integrated agreement other than a completely integrated agreement.
>
> § 213. Effect of Integrated Agreement on Prior Agreements (Parol Evidence Rule)
>
> (1) A binding integrated agreement discharges prior agreements to the extent that it is inconsistent with them.
>
> . . .
>
> (3) A binding completely integrated agreement discharges prior agreements to the extent that they are within its scope.

The difficulties with the parol evidence rule arise because, although the rule addresses the problem of the credibility of extrinsic evidence, it treats that problem as though the parties themselves had already resolved the question of whether extrinsic evidence should be considered. Whether a writing is integrated, completely or partially, depends on whether the parties adopted it as a final expression of one or more terms of an agreement. If so, then the parties intended it to discharge prior agreements. It does not matter whether the evidence of a prior agreement is credible or not. Even if the evidence is indisputable, the parties themselves decided that the prior agreement would be discharged, and so evidence of it is irrelevant.

One difficulty with this approach has been noted since Williston and Corbin squared off at the time of the *First Restatement*. It may be difficult to tell whether the parties intended their agreement to be completely or partially integrated without knowing whether the parties actually entered into a prior agreement. If they did, one can then ask whether it is likely that they intended the written agreement to supersede it. It would seem, then, that a court must determine whether a prior agreement was made in order to determine whether evidence of that prior agreement can be admitted to supplement or contradict the final agreement. In that event, a court must pass on the credibility of the evidence of the prior agreement. Yet the aim of the parol evidence rule is to prevent the introduction of extrinsic evidence because it might not be credible.

This difficulty can be dealt with in two ways, neither of which is satisfactory. Williston believed that, so far as possible, a court should determine the parties' intention without looking at extrinsic evidence. If the written agreement seems to be final and complete as to some matters, it is deemed to be partially integrated; if so as to all matters, completely integrated. The trouble with this approach is that the court will be ignoring evidence that is relevant to the very question it is trying to decide. Corbin concluded that the court should look at all the evidence bearing on the parties' intent, including extrinsic evidence. It should consider that evidence out of the hearing of the jury into order to decide whether the jury should be allowed to consider it.

The *Second Restatement* adopted Corbin's approach:

> Where the parties reduce an agreement to a writing which in view of its completeness and specificity reasonably appears to be a complete agreement, it is taken to be an integrated agreement unless it is established by other evidence that the writing did not constitute a final expression.[55]

The trouble with this approach is that it is hard to see how the court can consider extrinsic evidence without weighing its credibility. Yet the object of the parol evidence rule is to prevent consideration of the credibility of extrinsic evidence

[55] Restatement (Second) of Contracts § 209(3) (Am. Law Inst. 1981).

when the parties intended their final agreement to be completely or partially integrated.

A further problem is that the parol evidence rule is concerned with an intention as to the legal effect of a written agreement that the parties rarely have: the intention to make an agreement fully or partially integrated, or, to put it another way, the intention to exclude extrinsic evidence of their agreement completely or partially. If the parties did have such an intention, they decided themselves whether extrinsic evidence should be considered. It would be convenient if they had. But they may not have done so.

If they put a great deal of thought into drafting the final agreement, one might assume that they intended it to cover everything. But normally they did not. Justin Sweet has noted that "[t]he hallmark of a truly integrated agreement is that it is put together carefully and methodically. In this sense it resembles the creation of a statute or a treaty. A good deal has occurred before the act of integration: drafts have been prepared, read, reread, and redrafted." According to Sweet, so few contracts are made this way that to confine the parol evidence rule to them is almost to abolish it. "But these are the only types of written agreements that can confidently be assumed to integrate the entire transaction in one repository, and even they may not contain everything."[56]

Indeed, even when the parties expressly resolved the question of whether their written agreement is integrated, courts often disregard what they said. Contracts often contain an "integration clause" stating that the writing constitutes the entire agreement of the parties. As Eisenberg observed, "[t]he law on what effect should be given merger clauses is messy. In some cases, they have been given a great deal of weight; in some they have been given little weight; and in some the courts have said that the weight to be given such provisions varies with the circumstances."[57]

The source of the difficulty, according to John Calamari and Jospeh Perillo, lies "[i]n treating the matter of integration as a question of intent."[58] Williston made that mistake, and it laid him open to Corbin's criticism. According to Calamari and Perillo, "shorn of the rote language of fiction indicating a search for intention," Williston and his partisans "are advocating . . . a rule of form." "[T]he security of transactions require[s] that, despite occasional injustices, persons adopting a formal writing be required, on the penalty of voidness of their oral and written side agreements, to put their entire agreement in the formal writing."[59] But Calamari and Perillo would then be putting the parol evidence

[56] Justin Sweet, *Contract Making and Parol Evidence: Diagnosis and Treatment of a Sick Rule*, 53 Cornell L. Rev. 1036 (1968).

[57] Fuller & Eisenberg, *supra* note 24, at 602.

[58] John D. Calamari & Joseph M. Perillo, *A Plea for a Uniform Parol Evidence Rule and Principles of Interpretation*, 42 Ind. L.J. 333 (1967).

[59] *Id.*

rule to a strange use. As traditionally stated, the rule is a way of effectuating the intention of the parties. By their interpretation, the rule should be used to defeat the intention of parties who do not wish to put their entire agreement in a formal writing.

Another difficulty is that by excluding evidence of a prior agreement, the parol evidence rule collides with the doctrine of mistake. As we have just seen, if a writing executed by both parties fails to express their actual intention, not only may a court hear evidence of what that intention was, but it may order reformation of the written document so that it states their actual intention. According to the *Second Restatement*:

> Where a writing evidences or embodies an agreement in whole or in part fails to express the agreement because of mistake of both parties as to the contents or effect of the writing, the court may at the request of a party reform the writing to express the agreement.[60]

Thus the parties are bound by what they meant, not by what they said in their written agreement. As we have seen, if they agreed to an insurance policy that would pay the insured $500 per year after age 65, and by mistake the policy said that the insured would be paid $500 per month, the insured receives $500 per year.[61] If they agreed that the amount of a loan would be $25,000 and, due to a scrivener's mistake, the amount of the loan was written as $15,000, the loan is for $25,000. It would seem, if they failed to include the terms of an earlier agreement in a later writing that was not meant to supersede the earlier agreement. A party should be able to introduce evidence of the mistake and ask for reformation. And, indeed, according to the *Restatement Second*, evidence of mistake is admissible despite the parol evidence rule.[62]

One might be tempted to give up on the parol evidence rule entirely. Yet often parties do reduce their agreement to writing in order to avoid the uncertainties that may arise from the introduction of extrinsic evidence. They may do so because a written statement of its terms is clearer and more reliable than their memories of what they said to each other. They may wish to prevent the other party from concocting stories afterward about what they said to each other. The court should ask whether the parties had such an intention, and, if so, what extrinsic evidence they meant to exclude. The court would then be honoring an intention that the parties actually did have. It need not ask whether they intended the written agreement as a final expression of one or more terms of an agreement

[60] Restatement (Second) of Contracts § 155 (Am. Law Inst. 1981).
[61] Travelers Ins. Co. v. Bailey, 197 A.2d 813 (Vt. 1964).
[62] Restatement (Second) of Contracts § 214(d) (Am. Law Inst. 1981).

which supersedes any prior agreement. It need only ask whether they intended the written agreement to be trusted ahead of other evidence that they deemed less trustworthy.

To do so, the court must consider why the parties executed a written agreement. That purpose may vary from one written document to another. One can see how it might by considering two judicial opinions that are commonly thought to stand at opposite poles: Judge Andrews's opinion in *Mitchell v. Lath* and Judge Traynor's opinion in *Masterson v. Sine*. In *Mitchell v. Lath*,[63] Mrs. Mitchell signed a written contract to buy land from Lath that omitted Lath's promise to remove an unsightly icehouse. Andrews said that evidence of that promise was not admissible because the written contract was detailed and seemingly complete. In *Masterson v. Sine*,[64] the Mastersons conveyed land and retained an option to repurchase. Judge Traynor allowed extrinsic evidence to be admitted to show that the option was personal to the Masterson family and could not be exercised by a trustee in bankruptcy. Traynor said that the parties might not have mentioned that limitation in the conveyance because of "the difficulty of accommodating the formalized structure of a deed to the insertion of collateral agreements" and because the option "might well have been placed in the recorded deed solely to preserve the grantor's rights against any possible future purchasers." Here, his opinion is not in conflict with that of Andrews. Andrews said that he might have come to a different conclusion if the terms of sale had appeared in a deed conveying the land. "The fixed form of a deed makes it inappropriate to insert collateral agreements, however closely connected with the sale."[65]

Both Andrews and Traynor were trying to apply the parol evidence rule as traditionally formulated. Traynor said, "[t]he crucial issue in determining whether there has been an integration is whether the parties intended their writing to serve as the exclusive embodiment of their agreement." Both agreed the parties might not have so intended when they executed a deed. But it should not be an either–or question whether they intended to exclude all extrinsic evidence when they executed a written contract. What they intended to exclude depends on what they intended the writing to accomplish. Andrews and Traynor agreed that what they intend to accomplish in a deed is different than in a contract of sale.

In *Lopez v. Reynoso*,[66] Reynoso sold a car to Lopez in a document that contained an integration clause. It said that the price was $6,500 and that Lopez had made a down payment of $500. Reynoso was allowed to prove that the real price was $8,000, and that accordingly $2,000 received by him from Lopez was a not a down payment plus another $1,500 toward the purchase price. He had

63 160 N.E. 646 (N.Y. 1928).
64 Masterson v. Sine, 436 P.2d 561 (Cal. 1968).
65 *Mitchell*, 160 N.E. at 383.
66 Lopez v. Reynoso, 118 P.3d 398 (Wash. App. 2005).

written down a lower price at Lopez's request. In return, he had received $2,000 in cash. For personal reasons, Lopez did not wish the document to show that she had paid so much in cash. The trial court "found Mr. Reynoso's explanation more credible and reasonable," in part, because the price contained in the sales agreement was not much above the invoice price. In upholding that result, the appellate court said that the trial court had "implicitly concluded that the written agreement was only partially integrated." It would be better to say that the language of the sales agreement was not written to indicate the total price but only the amount still owing. For that reason, the language of the agreement should not be applied. It was not necessary to ask whether the agreement was fully integrated.

In *Brown v. Oliver*,[67] defendant sold plaintiff a hotel. The contract "written by a scrivener" included no mention of personal property although "there was ample oral evidence that the sale included the hotel furniture." The court admitted the oral evidence to determine what the document was meant to cover. It may be that the parties had reasons for putting the sale of the hotel in writing that did not apply to the sale of the furniture, and that the scrivener had been instructed accordingly. Whether the result is correct depends on whether they did.

If this approach is correct, then Andrews should have asked more questions about the written agreement in *Mitchell v. Lath*. According to Andrews, "she [Mrs. Mitchell] made a written contract to buy the property for $8,400, for cash and a mortgage and containing various provisions usual in such papers." How did Mrs. Mitchell do so? Did she draft these provisions for herself, did her lawyer draft them, or did she use a printed form that she had purchased somewhere? In the latter case, might it not have been hard to insert collateral agreements on the printed form however closely connected with the sale?

If the parties did make a written agreement because they thought the writing would be more trustworthy than other evidence of what they agreed, the court should consider what sort of evidence they regarded as less trustworthy. They may have thought that a writing is a more reliable record of their agreement than their memories or that it would prevent a party from concocting evidence later on. If that is all that they intended when they put their agreement in writing, they did not intend to exclude evidence that is more reliable than their memories and difficult or impossible for one party to concoct.

Consequently, in applying the parol evidence rule, a court should consider how reliable extrinsic evidence is likely to be. That view has been taken by Richard Posner and Steven Burton.[68] According to Judge Posner, "the key is the distinction between what might be called 'objective' and 'subjective' evidence of

[67] Brown v. Oliver, 256 P. 1008 (Kan. 1927).
[68] Steven J. Burton, Elements of Contract Interpretation (2006).

ambiguity. . . . By 'objective evidence' we mean that the evidence of ambiguity can be supplied by disinterested third parties. . . . By 'subjective' evidence we mean the testimony of the parties themselves to what the contract means." "Subjective" evidence is self-serving and easier to manufacture. In Posner's view, the policy of the parol evidence rule can best be served by screening it out and allowing "objective" evidence to be admitted.[69] In many cases, Posner's rule will effectuate the parties' intent. But the question should be what the parties were trying to accomplish when they put their agreement in writing. Suppose the reason was that they thought the writing is more reliable than their memories and that extrinsic evidence is easy to concoct. If so, "subjective" evidence should be excluded to the extent that it is testimony as to what a party remembered or it is evidence that is easy to concoct; objective evidence should be admitted to the extent that it is neither the one nor the other.

As mentioned earlier, as traditionally stated, the parol evidence rule collides with the doctrine of mistake. According to the doctrine of mistake, if a written contract does not include or conflicts with the parties' own understanding of their agreement, and a party can prove that it does, a court can grant reformation so that the writing corresponds to their actual intent. Here we have two principles in conflict: to give effect to the parties' actual intention which, by mistake, they did not express, or to give effect the intention they expressed because it is more trustworthy than what they did not express. A court should not invariably credit evidence of their unexpressed intention or invariably trust their writing. All it can do is to admit extrinsic evidence of mistake but insist that it be clear and substantial.

Sometimes courts have done so. In *Bollinger v. Central Pennsylvania Quarry & Construction Co.*,[70] according to the parties' written agreement, a construction company was permitted to deposit construction waste on plaintiff's property. The plaintiff claimed that the parties had agreed that the company would first remove the topsoil and then, after depositing the waste, place the topsoil on top of it. The court granted reformation on the ground that a term requiring the company to do so had been omitted by mistake. According to the court, the burden of proving such a mistake was "heavy" but the plaintiff had done so by "undisputed evidence" including the fact that for a while in performing the contract the company had been replacing the topsoil on top of the waste.

Sometimes, in similar cases, courts have applied the parol evidence rule and excluded extrinsic evidence. In *Gianni v. R. Russell & Co.*,[71] the plaintiff claimed

[69] AM International, Inc. v. Graphic Management Associates, Inc., 44 F.3d 572 (7th Cir. 1995). In that case, the court was applying Illinois law. In a later one, the Supreme Court of Illinois ignored Posner's formulation and applied the parol evidence rule in its traditional form. Air Safety v. Teachers Realty Corp., 706 N.E.2d 882 (Ill. 1999).

[70] Bollinger v. Central Pennsylvania Quarry & Construction Co., 229 A.2d 741 (Pa. 1967).

[71] Gianni v. R. Russell & Co. 281 Pa. 320 (1924).

that when he leased a store in defendant's building, the defendant promised that he would not lease to anyone else who sold soft drinks. The court excluded evidence of the promise, noting that the parties would "normally and naturally" have included such a term in the lease had they agreed upon it. In the classic case of *Thompson v. Libby*, the parties agreed on a sale of logs, and one party later alleged there had been an oral agreement for a warranty. Again, the evidence was excluded.[72] In these cases, to be sure, the reason for executing a written agreement was to avoid the disputes to which oral agreements give rise. For that very reason, if the parties had agreed to the additional term, they made a mistake in reducing their agreement to writing. Therefore the party claiming that there had been an oral agreement should have been allowed to prove that there was a mistake, although, as in *Bollinger*, subject to a heavy burden of proof.

It has often been noted, to quote Judge Posner, that the parole evidence rule provides "a further screen to protect the parties from the uncertainties of trial." Extrinsic evidence "must be first presented to the judge, and only if he concludes that there is a genuine ambiguity is the question of interpretation handed to the jury."[73] That is true, and the division of responsibilities between judge and jury provides an extra safeguard against placing too much trust in extrinsic evidence. The reason for distrusting extrinsic evidence in the first place, however, is to give effect to the intention of parties who regarded the written terms of their agreement as more trustworthy. The role of the judge in applying that rule is one more way to ensure that this intention is respected.

[72] Thompson v. Libby, 26 N.W. 1 (Minn. 1885).
[73] AM International, Inc. v. Graphic Management Associates, Inc., 44 F.3d 572 (7th Cir. 1995).

PART IV
REMEDIES

12
Compensation for Harm Suffered and Lost Gain

I. The conventional account

According to the standard account, contract remedies serve to protect one of three interests: the expectation interest, the reliance interest, or the restitution interest.

Lon Fuller and William Perdue identified these three interests in what has been called the most influential law review article ever written.[1] Their view became orthodox. As the *Second Restatement of Contracts* explained:

> Judicial remedies under the rules stated in this Restatement serve to protect one or more of the following interests of a promisee:
> (a) his "expectation interest," which is his interest in having the benefit of his bargain by being put in as good a position as he would have been in had the contract been performed,
> (b) his "reliance interest," which is his interest in being reimbursed for loss caused by reliance on the contract by being put in as good a position as he would have been in had the contract not been made, or
> (c) his "restitution interest," which is his interest in having restored to him any benefit which he has conferred on the other party.[2]

This chapter questions whether identifying these three interests makes any contribution to our understanding of contract remedies or why they are given. It suggests a different way of understanding contract remedies, one which answers the purposes of the parties entering into a contract.

Fuller and Perdue correctly pointed out that these three "interests" correspond to three types of remedies for breach of contract. As Samuel Williston observed in a passage quoted by Fuller and Perdue, "the normal rule" is "to put the plaintiff in as good a position as he would have been in had the defendant kept his

[1] Lon L. Fuller & William Perdue, Jr., *The Reliance Interest in Contract Damages*, 46 Yale. L.J. 52 (1936).

[2] Restatement (Second) of Contracts § 344 (Am. Law Inst. 1981).

Foundations of American Contract Law. James Gordley, Oxford University Press. © Oxford University Press 2023.
DOI: 10.1093/oso/9780197686089.003.0012

contract."[3] According to Fuller and Perdue, that remedy protects a party's expectation interest.

Instead, a remedy may put the plaintiff in as good a position as they would have been if the promise had never been made. A year before Fuller and Perdue published their article, Warren Shattuck suggested that this remedy should be given for an action based on promissory reliance..[4] That doctrine had been recognized in § 90 of the *First Restatement of Contracts*.

Finally, in some cases, the plaintiff can recover the amount that the defendant gained by breaching the contract. According to Fuller and Perdue, that remedy protects the plaintiff's restitution interest.

We will organize our discussion around these three "interests" because they are the landmarks of the standard account. In the process, however, we will need to rewrite that account.

II. The "expectation interest"

According to Fuller and Perdue, "[i]t is . . . no easy thing" to explain why the law protects the expectation interest. "In this case we 'compensate' the plaintiff by giving him something he never had. This seems on the face of things a queer kind of 'compensation.'[5] One justification, they said, may be found in the much-discussed 'will theory' of contract law."

Williston, in language they quoted, had defined what they called the expectation interest in these words: "In fixing the amount of these damages, the general purpose of the law is, and should be, to give compensation—that is, to put the plaintiff in as good a position as he would have been in had the defendant kept his contract."[6]

One justification that Fuller and Perdue gave for the protection of the expectation interest was new: it is an indirect way of protecting a party's reliance on a contract. Another justification which they described and rejected was old: it "may be found in the much-discussed 'will theory' of contract law." They thought that an implication of the will theory was that the expectation interest should be protected:

> [The will] theory views the contracting parties as exercising, so to speak, a legislative power, so that the legal enforcement of a contract becomes merely an

[3] 3 SAMUEL WILLISTON, CONTRACTS 1338 (1920), *cited in* Fuller & Perdue, *supra* note 1, at 52.

[4] Warrren L. Shattuck, *Gratuitous Promises—A New Writ?* 35 MICH. L. REV. 908 (1937)..

[5] Fuller & Perdue, *supra* note 1, at 52–53.

[6] WILLISON, *supra* note 3, at §1338, *cited in* Fuller & Perdue, *supra* note 1, at 52. Williston cites Lord Atkinson in *Wertheim v. Chicoutimi Pulp Co.*, [1911] A.C. 301, 307; Parke, B. in *Robinson v. Harman*, 1 Ex. 850, 855; *Federal Wall Paper Co. v. Kempner*, 244 Fed. 240, 243. *Id.* at n.1.

> implementing by the state of a kind of private law already established by the parties. If A has made, in proper form, a promise to pay B one thousand dollars, we compel A to pay this sum simply because the rule or *lex* set up by the parties calls for this payment.[7]

They cited one of the foremost will theorists, the great nineteenth-century German jurist Bernhard Windscheid:

> A legal transaction is the exercise of the creative power which the private will possesses in legal matters. The individual commands, and the law adopts his command as its own.[8]

In the nineteenth century, which was an age of will theories and of conceptualism, the German jurists were masters of both. Conceptualism, as noted earlier, was a method of legal reasoning that began with the definitions of terms, and then tried to extract as many conclusions from them as possible. Windscheid did define contract to require a "manifestation of will directed to bringing about a legal result."[9] His account of damages, however, was based on another conceptual simplification:[10]

> The party who is obligated must make compensation for the disadvantage (*Nachteil*) to the financial position of the other party that takes place as the result of a certain event.[11]

This formula was supposed to cover the maze of rules governing damages for breach of contract in the Roman texts Windscheid was interpreting, texts which remained in force until the enactment of the *German Civil Code* of 1900. It was supposed to cover damages in tort as well as contract.

Fuller and Perdue quoted the common law rule as formulated by Williston. It was not that of Windscheid:

> In fixing the amount of these damages, the general purpose of the law is, and should be, to give compensation—that is, to put the plaintiff in as good a position as he would have been in had the defendant kept his contract.[12]

[7] *Id.* at 58.

[8] 1 Bernhard Windscheid, Lehrbuch des Pandektenrechts § 68 (9th ed. 1906), *quoted id.* at 58.

[9] 1 Bernhard Windscheid, Lehrbuch des Pandektenrechts § 69 (7th ed. 1891).

[10] Here I am correcting the view I expressed in James Gordley, *The Myth of "Expectation Interest,"* 52 Univ. Pac. L. Rev. 77, 79–80 (2020).

[11] 3 Windscheid, *supra* note 9, at § 258.

[12] Willison, *supra* note 3, at §1338, *citing* Fuller & Perdue, *supra* note 1, at 52 (*see also supra* note 6 for the authorities Williston cited).

In 1848, in an option cited by Williston,[13] Baron Parke had formulated the rule is the same way as Willison, Fuller, and Perdue:

> The rule of the common law is, that where a party sustains loss by reason of a breach of contract, he is, so far as money can do it to be placed in the same situation, with respect to damages, as if the contract had been performed.[14]

In contrast, although Baron Alderson agreed with Parke, he formulated the rule in much the same way as Windscheid:

> I am of the same opinion. The damages have been assessed according to the general rule of law, that where a person makes a contract and breaks it, he must pay the whole damage sustained.[15]

When the rule is formulated as it was by Parke, Willison, Fuller, and Perdue, it does seem strange that "we 'compensate' the plaintiff by giving him something he never had."[16] In contrast, the formulation of Alderson and Windscheid suggests the plaintiff is compensated for the loss of a right: for "the whole damage sustained," for "the disadvantage (*Nachteil*) to the financial position . . . that takes place as the result of a certain event." The plaintiff who is compensated for that damage or detriment will receive the same amount as one who receives what Fuller and Perdue described as "expectation damages." But whether we say the plaintiff is receiving "something he never had" or being compensated for a loss depends on whether or not we believe that the plaintiff already had the right to the promised performance. Peter Benson and the other proponents of "transfer theories" believe that contracts are enforceable because at the time the contract was made the promisor gave the promisee the right to the promised performance.[17] If so, it would seem the promisee should be compensated for the loss of that right. It is like damages in tort. The plaintiff whose right to bodily integrity is violated can recover not only for past medical expenses but for the loss of future earnings. When Fuller and Perdue asked why we give the plaintiff "something he never had," they begged the prior question of what belonged to the plaintiff already.

[13] *Id.* at n.1 also citing Lord Atkinson in *Wertheim v. Chicoutimi Pulp Co.*, [1911] A.C. 301, 30, and *Federal Wall Paper Co. v. Kempner*, 244 Fed. 240, 243.

[14] Robinson v. Harman, (1848) 1 Ex. Rep. 850, 855.

[15] *Id.* at 855–56.

[16] Fuller & Perdue, *supra* note 1, at 52–53.

[17] Peter Benson, Justice in Transactions: A Theory of Contract Law 8 (2019). *See* Seana Valentine Shiffrin, *Promising, Intimate Relationships, and Conventionalism*, 117 Phil. Rev. 481, 507, 516 (2008); Arthur Ripstein, Force and Freedom: Kant's Legal and Political Philosophy 109 (2009).

Fuller and Perdue suggested that the reason the law protects the "expectation interest" is that to do so is an indirect way of protecting a party's reliance on a contract. Some losses due to reliance are hard to prove, for example "the gains prevented by reliance, that is, losses, involved in foregoing the opportunity to enter other contracts."[18] Protecting the expectation interest "is a cure . . . in the sense that [it] offers the measure of recovery most likely to reimburse the plaintiff for the (often very numerous and very difficult to prove) individual acts and forbearances which make up this total reliance on the contract."[19]

Why, then, should reliance be protected? According to Fuller and Perdue:

> [T]here is . . . a policy in favor of promoting and facilitating reliance on business agreements. . . . When business agreements are not only made but are also acted on, the division of labor is facilitated, goods find their way to the places where they are most needed, and economic activity is generally stimulated.[20]

Here they anticipated one feature of the contemporary law and economics movement. Their answer to why the law does something is not that it is fair or just to do so. Their answer is it is good economic policy.

A difficulty with their answer is that if is correct, then, in principle, contract law collapses into tort. Indeed, Grant Gilmore claimed the recognition of liability for promissory reliance meant "the death of contract."[21] As in tort, the defendant is liable for fault, or, at least for conduct which he knew or should have known could harm a plaintiff who relied on their promise. Some scholars believe that the plaintiff should recover only for the amount that they were hurt—the amount that Fuller and Perdue called the plaintiff's "reliance damages."[22] Some believe that the protection of reliance is based on tort principles.[23]

Another difficulty is that the claim that expectation damages are given to facilitate reliance by the promisee is deeply circular. According to Fuller and Perdue, the losses due to reliance include "the gains prevented by reliance, that

[18] Fuller & Perdue, *supra* note 1, at 60.

[19] *Id.*

[20] *Id.* at 61.

[21] Grant Gilmore, The Death of Contract (1974).

[22] Benjamin F. Boyer, *Promissory Estoppel: Principle from Precedents* (pts. 1 & 2), 50 Mich. L. Rev. 639, 873 (1952); Warren A. Seavy, *Reliance upon Gratuitous Promises or Other Conduct*, 64 Harv. L. Rev. 913 (1951).

[23] Melvin A. Eisenberg, Foundational Principles of Contract Law 117 (2018). Other scholars have taken the opposite position, that the doctrine concerns the enforcement of a promise, not compensation for harm suffered by relying on it. Randy E. Barnett, *The Death of Reliance*, 46 J. Legal Educ. 518, 528 (1996); Edward Yorio & Steve Thel, *The Promissory Basis of Section 90*, 101 Yale L.J. 111, 113 (1991).

is, losses, involved in foregoing the opportunity to enter other contracts."[24] Suppose a party insures a house against fire for $500,000 and sues to collect that amount when the house burns down. By Fuller and Perdue's account, the insurance company is liable because the plaintiff relied on its promise by giving up the opportunity to enter into a different insurance contract with a different insurance company on the same terms. But, by the same logic, the reason that that insurance company would have been liable is that the plaintiff would have given up the chance of entering into a contract on the same terms with yet another insurance company. And so forth. The earth rests on a turtle which rests on another turtle which rests on another, and it is turtles all the way down.

III. A fresh approach

Benson pointed out that his "transfer theory" is not new. He traces it to Hugo Grotius, who, as we have seen, borrowed it from the late scholastics. They were trying to explain why, as a matter of justice, the disappointed promisee should have a right to recover. The reason, Grotius said, is that the promisor might "want . . . to confer on another person a right of his own, which is called a perfect promise, and has an effect similar to the alienation of ownership."[25] As we saw, the theory is incomplete. It does not explain why a person would make one type of promise rather than another. The reason we suggested is that, in a contract of exchange, a promise must be enforceable if one party is compensating the other for assuming a risk.

If that is so, then the reason for giving a remedy is that a party who was compensated for assuming a risk should be responsible for the consequences if the risk materializes. Eisenberg said that "allowing a promisor to limit damages to less than the promisee's expectation would . . . have the same unfair quality as allowing a promisor to renege on a fair bet that he made and lost."[26] Eisenberg is correct but his use of the word "expectation" in this context is imprecise. The promisee has a right to be compensated only for the consequences of risks that the promisor was paid to assume. The promisor who disclaims responsibility is, indeed, "reneg[ing] on a fair bet that he made and lost."

[24] Fuller & Perdue, *supra* note 1, at 60.

[25] Hugo Grotius, De iure bellis ac pacis libri tres II.xi.1.6–2.1–4 (1688).

[26] Shawn J. Bayern & Melvin A. Eisenberg, *The Expectation Measure and Its Discontents*, Mich. St. L. Rev. 1, 53 (2013); Melvin A. Eisenberg, *Actual and Virtual Specific Performance, the Theory of Efficient Breach, and the Indifference Principle in Contract Law*, 93 Calif. L. Rev. 975, 980 (2005).

i. Direct and consequential damages

The allocation of risks

In some cases, the risks that each party assumed are assigned by the terms of the contract itself. The contract provides that one performance is to be exchanged for another. Knowing that much, one can tell how certain risks have been allocated, and therefore what the damages should be. We will call them "direct" damages. When damages are direct, the party in breach should be liable for them.

When the parties contract at an agreed price, each gives up the chance of entering into a more favorable bargain. Each does so in order to avoid the risk of entering into one that is less favorable. If the contract is for the sale of a fungible commodity with a market price, the seller is giving up the chance to sell for more if the market price rises to avoid the risk of selling for less if it falls. The buyer is giving up their chance to buy for less if it falls in order to avoid the risk of buying for more if it rises.

If the parties contract for a unique item such a house, the seller gives up the chance of getting a higher offer. The buyer gives up the chance of finding a house that is just as satisfactory for a lower price.

When the parties contract at a fixed price for a performance which has yet to be made, one takes the risk that the performance will cost more than they estimate, and the other than it will cost less. Specific performance requires the breaching party to assume these risks. So does a damages award that holds him responsible for the risks allocated by the terms of the contract.

Because these risks are allocated by the terms of the contract itself, one can tell which party has assumed them without speculating about the parties' intentions. If they contract at a certain price, each one takes the risk of losing out on a better deal. Eisenberg has said that the reason parties contract in advance for what he calls "off-the-shelf" goods or services "would seldom be to allocate the risk of price changes or to speculate on prices: consumers normally do not make contracts to purchase off-the-shelf services for either purpose."[27] An example is a yoga studio signs up a would-be student for a year-long class that that is limited to twenty and will be cancelled if fewer than twelve students enroll. The student agrees to pay a fee of $800. Their reason for doing so most likely is "to ensure a place in the class."[28] Another example is a dealer sells a new Camry for future delivery for $30,000. Eisenberg argued—correctly, as we will see later on—that the student who decides not to take the course after sixteen students have signed up should not be liable. Neither should the car buyer. Nevertheless, it would be unfair if the student did not drop out and the studio tried to charge $900, or if

[27] EISENBERG, *supra* note 22, at 218.
[28] *Id.*

the buyer wanted the car and the dealer refused to deliver it for less than $35,000. In setting the price, the studio and the dealer gave up the chance of charging a higher price in order to attract more customers. It would also be unfair for the student or the car buyer to repudiate the contract because they found that they could get lessons or a car more cheaply elsewhere. They would be acting like someone who accepted a job on a five-year contract and then tried to escape when someone offered more.

It may happen, of course, that the price in the contract is not meant to bind the parties. In the case of the five-year employment contract, there might be an understanding that if the employee's services were of exceptional value, the employer would raise their salary, and in doing so, the employer would take into account other offers that the employee has received. But then, whatever the contract says, we are no longer speaking of a commitment to exchange at a price agreed in advance. In that event there ought to be clear evidence that the contract does not mean what it says.

Other risks are not allocated by the terms of the contract. We will call the damages for the harm that such risks may cause "consequential damages." The party in breach may or may not have assumed these risks. For example, the breach may prevent the non-breaching party from entering into favorable transactions with other people. The damages are "consequential." If the parties have not allocated that risk expressly, we must ask about their "hypothetical intent": how they would have allocated it had they considered the matter. The answer depends on which party can bear the risk at the lowest cost.

Which party is best able to bear a risk, economists tell us, and as we noted earlier, depends on three factors. One factor is who can best foresee the magnitude of the risk. A risk is lower for the party who can best foresee it for roughly the same reason that the risk of playing poker is lower for someone who can peek at the other players' cards. Another factor is who can best control the risk. If the party who can do so must bear the cost if the risk eventuates, then the further risk is reduced that too few precautions will be taken. A third factor is who can best spread the risk over similar transactions, whether by buying insurance or by self-insuring. The risk of a house catching fire is less for an insurance company than for a homeowner because it can spread that risk over the many houses it insures. The risk of a streak of bad luck is less for a casino than for an individual gambler.[29]

The party who is in the best position to foresee and control the risk of a breach of contract is often the party who breaches it. Which party is in the best position

[29] On the first and last of these factors, see Richard A. Posner & Andrew M. Rosenfield, *Impossibility and Related Doctrines in Contract Law: An Economic Analysis*, 6 J. LEGAL STUD. 83 (1977). On the second, see GUIDO CALABRESI, THE COSTS OF ACCIDENTS: A LEGAL AND ECONOMIC ANALYSIS (1970).

to spread that risk among similar transactions depends on whether the risk is much the same for the other clients and customers of the party in breach. If not, then to be compensated for bearing it, that party would have to charge a higher price to those customers for whom the adverse consequences are likely to be abnormally large.

The eclipse of the distinction

Some courts distinguish between damages that are "direct," "general," or "natural" and those that are or "consequential" or "special." As Victor Goldberg has noted, however, that distinction has fallen into disuse. "A Westlaw search for ['consequential damages' and synonymous and 'special damages'] yielded 35 cases, and a similar search [for 'general damages' and synonymous and 'direct' damages'] yielded 40."[30]

As he noted, "[t]he Restatement (Second) is unhelpful."[31] It discusses the distinction only as a misleading way of expressing the requirement that damages must be foreseeable when the contract was made—a requirement we will discuss later. According to the *Restatement*, courts have called a loss "natural" or damage "general" when it "it results from a breach in the ordinary course of events" and therefore is foreseeable. "The damages that are recoverable for loss that results other than in the ordinary course of events are sometimes called 'special' or 'consequential' damages." According to the *Restatement* "these terms are often misleading"—which is to say, courts sometimes use them in a different sense, and one that the drafters of the *Restatement* did not like. They concluded that "it is not necessary to distinguish between 'general' and 'special' or 'consequential' damages for the purpose of the rule."[32]

Common law courts borrowed that distinction from civil law which had traditionally distinguished between damages that are *circa rem* and those that are *extra rem*. A party's damages were *circa rem* if they were simply due to the loss of the performance they had contracted for. If they suffered further damages because of the breach, they were *extra rem*. As Reinhard Zimmermann observed, this distinction "dominated the discussion for centuries."[33] By the eighteenth century, he noted, "it had become became imprecise and muddled with other criteria.[34] Windscheid rejected it when he adopted his simpler formula: a "party,,, must make compensation for the disadvantage (*Nachteil*) to the financial position of the other party that takes place as the result of a certain event."[35]

30 Victor P. Goldberg Rethinking the Law of Contract Damages 171–72 (2019).

31 *Id.* at 172.

32 Restatement (Second) of Contracts § 351 cmt. b (Am. Law Inst. 1981).

33 Reinhard Zimmermann, The Law of Obligations Roman Foundations of the Civilian Tradition 831 (1990).

34 *Id.* at 832.

35 3 Windscheid, *supra* note 9, at § 258. "It is not required that the disadvantage that takes place be the immediate result of the event that occurred." *Id.* He referred in a footnote to the contrary "opinion

The distinction goes back to medieval jurists' interpretation of the Roman legal texts that were then in force in much of continental Europe. One Roman text said that a seller of wine who fails to deliver it on time is liable for the highest price the wine would command.[36] The reason, according to the text, is that "when the seller is liable for non-delivery of an object, every benefit to the buyer is taken into account that concerns the thing itself" (*circa rem ipsam consistit*). Citing this text, medieval jurists taught that whether damages were recoverable depended in part on whether damages were *circa rem* or *extra rem*.

According to Accursius (*c.*1182–1263), one of the most influential medieval jurists, damages can be recovered for non-performance when they are *circa rem* but not when they are *extra rem*.[37] According to Bartolus of Sassoferrato (1313–57), damages are *circa rem* or "intrinsic" when they concern "that which pertains to the thing [the performance] itself, or its value, and that which is immediately from it, such as fruits and offspring. But that which arises circumstantially (*occasione rei*) and not *ex re ipsa* should be called extrinsic."[38] The lost gain (*lucrum cessans*) that is intrinsic or *circa rem* is the difference between the contract price of a performance and its common value, or, as we would say, its market price: for example, "a basket of grain was worth 10 and five months later worth 20." The *lucrum cessans* is 10. When the damages are extrinsic or *extra rem*, the lost gain can be recovered only in certain cases. One such case is a gain that would have accrued to any party who had contracted for the same performance.[39] It is a gain, as Bartolus put it, that "follows the object regardless of to whom it goes" (*sequitur rem penes quaecumque vadat*).[40]

We will see that Bartolus was right. A party should recover as damages the difference between contract and market price. Such damages are direct in the sense that they compensate a party for a risk assigned by the terms of the contract itself. The loss of any other profit a party might have made is consequential. They

that the so-called indirect damages (damages *xtra rem* as opposed to the damages *circa* rem) need not be paid in all cases." *Id.* at n.10.

[36] DIG. 19.21.3.3.

[37] ACCURSIUS, GLOSSA ORDINARIA to C. 7.47.2 to *dupli* (1581).

[38] BARTOLUS DE SAXOFERRATO, COMMENTARIA CORPUS IURIS CIVILIS to C. 7.47.2 (1615).

[39] He took this distinction from Petrus de Bellapertica who, however, used it to define when damages were intrinsic rather than extrinsic. REPETITIO IN L. SI RES VENDITA § CUM PER VENDITOREM. ms. Vaticano Borghese 277 fol. 76 vb–fol. 77 ra, *quoted in* RAFFAELE VOLANTE, ID QUOD INTEREST IL RISARCIMENTO IN EQUIVALENTE NEL DIRITTO COMMUNE 99 (2012). As Volante noted, Petrus had replaced the distinction between damages *circa rem* and *extra rem* with this distinction between intrinsic and extrinsic damages. *Id.* at 99.

[40] BARTOLUS, COMMENTARIA to C. 7.47.2. He cited Roman texts which dealt with the sale of slaves who would have brought money with them to whoever became their owner. DIG. 21.2.8; DIG. 9.2.23. Another example was a case in in which the profits were derived from the ownership of the thing rather than from "reselling it or some other human activity". He noted that sometimes "the nature of the thing plays a greater part" in producing a profit than human industry, as it the profit from a farm (*ex fundo*)."

should recover for it only if a similar loss would have been suffered by anyone with whom the party in breach had contracted.

Liability for the contract–market differential

When parties enter into a contract at an agreed price, each of them gives up their chance to contract at a price that is more favorable in order to avoid the chance of having to accept a less favorable price. Consequently, the typical remedy for the non-breaching party is to obtain the benefit of the price that party locked in when the contract was made. Specific performance allows a party to receive the promised performance at the contract price. Damages should award the difference between the less advantageous price now available to the non-breaching party and the contract price. The formulas are well known. In a contract to buy or sell goods, the buyer receives the difference between the higher market price and the contract price. The seller receives the difference between the contract price and the lower market or resale price.

These remedies happen to protect what Fuller and Perdue called the plaintiff's "expectation interest." But doing so is not the purpose of giving a remedy. The purpose is to hold each party responsible for the risks that they were compensated to assume. Sometimes that purpose is achieved when a party is made as well off as if the contract had been performed. But sometimes it is not.

We will examine three situations in which it is not.

The lost-volume seller

The non-breaching party may not have accepted a less favorable price but lost an extra sale. Orthodox doctrine allows a seller who would have made an additional sale but for the breach to recover the lost profit. That would be the proper result if protecting the "expectation interest" were the purpose of giving a remedy. By our approach it is not. The risk of losing an extra sale is not one for which the seller would have compensated the buyer to assume. Section 2–708(2) of the *Uniform Commercial Code* (*UCC*) allows recovery of "the profit (including reasonable overhead) which the seller would have made from full performance by the buyer." An example is *Neri v. Retail Marine Corp.*[41] The defendant contracted to buy a new boat of a specified model from the defendant, a dealer. Six days later, the defendant notified the plaintiff that he wished to rescind the contract because he was about to undergo hospitalization and surgery. Four months later, the boat ordered for the defendant and received by the plaintiff was sold to another buyer for the price that the defendant had agreed to pay. The defendant was held liable for the contract price minus the costs that the plaintiff saved because he did not

[41] 285 N.E.2d 311 (N.Y. 1972).

have to purchase another boat. Thus, the plaintiff was made no worse off than he would have been if the contract with the first customer had been performed.

The parties who contract at a certain price are protected against the risk of having to accept a less favorable price. In *Neri*, the seller did not receive a less favorable price. If the contract is enforced, it will protect the seller against a different risk: the risk that the buyer will not pay for merchandise that the buyer does not want. That risk is not one that the seller would pay the buyer to assume if both parties are risk averse. It is like the risk that gamblers create when they bet on a coin flip. If neither party were bound by the terms of the wager, neither would be harmed. Risk-averse parties will not enter into a contract that creates a risk of harm that exists only if the contract is binding.

Suppose there were two competing boat dealers located next door to each other, and a would-be buyer went first to one, then to the other, and then back again, seeking the most favorable terms. The buyer offered to pay extra for the privilege of backing out and thereby costing the dealer an extra sale. The pressure of competition would lead each dealer to allow the buyer to do so at no extra charge. The dealer would sell an extra boat if the buyer did not back out and would lose nothing if the buyer did.

Victor Goldberg began his discussion of the lost-volume seller by quoting James White and Robert Summers: a remedy for lost profits is "the recovery which all right-minded people would agree that the lost volume seller should have."[42] According to Goldberg, "all those right-minded people are wrong." "By cancelling the order, the buyer in effect invokes an implied termination clause. The remedy would be the price that the buyer would need to pay for termination (cancellation)."[43] Goldberg is correct, but we would take this argument a step further. As we have shown, assuming competition among the sellers, unless the seller might suffer some harm other than the loss of an additional sale, the price the buyer would need to pay for such a clause is zero.

Eisenberg maintained that the lost-volume seller should recover for lost profits because it is a consequence of the "expectation principle."[44] Yet he would not allow the seller to recover when the buyer backs out of a contract for "off-the-shelf" goods and services. His arguments concerning sellers of "off-the-shelf" goods apply equally well to lost-volume sellers.

Earlier, we described the two hypothetical cases he used to illustrate his point. Suppose a dealer sells a new Camry for future delivery. Or suppose a yoga studio signs up a would-be student for a class that is undersubscribed. In such cases, Eisenberg observes:

[42] 1 James J. White & Robert S. Summers, Uniform Commercial Code 381 (6th ed. 2010), *quoted in* Goldberg *supra* note 29, at 47.

[43] Goldberg, *supra* note 29, at 47.

[44] Eisenberg, *supra* note 22, at 190–91.

> it is unlikely that a consumer would knowingly enter into a ... contract in which she would be required to pay the entire contract price if she cancelled, because damages measured that way would be highly disproportionate to both the benefit to the consumer from making the contract now rather than waiting ... and the cost to the provider of resulting from a breach by the consumer.[45]

According to Eisenberg, the consumer did not benefit by contracting in advance because "the reason for doing so would seldom be to allocate the risk of price changes."[46] We noted earlier that the contract should guarantee the consumer that the studio or dealer would not raise its price. But it should not matter whether or not the parties allocated the risk of price changes as long as the price never changed. Moreover, in Eisenberg's examples, the cost to the yoga studio is zero. It is zero to the car dealer who has not ordered the Camry before the customer cancels or who can sell it to someone else. The same can be said of the lost-volume seller.

The supplier with excess capacity

If the buyer breaches and the seller must sell the goods or services to someone else for less, the buyer is liable for the difference in price. Suppose, however, that the goods or services cannot be sold to anyone else. The party in breach who agreed to pay for them was the only possible customer.

According to conventional doctrine, if the buyer breaches, the seller recovers the contract price minus the scrap value of the goods and any costs saved by not having to perform. That remedy makes the seller as well off as if the contract had been kept, and so protects the "expectation interest." The proper remedy, however, should depend on what risks the breaching party assumed. The buyer who assumed the risk that the seller might have to accept a less favorable offer from a third party, need not have assumed the risk that the seller would have no other offers at all. If the designer of a machine specially ordered parts of no use to anyone else, or a producer hired a cast to rehearse and present a play to which no one comes, surely the risk falls on them. But if an entrepreneur invests in an enterprise and finds that there is only one person to whom they can sell, that person need not have assumed the risk of being the entrepreneur's only possible customer.

In *Vitex Mfg. Corp. v. Caribtex Corp.*,[47] the plaintiff had invested a large amount in a factory to waterproof material for shower curtains. The factory would have stood idle except that the defendant contracted for enough material

[45] *Id.* at 218.
[46] *Id.*
[47] 377 F.2d 795 (3d Cir. 1967).

to be waterproofed for it to operate at full capacity. The defendant breached his contract and provided no material to waterproof. As it happened, he was the plaintiff's only possible customer. The plaintiff was awarded the amount of his fixed costs or overhead plus his lost profit, or, to put it another way, the contract price minus the variable costs, that is, the costs that were saved because the plaintiff did not have to process any material. That would be the right result if the goal is to protect the parties' expectation interest. The result, however, was to transfer the risk of the plaintiff's bad investment to the one customer that he happened to find.

There is no reason that loss should be borne by that customer. The customer who happened to contract with a less successful entrepreneur with no discount in price should not be liable for the risk of being the only possible customer. It is also unlikely that, as a risk-averse party, a buyer would have been willing to bear this risk for any discount in the price to which the seller would have agreed.

The hedged bet

In the cases we have just discussed, the non-breaching party did not receive a less favorable price but nevertheless was worse off because the contract was not performed. In another, although rare situation, the non-breaching party who accepted a less favorable price may be no worse off, having hedged against the risk that the price would change.

An example is *KGM Harvesting Co. v. Fresh Network.*[48] The defendant contracted to sell lettuce to the plaintiff at 9 cents per pound. When the price rose, the defendant breached its contract and sold the lettuce to a third party at the higher price. The plaintiff covered by buying lettuce at the higher price, which it processed and resold to third parties. The plaintiff was no worse off, however, because its contracts to resell the lettuce were not fixed price but cost plus. Consequently, it was able to pass along the higher price that it paid to its customers.

The court awarded the plaintiff the difference between the higher price it paid for the lettuce and the contract price.

That is the correct result. It would be the wrong one if the goal were to put the plaintiff in as good a position as he would have been in had the contract been performed. It is correct because the parties bet on whether the price of lettuce would rise or fall, and the non-breaching party won the bet. Because he hedged his bets, he received a windfall. If he were not allowed to recover, however, the windfall would go to the breaching party who was the party who lost the bet. Moreover, the contract guaranteed the breaching party that he would receive the contract price even if the market price of lettuce fell. The non-breaching

[48] 42 Cal. Rptr. 2d 286 (Cal. App. 1995).

party provided that guarantee. It should not matter that, by entering into another transaction, the non-breaching party provided that guarantee at no risk to himself.

ii. The requirement that damages be foreseeable

According to conventional doctrine, the party in breach is liable for harm that he could reasonably have foreseen at the time they contracted. Section 351 of the *Second Restatement* provides:

(1) Damages are not recoverable for loss that the party in breach did not have reason to foresee as a probable result of the breach when the contract was made.
(2) Loss may be foreseeable as a probable result of a breach because it follows from the breach
 (a) in the ordinary course of events, or
 (b) as a result of special circumstances, beyond the ordinary course of events, that the party in breach had reason to know.

We will see, however, what should matter, and usually does, is not whether damages are foreseeable. What should matter is whether the damages are direct or consequential, and, if they are consequential, whether the party in breach was compensated for assuming the risk that they would occur. That is unlikely if the damages are disproportionately high compared with the contract price and the damages that other customers of the breaching party are likely to suffer. When the damages are disproportionately high, courts have called them "unforeseeable" even when they were not particularly hard to foresee.

The origin of the foreseeability rule

The foreseeability requirement was set forth in England in 1854 in the famous case of *Hadley v. Baxendale*.[49] In that case, the plaintiff's mill was stopped because a shaft was broken. The plaintiff hired the defendant to transport the shaft to a manufacturer so that it could serve as a model for a new one. Transportation was delayed due to the defendant's breach of contract, and the plaintiff sued for the profits he had lost because the mill was stopped for a longer period of time. The court denied recovery on the grounds that this harm was not foreseeable at the time that the contract was made.

[49] 9 Ex. 341 (1854).

The court in *Hadley* adopted a rule that had been proposed by the French jurist Robert Pothier (1699–1772) and was enacted by the *French Civil Code* of 1804.[50] Pothier had borrowed the idea that foreseeability should limit liability from an earlier century French jurist, Charles du Moulin (1500–56). Du Moulin and Pothier arrived at their conclusion by combining two rules of Roman law, neither of which concerned foreseeability.

One has already been described. The party in breach is liable for damages *circa rem*, or in Pothier's words, *propter rem ipsam*, but for damages *extra rem* only in special situations According to Pothier, the reason for this limitation is that damages *circa rem* or *propter rem ipsam* were foreseeable by the party in breach at the time he contracted.[51]

Du Moulin had explained another Roman rule that limited damages in the same way. According to a poorly drafted Roman text, in contracts for a *certum*, the non-breaching party could recover no more than "twofold."[52] Since the Middle Ages, jurists had spent much effort discussing what was meant by *certum* (certain) and what must be multiplied by two to determine the limit of recovery. Du Moulin suggested a rationale for the rule: "most likely it was not foreseen or thought that greater damage would be suffered or that there was a risk beyond the principal object than the principal object itself."[53] Pothier presented du Moulin's rationale as though it were not an explanation but a rule in its own right: "The person who owes a performance is only liable for the damages that one could have foreseen at the time of the contract that the party owed a performance would suffer."[54]

Thus, a Roman rule against recovering damages that are disproportionately high became a rule against recovering damages that are unforeseeable. Moreover, a rule providing for the recovery of damages that were *circa rem* became a rule that provided for the recovery of these damages because they were foreseeable. As we have seen, the *Second Restatement* claimed that the distinction between damages that are "general" from those that are "special" or "consequential" is misleading: they are imprecise attempts to distinguish between damages that are foreseeable because they occur "in the ordinary course of events" and damages that are not.[55]

That is one way of reading the language in *Hadley v. Baxendale*: all that matters is whether damages were foreseeable when the contract was made. Baron Parke described the damages that are recoverable as those which are "directly

[50] Zimmermann, *supra* note 32, at 830.

[51] Carolus Molinaeus, Tractatus de eo quod interest no. 60 (1574); Robert Pothier, Traité des obligations no. 160, *in* 2 Oeuvres de Pothier 497 (Bugnet ed., 2d ed. 1861).

[52] C. 7.47.1.

[53] Molinaeus, *supra* note 50, at no. 60.

[54] Pothier, *supra* note 50, at n.160.

[55] Restatement (Second) of Contracts § 351 cmt. b (Am. Law Inst. 1981).

and immediately results from the non-performance of the contract,"[56] quoting Sedwick's translation of the version of Pothier's rule.[57] Baron Alderson, delivering the judgment of the court, described these damages as "arising naturally, i.e., according to the usual course of things, from such breach of the contract itself."[58] Perhaps, as the *Second Restatement* suggests, all that matters is whether damages arise "according to the usual course of things," since in that event they were foreseeable. As Lord Asquith said in *Victoria Laundry (Windsor) Ltd. v. Newman Industries, Ltd.*, "Everyone, as a reasonable person, is taken to know the 'ordinary course of things' and consequently what loss is liable to result from a breach of contract in that ordinary course."[59]

If that is so, then if the damages were foreseeable when the contract was made, they should be recovered even if they do not "aris[e] naturally, i.e., according to the usual course of things, from [the] breach of the contract itself." That would seem to be the view of Baron Alderson. He said:

> if the special circumstances under which the contract was actually made were communicated by the plaintiffs to the defendants . . . the damages resulting from the breach of such a contract, which they would reasonably contemplate, would be the amount of injury that would ordinarily follow from a breach of contract under these special circumstances so known and communicated.[60]

Nevertheless, Victor Goldberg has shown that *Hadley* need not be read that way, and that, for a long time, it was not. In *Hadley*, surprisingly enough, the special circumstances under which the contract was made actually were communicated to the defendants. A headnote to the case said: "The plaintiff's servant told the [defendant's] clerk that the mill was stopped and that the shaft must be sent immediately."[61] Goldberg has shown that the headnote was "almost certainly not" a reporter's error.[62] In 1856, two years after the decision, James William Smith and Sir Henry Singer Keating, who had been the attorneys for Hadley and Baxendale respectively, mentioned the communication to the clerk in their book, *A Selection of Leading Cases on Various Branches of the Law*.[63] Sir Roger Crompton, the trial court judge in *Hadley v. Baxendale*, said, in a later opinion: "The curious part of the case is that there was a distinct notification to the carrier of the consequences that would follow

[56] *Hadley*, 9 Ex. at 346.
[57] FRENCH CIVIL CODE (CODE CIVIL) art. 1231–3.
[58] *Hadley*, 9 Ex. at 354.
[59] [1949] 2 K.B. 528 (Ct. App.).
[60] *Hadley*, 9 Ex. at 354–55.
[61] *Id.* at 156.
[62] GOLDBERG, *supra* note 29, at 166.
[63] 431 (4th ed. 1856), at 166.

the non-delivery of the shaft, and the Court held that these consequences could not be taken into consideration."[64] In spite of what he said, could Baron Alderson have thought that the communication of these special circumstances did not matter?

Whatever he meant, Goldberg has shown that "[f]or almost a century, the courts relying on *Hadley v. Baxendale*, restricted recovery for consequential damages to those damages to which the promisor had tacitly agreed."[65] Twelve years after *Hadley*, in *British Columbia Saw Mill Co. v. Nettleship*, the court held that "the mere fact of knowledge cannot increase liability. The knowledge must be brought home to the party sought to be charged, under such circumstances that the person he contracts with reasonably believes that he accepts the contract with the special condition attached to it."[66] Goldberg quoted the 11th edition of Mayne's *Treatise on Damages* published in 1946 in which the authors asked, "Is mere knowledge or communication sufficient to impose liability?" They thought that conclusion unlikely, given that the carrier in *Hadley* had been told that the mill was stopped, and that the result would be that a "party, by acquainting [the other party] with further consequences which the law would not have implied, [could] enlarge his responsibility to the full extent of those consequences, without a contract to that effect."[67]

According to Goldberg, the rule changed abruptly in 1949 with Lord Justice Cyril Asquith's opinion in *Victoria Laundry v. Newman*. Asquith denied that in *Hadley*, the plaintiff's servant had communicated that the mill was stopped. The headnote was "misleading." Asquith distinguished the "first rule" and the "second rule" of *Hadley v. Baxendale*. According to the first rule, "[e]veryone, as a reasonable person, is taken to know . . . what loss is liable to result from a breach of contract in [the] ordinary course." According to the second rule, "he actually possesses [knowledge] of special circumstances outside the 'ordinary course of things, of such a kind that a breach in those special circumstances would be liable to cause more loss." In that event, the "additional loss is also recoverable."[68]

By this route, the common law arrived at the rule formulated in the *Second Restatement*. As long as the damages were foreseeable in the ordinary course of events it does not matter whether they are *circa rem*, "natural," "general," or "direct." Nor does it matter whether they were disproportionately high.

[64] Simmons v. Patchett, [1857] 26 LJQB 195, 197 *in* Goldberg, *supra* note 29, at 166.
[65] *Id.* at 165.
[66] [1868] LR 3 CP 499, 508–09, *quoted id.* at 167.
[67] W.E. Earnengy ed., Mayne's Treatise on Damages 28–29 (11th ed. London, 1946) *quoted in* Goldberg, *supra* note 29, at 165.
[68] Victoria, 2 K.B. at 539.

An alternative

The rationale for the rule, according to Baron Alderson, is that "had the special circumstances [leading to unforeseen injury] been known, the parties might have specially provided for the breach of contract by special terms, as to the damages in that case."[69] That may be. But why assume that the parties are willing to be liable for the damages they do foresee unless they agree to be? Why would they have agreed unless they charged an extra amount?

Nevertheless, sophisticated economic defenses of the rule have been based on the same assumption. According to Richard Posner, the foreseeability rule "induces the party with knowledge of the risk either to either to take appropriate precautions himself, or, if he believes that the other party might be the more efficient preventer or spreader (insurer) of the loss, to reveal the risk to that party and pay him to assume it."[70] According to Ian Ayres and Robert Gertner, the foreseeability rule will force the party who knows that harm may occur to accept liability for it or to convey that information to the other party who may be best able to prevent it.[71] Perhaps, but at be liable, a party ought to accept responsibility for the risk and charge an extra amount for doing so. The trouble is that the foreseeability rule does not require that this party agree but merely to be informed.

What should matter is whether the harm is disproportionately high compared with the contract price and the harm that other customers of the breaching party are likely to suffer. If so, it should not be recoverable because the risk of liability is one for which the breaching party is unlikely to have been compensated. The best rule was formulated by Bartolus nearly seven hundred years ago. Damages should be recoverable if the harm is direct (*circa rem*), or if it would typically be incurred by any non-breaching party (*sequitur rem penes quecumque vadat*).

In the case of direct damages, responsibility for a risk is allocated by the terms of the contract. If the damages are direct, they will have been expected to occur in the ordinary course, and so may be recoverable under what Lord Asquith called the first rule of *Hadley v. Baxendale* and under the *Restatement Second* § 351(2)(a). But that is not why they should be recoverable. They should be recoverable because the risk was assumed by the other party. When the parties contract at a fixed price, each party takes the risk of missing out on a better bargain in return for a guarantee against having to accept a worse one. The direct damages are normally the difference between contract price and lost profits, and they should be recoverable. The party in breach may or may not have assumed the risk of indirect or consequential damages. That loss for one customer may be disproportionately high compared with the contract price and the harm that other customers

[69] *Hadley*, 9 Ex. at 354–55.

[70] Richard A. Posner, Economic Analysis of Law 141 (7th ed. 2007).

[71] Ian Ayres & Robert Gertner, *Filling Gaps in Incomplete Contracts: An Economic Theory of Default Rules*, 99 Yale L.J. 87 (1989).

of the breaching party are likely to suffer. If so, the party in breach should not be liable unless that customer was charged an extra amount.

Despite Lord Asquith's statement of the second rule in *Hadley v. Baxendale*, and despite §351(2)(b) of the *Second Restatement*, courts have refused to hold the defendant liable for damages that may well have been foreseeable but are disproportionately large. An example is *Hadley v. Baxendale* itself. The plaintiff's servant told the defendant's clerk that the mill was stopped. Nevertheless, the plaintiff should not recover unless he paid the defendant an extra amount to assume the risk that a late delivery would cause a loss of profits. Very likely, he did not. He was charged the same amount as other customers who were shipping a package of the same weight or volume the same distance.

The *Second Restatement* gives an illustration based on *Hadley* in which recovery is denied event though a carrier knows that a factory will lose profits if delivery is delayed:

> A, a private trucker, contracts with B to deliver to B's factory a machine that has just been repaired and, without which B's factory, as A knows, cannot reopen. Delivery is delayed because A's truck breaks down. In an action by B against A for breach of contract the court may, after taking into consideration such factors as the absence of an elaborate written contract and the extreme disproportion between B's loss of profits during the delay and the price of the trucker's services, exclude recovery for loss of profits.[72]

Presumably, the absence of an elaborate written contract matters because such a contract would have placed the risk on the trucker, if he has wished to assume it, in which case, presumably, it would have charged a higher price. But why should the extreme disproportion and the absence of a written contract make the damages unforeseeable?

Indeed, there is a line of cases stretching back almost to *Hadley v. Baxendale* that deny recovery when damages were disproportionate but seem to have been foreseeable.[73] Recovery was denied for a loss of profits caused by providing a ship with defects,[74] by providing tires with defects,[75] for failing to provide boilers on time,[76] for failing to finish building a railroad,[77] for failing to provide a machine for drying bricks with as much capacity as promised,[78] for

[72] Restatement (Second) of Contracts § 351, illus. 17 (Am. Law Inst. 1981).

[73] Larry T. Garvin, *Disproportionality and the Law of Consequential Damages: Default Theory and Cognitive Reality*, 59 Ohio St. L. Jour. 339, 345–60 (1998).

[74] Sundance Cruises Corp. v. American Bureau of Shipping, 7 F.3d 1077, 1084 (2d Cir. 1993).

[75] Armstrong Rubber Co. v. Griffith, 43 F.2d 689, 691 (2d Cir. 1930).

[76] McEwen v. McKinnon, 11 N.W. 828, 830 (Mich. 1882).

[77] Snell v. Cottingham, 72 Ill. 161, 170 (1874).

[78] Moulthrop v. Hyett, 17 So. 32, 33–34 (Ala. 1895) (although the court added that damages were remote and speculative).

failing to dress stones for the plaintiff's mill,[79] and for failing to return machinery on time.[80] It is true that some courts have held it to be enough that there are, indeed, courts held that it to be enough that the plaintiff informed the defendant of the loss it would suffer in the event of breach. For example, in *Cook Associates v. Wanick*,[81] the Utah Supreme Court awarded damages for lost profits when the late delivery of parts by a supplier prevented a manufacturing plant from opening on time. It is not surprising when a rule is repeated often enough, a court sometimes will follow it even when it leads to a bad result. The court noted in *Cook*, the defendant "asserts that there was no evidence that the parties 'mutually [understood] that lost profits [would] be included in damages should breach occur.' "[82] According to the court, it did not matter. It should have.

As we have seen, Pothier said that the reason for limiting recovery to damages that are *circa rem* or *propter rem ipsam* is that they are foreseeable. He recognized one exception: these damages could be recovered from a party who breached the contract wrongfully (through *dol*).[83] In tort law, a person may be held responsible even for the unforeseeable consequences if a wrongful act.[84] We noted earlier that this principle can explain why a party who made a fraudulent misrepresentation should be bound even if the misrepresentation was unlikely to have induced the other party to consent. The same principle implies that Pothier was correct: a party who wrongfully breaches should be liable even for damages that are *extra rem*, which Pothier characterized as unforeseeable.

Although English and American courts adopted Pothier's rule as to foreseeability, they never formally adopted this exception. Yet it may explain the result in *Koufos v. C. Czarnikow, Ltd.* [the *Heron II*].[85] The plaintiffs chartered the defendant's ship *Heron II* to carry a cargo of 3,000 tons of sugar from Constanza to Basra which would normally have taken twenty days. In breach of the contract, the ship made deviations that caused a delay of nine days. During that time, the market price for sugar in Basrah had fallen from £32 10s to £31 2s 9d. The House of Lords allowed the plaintiff to recover the difference on the grounds that it was foreseeable that the sugar would be sold at the market price on arrival and that this price might fluctuate. The case is a good illustration of why what matters should not be foreseeability. The loss caused by the delay might have been much greater if the plaintiff had been shipping 3,000 tons of some much more valuable

[79] Fleming v. Beck, 48 Pa. 309, 312 (1864).
[80] Armstrong & Latta v. City of Philadelphia, 94 A. 455, 458 (Pa. 1915).
[81] 664 P.2d 1161 (Utah 1983).
[82] *Id.* at 1167.
[83] Pothier, *supra* note 50, at no. 166.
[84] James Gordley, *Responsibility in Crime, Tort, and Contract for the Unforeseeable Consequences of an Intentional Wrong: A Once and Future Rule?* in The Law of Obligations Essays in Celebration of John Fleming 175 (P. Cane & J. Stapleton eds., 1998).
[85] [1969] A.C. 350 [H.L. 1967].

commodity or goods whose price was more volatile such as gold or silk. Yet the charter fee would have been the same. Since the defendant did not charge less or more to reflect the risk, he should not normally be liable for it.

In *Koufos*, perhaps he should. He breached the contract willfully for reasons of his own by deviating from the prescribed route. Under Pothier's rule, he would be liable.

iii. The requirement that damages be established with certainty

Another limitation on damages recognized by conventional doctrine is that they must be proven with a higher degree of certainty than damages in tort or the other elements of the plaintiff's claim in contract. Although courts speak of certainty, again, what should matter is whether the damages are direct or consequential. In some cases, the risks that each party assumed are assigned by the terms of the contract itself. As we have been using the term, when a party is held liable for these risks, the damages are "direct." The amount of these damages need not be established with any higher degree of certainty than any other element of the plaintiff's case. Indeed, as we will see, sometimes courts require a lesser degree of certainty. In contrast, what we have called "consequential damages" are not allocated by the terms of the contract. The defendant may or may not have assumed these risks. What should matter is not whether these damages can be established with certainly but whether the defendant assumed them or not.

One risk that is allocated by the terms of the contract is the risk of losing a more favorable bargain. When the parties contract for goods or services, they assume the risk that the market price may rise or fall. Problems of certainty can arise in long-term contracts in which a commodity is sold for delivery over a period of years. They can also arise when the performance a party is to receive is the profits or a share in the profits of some enterprise. The amount of these profits may be uncertain. In these cases, there is no reason why difficulties of proof should be any more of an obstacle to recovery than with any other element of the plaintiff's case. We will see that courts do not require any greater degree of certainty.

Another risk that is allocated by the terms of the contract is the risk that a performance may cost more than estimated. That risk, like the first, is allocated by the terms of the contract. We will see, surprisingly enough, that courts require a lesser degree of certainty in the proof of lost profits than they would otherwise. We will see why they are correct to do so.

These damages are direct. Risks that are not allocated by the terms of the contract are consequential. An example is the risk that the non-breaching party will lose the opportunity to enter into profitable transactions with third parties.

Whether damages should be awarded should not depend on the degree of certainty with which they can be established. It should depend on whether the party in breach assumed the risk of liability for consequential damages. Whether they did depends on the same considerations which we discussed in dealing with foreseeability.

The risk of a change in the value in the performance for which the parties contracted

As discussed earlier, if parties contracted to give or receive a commodity with a market price, one party will gain if the market price rises and the other if the market price falls. Having assumed that risk, the breaching party should be liable for the difference between the contract price and the market value at the time of breach.

This amount may be hard to estimate. Nevertheless, there is no reason for requiring that it be established with any greater certainty than any other element in the plaintiff's case. In *Tractebel Energy Mtg. Inc. v. AEP Power Mktg, Inc.*, the Second Circuit, applying New York law, allowed the plaintiff to recover lost profits on a long-term contract. AEP had contracted to build a plant to sell steam to Dow Chemical and electricity to Tractebel. Tractebel agreed to buy at least $50,000,000 of electricity and repudiated the contract when the price of electricity fell. The district court had refused to award damages because "[a]ny projection of lost profits would necessarily include assumptions regarding the price of electricity and the costs of operating over twenty years."[86] The Court of Appeal reversed, noting that "[t]he variables identified by the district court exist in every long-term contract."[87] The non-breaching party should recover because the damages are "general," as the court said, or, as we would say, "direct."

[W]hen the non-breaching party seeks only to recover money that the breaching party agreed to pay under the contract, the damages sought are general damages. . . . The damages may still be characterized as lost profits . . . [b]ut, in this case, the lost profits are the direct and probable consequence of the breach. . . . AEP seeks only what it bargained for—the amount it would have profited on the payments TEMI promised to make for the remaining years of the contract. This is most certainly a claim for general damages[88].

It may happen that, in return for its own performance, a party is to receive profits or the share of the profits in some enterprise. It assumes the risk that the profits will be higher or lower. The damages are direct. As before, if the other party breaches the contract, it should recover the profits to which it was entitled.

[86] 487 F.3d 89, 111 (2d Cir. 2007).
[87] *Id.* at 112.
[88] *Id.* at 112.

Again, there is no reason that the non-breaching party should have to prove these profits with any greater degree of certainty than any other element of its case. The court's estimate, like that of the parties, may be too high or too low, but it is more likely to correspond to the amount of lost profits than if the court required greater certainty. Such a requirement always means an aard of less than the amount that profits are estimated to be. A refusal to give any relief on the grounds of uncertainty would mean an award of zero damages

Of course there are difficulties of proof. As Victor Goldberg noted, even though proof may require "some sophisticated work by economic experts," "this is an exercise that the parties routinely go through in negotiating a settlement."[89] Melvin Eisenberg pointed out that when the parties themselves estimate the future value of an investment, they make the same projections that a court would make in awarding damages.[90]

At present, the rules are unclear. Goldberg noted that "some case law suggests that the standard of proof is higher for consequential damages" than it is for "direct damages."[91] The *Second Restatement of Contracts* does not recognize this distinction. Yet the rule of the *Second Restatement* is not clear. "Damages are not recoverable for loss beyond an amount that the evidence permits to be established with reasonable certainty." That rule is said to be a "limitation" on the recovery of damages. According to the Official Comment this "limitation" "merely excludes those elements of loss that cannot be proved with reasonable certainty" and, moreover, is compatible with the decisions of "[c]ourts [which] have traditionally required greater certainty in the proof of damages for breach of a contract than in the proof of damages for a tort."[92] It cannot be both.

According to Eisenberg, the requirement of greater certainty is a holdover from nineteenth-century contract law. "Under classical contract law the degree of certainty required was typically set at a high level." This approach, which has been carried over into some modern cases, is exemplified, according to Eisenberg,[93] by two decisions of the New York Court of Appeals, *Freund v. Washington Square Press* .[94], and *Kenford Co. v. Erie County* [95]

In *Freund*, Washington Square Press agreed to publish a book which Freund was to write, and the parties were to share the royalties. In *Kenford*, Erie County agreed to construct a domed stadium and to lease it to an affiliate of Kenford, or, if the parties were unable to agree on the terms, to hire the affiliate to manage the stadium

[89] GOLDBERG, *supra* note 29, at 25.
[90] EISENBERG, *supra* note 22, at 233–34.
[91] GOLDBERG, *supra* note 29, at 171.
[92] RESTATEMENT (SECOND) OF CONTRACTS, § 352 cmt. a (AM. LAW INST. 1981).
[93] EISENBERG, *supra* note 22, at 227.
[94] .314 N.E.2d 419 (N.Y. 1975)
[95] 493 N.E.2d 234 (N.Y. 1986).

in return for a percentage of the stadium's gross revenues. In both cases, the court denied recovery on the ground that the plaintiff's damages were too uncertain.

According to Eisenberg, "[t]his approach is dramatically out of touch with the reality of probability."[96] "Many modern courts have properly broken away from the binary, economically uniformed, all-or-nothing approach taken by classical contract law."[97] To illustrate the modern approach, he cited three cases applying New York law. In *Ashland Management, Inc. v. Janien*,[98] the plaintiff had been promised royalties of 15 percent on a computerized investment model he had developed for the defendant. In *Contemporary Mission v. Famous Music Corp.*,[99] the plaintiff had been assigned the exclusive right to the master tape of a rock opera and records made from the master to the plaintiff. He was to receive royalties on the sales. The defendant was to promote the records. In *Lexington Products Ltd. V.B.D. Communications, Inc.*,[100] in return for an exclusive license, the defendant agreed to market the plaintiff's toothbrush, to purchase 200,000 toothbrushes a year, and to pay royalties on each brush sold. He also cited a Massachusetts case, *Rombola v. Consindas*,[101] in which the plaintiff agreed to train, maintain, and race the defendant's horse in return for 75 percent of the gross amount of all purses that the horse won. In all of these cases, the plaintiff recovered on the basis of evidence of the profits he would have made: projections on the success of the investment model; data about the success for other records that had done as well as the one that the plaintiff had recorded but defendant failed to promote; estimates of the sales of toothbrushes; the past track record of the horse.

Eisenberg is right that in *Freund* and *Kenford*,[102] the court should not have required a greater degree of certainty in the proof of damages.[103] But these decisions are not relics of the past. They are two relatively rare and recent instances in which the plaintiff was promised a share in the proceeds of a venture and in which recovery was denied.

Nor is the requirement of greater certainty a relic of the nineteenth century. In 1817, in *Gale v. Leckie*, the defendant breached an agreement to provide a manuscript which the plaintiff would publish. The profits were to be equally divided.

[96] Eisenberg, *supra* note 22, at 229.
[97] *Id.* at 234.
[98] 624 N.E.2d 1007 (N.Y. 1993).
[99] 557 F.2d 918 (2d Cir. 1977).
[100] 677 F.2d 251 (2d Cir. 1982).
[101] 220 N.E.2d 919 (Mass. 1966).
[102] Or if the result was right, it was not because damages were uncertain.See Eisenberg, *supra* note 22, at 236 (construing Rombola v. Consindas, 220 N.E.2d 919, 922 (Mass. 1966)).
[103] Goldberg noted that *Kenford* may have been rightly decided but for a different reason. The plaintiff was trying to recover the profits that they would have made by investing in a domed stadium. The court held that the lost profits were too uncertain. The mistake, according to Goldberg, was to neglect the possibility that the plaintiff was then free to invest in some other project that might have been equally profitable. GOLDBERG, *supra* note 29, at 228–31.

Lord Ellenborough allowed the jury to estimate the plaintiff's lost profits.[104] In *McNeil v. Reid*, the defendant breached a contract to make the plaintiff a partner in the defendant's firm. The jury was allowed to estimate the profits the plaintiff would have made as a partner.[105] Both of these English cases were cited by the New York Court of Appeals in 1853 in *Bagley v. Smith*. There, the court allowed the plaintiff to recover the profit he lost when the defendant breached a contract to continue a partnership with him for a fixed period.[106] Similarly, in 1868, in *Taylor v Bradley*, the Court of Appeals awarded the profit the plaintiff lost when the defendant breached a contract to lease him a farm and share the profit. The court acknowledged that the profit "depends upon details more or less contingent and speculative." Yet "the plaintiff is entitled to the value of his contract. . . . [H]e is deprived of his adventure."[107] In 1908, in *Nash v. Thousand Island Steamboat Co.*, the New York Appellate Division allowed the plaintiff to recover the profits that he would have made had the defendant not breached a contract giving him "the exclusive souvenir, confectionery, view book, news, and parcel checking privileges on these six steamers during the three years named."[108] The trial court denied the plaintiff's recovery "upon the ground that they did not and could not show what profits they would have made if the contract had been performed by the defendants." The Appellate Division reversed, noting that "[t]here must always be difficulty in determining what future profits would arise from conditions that never come about."[109]

These cases were correctly decided. In all of them, as in the cases that met with Eisenberg's approval, a party contracted in return for a share of the profits of some enterprise: the profits of a partnership (*McNeil*, *Bagley*), the profits from publishing a manuscript (*Gale*), or the purses won by racing a horse (*Rombola*). In some, the parties were to share royalties (*Ashland*, *Contemporary Mission*, *Lexington Products*), and one can cite others.[110] The damages were direct. There is no reason that the non-breaching party should have to prove these profits with any greater degree of certainty than any other element of their case.

Goldberg believed that in such cases the non-breaching party should recover these profits as what he called "direct damages." His reason is that the non-breaching party is entitled to what he called the value of their contract as an asset. When a party contracts to give or receive a fungible commodity, the value of the asset at the time of breach is the difference between the market price and the

[104] Gale v. Leckie (1817) 2 Stark. 107.
[105] McNeil v. Reid (1832) 9 Bing. 68.
[106] Bagley v. Smith, 10 N.Y. 489 (1853).
[107] Taylor v. Bradley, 39 N.Y. 129, 144 (1868).
[108] Nash v. Thousand Island Steamboat Co., 108 N.Y. Supp. 336, 337 (A.D. 1908).
[109] *Id.* at 342.
[110] Perma Research & Devel. Co. v. Singer Co., 542 F.2d 111 (2d Cir. 1976); MindGames Inc. v. Western Publ. Co., Inc., 218 F.3d 652 (7th Cir. 2000).

contract price of the commodity. When a party contracts in return for a share of profits, the value of the asset is the estimated value of those profits at the time of breach. "Contracts assign the risks of market change. If the market price goes up and the seller breaches, the buyer's damages are the difference between the contract and market price." Some " 'lost profits' are clearly direct damages. They give the claimant the benefit of the bargain."[111]

His analysis is like ours. We have said that contract remedies should hold each party responsible for the risks that they have been compensated to assume. The seller of goods at a fixed price gives up the chance to profit if the market price rises in order to avoid the risk of losing if the market price falls. The party in breach is liable for the difference between contract and market price. A party who contracts for a share of profits is entitled to that share.

Moreover, American courts dealt with such cases by asking if damages were direct before they began asking whether they were certain. Some courts were borrowing directly or indirectly from Pothier. He said that the recovery of damages should be limited to those that are, in his words, *propter rem ipsam*, or, in Evans's translation, "in respect to the particular thing which is the object of it." The reason, he claimed, was that such damages were foreseeable. Courts that borrowed these words often treated them as a limitation in themselves with little or no attention to the question of whether they were foreseeable. The New York Supreme Court quoted these words in *Blanchard v. Ely*. The New York Supreme Court denied recovery for the profit the buyer would have made from the timely delivery of a steamboat.[112] It quoted them in 1845, in *Masterton & Smith v. Mayor of Brooklyn* to allow the seller to recover for breach of contract for the manufacture and delivery of marble.[113] The court added that such damages were "contemplated" by the parties. It quoted them again in 1848, in *Freeman v. Clute*, to deny the buyer damages for the profits he lost during a three-month delay in providing a suitable steam engine.[114] In time, New York courts supplemented[115]

[111] Goldberg, *supra* note 29, at 175. Goldberg was speaking of the special case of "indirect compensation," in which, for example, instead of paying a distributor a set price for retailing services, a manufacturer sells to them for resale at a markup. His argument carries over to any case in which the benefit of the bargain is to obtain profits or a share in the profits. He mentions the case of licensing for a share in the royalties. *Id.* at 173.

[112] Blanchard v. Ely, 21 Wend. 342, 348 (S. Ct. N.Y. 1839).

[113] Masterton & Smith v. The Mayor &c of the City of Brooklyn, 9 Hill 61, 68 (S. Ct. N.Y. 1845), citing *Evans' Poth.* 91. Damages cannot be recovered when they have "no legal or necessary connection with the stipulations between the parties, and cannot therefore be presumed to have entered into their consideration at the time of contracting." *Id.* at 68. "[P]rofits or advantages which are the direct and immediate fruits of the contract entered into between the parties, stand upon a different footing. These are part and parcel of the contract itself, entering into and constituting a portion of its very elements." *Id.* at 69.

[114] Freeman v. Clute, 3 Barb. 424, 427 (S. Ct. N.Y. 1848).

[115] Masterton & Smith v. The Mayor &c of the City of Brooklyn, 9 Hill 61, 67 (S. Ct. N.Y. 1845); Wakeman v. Wheeler & Wilson Manufacturing Co., 4 N.E. 264, 266 (N.Y. 1886).

or replaced[116] this limitation by the rule that the plaintiff must prove their damages with a greater degree of certainty.

The risk of the cost of performance

Sometimes the parties contract at a fixed price when it is not certain what the cost of providing the goods or services required by the contract will be. The goods have yet to be manufactured, and it is not certain how expensive it will be to make them. The services have yet to be performed, and it is not certain how much it will cost to furnish them. The damages that ensue if the estimate is wrong are direct. By agreeing to a fixed price contract, the party who is to provide the goods or services assumes the risk of a cost overrun but can keep the extra profit if costs are less than they were estimated to be. If they had made a cost-plus contract, the risk that costs will be greater than estimated is placed on the party who is to receive them.

If the contract is fixed price, and the recipient of the goods or services breaches, the recipient should be liable for the profit the other party would have made. The reason is not to put that party in as good a position as if the contract had not been breached. The reason is the allocation of risks established by the terms of the contract. That party would have lost in the event of a cost overrun, so should win if the work could have been completed for less than the contract price. Here again, we are dealing with a risk allocated by the terms of the contract.

The standard for proving the damages should be no higher. Indeed, according to some courts, it should be lower. Some have said that the reason is that the profits in this situation are direct. But that is not a satisfactory explanation since the damages were also direct in the cases we discussed earlier.

In 1851, in *Philadelphia, W. & B.R. Co. v. Howard*, the plaintiff contracted "to furnish . . . building materials . . . [w]orkmanship and labor" to a railroad.[117] In holding the defendant liable for the plaintiff's lost profits, the United States Supreme Court said, quoting the language of Pothier:

> Actual damages clearly include the direct and actual loss which the plaintiff sustains *propter rem ipsam non habitam*.
>
> And in case of a contract like this, that loss is, among other things, the difference between the cost of doing the work and the price to be paid for it. This difference is the inducement and real consideration which causes the contractor to enter into the contract. For this he expends his time, exerts his skill, uses his capital, and assumes the risks which attend the enterprise. And to deprive him of it, when the other party has broken the contract and unlawfully

[116] Griffen v. Colver, 16 N.Y. 489, 493 (Ct. App. 1858).
[117] 54 U.S. (13 How.) 307, 310.

> put an end to the work, would be unjust. There is no rule of law which requires us to inflict this injustice. Wherever profits are spoken of as not a subject of damages, it will be found that something contingent upon future bargains, or speculations, or states of the market, are referred to, and not the difference between the agreed price of something contracted for and its ascertainable value, or cost.[118]

More recently, in *Franklin v. Demico, Inc.*,[119] the defendant breached a contract in which the plaintiff was to manufacture circuit boards to its specifications. The court said:

> There is no merit in Franklin's argument that the amount is not proved because it includes profits, which must be shown with a requisite degree of certainty. . . . Franklin is confusing the legal concepts appropriate to profits which might accrue collaterally as a result of the contract's performance and profits necessarily inherent in the contract, which are always provable. . . . Although we acknowledge that, as the dissent contends, the complex and confusing mathematical methodology used in this case does not produce exact arithmetical accuracy, we must nevertheless presume that the trial judge, as trier of the facts, separated the wheat from the chaff.[120]

It might seem that in this situation, lost profits should be established with at least the same degree of certainty as in other cases of direct damages. Indeed, one could make an argument that they should be established with a greater degree of certainty. Yet the opposite is true. The degree of certainty that courts require is less, and rightly so.

The argument that damages should be established with a greater degree of certainty is that when a party is compensated by a receiving or sharing in the profits of an enterprise, the parties are not betting against each other. Each party will receive more if the profits are larger than expected and less if they are not. Each party' gain is not the other party's loss. That is so even though, if the profits had been more accurately estimated in advance, that estimate would have affected the share of the profits that a party could have successfully demanded as compensation. For example, if the profits on a book are much greater than expected, both the author and the publisher will win out, although, if the parties had known in

[118] *Id.* at 344.

[119] 347 S.E.2d 718 (Ga. App. 1986).

[120] *Id.* at 779. According to the dissent, "Having essentially laid the foundation for the recovery of damages resulting from the breach, plaintiff needed only to attach some relevant figures regarding the costs of production and costs of material purchased, less the amounts received from salvage or other utilization of such materials, but it did not do so." *Id.* at 722.

advance how successful the book would be, the author could have demanded a greater share of the royalties.

In contrast, in a contract to pay a fixed price for goods that have yet to be manufactured or a service yet to be performed, the parties are betting against each other. The party who is to manufacture or to perform assumes the risk of a cost overrun but can keep the extra profit if costs are less than they were estimated to be. The reason for making a fixed price contract is that it is uncertain in advance what the costs will be. It would seem that to allow the non-breaching party to recover lost profits is to allow them to recover on a bet he made but never won.

Nevertheless, courts have correctly required less certain evidence of lost profits. The party in breach has made it impossible to determine precisely what the profits would have been. The party who hired the contractor should not be allowed to walk away from that commitment. The contractor took a risk. It is true that the contractor, like a lost-volume seller, did not give up the opportunity to accept other offers. Since they subcontract the work out to others, they can accept as many offers as they receive. Nevertheless, the contractor took the risk of a cost overrun, and could have reduced the risk by offering to do the work at a higher price. The purpose of offering a lower price was to induce the other party to make a commitment. The other party should not be able to accept a more favorable offer from someone else, and then, having prevented the contractor from performing, to refuse to pay because the cost of performance is uncertain.

Consequently, courts have correctly allowed contractors to recover lost profits based on no more evidence than the estimates they used to compile their bids. In *American Fidelity Fire Ins. Co. v. Kennedy Bros. Construction, Inc.*,[121] the defendant breached its contract by rejecting the plaintiff's low bid. The plaintiff was allowed to recover by presenting in evidence "its calculated cost and profits for each item listed in the . . . bid form."[122] In *Alaska Children's Services, Inc. v. Smart*,[123] the jury found that the plaintiff had been awarded a roofing contract after making the lowest bid. The defendant breached by firing him and hiring a competing bidder who was allowed to rebid. "The evidence as to lost profits in this case was Smart's testimony that his profit on the ACS job would have been between $15,000 and $18,000 and that his normal profit percentage was 'usually anywhere from 18 to 25%.'"[124] Similarly, in *Foster v. United Home Imp. Co., Inc.*,[125] the defendant contracted with one developer, and then before he could begin work, contracted for the same project with another. The court allowed the

[121] 670 S.W.2d 798 (Ark. 1984).
[122] *Id.* at 799.
[123] 677 P.2d 899 (Alaska 1984).
[124] *Id.* at 902. The court said this evidence was "bolstered" by testimony from the competing bidders that they included a similar profit margin in their bids.
[125] 428 N.E.2d 1351 (Ind. App. 1981).

first developer to recover on the basis of his own testimony as to "his expected profit on the total job—based on his experience in construction work since 1954. . . . [He] explained such figure was calculated as the difference between the contract price and his anticipated expenses." The court dismissed the defendant's objection that "(t)he only evidence in the record is the bald assertion by [the plaintiff] that he would have made such profit."[126]

The problem is similar when a manufacturer contracts to produce custom-made goods of use only to the buyer. If the buyer breaches the contract before the manufacturer has a chance to produce them, there may be little evidence of what it would have cost them to perform beyond the estimates it used to set the price it offered. Yet, again, the reason the plaintiff could not prove tits cost of performance was that the defendant prevented it from doing so by breaching the contract. In *Bead Chain Mfg. Co. v. Saxton Products, Inc.*,[127] the Connecticut Supreme Court allowed such a manufacturer to recover lost profits based on the plaintiff's testimony "about the elements he considered in pricing the job."[128] The court admitted that "his cost and price estimates about the actual production run were necessarily theoretical, since [the defendant's] breach made it impossible to go forward with the production that would have made historically accurate figures available."[129] But he should recover precisely because "the plaintiff's difficulty in quantifying his damages often flows directly from the defendant's breach," and therefore the court would "require that degree of proof of damages which the facts permit, but no more."[130]

The risk of losing profits on other transactions

Another risk is that because of the breach of contract, a party will lose the opportunity to enter into profitable transactions with third parties. The plaintiff who seeks to recover lost profits is seeking damages that are not direct but consequential.

In such cases, courts have sometimes denied recovery on the grounds that the damages were not established with certainty. The reason that recovery should sometimes be denied is not that the damages are uncertain. What should matter is whether the party in breach assumed the risk that the non-breaching party would lose the profit they would otherwise make by entering into transactions with others.

Whether the party in breach assumed that risk depends on the same considerations that we discussed in dealing with the requirement of

[126] *Id.* at 1357.
[127] 439 A.2d 314 (Conn. 1981).
[128] *Id.* at 320–21.
[129] *Id.*
[130] *Id.* at 320.

foreseeability. Often, the party in breach can best foresee and control a risk in the best position, not only to foresee and controlit, but to spread the risk among similar transactions, charging each customer or client a bit more. But if the adverse consequences differ from one customer or client to the next, to be compensated, those for whom these adverse consequences are abnormally large must pay a larger amount.

The "new business rule" denies recovery for loss of profits when a breach of contract prevented the opening of a new business on the grounds that the profits cannot be proved with sufficient certainty. Some scholars have said the rule is foolish,[131] and others that it has been nearly abandoned.[132] What should matter, as in the case when recovery is denied when damages are unforeseeable, is whether recovery would impose a disproportionate risk on the breaching party.

Victor Goldberg pointed out that the rule often serves the same purpose as the foreseeability rule. For example, in *Cramer v. Grand Rapids Show Case Co.*,[133] the court denied damages for the profits that were lost when the late delivery of furniture priced at $1,376.75 delayed the opening of a retail store. In *Marvell Light & Ice Co. v. General Electric Co.*,[134] the court denied damages for the profit lost when the delivery of ice-making machinery was delayed. As Goldberg noted, the problem was not that proving the amount of lost profits was difficult. It was whether the foreseeability rule of *Hadley v. Baxendale* had been satisfied. In *Cramer* it was not. In *Marvell* it may have been. The buyer of the ice-making machinery had notified the seller when the contract was made of the consequences of delay. As we have seen, what should matter is not foreseeability but whether the buyer was apt to suffer an abnormally large amount of harm and, if so, whether the seller charged extra for assuming that risk.[135]

In contrast, suppose the seller provides a commodity for resale.[136] Under the *UCC*, "consequential damages" may be recovered[137] when they result from "needs of which the seller at the time of contracting had reason to know and

[131] Eisenberg, *supra* note 22, at 234–35; Robert L. Dunn, The Recovery of Damage for Lost Profits 392 (6th ed. 2005).

[132] E. Allan Farnsworth, Contracts 833 (3d ed. 1999).

[133] 119 N.E. 227 (N.Y. 1918).

[134] 259 S.W. 741 (Ark. 1924).

[135] Goldberg also pointed to cases in which damages for lost profits should be recovered, not because a business is new, but because the plaintiff who was unable to open their business in one location could have made a similar profit by investing the same resources in opening their business elsewhere. Goldberg, *supra* note 29, at 231–39. Examples are Fera v. Village Plaza, 242 N.W.2d 372 (Mich. 1976), Super Valu Stores, Inc. v. Peterson, 506 So.2d 317 (Ala. 1987), and cases in which a would-be franchisee never proved he would do better in one location than another. Goldberg, *supra* note 29, at 237–38. Goldberg also discusses how the new business rule should apply to non-payment of royalties. By our approach, in these cases, damages in these cases concern the value of the performance contracted for, and so need not be proven with any greater degree of certainty than any other element of the plaintiff's case.

[136] Goldberg, *supra* note 29, at 184.

[137] U.C.C. § 2-714(3) (Am. Law Inst. & Unif. L. Comm'n 1977).

which could not reasonably be prevented by cover or otherwise."[138] According to an Official Comment: "in the case of a sale of wares to one in the business of reselling them, resale is one of the requirements of which the seller has reason to know."[139] In the situation to which that provision normally applies, the seller is providing similar goods to a number of purchasers who will resell them at a similar markup. The damages that they will suffer if it breaches its contract are likely to be much the same. In that situation, the seller is likely to be in the best position to assume the risk.

Alan Farnsworth said, citing Fuller and Perdue:[140] "If the test of foreseeability is met, but the court concludes that liability would impose on the party in breach a risk disproportionate to the rewards that the party stood to gain by the contract, 'the test of certainty is the most usual surrogate.' "[141] If that is so, one might ask Farnworth, or Fuller and Perdue, what is the significance of the "expectation interest" if what matters is the risks the parties assumed, which depends in turn on whether the risk was disproportionately high?

iv. Unique performances

When performance is unique, it may have a value to the recipient that cannot be measured by money damages. The court should award specific performance.[142]

That remedy is usually explained as a means of protecting the "expectation interest" of the non-breaching party. Because the promised performance may have unique features that no substitute performance will have, a damage award is not enough. Only a decree of specific performance will put the plaintiff in as good a position as if the contract had been performed.

The result is correct. The reason, however, is not that the purpose of giving a remedy should be to protect a party's "expectation interest." The purpose should be to respect voluntariness and economic fairness. Contracts of exchange should be not only economically fair but also voluntary. They are voluntary so long as the parties each place a higher value on what they are to receive than on what they are to give in return. An adequate remedy deprives neither party of compensation for a risk they paid to assume nor foists on either of them a bargain to which they never consented.

When performance is unique, damages will not enable the party who contracted for the promised performance to obtain an equivalent. Damages

138 *Id.* at § 2-715(2)(a).
139 *Id.* at § 2-715 cmt. 6.
140 Fuller & Perdue, *supra* note 1, at 376.
141 Farnsworth, *supra* note 131, at 831–32.
142 *See* Restatement (Second) of Contracts §359(1) (Am. Law Inst. 1981).

would be measured by the difference in market value between the promised performance and one that is similar but not identical. The party who voluntarily contracted for the one promised might not voluntarily pay that amount for the other.

When a performance is unique, a damage remedy is unfair as well. The value of unique goods depends on the value they may have in the future to a buyer who cannot obtain a substitute performance that is just the same. When the parties contract, the opportunity to profit from the unique characteristics of the goods passes from the seller to the buyer. For the seller to breach the contract is to take back that opportunity. By hypothesis, a damage award will not reflect the value that the unique item may have on account of its unique characteristics to someone in the future. The buyer who was promised a certain house or painting and cannot obtain it is like one who was promised shares in a closely held company. An investment in another house or painting or in other stock may be profitable but it will be subject to different risks of gain or loss than the house, th painting or the stock contracted for.

This explanation of why a party has a right to specific performance poses a challenge to the theory of "efficient breach." That theory may have been inspired by the idea that the purpose of a remedy for breach of contract is to protect a party's "expectation interest." For those who explain contract law in terms of efficiency, the protection of a party's "expectation interest" is a consequence of the "indifference principle." Under that principle, the remedies for breach of contract should "leave the [promisee] absolutely indifferent, in subjective terms, between having the defendant breach and pay damages or having the defendant perform."[143]

Suppose Ann agrees to sell something to Bart for a certain price and then discovers that Claire will pay much more for it than Bart ever would, and indeed, more than the amount Bart will suffer if the contract is breached. According to Richard Posner, it is "efficient" for Ann to breach her contract with Bart. Bart is no worse off because he will receive damages sufficient to put him in as good a position as if the contract had been performed. Ann and Claire are better off. Therefore the breach is efficient. If "[a] party's profit from breach would exceed . . . the expected profit to the other party from completion of the contract, and if damages are limited to the loss of that profit, there will be an incentive to commit a breach. But there should be."[144]

Admittedly, if Claire knew of the contract between Ann and Bart, she could have contacted Bart herself and asked Bart to resell to her. If Claire did not

[143] Richard Craswell, *Contract Remedies, Renegotiation, and the Theory of Efficient Breach*, 61 S. Cal. L. Rev. 629, 636 (1988).
[144] Richard Posner, Economic Analysis of Law 133 (5th ed. 1998).

know of that contract, Ann could have contacted Bart and offered to tell him about Claire's interest in return for a finder's fee. Either way, Claire will end up owning the object in question, which is the efficient result. But a resale by Bart, according to Posner, "would have introduced an additional step, with additional transactions costs."[145] One can raise questions about the significance of these "transactions costs." Posner acknowledged that if the original buyer (Bart) resells "litigation costs would be reduced." But he expects transaction costs to be "high . . . because it would be a bilateral monopoly negotiation."[146] One difficulty with this argument is that there would also be a "bilateral monopoly negotiation" if Ann sells directly to Claire. There is no reason to suppose, as Posner does, that Ann will tamely accept Claire's first offer.[147] Nor is it clear that transactions costs will be particularly high given that the parties have an incentive to minimize them. It is true that, from the standpoint of efficiency, all that matters is that Claire ends up with the object in question, that Ann and Bart are no worse off, and that transactions costs are minimized. From this standpoint, if Claire were willing to pay a vastly greater amount for the object than Bart—a million dollars—and the transactions were $1,000 greater if Bart were to negotiate directly with Claire, for that reason alone, Ann would be entitled to so much of the million dollars as he could persuade Claire to pay. The question of who has the right to an enormously valuable asset would turn on how to avoid a trivial increase in transactions costs. Such an approach would appeal only to those who are so committed to economic explanations of law that they believe nothing but efficiency could matter.

Suppose instead we ask how the parties allocated the risk that the object can be resold to a third party for more than the contract price. If the object in question is not unique and is readily available on the market, the issue of efficient breach does not arise since the third party would buy such an object on the market at the market price. If the object is unique, such as a house or a painting, the opportunity to profit if a third party becomes interested in its unique characteristics was bought by the buyer along with the object. When Bart bought the object, he bought the opportunity to resell it someday if a person such as Claire is willing to pay more for it. It does not matter that Claire came along sooner rather than later.

To make his claim plausible, Posner described a situation in which an object is one which is unique but which, at the time of contracting, the parties believed would be of interest to only one buyer. The object is custom-made by the seller for the buyer. In Posner's hypothetical case, a seller agreed to deliver 100,000 "custom-ground widgets" for 10 cents apiece for use in the buyer's boiler

[145] *Id.*
[146] *Id.*
[147] *Id.*

factory. After he has delivered 10,000 to the buyer, a third party comes to him and "explains that he desperately needs 25,000 custom-ground widgets at once, since otherwise he will be forced to close his pinola factory at great cost," and offers to pay 15 cents apiece. The seller sells him the widgets, causing the original buyer to lose $1,000 in profits, but making for himself an additional profit of $1,250.

Earlier, we discussed contracts for the manufacture of custom-made goods that are expected to be of use only to the buyer. The risk that the parties normally assume is whether the cost of performance will be greater or lesser than the contract price. In contrast, when the performance is unique but is expected to be of value to a number of buyers, as in the sale of the oriental rug, the racehorse, or the Fragonard, the risk that the parties normally assume is whether either will receive an offer that is greater or lesser than the contract price. Posner picked an example which concerns a risk—the unexpected advent of a third party who will pay more than the contract price—that parties to a contract for custom-made goods normally do not consider when they expect the goods to be of use only to person.

Posner devised a hypothetical case in which it is hard to find a principled solution. The risk is not one allocated by the contract for the widgets. Since the purpose of the contract was to manufacture widgets custom made for buyer's needs, the opportunity to sell to a third party could not have been priced into the contract. Neither party would have agreed, even hypothetically, to whom this opportunity should belong. Whichever party should prevail, it is unwise to found a general theory on a type of case in which a principled result is so elusive.

v. Partial or defective performances

A party whose performance is partial or defective, may no longer be entitled to damages measured by the contract price. The recipient of the performance may be entitled to cancel or terminate the contract. The recipient who exercises this right is not responsible for the risks that normally accompany a fixed price contract. The party whose performance was partial or defective can recover, at most, the fair value of any benefits conferred on the recipient.

Whether a party has the right to cancel or terminate should depend on the principles of voluntariness and fairness which we have described. On the one hand, a party who would never have agreed to accept a partial or defective performance even at a discounted price should not be obligated to do so. On the other hand, it would be unfair to allow a party who was compensated for assuming a risk to escape from a disadvantageous bargain on the excuse that the performance was partial or defective. A party who would have accepted a partial or defective performance at a discounted price should not be able to escape the bargain.

Such a solution reconciles the principles of voluntariness and fairness but only if we speak of "voluntariness" in a more extended sense. When the parties contract, the exchange is voluntary in the sense that each party gives up something they value less to receive something they value more. Here, one must ask whether a party would have valued a partial or defective performance sufficiently to have agreed to pay a reduced price for it. That is a choice the recipient of the performance never made. To say it is voluntary because the recipient would have made that choice strains the normal meaning of the word "voluntary." Moreover, to decide what the recipient would have been willing to do requires guesswork. Eisenberg observed that "[i]f A has rendered a bargained-for performance to B, we know that A was willing to render that performance to B for the agreed-upon price. We cannot know whether A would have rendered that performance to B for any lesser price."[148] Conversely, if A has rendered less than the bargained-for performance, it we cannot know whether B would have been willing to pay less for it than the price agreed. We can guess. Although the guess may be inaccurate, the solution that comes closest to reconciling voluntariness and fairness does not allow a party who would have agreed to pay a reduced price to escape if the bargain happens to become disadvantageous.

Except in contracts for the sale of goods, the effect of partial or defective performance is governed by the doctrines of substantial performance, material breach, and total breach.

These doctrines reconcile voluntariness and fairness in the way just described. Sales of goods are governed by the perfect tender rule. As critics have pointed out, it allows a buyer to escape from a disadvantageous bargain by using a flaw in the promise performance as an excuse.

Substantial performance, material breach, total breach

As we have seen, when the parties contract at a fixed price, they allocate a risk. They each give up the opportunity of finding a better offer in return for a guarantee that they have to accept one that is worse. In a contract for a service, they allocate the risk that the cost of performance will be higher or lower than they estimate. The service recipient takes the risk that the job will cost less than expected and the service provider takes the risk that it will cost more. Sometimes, a party who does not perform or fully perform can no longer claim damages measured by the contract price. If not, it is said that the party did not "substantially perform," that the breach was "material," or that it was "total." The question

[148] Bayern & Eisenberg, *supra* note 25, at 5.

is always the same. But some courts and scholars use these terms synonymously and some do not.

The *Second Restatement* uses the term "substantial performance" to mean the flip side of a "material breach." A party who did not substantially perform has breached the contract materially.[149] Melvin Eisenberg uses the term "substantial performance" to refer to a situation in which a party claims their performance is sufficient to allow them to hold the other party to their duties under the contract. He uses the term "material breach" to refer to a situation in which the party to whom the performance is due claims it is insufficient for them to be bound.[150]

The *Second Restatement* uses the term "material breach" to mean that the party to whom performance is due is entitled to refuse to perform their duties until the breach is cured. It uses the term "total breach" to refer to a situation is which that party can terminate the contract because of the other party's material breach. Eisenberg uses the term "material breach" to mean "a breach that justifies a promisee in terminating a contract."[151] "Once the term material breach is property defined, the term total breach becomes unnecessary and should not be employed."[152] In the event of a material breach, however, the promisor may be entitled to cure.[153] Perillos's terminology is like Eisenberg's although he uses the term "total breach": "if a breach is material and no cure is forthcoming, the aggrieved party may cancel the contract and may sue for total breach."[154]

The questions, however, are the same. One is when a breaching party can no longer hold the other party to the terms of the contract. The second is when such a party has the right to cure the failure by completing performance or correcting defects.

For the reasons suggested earlier, a party who would not have agreed to pay for a partial or incomplete performance even at a reduced price should not be required to accept it. A party who would have agreed should be required to accept the reduced price and not be permitted to escape from the bargain. With one qualification, that approach is consistent with standard doctrine as summarized by the *Restatement Second*. It lists a series of factors to be taken into account in determining whether a party has substantially performed or is in material breach. Two of them concern the amount by which the value of the performance to the party who is to receive it has been diminished: "(a) the extent to which the injured party will be deprived of the value which he reasonably expected to receive;

[149] *See* Restatement (Second) of Contracts §237 illus. 11 (Am. Law Inst. 1981), *quoted in* Lon L. Fuller & Melvin Aron Eisenberg, Basic Contract Law 992–93 (8th ed. 2006).

[150] *Id.* at 993.

[151] Eisenberg, *supra* note 22, at 689.

[152] *Id.* at 688.

[153] *Id.* at 691.

[154] John D. Calamari & Joseph M. Perillo, Calamari and Perillo on Contracts 374 (6th ed. 2009).

(b) the extent to which the injured party can be compensated for the part of that benefit of which he will be deprived."[155] A third is "(c) the extent to which the party failing or perform . . . will suffer forfeiture." These factors should be taken into account in answering the question, would the injured party have agreed to receive a performance which deprives them of the value which they reasonably expected to receive at a reduced price?

The qualification concerns the meaning of "forfeiture." When the parties contract at a fixed price, one party assumes the risk that the performance will cost more than estimated, and the other party the risk that it will cost less. As just noted, the party who has not substantially performed loses the right to profit if the work does cost less. The *Second Restatement* does not count that loss as a "forfeiture." By "forfeiture," it means that a party suffered a loss because by "relying substantially on the expectation of the exchange, as through preparation or performance."[156] By that definition, "forfeiture" does not include loss of the benefit of the bargain. But that is irrational. The doctrine of substantial performance determines when, by failing to substantially perform, a party loses the benefit of their bargain and cannot hold the other party damages based on the contract price. At most, that party has a claim for restitution, which is the value of the work done. According to the *Second Restatement*, "the potential forfeiture may be mitigated if the builder has a claim in restitution."[157] The builder's claim in restitution allows the builder to recover for the fair value of the work that has been completed. The builder cannot recover neither the difference between the contract price allocable to the work completed nor the profit lost on work that was never done.[158]

It may be difficult to tell when the party would have been willing to accept such a performance at a reduced price. Judge Cardozo, in his classic decision in *Jacob & Youngs v. Kent*, noted that the defects in performance were "of trivial or inappreciable importance" and "insignificant in . . . relation to the project."[159] The contractor, making an innocent mistake, had installed Coulter Pipes when the specifications called for Reading Pipes. The quality and cost of the two brands of pipe was much the same. In other cases, the defects were so substantial that the court questioned whether the party owed performance would have accepted them at any reduction in price: for example, when a contractor installed

[155] Restatement (Second) of Contracts § 241 (Am. Law Inst. 1981).

[156] *Id.* at cmt. d.

[157] *Id.*

[158] The *Second Restatement* defined "forfeiture" in this way to be consistent with its explanation of when a condition is excused by "forfeiture." Because the failure of one party to perform "acts as the non-occurrence of a condition, the same risk of forfeiture obtains as in the case of conditions generally." *Id.* As we will see, the definition is incorrect when it is applied to conditions, and for the same reason.

[159] Jacob & Youngs, Inc. v. Kent, 129 N.E 889, 890, 892 (N.Y. 1921).

a russet-colored shingle roof with yellow streaks that could not be removed without rebuilding the roof.[160] In intermediate cases, there will be guesswork as to whether a party would have been willing to accept an imperfect performance. Nevertheless, there is no way to avoid the guesswork and still have a rule that reflects both of the concerns just described. A party who would not have agreed to exchange should not be forced to accept it. A party who would have been willing to do so should not be able to escape the risks allocated by a contract to exchange at a fixed price.

In two situations, however, this rule needs to be qualified. In one, the contractor has done very little. Courts have recognized that completing a small portion of the work does not constitute substantial performance.[161] It may be that the other party can receive exactly the performance called for by the contract by hiring someone else to complete the work. But a party who enters into a fixed price contract assumes the risk of whether the work could be completed for the cost estimated. When a contractor quits after doing little of the work, it may be impossible to determine what the cost of completing the job would have been. A contractor who could recover the contract price minus the cost to the other party of completing the work, might enter into a contract, breach it immediately, and then recover a lost profit by claiming that the other party overbid.

In another situation, the contractor acted in bad faith. As the *Second Restatement* notes, in determining whether a party has substantially performed, another factor to consider is "the extent to which the behavior of the party failing to perform comports with standards of good faith and fair dealing."[162] An example of bad faith would be deliberately to substitute different and cheaper materials than those called for by the contract in order to lower the cost of performance. The contractor is not entitled to damages measured by the contract price even if the other party would have been willing to accept a performance using these cheaper materials at a suitably reduced price. Under the contract, the contractor assumed the risk of how much it would cost to complete the project using the materials the contract specified. A party who cheats should not be able to hold the other party to the terms of their bet. The reason for requiring the other party to take a performance that is different than the one contracted for is to avoid unfairness to the party who did not fully perform. A party who cheats should not be able to complain of unfairness.

[160] O.W. Grun Roofing & Constr. Co. v. Cope, 529 S.W.2d 258 (Tex. Civ. App. 1975).

[161] Keyer v. Driscoll, 159 N.W.2d 680 (Wisc. 1968).

[162] Restatement (Second) of Contracts § 241(e) (Am. Law Inst. 1981). The remaining factor is "(d) the likelihood that the party failing to perform . . . will cure the failure." As the Official Comment to that provision notes, that factor concerns, not the right of the non-breaching party to repudiate the contract, but his "right to withhold further performance as a means of securing his expectation of an exchange of performances."

A party whose performance is too partial or incomplete to hold the other party to the contract may have the right to cure. It does not matter whether we say that when one party is in material breach, the other has the right to terminate unless they are entitled to cure, or that a party is entitled to cure who is not in material breach. The factors we have just considered in determining whether a breach is sufficiently serious that the other party can terminate should determine whether a party can cure. As we saw, according to the *Second Restatement*, whether a breach is sufficiently serious to entitle the other party to suspend performance depends on "(a) the extent to which the injured party will be deprived of the value which he reasonably expected to receive; (b) the extent to which the injured party can be compensated for the part of that benefit of which he will be deprived." Whether there is a "total breach" which entitles the other party to terminate depends on two additional factors:

(b) the extent to which it reasonably appears to the injured party that delay may prevent or hinder him in making reasonable substitute arrangements;
(c) the extent to which the agreement provides for performance without delay, but a material failure to perform or to offer to perform on a stated day does not of itself discharge the other party's remaining duties unless the circumstances, including the language of the agreement, indicate that performance or an offer to perform by that day is important.[163]

Those considerations bear on whether, if the contract is not terminated, the injured party will be deprived of the value which they reasonably expected to receive and, if so, can be compensated for that loss. The answers may depend on whether a substitute agreement can be made and whether the timeliness mattered.

Sale of goods

We have seen that, in a contract to provide services, a party who has substantially performed does not lose the benefit of their bargain. As just mentioned, among the factors that determine whether they have substantially performed is: "the extent to which the injured party will be deprived of the value which he reasonably expected to receive; (b) the extent to which the injured party can be compensated for the part of that benefit of which he will be deprived."[164]

Had this rule been applied to the sale of goods, the result would have been like the traditional rule at civil law. In Roman law, if goods were defective, the buyer might have the right to return them and recover the purchase price. Or he might have the right to recover for the amount by which the defects

[163] *Id.* at § 242.
[164] *Id* at § 241.

diminished the value of the goods. At first, these remedies were provided for the buyer of slaves and animals, and later they were granted to buyers in general. There was a continuing discussion over when a buyer was entitled to rescission and when to the diminution of value. The prevailing opinion among early modern jurists was that the buyer should only be able to seek rescission if he would not have bought the object had he known of the defect.[165] The same option was given the buyer by the *French Civil Code* of 1804[166] and the *German Civil Code* of 1900.[167]

The nineteenth-century treatise writers tried to bring order to a common law that was less clear. When goods were not as they were supposed to be, English courts had sometimes discharged the contract and sometimes allowed the buyer to claim damages. The treatise writers explained that the first remedy was proper when the term of the contract describing the goods was a condition precedent to the duty of the buyer to pay for them. The reason, Judah Benjamin said, was that "the vendor fails to comply . . . with the contract itself."[168] A remedy in damages was appropriate for breach of warranty. A warranty was not a condition but a promise. Sometimes, however, a term could be both a condition and a warranty, and then either remedy was appropriate.

One consequence of their work was the idea that a breach of warranty might also be the non-fulfillment of a condition precedent of the buyer's obligation to pay the price. "The vendor fails to comply . . . with the contract itself. . . anymore than if he delivered peas when the contract called for beans." One consequence of this idea was the "perfect tender rule." The buyer could refuse to accept goods regardless of the importance of the defect. In sales of goods, there was no doctrine of substantial performance.

Another consequence was the idea that a warranty was a promise, and that, therefore, the remedy for a breach of warranty should be the recovery of damages for breach of contract. English courts had also recognized a third remedy which they considered to be different than recovering damages for breach of warranty. The buyer might ask for the sales price to be diminished to reflect the decreased value of the defective goods. This remedy either disappeared or lost its distinctiveness when the idea became accepted that the goal of remedies for breach of contract is to protect a party's expectation interest.

We have suggested that when a performance is partial or incomplete, the party who would have agreed to accept it for a reduced price at the time that the parties contracted should be required to do so. One unfortunate result of the work of the

[165] Zimmermann, *supra* note 32, at 325.
[166] French Civil Code (Code civil) art. 1644.
[167] German Civil Code (Bürgerlichesgesetzbuch) § 480 (1900).
[168] Judah Philip Benjamin, Treatise on the Law of Sale of Personal Property 634 (4th ed. 1888).

nineteenth-century treatise writers was to lose track of the idea that requiring the buyer to accept a reduced price is a distinct remedy with a distinct justification. Another unfortunate result was the "perfect tender rule."

Diminution in price

The English courts had regarded the remedy of requiring the buyer to accept a reduced price as distinct from allowing him to recover damages for breach of contract. Before the enactment of the *Judicature Acts* these remedies had to be sought in separate actions. When sued by the seller, the buyer might counterclaim for a diminution of the price. Or he might bring a cross-action to claim damages, an action which was not barred if he had made a counterclaim for a reduced price in a previous action.[169] Under the *Judicature Acts* he can "set up by way of set off or counterclaim any claim, whether sounding in damages or not, which he has against the claim of the plaintiff" (*Order XIX*, r. 3) and "is enabled to recover consequential damages that may far exceed the amount of the price sued for by the plaintiff" (*Order XXII*, r. 10).[170]

The two remedies were still conceived to be distinct in the *English Sale of Goods Act* of 1893 and the *American Uniform Sale of Goods Act* of 1906. According to the *Sale of Goods Act* 53(i), the buyer "may (a) set up against the seller the breach of warranty in diminution or extinction of the price; or (b) maintain an action against the seller damages for the breach of warranty." According to § 69(a) of the *Uniform Sales Act*:

> Where there is a breach of warranty by the seller, the buyer may, at his election—
>
> 1. Accept or keep the goods and set up against the seller, the breach of warranty by way of recoupment in diminution or extinction of the price;
> 2. Accept or keep the goods and maintain an action against the seller for damages for the breach of warranty.

Both Acts provided that if the buyer sued for damages, "the measure of damages" is "the difference between the value of the goods at the time of delivery to the buyer and the value they would have had if they had answered to the warranty."[171]

The nineteenth-century treatise writers had described a warranty as a promise like any other. After the view became accepted that the object of a remedy for breach of a promise was to protect a party's "expectation interest" it no longer

[169] *Id.* at 906.

[170] *Id.*

[171] Sale of Goods Act 1893, 56 & 57 Vict. Ch. 71, § 53(i); Uniform Sales Act § 69(f) (Unif. L. Comm'n 1906).

made sense to distinguish diminution in price from the recovery of damages for breach of contract. The *UCC* provides:

> The measure of damages for breach of warranty is the difference at the time and place of acceptance between the value of the goods accepted and the value they would have had if they had been as warranted, unless special circumstances show proximate damages of a different amount.[172]

We have seen that the purpose of giving a remedy should not be to protect a party's expectation interest. It should be to hold the parties responsible for the risks that each of them assumed. Consequently. when seller's performance is partial or incomplete, the buyer should be required to accept it at a reduced price rather than being be permitted to escape responsibility for a such a risk. The purpose of the remedyis not to put the buyer in as good a position as if the seller not breached the contract. It is to compensate a buyer for having received a performance worth less than the one bargained for.

This purpose is not reflected in the description of the damages for breach of warranty in the *Sale of Goods Act*, the *Uniform Sales Act*, and the *UCC*. The measure of damages should not be "the difference at the time and place of acceptance between the value of the goods accepted and the value they would have had if they had been as warranted." That would be the correct measure if, as the *UCC* assumed, the remedy should protect the buyer's expectation interest. Consequently, it is odd to find it appearing side by side with the remedy of diminution of price in the *Sale of Goods Act* and the *Uniform Sales Act*. Suppose that goods that were sold for $100,000 which was their market value at the time of sale, but that they were defective, and would only have had a market value of $90,000 at that time had the defect been known. If the parties would have been willing to contract at that price, the proper remedy would be to allow them to pay $90,000. Suppose that at the time and place of acceptance, the price for the goods, defective or not, fell by 30 percent. They were worth $63,000 and would have been worth $70,000 had they conformed to the contract. Each party should bear the risk that the price will fluctuate after they contract. The seller should receive $90,000 for their goods, not $63,000, and by the same token, the buyer should receive a discount of $10,000, not $7000.

Another unfortunate consequence of the formula of the *UCC* is that it takes no account of whether the parties would have been willing to contract at a mutually acceptable price had they known of the defect. It may be, for example, that the goods are worthless unless they are repaired, and that the cost of repairing them exceeds

[172] U.C.C. § 2-714(2) (AM. LAW INST. & UNIF. L. COMM'N 1977).

the contract price. In *Continental Sand and Gravel v. K & K Sand and Gravel*, the defendant sold front-loaders, cranes, and other equipment for $50,000[173] An express warranty was breached, and the plaintiff recovered $104,206.75, which was the cost of the repairs necessary to put the equipment in the condition warranted. The court allowed recovery of that amount under § 2–714(2) of the *Code*, rejecting the defendant's argument that recovery should be "diminution in value from the purchase price as the result of the breach of warranty." "The result is logical," the court said, "since to limit recoverable damages by the purchase price . . . would clearly deprive the purchaser of the benefit of its bargain.".[174] At the time the parties contracted, the seller gave up his chance that if he sold later he would receive more than $50,000 for the equipment to avoid the risk that he would have to sell it for less. Had he known of the defect, presumably, he would have been willing to sell the equipment at a discounted price in order to avoid the similar risk that later he would have to sell the defective goods for less. But there is no reason to think that he was willing to assume the risk of paying twice the contract price to the buyer if the equipment was defective. There is no reason to think that the buyer would have been willing to pay that much to acquire it.

In another such situation, the goods will not do the job that they were warranted to do, and the cost of goods that can do that job exceeds the contract price. In *Chatlos Systems, Inc. v National Cash Register Corp.*,[175] the plaintiff purchased a computer for $45,000 that was warranted to run an accounting program that the plaintiff wished to use. The computer was unable to do so. The value of a computer that would was $205,000.31.[176] The court awarded that amount, which was correct if the true goal of remedies for breach of contract is to protect the non-breaching party's expectation interest.

To avoid the evident unfairness of the result, as Christopher Wonnel observed, some scholars have suggested that the expectation interest is protected if we read in an implied or gap-filling term that limits the damages to those to which the parties would have agreed.[177] As he noted:

> The problem with this argument is that any remedial scheme can be made consistent with expectation theory in this way, by saying that parties would have

[173] 755 F.2d 87 (7th Cir. 1985). I thank Mark Gergen for noting how unlikely it is that $50,000 was a genuine sales price. It was the price set for the equipment in a larger deal which included the transfer of other assets, and may have been artificially low. The court, however, treated is as a genuine price.

[174] 755 F.2d at 91–92. .

[175] 670 F.2d 1304 (3d Cir.1982).

[176] At least, the court accepted that figure although the dissent pointed out there was little evidence to support it. *Id.* at 1307.

[177] E. ALLAN FARNSWORTH & JOHN HONNOLD, CASES AND MATERIALS ON COMMERCIAL LAW 690 (4th ed. 1985), *cited by* Christopher Wonnell, *Expectation, Reliance and the Two Contractual Wrongs*, 8 SAN DIEGO L. REV. 53, 74 n.63 (2001).

wanted it. The interesting question is what kind of substantive and remedial scheme the parties to a contract would want.[178]

So we come back to the question: what risks did the parties assume when they contracted? In *Chatlos*, if the parties had known about the defect at the time that they contracted, there is no reason to believe that the seller would have been willing to assume the risk of having to pay the amount necessary to purchase a computer that would run the buyer's accounting program. There is no reason to believe that the buyer would have been willing to pay that much to have a computer that would.

Perfect tender

As we have seen, the nineteenth-century treatise writers explained that a term of the contract could be both a warranty and a promise and also a condition precedent to the duties of the buyer to accept the goods and pay for them. The reason that English courts sometime discharged the duties of the buyer, they said, was that, in these cases, the term in question was a condition.

Pollock said, "Whether any term of a contract is in fact a condition or a warranty is a question of construction depending on the language used and to some extent on the nature and circumstances of the transaction."[179] According to the English *Sale of Goods Act* of 1893:

> Whether a stipulation in a contract of sale is a condition the breach of which may give rise to a right to treat the contract as repudiated, or a warranty, the breach of which may give rise to a claim for damages but not to a right to reject the goods and treat the contract as repudiated, depends in each case on the construction of the contract.[180]

This approach was not taken in the United States. The *Uniform Sales of Goods Act* of 1906 provided that "where there is a breach of warranty by the seller, the buyer may, at his election . . . [r]efuse to accept the goods, if the property therein has not passed, and maintain an action against the seller for damages for the breach of warranty." The buyer may "[r]escind the contract to sell or the sale and refuse to receive the goods, or if the goods have already been received, return them or offer to return them to the seller and recover the price or any part thereof which has been paid" (§ 69).

[178] Wonnell, *supra* note 176, at 74.

[179] Frederick Pollock, Principles of Contract: Being a Treatise on the General Principles Concerning the Validity of Agreements in the Law of England 488–89 (4th ed. 1885).

[180] Sale of Goods Act, 1893, 56 & 57 Vict. Ch. 71, §§ 11(i)(a) & 11(i)(b).

The *UCC* provides: "If the goods or the tender of delivery fail in any respect to conform to the contract, the buyer may . . . reject the whole."[181] Thus we have moved from the position that the term warranting goods might also be a condition, depending on the circumstances, to the position that warranty will have the same effect as a condition—non-conformity will discharge a contract—to the position that if the goods "fail in any respect to conform to the contract, the buyer may . . . reject the whole"—which is an application of the general rule which, as we have seen, requires "perfect fulfillment" of a contract.

In a contract to provide services, one party's performance is also deemed to be an implied condition which means that it that must be fulfilled for the other party to be obligated. It is a condition that need not be perfectly fulfilled. Courts have altered the rule that requires conditions to be perfectly fulfilled by adopting the doctrine of "substantial performance." In contrast, the *UCC* adopted a perfect tender rule. It allows the buyer to refuse to accept a price discount and reject goods that are defective in any way.[182] If the market has fallen, the buyer can use the excuse that the goods are defective to buy at cheaper price.

The drafters of the *Code* tried to ameliorate the effects of the perfect tender rule by imposing a series of limitations. The limitations only show what a bad rule it is, and remains despite their efforts.

One limitation is that the buyer who accepts goods may reject them afterward only if their "nonconformity substantially impairs its value to him."[183] A similarly worded limitation applies to installment contracts. The buyer may reject a single installment only if its nonconformity substantially impairs its value even the seller cannot cure. The buyer may cancel the entire contract if the nonconformity of one or more shipments substantially impairs the value of the whole.[184]

By our approach, the rule should be that the buyer must accept nonconforming goods at a discount if he would have done so had such an offer been made originally. The rule allowing the buyer to reject the goods only if they substantially impair their value is a step in that direction. The test, however, should not be "substantial impairment": at a sufficient discount, the buyer might have been willing to accept goods even if their value is substantially impaired.

Another limitation on the perfect tender rule is that the seller may have the right to cure by making a conforming delivery. The right to do so, however, is

[181] U.C.C. § 2-601 (Am. Law Inst. & Unif. L. Comm'n 1977).

[182] One limitation on the buyer's right to refuse the goods is the general requirement that rights under the *Code* must be exercised in good faith. *Id.* at §1-304. But it does not prevent a buyer from rejecting goods on account of a defect that does not "substantially impair" their value to them. *Id.* at § 2-608(1). The *Code* deems them to be acting in good faith even if they do so to obtain a price that is more favorable to them, and less favorable to the seller, than the contract price.

[183] *Id* at § 2-608(1).

[184] *Id.* at § 2-612(2)-(3).

restricted in two ways. First, delivery must be made when "the time for performance has not yet expired."[185] Second, if the time for performance has expired, a conforming tender may be made within a "reasonable time" only if the seller "had reasonable grounds to believe it would be acceptable with or without money allowance."[186]

In either case, even a buyer who would originally have agreed to accept the non-conforming goods at a lower price is entitled to a conforming tender. The first restriction allows the seller's right to cure to depend on whether they can promptly be purchased. If not, the buyer is free to reject goods when their market price has fallen since the contract was made even if the lack of conformity does not in any way impair their value.

The second limitation is strange. It allows the right to cure to depend on the seller's expectations of what goods the buyer would have been willing to accept with a discount. Why should the seller's reasonable expectations matter? Good faith should matter. But good faith is not the same as a belief that the goods would be acceptable to the buyer. The seller may not know of the defect. The seller may know of the defect and suspect that they are not acceptable. The seller who acts in bad faith by trying to cheat the buyer should lose the benefit of the bargain. A seller who is being honest with the buyer about the condition of the goods is not trying to do so.

Consider some variations on the facts of *T.W. Oil, Inc. v. Consolidated Edison Co.*[187] There, the seller was under contract to deliver fuel oil with a sulfur content of less than 0.5 percent. It did not realize that the oil he was delivering had a sulfur content of 0.9 percent but, had it known, it would have reasonably believed that the buyer would find oil of that sulfur content acceptable. The court ruled that the seller did not have to believe that its oil was non-conforming in order to be allowed to cure. That result is sensible. There is no reason that the seller should be in a better position if it thinks it is delivering non-conforming goods than if it thinks it is not. Suppose, however, that the facts were the same but that the seller did not know that the buyer could use oil with a sulfur content of .9 percent. It would seem that the result should be the same as long as the buyer would reasonably have found oil of that sulfur content acceptable. What the seller believed, reasonably or not, did not affect what the seller did. It delivered oil that it reasonably believed had a sulfur content of 0.5 percent.

Suppose, then, that the seller had no information as to the maximum sulfur content of the oil that the buyer could use, that it had learned that the oil it had already purchased had a sulfur content of 0.9 percent. It delivered the oil anyway,

[185] Id. at § 2-508(1).
[186] Id. at § 2-508(2).
[187] 443 N.E.2d 932 (N.Y. 1982).

informing the buyer of the discrepancy, in the hope that that the buyer would accept the shipment. Can the buyer reject the oil anyway? If so, then the seller is worse off because he made the wrong guess about the buyer's needs than, as in the previous hypothetical, in which he made no guess at all. If not, then despite subsection 2, the seller's expectations do not matter. What matters is whether it delivers goods that meet the buyer's needs.

IV. Alternatives when damages are hard to establish

i. Liquidated damages clauses

When the parties know that damages will be hard to establish if one of them breaches the contract, they may insert a liquidated damage clause which specifies the damages that a party who breaches the contract must pay. Such a clause is enforceable if it a reasonable estimate at the time the contract is made of what the damages are likely to be.[188] If it is not a reasonable estimate, it is a "penalty clause," and it is not enforceable.

A liquidated damages clause should be enforceable because it enables a party to obtain compensation for the consequences of risks that the other party assumed even when the compensation is hard to establish. A penalty clause should not be enforceable because it is like a gamble. It imposes liability for a risk that neither party would be willing to assume. Risk-averse parties do not gamble.

An insurance company would not insure a house for more than it is worth, not simply because the insured might burn it down to collect the insurance, but because anything over that amount would be a windfall for the insured, and there is no amount that the insured would be willing to pay for the chance of obtaining that windfall that the insurance company would accept. It would be as though the parties made a bet on whether a neighboring house would burn down or whether lightning would strike a certain tree in a nearby park. Similarly, in a sales contract, the seller assumes the risk of losing out if the market price should rise and is compensated for doing so by the borrower who assumes the risk of losing out if the market price should fall. The breaching party owes the difference between the market and the contract price at the time of breach. But if the parties are risk averse, they will not agree that one would compensate the other for twice the difference between the market and the contract price at the time of breach. If the contract contained a clause requiring one of the parties to do so, that party could not have been fairly compensated for bearing that risk.

[188] *See* RESTATEMENT (SECOND) OF CONTRACTS § 356 (AM. LAW INST. 1981).

An example of how the rule should be applied is *Wasserman's Inc. v. Middletown*.[189] A commercial lease contained a clause which provided that if the lease were cancelled, the lessor would pay the lessee damages equal to 25 percent of its gross receipts. Absent the clause, the lessee would be entitled to recover the loss of its profits. For it to recover gross receipts in excess of net profits would be a "windfall."[190] The Supreme Court of New Jersey correctly refused to enforce the provision.

An example of how this rule should not be applied is *NPS, LLC v. Minihane*.[191] A ten-year license agreement for luxury seats for the New England Patriots football games contained an acceleration clause which provided that if the licensee defaulted, he had to pay the full amount for all the years remaining on the license. In upholding the provision, the Massachusetts Supreme Court said:

> The sum provided for . . . bears a reasonable relationship to the anticipated actual damages arising from a breach. It anticipates a worst-case scenario, that is, NPS's inability to resell the seats for the remaining term of the license. However, the defendant has not shown that this outcome is sufficiently unlikely that it renders the amount grossly disproportionate to a reasonable estimate of actual damages.[192]

A reasonable estimate is the amount of the loss discounted by the probability of its occurring. It is fanciful to think that there was no significant chance of reselling the luxury seats. The court claimed that "in the case of an enforceable liquidated damages provision, mitigation is irrelevant and should not be considered in assessing damages."[193] That cannot be. A liquidated damages clause is supposed to be a reasonable estimate of damages. The damages that occur if feed is not delivered to a chicken farmer is not the loss if the chickens die because the farmer failed to mitigate damages by buying feed elsewhere. It is the difference between the price the farmer paid to buy feed elsewhere and the contract price.

There is a conflict of authority as to whether such a clause should be enforced when the damages that will result from a breach are uncertain at the time that the contract is made but will be easy to establish afterward.[194] Suppose a party sells land or goods. The damages if the buyer breaches will be the contract price minus the amount the seller receives by reselling them. Neither party may know how much that will be in advance but afterwards the court can merely subtract

[189] 645 A.2d 100 (N.J. 1994).

[190] *Id.* at 110.

[191] 886 N.E.2d 670 (Mass. 2008).

[192] *Id.* at 675.

[193] *Id.*

[194] *Compare* Lee Oldsmobile v. Kaiden, 363 A.2d 270 (Md. App. 1976) (clause unenforceable) *with* Hutchison v. Thompkins, 259 So.2d 129 (Fla. 1972) (clause enforceable).

the resale from the contract price. If the contract provides that the seller should recover a greater amount it is imposing a penalty as much as one that provides the seller should recover a thousand dollars more than the difference between the contract and the resale price.

ii. So-called reliance damages

A party who lost profits because of a breach of contract but cannot prove the amount may recover the amount spent in order to make these profits.[195] As Allan Farnworth put it, "one who fails to meet the burden of proving prospective profits . . . can usually meet the burden of proving with sufficient certainty the extent of that reliance. . . [and] can then recover damages based on reliance."[196] For example, as we have seen, a party who fails to deliver goods sold for resale is liable for the buyer's lost profits. The buyer who cannot prove the amount for which the goods would have been resold can still recover, for example, the amount spent advertising them for sale.

The reason is that the buyer expected to make that amount back and more if the goods were delivered. The reason for accepting it as a good estimate of the lost profits is that the buyer spent that amount with that expectation. To award reliance damages is a surrogate for awarding damages based on lost profit.

For that reason, it is misleading to call them "reliance damages." Ordinarily, reliance damages are the amount necessary to make a party as well off as if the promise that was broken had never been made. Farnworth concluded that the rule allowing recovery of reliance damages will not "allow a party to recover costs incurred *before* a contract was made."[197] Nevertheless, the reason for allowing a party to recover costs is that they were incurred in the expectation of making at least that much if the contract were performed. As long as that was the buyer's expectation, it should not matter if these costs were incurred before the contract was made.

Some courts have held that it does not. In *Security Stove & Mfg. Co. v. American Ry. Express Co.*,[198] a stove company was unable to exhibit its product at a show because a shipper failed to deliver one of the parts necessary for the stove to work. How much more it would have sold if the stove had been exhibited could not be determined, and consequently neither could its additional profits. The court awarded the company the amount it had spent setting up the show before and after the contract with the shipper had been made. In an English case,

[195] DPJ Co. Ltd. Partnership v. F.D.I.C., 30 F.3d 247 (1st Cir. 1994).

[196] FARNSWORTH, *supra* note 131, at 835.

[197] *Id.*

[198] 51 So.2d 572 (Mo. App. 1932).

Anglia Television Ltd. v. Reed,[199] because of a mixup in his bookings, the actor Robert Reed breached his contract with a studio to star in a film it was making. It abandoned the film because it could not find an adequate alternative for the male lead. It recovered the expenses it had incurred before Reed entered into the agreement.

These cases may have been incorrectly decided but the reason is not that the plaintiffs recovered money that they spent before the contract was made. The courts assumed that the plaintiffs should have recovered their lost profits if only they could prove what the profits would have been. It is unlikely, however, that the shipper or Robert Reed assumed the risk of liability for profits that the stove manufacturer or the studio would lose if the contract were breached. Very likely, the shipper charged according to the weigh and volume of the containers and the distance that they had to be transported. Presumably, Robert Reed was not paid extra for assuming the risk that all of the studio's prior expenses would be wasted. These are like the cases we considered earlier where the damages would vary greatly from one person to the next.

iii. Specific performance

As we have seen, a court will award specific performance rather than damages when the plaintiff would be unable to purchase an equivalent for the performance promised. The land or goods promised were unique. Specific performance may also be awarded when the damages that the plaintiff should recover are too difficult to prove. For example, in *Laclede Gas Co. v. Amoco Oil Co.*,[200] the court specifically enforced a long term contract to supply propane for resale to a yet-to-be determined number of residential developments. The plaintiff "probably could not find another supplier of propane willing to enter into a long-term contract such as the Amoco agreement, given the uncertain future of world-wide energy supplies," and if it could "it would still face considerable expense and trouble which cannot be estimated in advance in making arrangements for distribution to its subdivisions."[201] The Eighth Circuit Court of Appeals granted specific performance..

In cases such as *Amoco*, however, the damages to which the plaintiff was entitled were the difference between market and contract price, which compensated it for the risk that it had assumed. As we have seen, the profits that a party loses if a contract is breached may not correspond to any risk that it

[199] [1971] 2 All E.R. 690 (C.A.).
[200] 522 F.2d 33 (8th Cir. 1975).
[201] *Id.* at 40.

assumed. In that event, a court should not award specific performance in lieu of damages for the lost profits.

In *Walgreens Co. v. Sara Creek Property Co.*,[202] Sara Creek had leased property in a shopping mall to Walgreens and promised not to lease space in the mall to anyone else who operated a pharmacy or to a store that contained one. Sara Lee wished to lease to Phar-Mor, a store that would contain a pharmacy as large as Walgreens. The clause was intended to secure Walgreen against competition. Presumably, the rent it paid compensated Sara Lee for assuming liability for the loss Walgreen would suffer if the clause were breached. A damage remedy would have compensated Walgreen for that loss.

Damages would be hard to ascertain. To grant specific performance, however, might not merely compensate Walgreen for its loss. It might force Phar-Mor and Sara Lee to disgorge much of the profit that it would make by competing with Walgreen. Walgreen would demand a share of that profit in return for declining to enforce the degree of specific performance. There are cases in which a party in breach should pay "disgorgement damages"—as Melvin Eisenberg calls them—which is the profit he makes from breaching the contract. As we will see, the breach of a covenant not to compete is not among them. Although a decree of specific performance would avoid the difficulty of estimating the loss that Walgreen would suffer from competition, it could allow Walgreen to recover more than the most extravagant estimate of its loss. It is not entitled to do so.

Walgreens Co. v. Sara Creek Property Co. was decided by Judge Posner, a key figure in the law and economics movement. Like others who take an economic approach to law, he was concerned, not with justice, but with efficiency. The efficient result depended on whether the cost to Walgreens of competition from Phar-Mor was greater or lesser than the benefit to Sara Creek of leasing to Phar-Mor. Sara Creek argued that its breach of contract would be efficient. It could pay the damages equal to the cost that Walgreens suffered from increased competition and still make a profit on the lease to Phar-Mor. "If so," it argued, "society will be better off if Walgreens is paid its damages, equal to that cost, and Phar-Mor is allowed to move in rather than being kept out by an injunction."[203] Posner pointed out that if Sara Creek could pay Walgreens's damages and come out ahead, Sara Creek would lease to Phar-Mor even if an injunction were issued. It would pay Walgreens to set aside the injunction:

> Suppose the cost to Walgreens of facing the competition of Phar-Mor . . . would be $1 million, and the benefit to Sara Creek of leasing to Phar-Mor would be $2 million. Then at any price between these two figures for a waiver of

[202] 966 F.2d 273 (7th Cir. 1992).
[203] *Id.* at 274.

> Walgreens's injunctive rights both parties would be better off, and we expect parties to bargain around a judicial assignment of legal rights if the assignment is inefficient.[204]

The question, for Posner, was which remedy has the lower costs: damages or an injunction. It would be more costly and less reliable for the court to determine Walgreen's damages Nevertheless, there were costs to issuing an injunction. "Many injunctions require continuing supervision by the court, and that is costly," although that would not be the case here. "A more subtle cost of relief arises from the situation that economist's call 'bilateral monopoly,' in which two parties can only deal with each other: the situation that an injunction creates."[205] "With so much at stake, both parties will have an incentive to devote substantial resources of time and money to the negotiation process. The process may even break down, if one or both parties want to create for future use a reputation as a hard bargainer."[206]

Consequently, by this approach, whether Walgreens should receive damages or an injunction should depend on whether the "costly processes of forensic fact determination" outweigh the "time and money of the negotiation process." If the negotiation process is less costly, then Sara Creek must purchase the right to compete from Walgreens. That right, on Posner's hypothetical figures, could be worth $1,000,000. Posner was not concerned with whether Walgreen had a right to any portion of that amount. As we have seen, it did not. Any portion it obtained would be equivalent to a recovery of disgorgement damages, to which it was not entitled. What mattered to Posner was a comparison of the costs of "forensic fact determination" and negotiation. If the cost of negotiation were $10,000 cheaper, Walgreen would have a right worth $1,000,000. From the standpoint of efficiency, the fact that Walgreen would then be a million dollars better off does not matter. All that matters is the possible saving in costs.

[204] *Id.* at 276.
[205] *Id.*
[206] *Id.*

13
Compensation for the Value of Benefits Conferred

I. Past consideration: benefits conferred before a promise was made

By the bargained-for-detriment formula, a promise cannot have consideration if it is made in return for some benefit conferred by the promisee in the past. Since the benefit has already been received, the promise was not made to induce the promisee to confer it.

There are three traditional exceptions and a more recent one that is more general. The three traditional exceptions are promises to pay obligations that the promisor incurred as a minor, obligations that are no longer actionable because the statute of limitations has run,[1] and obligations that were discharged in bankruptcy.[2] In each of these situations, when the law interposed a barrier to recovering damages on a contract that had been breached, it sanctioned a result that would otherwise be unfair. The law tolerates the unfairness to prevent some greater evil. When the threat of that evil is removed, the law permits the fair result. If fairness did not matter, the law would not do so.

Contracts by minors are not enforced in order to protect young people against their own bad judgment. Once they are of legal age, their judgment is deemed to be sound enough to enter into a contract.

An obligation cannot be enforced after a period of time has passed that is fixed by the statute of limitations. The reason is that evidence may have been lost, and the party who incurred the obligation may have acted on the assumption that a suit would never be brought. A party who promises to pay a debt is acknowledging that the debt is genuine and presumably is in a position to pay. The reasons for barring its enforcement disappear.

Obligations are discharged in bankruptcy to give the debtor a new start. Presumably, a debtor who later promises to pay has successfully made a new start and is now in a position to do so. The reason that the debt was enforceable have disappeared. This exception, however, was subject to abuse. After a discharge

1 Restatement (Second) of Contracts § 82(1) (Am. Law Inst. 1981).
2 *Id.* at § 83.

Foundations of American Contract Law. James Gordley, Oxford University Press. © Oxford University Press 2023.
DOI: 10.1093/oso/9780197686089.003.0013

in bankruptcy, a former creditor would try to lure the former into promising to pay the debt. The former debtor might do so rashly without realizing the legal consequences. The federal bankruptcy statute has been amended to make a promise to pay a debt discharged in bankruptcy unenforceable unless it is approved in court.[3]

In these three cases, the amount the promisee recovers is the amount that was owed under a previous contract.

The broader exception is based on the principle against unjust enrichment. A person who has been unjustly enriched at another's expense may recover the amount of the enrichment in the absence of any contract. For example, a medical doctor who stops on the highway to treat the unconscious victim of an accident can recover the fee that a doctor would usually charge. Sometimes, however, the plaintiff cannot recover in unjust enrichment because it is not clear that a benefit was conferred or what the defendant would have paid for it. A volunteer who is injured saving a person who seems to be drowning may not recover because that person may not have needed the rescue and may have been unwilling to pay for the volunteer's injury. A plaintiff who mistakenly builds a house on the land of another person cannot recover because the person may not have wanted the house and would not have been willing to pay the cost of building it. This obstacle can be cured if the defendant promises to pay for the benefit conferred. The promise shows a desire for the benefit and a willingness to pay that amount. The obstacle to allowing the plaintiff to recover on principles of unjust enrichment is thus removed.[4]

The *Second Restatement* provides: "A promise made in recognition of a benefit previously received by the promisor from the promisee is binding to the extent necessary to prevent injustice."[5] Such a promise is not binding "if the promisee considered the benefit as a gift."[6] The reason, as the *Second Restatement* noted, is that "a subsequent promise to make restitution removes the reason for the denial of relief, and the policy against unjust enrichment then prevails."[7]

The drafters formulated this rule by generalizing the result in a 1936 Alabama Court of Appeal case, *Webb v. McGowin*.[8] There a worker in a warehouse became permanently disabled and unable to work when he rescued an officer and owner of his employer from serious injury or death. The man he had saved promised him a modest monthly amount for the rest of his life. When the man died and

[3] Bankruptcy Code, 11 U.S.C. § 524.
[4] *See* Melvin A. Eisenberg, Foundational Principles of Contract Law 113 (2018).
[5] Restatement (Second) of Contracts § 86(1) (Am. Law Inst. 1981).
[6] *Id.* at § 86(2)(a).
[7] *Id.* at § 86 cmt. b.
[8] 168 So. 196 (Ala. Ct. App. 1935), *cert denied*, 169 So. 199 (Ala. 1936).

his executors refused to pay, the rescuer brought suit, and the court enforced the promise.

When the law of unjust enrichment does give a remedy, it is for a benefit conferred on the plaintiff themself. The medical doctor can recover against the unconscious victim they treated. The doctor cannot recover against the victim's parents or spouse. This rule has been carried over to cases in which parents or a spouse later promise to pay for a benefit conferred on the victim. In an illustration in the *Second Restatement*, "A gives emergency care to B's adult son while the son is sick and without funds far from home. B subsequently promises to reimburse A for his expenses. The promise is not binding."[9] In contrast: "A finds B's escaped bull and feeds and cares for it. B's subsequent promise to pay reasonable compensation to A is binding."[10]

Eisenberg asked, "Is there a world in which people would believe that a promise to reimburse a stranger for the costs of having cared for the promisor's bull should be enforceable, but a promise to reimburse a stranger for the costs of having cared for the promisor's ill adult son should not be enforceable?"[11] There shouldn't be. The reason that the law of unjust enrichment will not give a remedy against parents to a medical doctor who treated their adult son is, again, the problem of uncertainty. The parents are under no legal obligation to pay for his cure. Whether or not the parents should have been willing to pay for his cure, it is not clear that they were willing to do so and how much they would have paid. Consequently, a "subsequent promise" by a parent "removes the reason for the denial of relief" in unjust enrichment as surely as it does in the case of the rescue. Their promise should be enforceable.

II. Restitutionary remedies: benefits conferred when a promise has been broken

If a party contracts to provide services at a fixed price, the service provider assumes the risk that the cost will be higher than estimated, and the recipient assumes the risk that it will be lower. It is like a bet on what the cost of performance will be. Consequently, if the service provider breaches the contract, the recipient can recover the difference between the cost of completing the work and the contract price. If the service recipient breaches the contract, the provider can recover the lost profit plus costs already incurred, or, to put it another way, the

9 Restatement (Second) of Contracts § 86 illus. 1 (Am. Law Inst. 1981). The illustration is based on *Mills v. Wyman*, 20 Mass. (3 Pick.) 207 (1825).

10 *Id.* at illus. 6.

11 Lon L. Fuller, Melvin Aron Eisenberg, & Mark P. Gergen, Basic Contract Law 54 (10th ed. 2018).

contract price minus the costs that would have been incurred had performance been completed.

As we have seen, the doctrine of substantial performance determines when a non-breaching party can be held to the terms of the bet despite the other party's breach. If that party has not substantially performed, the bet is off. The recipient who had received the incomplete performance need not pay for it at the contract rate. The service provider cannot recover the contract price minus the cost to the recipient of completing performance.

Nevertheless, the principle against unjust enrichment may require the recipient who has received a benefit to pay its fair value. According to the *Restatement (Second) of Contracts*, "on a breach by non-performance that gives rise to a claim for damages for total breach or on a repudiation, the injured party is entitled to restitution for any benefit that he has conferred on the other party by way of part performance or reliance."[12] The reason is "to prevent the unjust enrichment of the other party."[13]

Only a party who was actually benefited is liable. In *G.W. Grun Roofing & Construction Co. v. Cope*, a contractor installed "a roof which so lacks uniformity in color as to give the appearance of a patch job." The court held that he had not substantially performed because the owner may "choose for himself and . . . contract for something which exactly satisfies that choice and [is] not to be compelled to accept something else." The contract could not recover "for the benefit conferred" because it had not shown that "the plaintiff has received any benefit from the defendant's defective performance."[14]

If the defendant does not substantially perform, the plaintiff may escape from a losing contract. He may then be better off than if the defendant had substantially performed. In *United States v. Algernon Blair*,[15] a subcontractor underbid a contract to erect the steel structure of a building. The Fourth Circuit held that the general contractor had failed to substantially perform when it refused to pay for the cost of renting cranes to be used in erecting the structure. Consequently, the plaintiff was justified in refusing to complete performance. The general contractor was liable for the reasonable value of the subcontractor's part performance even though, if it had not breached the contract, the subcontractor would have lost more than the unpaid balance of the contract price. The subcontractor's claim was for restitution of a benefit conferred. "While the contract price may be evidence of the reasonable value of the services, it does not measure the value performance or limit recovery."[16]

[12] RESTATEMENT (SECOND) OF CONTRACTS § 373(1) (AM. LAW INST. 1981).
[13] *Id.* at cmt. a.
[14] 529 S.W. 2d 258, 262, 263 (Tex. Civ. App. 1975).
[15] 479 F.2d 638 (4th Cir. 1973).
[16] EISENBERG, *supra* note 4, at 326–27 (2018) (chapter coauthored by Mark Gergen). *Id.* 319 n.1.

Thus the principle for giving a remedy for unjust enrichment is, as noted by the *Restatement (Third) of Restitution and Unjust Enrichment*, "that a party confronted by a material breach is entitled to disregard the contract and deal with the breaching party as if the performance in question had been rendered in the absence of contract."[17] The *Third Restatement* claimed, however, that such a principle "is inconsistent with the rest of the law of contract."[18] Therefore, it rejected the rule of *Algernon Blair*[19] although, it acknowledged that rule is supported by *Second Restatement of Contracts* and a good deal of case law.[20] It claimed that the rule "is contrary to fundamental objectives of contract law and inconsistent with the other remedies for breach of contract, all of which take the parties' agreement as the benchmark by which the plaintiff's remedies are measured."[21]

Melvin Eisenberg and Mark Gergen agreed. Otherwise, there would be a "windfall to the promisee on the breach of what would be a losing contract."[22] This argument, like that of the *Third Restatement*, is circular. If the promisor should be liable on the contract despite the promisee's failure to substantially perform, of course the terms of the contract should be "the benchmark" for determining their obligations and for them to escape these obligations would be a windfall. As the *Third Restatement* noted, "allowing damages measured by the value of performance unlimited by the contract price . . . reallocate[s] or revalue[s] risks that it is the function of contract to price and to assign." If our analysis of the doctrine of substantial performance is correct, however, the function of that doctrine is to determine when these risks ought to be reallocated. If one party has not substantially performed, the other party should not be required to perform at the contract rate. If the result in *Algernon Blair* is wrong, it is because the court mistakenly held that the general contractor failed to substantially perform. But if that finding was correct, so was the result. It is true, as Eisenberg and Gergen observed, that the *Algernon Blair* rule gives the "promisee an incentive to find grounds for declaring a total breach in order to avoid a losing contract."[23] But whether the promisor committed a total breach—whether they failed to substantially perform—depends on the promisor, not on the desires of the promisee.

[17] RESTATEMENT (THIRD) OF RESTITUTION AND UNJUST ENRICHMENT II 4 2 Intro. Note (AM. LAW INST. 2011).

[18] *Id.*

[19] *Id.* at § 38.

[20] *Id.* at II 4 2 Intro. Note. *See id.* § 38 cmt. d. According to George Palmer, "When there is a breach of contract that justifies the innocent party in putting an end to the contract after part performance, and he does so, the overwhelming weight of authority grants restitution in his favor not limited by the contract price or rate." 1 GEORGE PALMER, THE LAW OF RESTITUTION 389 (1978).

[21] RESTATEMENT (THIRD) OF RESTITUTION AND UNJUST ENRICHMENT § 38 cmt. d (AM. LAW INST. 2011).

[22] *Id.* at § 38.

[23] EISENBERG, *supra* note 4, at 326.

Nevertheless, according to the *Third Restatement*, "a plaintiff who is entitled to a remedy for material breach or repudiation may recover . . . the market value of the plaintiff's uncompensated contractual performance, not exceeding the price of such performance as determined by reference to the parties' agreement."[24] The contract price thus serves as a cap on the recovery. In Illustration 17, the contract price is $50 million. The plaintiff has completed half of the work at a cost to him of $50 million. The cost to him to complete the work is $30 million. The market value of the work he has done is $40 million. According to the rule of the *Third Restatement*, since he has done half the work, he is entitled to "$40 million capped at 50 percent of contract price = $25 million."[25]

One might ask why the market value of the work completed should matter at all if, according to the *Third Restatement*, damages should be measured by the contract price. To quote Eisenberg and Gergen, "[W]hy not abolish the claim for restitution damages entirely . . . ? Why retain a rule that could put the promisee in a better position than he would have been if the contract had been fully performed, once the decision has been made to calculate expectation damages?"[26] Their answer is that "expectation damages" may be uncertain. Indeed, according to the *Third Restatement*, the "usual application" of the rule:

> is either to a case in which the plaintiff's contractual expectation cannot be established at all, or to a case in which—although the plaintiff's expectancy cannot be known with certainty—it can be shown to lie somewhere within an upper limit. In either case, an alternative damage calculation by the rule . . . protects the plaintiff's expectancy so far as the evidence permits.[27]

The question then becomes: Why would the uncertainty of "expectation damages" be a reason for awarding damages measured by the market value of the work completed? "Expectation damages" are uncertain when it is difficult to estimate the cost of completion. According to Eisenberg and Gergen:

> The restitutionary rule reduces the impact on the damage award of an error in predicting the cost to complete by subtracting a fraction of the estimated cost on full performance from the estimated cost rather than the full amount of the estimated loss. Subtracting a fraction of the estimated loss put a thumb on the scale in favor of the promisee.[28]

24 Restatement (Third) of Restitution and Unjust Enrichment § 38 (Am. Law Inst. 2011).
25 *Id.* at illus. 17.
26 Eisenberg, *supra* note 4, at 327.
27 Restatement (Third) of Restitution and Unjust Enrichment § 38 cmt. a (Am. Law Inst. 2011).
28 Eisenberg, *supra* note 4, at 327.

That reasoning cannot explain the rule of the *Restatement Third* as it applies, for example, in a case like the *Restatement's* Illustration 17. In that illustration, we know the cost of completion: it is $30 million. If the defendant had not breached, the plaintiff would have lost $30 million: the contract price of $50 million minus the $80 million it cost him to perform. If Eisenberg and Gergen are right, there is no reason to award damages measured by market value. Indeed, there would be no reason to do so whenever it is clear, in Eisenberg's words, that damages will "put the promisee in a better position than he would have been if the contract had been fully performed."

Be that as it may, to say that we base damages on market value because market value is more certain than the cost of completion is like the drunk person looking under a streetlight for the wallet he lost several blocks away. When asked why, he said "because the light is better here." The rule of the *Third Restatement* gives the plaintiff the market value times the contract price multiplied by the percentage of the work completed. Why is that supposed to approximate the contract price minus the cost of completion? It does, indeed, "put a thumb on the scale in favor of the promisee." But that is about all one can say for it.

The principle against unjust enrichment also explains the result when the plaintiff fails to substantially perform the contract and seeks to recover the value of the benefit conferred on the defendant. The defendant has not breached the contract and therefore should be protected against the risk that the performance will be less or more than estimated. Consequently, the plaintiff can recover no more than the contract price minus the cost to the defendant of completing the work the plaintiff agreed to do.[29] Moreover, although judicial authority is split, the defendant should pay no more than the contract rate which is the pro rata share of the contract price for the work the plaintiff has done.[30] Subject to those limitations, the plaintiff should recover the value of the benefit conferred on the defendant. The contract protects the defendant against the risk of paying more for the performance than the contract price. But the principle against unjust enrichment does not allow the defendant to receive a benefit without paying for it, when it is clear how much the defendant would have been willing to pay.

[29] RESTATEMENT (SECOND) OF CONTRACTS § 374, cmt. a (AM. LAW INST. 1981) ("The party in breach is, in any case, liable for the loss caused by his breach. . . . If the benefit received exceeds that loss, the rule stated in this Section generally gives the party in breach the right to recover the excess in restitution").

[30] 1 PALMER, *supra* note 20, at 580–83.

14
Disgorgement of the Value of Benefits Received

I. The problem of disgorgement

According to the *Second Restatement*, remedies for breach of contract protect three interests: expectation, reliance, and restitution. As Melvin Eisenberg pointed out, there is a "striking omission": "the disgorgement interest, which is the promisee's interest in requiring the promisor to disgorge a gain that was made possible by her breach but does not consist of a benefit conferred upon her by the promisee."[1] The omission, he observed, "was plainly deliberate." "[S]hortly after publication of Restatement Second, Allan Farnsworth, the Reporter . . . wrote a leading article . . . arguing, on normative grounds, against the recognition of the disgorgement interest."[2]

The disgorgement interest, although ignored by the *Restatement Second of Contracts*, is recognized by the *Restatement Third of Unjust Enrichment and Restitution*. According to Section 39(1):

> If a deliberate breach of contract results in profit to the defaulting promisor and the available damage remedy affords inadequate protection to the promisee's contractual entitlement, the promisee has a claim to restitution of the profit realized by the promisor as a result of the breach. Restitution by the rule of this section is an alternative to a remedy in damages.

One issue that this provision raises is the relationship between disgorgement and the normal remedies for breach of contract. According to § 39(1), it is to be given if "the available damage remedy affords inadequate protection to the promisee's contractual entitlement." Another issue is whether the breach must be conscious or willful for the remedy to be given. Section 39(1) provides that it must be "deliberate."

[1] Melvin A. Eisenberg, Foundational Principles of Contract Law 335 (2018).
[2] *Id.* at 336 *citing* E. Allan Farnsworth, *Your Loss or My Gain? The Dilemma of the Disgorgement Principle in Breach of Contract*, 94 Yale L.J. 1339 (1985).

Foundations of American Contract Law. James Gordley, Oxford University Press. © Oxford University Press 2023.
DOI: 10.1093/oso/9780197686089.003.0014

In both instances, the *Third Restatement* reached the wrong conclusion. As it recognized, there are two fundamental principles underlying the law of unjust enrichment. The first principle is that "[a] person who is unjustly enriched at the expense of another is subject to liability in restitution."[3] The second is that "[a] person is not permitted to profit by his own wrong."[4] The *Third Restatement* explained disgorgement for breach of contract by the second principle.

In some cases, that explanation is correct. For example, in *Snepp v. United States*, Snepp, a former CIA employee, published an account of CIA activities in South Vietnam during his term of employment without securing the prior permission from the CIA, as required by his contract. The Supreme Court held that he must disgorge his profits. He had "violated his trust" and so profited by his own wrong. That principle may be one of morality, or it may rest on the deterrence of wrongdoing. In either case the government should have prevailed.

In *Snepp*, the defendant had not been enriched by appropriating something that belonged to the United States. In other cases, however, disgorgement damages should be awarded because the defendant was unjustly enriched at the expense of the plaintiff and therefore "is subject to liability in restitution."[5] The mistake of the *Third Restatement* is that it tried to explain these cases by the principle that the defendant should not profit from his own wrongdoing. It concluded that the breach must be "deliberate." The defendant's "wrongdoing" entitles the plaintiff to disgorgement because it is an "opportunistic breach of contract."[6] For that reason, the remedy should be given only for "deliberate" breach.[7] According to the Official Comments:

> The extent of liability in restitution for benefits wrongfully obtained depends significantly on the culpability of the defendant. . . . The conscious wrongdoer . . . is liable to disgorge profits (including consequential gains) derived from interference with the claimant's protected interests.[8]

[3] RESTATEMENT (THIRD) OF RESTITUTION AND UNJUST ENRICHMENT § 1 (AM. LAW INST. 2011). The language of the *First Restatement* is identical. RESTATEMENT (FIRST) OF RESTITUTION § 1 (AM. LAW INST. 1937).

[4] RESTATEMENT (THIRD) OF RESTITUTION AND UNJUST ENRICHMENT § 3 (AM. LAW INST. 2011). The *First Restatement* added the words "at the expense of another." RESTATEMENT (FIRST) OF RESTITUTION § 3 (AM. LAW INST. 1937). The *Restatement Third* omitted them "to avoid any implication that the defendant's wrongful gain must correspond to a loss on the part of the plaintiff." RESTATEMENT (THIRD) OF RESTITUTION AND UNJUST ENRICHMENT Reporter's note a (AM. LAW INST. 2011).

[5] RESTATEMENT (THIRD) OF RESTITUTION AND UNJUST ENRICHMENT § 1 (AM. LAW INST. 2011). The language of the *First Restatement* is identical. RESTATEMENT (FIRST) OF RESTITUTION § 1 (AM. LAW INST. 1937).

[6] RESTATEMENT (THIRD) OF RESTITUTION AND UNJUST ENRICHMENT § 1 cmt. a (AM. LAW INST. 2011).

[7] *Id.* at § 39(1).

[8] *Id.* at cmt. e.

II. Disgorgement and the principle against unjust enrichment

In the law of unjust enrichment, "[a] person who is unjustly enriched at the expense of another is subject to liability in restitution."[9] A person who is mistakenly undercharged by a shopkeeper or overpaid by an employer is liable for the benefit received. A person who profits by using another's resources is liable even though that person lost nothing. A person who profits from using another's land must disgorge the profit even if the owner was not using it.[10] A person who uses another's machine must pay its rental value even if the owner would not have used it.[11] A physician who incurs no costs treating an unconscious accident victim can recover a fee.[12] To say that one person has been enriched at another's expense means that one person gained by taking or using resources that belonged to another person. The other person need not have become worse off.

The same principle should apply when there has been a breach of contract. A party must disgorge any gain made by taking or using the property or services which, according to the contract, belong to the other party. That is the best explanation of the cases in which courts have required disgorgement of a profit made by breaking a contract. As Daniel Friedmann explained:

> Contract relations may . . . give rise to interests that come within the ambit of "property" for purposes of restitution. . . .
>
> Under the approach advocated here, the central issue in evaluating a claim for restitution of benefits obtained through a breach of contract can be presented as follows: When performance is promised under a contract, is the promisee "entitled" to it in such a way that if performance is withheld, appropriated or otherwise "taken," the promisee can be regarded as having been deprived of an interest that "belonged" to him?[13]

In *Laurin v. DeCarolis Construction Co.*, the plaintiff bought a house which the defendant was then constructing. After the contract was signed but before delivery, the defendant bulldozed trees and removed gravel and loam worth $6,480. The plaintiffs recovered the value of the trees, gravel, and loam that the defendant

[9] *Id* at § 1. The language of the *First Restatement* is identical. RESTATEMENT (FIRST) OF RESTITUTION § 1 (AM. LAW INST. 1937).

[10] Edwards v. Lee's Administrator, 96 S.W.2d 1028 Ky 1936 (commercial use of cave under the plaintiff's land).

[11] Olwell v. Nye & Nissen Co. 173 P.2d 652 (Wash. 1956).

[12] Cotnam v. Wisdom, 104 S.W. 164 (Ark. 1907).

[13] Daniel Friedmann, *Restitution of Property Obtained Through the Appropriation of Property or the Commission of a Wrong*, 80 COLUM. L. REV. 504, 513 (1980).

had removed even though the value of their property had not been diminished. The court reached the right result. The defendant had appropriated property to which the plaintiff was entitled by their contract. The court was confused, however, by the fact that the plaintiffs did not yet own the property. They had a contract right to it. The court concluded that because the action was in contract, rather than for the conversion of the plaintiff's property, the defendant was liable only because the breach was "deliberate and willful."

That is the approach of the *Restatement (Third) of Restitution and Unjust Enrichment*. Illustration 2 to § 39 is modeled on *Laurin*. Like the court, the *Restatement* said that the remedy is given because the breach was "deliberate." But it should not matter whether the right that was violated is classified as one in property or contract. The result should be the same if the defendant had innocently taken the trees, gravel, and loam mistakenly believing that they were located on a parcel that had not yet been sold. In Friedmann's words, they would still have deprived the plaintiff of "an interest that 'belonged' to him."

In *EarthInfo, Inc. v. Hydrosphere Resource Consultants, Inc.*,[14] the defendant agreed to pay the plaintiff a fixed hourly development fee as well as royalties, calculated as a percentage of net sales, for "inventive product ideas." All rights of ownership, copyrights, and patents were vested in the defendant. The defendant suspended royalty payments, putting it in substantial breach of its contract. The court required it to disgorge all profits it had made as a result of the breach since the breach was "conscious" as well as "substantial."[15] In this case, the profits that the defendant was required to disgorge were those it made using the ideas developed by the plaintiff and given to the defendant in return for royalties. Because the defendant was in substantial breach, it was no longer entitled to use those ideas in return for the royalties. It had, in effect, appropriated them. If it had appropriated intellectual property such as a patent or copyright, it would have to disgorge its profits. For that reason, however, there should be no additional requirement that the breach was "conscious."

A more difficult case arises when the defendant breaches an agreement not to compete with the plaintiff. Suppose a shopping center leases space to a grocery store or a pharmacy which is promised it will be the only one allowed to sell groceries or drugs, and which promises in return that it will not sell products that compete with those of any other lessee.[16] The lessor who breaches will not be required to disgorge its profits. The lessee's damages will be the profits it lost on account of competition. That is so even if the lessor acted in "bad faith."[17]

14 900 P.2d 113 (1995).

15 *Id.* at 120.

16 *See* Walgreen Co. v. Sara Creek Property Co., 966 F.2d 273 (7th Cir. 1992).

17 Olympus Hills Shopping Center, Ltd. v. Smith's Food & Drug Centers, Inc., 889 P.2d 445 (Utah 1994).

It is different, however, if the defendant sells an ongoing business to the plaintiff and promises not to compete. The relationships that have been established with customers are part of the asset the defendant is selling. Friedmann gave an example:

> A, a restaurant owner, sells his business, including its goodwill, to B. A undertakes not to open a restaurant in an area within ten miles of the present one. In breach of the contract, A opens a restaurant in the vicinity of the restaurant he sold to B.[18]

He noted that "B acquired the prospect of getting the clients that would have come to A's restaurant. Therefore, the profits made by A derive from the appropriation of an interest that he sold to B."[19] To sell a going concern and then lure away its customers is to appropriate in part what the other party bought.

Again, the *Restatement Third* reached the right result but for the wrong reason. It allowed the result to depend on a party's "deliberate disregard" of his contractual obligations. According to Illustration 6 to § 39:

> Buyer pays Seller $500,000 cash in exchange for (i) Seller's existing business as a going concern and (ii) Seller's promise not to compete with Buyer for a period of three years. The restraints thus imposed on Seller are reasonable, and the promise not to compete is enforceable under local law. Acting in deliberate disregard of his contractual obligations, Seller operates a new business in competition with Buyer for the final year of the three-year term, realizing profits of $50,000. Buyer is entitled to recover $50,000 from Seller by the rule of this section. It is not a condition of restitution that Buyer prove damages as a result of Seller's breach.

It should matter that Buyer purchased "Seller's existing business as a going concern," although the *Third Restatement* does not explain why it matters. The cases on which this illustration was modeled, according to the Reporter's Note, are similar. The defendant violated a covenant not to compete after selling him a store[20] or a drapery shop.[21]

In *Ingram v. Bigelow*,[22] cited in the same Reporter's Note, the situation was reversed. The defendant licensed the plaintiff's business which was "the sale of patented and copyrighted courses and materials and of services in connection

[18] Friedmann, *supra* note 13, at 1902–03.
[19] *Id.* at 1903.
[20] Y.J.D. Restaurant Supply Co. v. Dib, 98 Misc.2d 462, 413 N.Y.S.2d 835 (S. Ct. 1979).
[21] Morgan v. Stagg, 1987 WL 18703 (Tex. Ct. App.).
[22] 138 N.Y.S.2d 217 (S. Ct. 1954).

therewith." After the license was terminated, he continued to operate the business in competition with the plaintiff. The court held, correctly, that he had to disgorge the profits he made by doing so. As in Friedman's example, the profits he made "derive from the appropriation of an interest" although in this case, an interest in a business which once more belonged to the plaintiff.[23]

Now we can better understand the decision of the Second Circuit in *United States Naval Institute Press v. Charter Communications, Inc.*[24] Tom Clancy's first novel, *The Hunt for Red October*, was published in hardcover by Naval Institute, which owned the copyright. It licensed Berkeley Publishing Group to publish the paperback edition. The contract provided that Berkeley would not publish the paperback sooner than October 1985. The purpose was to allow Naval Institute to sell the hardback edition for a period of time without the competition of the cheaper paperbacks. Berkeley breached the contract by starting to sell paperbacks on September 15 rather than in October. The court awarded Naval Institute the damages it suffered because fewer people bought the book in hardback during that period. It refused to require Berkeley to disgorge the profits it made selling before the date permitted by its contract. Eisenberg thought that this result supported the position of the *Restatement Second of Contracts*. He argued that it was wrong.[25]

Berkeley would have been required to disgorge its profits if it had infringed Naval's copyright. The court held that it did not. In the court's view, Berkeley had acquired the right to publish *The Hunt for Red October*. Its acquisition of that right, in the court's view, was not conditional on compliance with the clause limiting when it could sell paperbacks. The court read that clause as a shield that protected Naval against competition in its sale of hardback books, much as a non-competition clause in a shopping center lease shields a pharmacy against losing sales to competing stores. Given that reading of the contract the result was correct. Naval was no more entitled to disgorgement than the pharmacy would be.

According to Eisenberg, "the decision rested on a scholastic and unconvincing distinction between contract rights, on the one hand, and property rights on the other."[26] Not so. It depends on the purpose of the non-competition clause. Even

[23] In another case cited in the same Reporter's note, *Oscar Barnett Foundry Co. v. Crowe*, 80 N.J.Eq. 258, 86 A. 915 (Err. & App. 1912), an inventor gave complainant sole right to manufacture his invention. The court held that whether the invention was patentable or not, the inventor "has no right whatever to enter into the manufacture of that very same article in competition" with him. The plaintiff was entitled to an accounting of the inventor's profits. The court attached no significance to whether the breach was deliberate. *Id.* at 916. What mattered, again, was that the defendant tried to reappropriate an exclusive right he had conferred on the plaintiff.

[24] 936 F.2d 692 (2nd Cir. 1991).

[25] Eisenberg, *supra* note 1, at 341.

[26] *Id.*

if the court were wrong about that purpose, the decision would not support the position of the *Restatement Second of Contracts*. It would not mean that, in principle, disgorgement damages should not be awarded.

In the cases we have considered thus far, the defendant gained by depriving the plaintiff of something to which the plaintiff was entitled and for which the defendant never paid. In another class of cases, the defendant gained by receiving payment from the plaintiff for a performance that the plaintiff never made. The plaintiff may not have suffered a loss. Nevertheless, the defendant has been enriched at the plaintiff's expense.

As before, the *Restatement (Third) of Restitution and Unjust Enrichment* recognized that the plaintiff should recover in such cases. Again, however, it did so for the wrong reasons: the plaintiff's recovery depends on whether the breach is "deliberate." In Illustration 7 to § 39:

> City contracts with Firefighters' Association for fire protection services to be furnished during the ensuing 12 months. The contract specifies the number of men, horses, and wagons to be kept in readiness at specified times and places, and the contract price is negotiated as a function thereof. After the 12 months have elapsed and the full contract price has been paid, City discovers that Association consistently devoted fewer men, horses, and wagons to City's fire protection than the numbers required by contract. Association acted in deliberate breach of its contractual obligations, calculating—accurately as it turned out—that the resources specified by contract were in excess of City's firefighting needs. In consequence, Association saved $100,000 over the life of its contract with City; while City suffered no increased loss from fire as a result of Association's disregard of the contract specifications. City is entitled to recover $100,000 from Association by the rule of this section.

As the Reporter's Note observes, "Illustration 7 adopts the facts and reverses the result in *City of New Orleans v. Firemen's Charitable Association*."[27]

> In Illustration 5:
> Landowner and Mining Company enter a contract for strip-mining. The agreement authorizes Mining Company to remove coal from Blackacre in exchange for payment of a specified royalty per ton. A further provision of the agreement, included at Landowner's insistence, obliges Mining Company to restore the surface of Blackacre to its preexisting contours on the completion of mining operations. Mining Company removes the coal from Blackacre, pays the stipulated royalty, and repudiates its obligation to restore the land. In

[27] 43 La. Ann. 447, 9 So. 486 (1891).

> Landowner's action against Mining Company it is established that the cost of restoration would be $25,000, and that the diminution in the value of Blackacre if the restoration is not performed would be negligible. The contract is not affected by mistake or impracticability. The cost of restoration is in line with what Mining Company presumably anticipated, and the available comparisons suggest that Mining Company took this cost into account in calculating the contractual royalty. Landowner is entitled to recover $25,000 from Mining Company by the rule of this section. It is not a condition to Landowner's recovery in restitution that the money be used to restore Blackacre.

A key fact is that "Mining Company took this cost into account in calculating its contractual royalty." Consequently, Landowner paid that amount for work that Mining Company never did. It does not matter, any more than in Illustration 7, how much, if at all, its failure to do so harmed the plaintiff.

Again, because the defendant was enriched at the plaintiff's expense, it should not matter whether the defendant's breach was deliberate. Indeed, in Illustration 13, it does not:

> Builder and Owner agree on the construction of a house at a price of $2 million. The specifications call for foundations to be made of Vermont granite, and the work has been bid and priced on that basis. By mistake and inadvertence, Builder constructs the foundations of granite quarried in New Hampshire. This fact comes to light when construction has been completed. The difference in the appraised value of Owner's property as a result of the nonconformity is nil. The cost to cure the default would far exceed the total price of the house. Because New Hampshire granite is less expensive than comparable stone from Vermont, Builder has saved $15,000 as a result of his negligent breach of contract. Owner may recover damages of $15,000 for Builder's breach.

As in Illustrations 5 and 7, the defendant was paid for work it never did. The *Restatement* admitted that "[t]he case is not within the rule of § 39 (because Builder's default is unintentional)." "But," it said, "principles of unjust enrichment reinforce the conclusion that saved expenditure makes an appropriate measure of contract damages in such a case." As Eisenberg noted:

> this "explanation" only underlines the defects in Section 39. If disgorgement for breach of contract should be allowed outside the limit of the text of Section 39, as should be and is, then the artificial limit of Section 39 serves no function, as it should not and does not.[28]

[28] EISENBERG, *supra* note 1, at 347 n.34.

III. The benefit of a bargain and the principle against unjust enrichment

In chapter 12, we saw that the normal remedy for breach of contract is to hold a party who was compensated for assuming a risk liable for the consequences. Otherwise, the party that was compensated for assuming the risk would be enriched at the promisee's expense. In such cases, it would also be correct to say that the party in breach is made to disgorge a gain made at the promisee's expense. It is not surprising that the *Restatement (Third) of Restitution* considers the remedy in the following case to be for disgorgement:

> Vendor and Purchaser agree on a sale of Blackacre for $100,000. Two weeks before the scheduled closing date, Vendor conveys Blackacre to a second purchaser for $110,000. Purchaser is entitled to recover $10,000 from Vendor by the rule of this section. Purchaser need not prove the value of Blackacre on the scheduled closing date; nor could Vendor reduce or avoid his liability under this section by proving that the market value of Blackacre on that date was something less than $110,000. § 39, illus. 1.

According to the *Restatement*, this remedy should be given because the breach is "opportunistic."

Daniel Friedmann gave this example:

> A, an opera singer, undertakes to perform in B's opera house during one opera season. In breach of the contract, A accepts an offer from C to sing in a competing opera house during the same season. B should be entitled to recover the amount which A received from C in excess of the payment he would have received from B.[29]

According to Friedmann, this remedy should be given because the defendant took something that "belong[s] to the plaintiff."[30]

Eisenberg explained that in such cases, the remedy should be given because the non-breaching party is entitled to the benefit of the bargain. The "Overbidder Paradigm" is a clear case of "opportunistic breach." The plaintiff purchases a commodity for which there is no readily available substitute. The defendant then sells it to someone who will pay more. As Eisenberg observed, "what looks like a

[29] Friedmann, *supra* note 13, at 1902. His citation is "Lumley v. Gye, 118 Eng. Rep. 749 (Q.B. 1853); Lumley v. Wagner, 42 Eng. Rep. 687 (Ch. 1852)." *Id.* at n.115.

[30] *Id.*

disgorgement case" is actually one in which the damages give the buyer the benefit of their bargain.[31]

We have seen that Eisenberg is right. The Overbidder Paradigm is the one we considered in discussing the theory of efficient breach.[32] One who buys a unique item buys the opportunity to profit if a third party appears who values its unique features much more. If the seller breaches their contract by selling to that third party, awarding the extra amount that the third party paid is giving the buyer the benefit of their bargain. In such cases, "the promisee has bargained for the promisor's gain from breach":

> [T]he promisor has paid for the right to any profit derived from selling to an overbidder. Making a forward contract for an undifferentiated commodity reflects a decision by the seller . . . that her best bet is to take the buyer's present offer . . . rather than waiting for a possible higher offer in the future. If the seller accepts the higher offer she is reneging on her bet.[33]

When a party bets and wins, for the other party to renege, as Friedmann would say, deprives the winner of something to which they are entitled. Consequently, as we have seen, the court reached the right result in *KGM Harvesting Co. v. Fresh Network*,[34] in which the defendant breached a contract to sell a fungible commodity. It sold lettuce to a third party for more than the contract price. Although the plaintiff covered by buying lettuce at a higher price, it was no worse off because its contracts to resell the lettuce were not fixed price but cost plus. Consequently, it was able to pass along the higher price that it paid to its customers. The parties bet on whether the price of lettuce would rise or fall, and the non-breaching party won the bet. By hedging the bet, that party received a windfall. If it were not allowed to recover, the windfall would go to the breaching party who was the party who lost the bet.

That case is a puzzle to those who hold the conventional view that contract remedies should put the promisee in as good a position as if had the contract been performed. It makes sense by the approach we have suggested in which a party should be liable for the risks that they assumed. A party who reneges when that risk materializes, is enriched at the other party's expense. For that reason, the remedy in such a case can equally well be described as disgorgement.

We saw in Part I that a contract is fair when, ex ante, neither party is enriched at the other's expense. Ex post, one party may become richer and the other poorer.

[31] Eisenberg, *supra* note 1, at 346.
[32] [00].
[33] Eisenberg, *supra* note 1, at 346.
[34] 42 Cal. Rptr. 2d 286 (Cal. App. 1995).

Ex ante, neither does because each party is compensated for the risk that they assume. In that sense, the exchange is equal. We saw in Part II that the terms implied in a contract preserve that equality. We have now seen that the same principle explains much of the law of remedies for breach of contract. The principle is one of commutative justice. In an exchange, neither party should be enriched at the other's expense.

Index

For the benefit of digital users, indexed terms that span two pages (e.g., 52–53) may, on occasion, appear on only one of those pages.